NIGHT IN THE AMERICAN VILLAGE

NIGHT IN THE AMERICAN VILLAGE

WOMEN IN THE SHADOW OF THE
U.S. MILITARY BASES IN OKINAWA

AKEMI JOHNSON

NEW YORK
LONDON

Requests for permission to reproduce selections from this book should be mailed to: Permissions
Department, The New Press, 120 Wall Street, 31st floor, New York, NY 10005.

Published in the United States by The New Press, New York, 2019
Distributed by Two Rivers Distribution

ISBN 978-1-62097-331-8 (hc)
ISBN 978-1-62097-332-5 (ebook)
CIP data is available.

The New Press publishes books that promote and enrich public discussion and understanding of
the issues vital to our democracy and to a more equitable world. These books are made possible
by the enthusiasm of our readers; the support of a committed group of donors, large and small;
the collaboration of our many partners in the independent media and the not-for-profit sector;
booksellers, who often hand-sell New Press books; librarians; and above all by our authors.

www.thenewpress.com

Book design and composition by Bookbright Media
This book was set in Fournier and Questa Grande

Printed in the United States of America

2 4 6 8 10 9 7 5 3 1

For Nadine and Nick

CONTENTS

Okinawa Island

CAPE HEDO

Ie Island
Auxiliary Airfield

IE ISLAND

EAST CHINA SEA

Camp Gonsalves
Jungle Warfare
Training Center

Nago

Camp Schwab

Hedoko

OURA BAY

Camp Hansen

Kin

Yomitan

Uruma

Camp Courtney

Torii Station

Kadena Town

Okinawa City

Chatan

Camp Foster

White Beach Naval Facility

Camp
Kinser

Ginowan

Naha

Camp
Lester

Kadena Air Base

MCAS Futenma

Nishihara

PACIFIC OCEAN

Itoman

Yonabaru

Urasoe

1

RINA

A YEAR AFTER HER DEATH, PEOPLE STILL BROUGHT HER FLOWERS. A makeshift memorial had been set up near the place where they had found her body, on the side of a twisting two-lane road in Onna Village. The road, flanked by dense forest, hugged the back of a luxury golf resort. On the bright afternoon I visited, the air smelled clean, and the area was quiet except for the wind in the trees, the occasional truck on the road, and the calling of crows.

The memorial stood in a clearing beside a path leading into the woods. Someone had brought a table, and people had filled the table with gifts. There were orchids and coins, cans of soda, bottles of tea, and glasses of water. There were bouquets of daisies and the red hibiscuses that grow everywhere on Okinawa, along with an alarm clock, a Christmas trinket, and potted houseplants. A stuffed Snoopy, clutching a red heart ("I LOVE YOU!"), had fallen to the ground and lay, looking forlorn, next to some cans of coffee. Beside the table, someone had built a little structure out of bricks to house a pot of incense. Rain on Okinawa can come on suddenly and with great intensity, followed by searing sun. The whole tableau was soggy, faded, softened by the elements. But there were fresh flowers, too. People had come very recently.

Soon after my visit, on the anniversary of her death, two more tables would be brought in to hold the dozens of bouquets, wrapped in cellophane, that people would bring. One activist would tweet a photo of the bunch she was leaving—as pink and perfect as a bridesmaid's bouquet. Even with the added tables, the flowers and drinks would spill to the ground.

I walked beyond the table toward the edge of the woods. Okinawa is a subtropical island where plants thrive. In cities, vines creep up the sides of buildings and weeds sprout on rooftops. In the northern forests, infinite shapes of green crowd together at all heights—low ferns, waving grasses, giant heart-shaped leaves, towering trees whose tops are said to look like broccoli. Here, the forest had been cut back. Cleared branches were piled beneath the roots of a felled tree. Yellow and black police tape wound around the trunk of another tree amid a riot of ferns. The path continued, but a wire fence blocked me from going further. Beyond the fence, people had discarded things: cinderblocks and boxes, a television set.

Walking back to my car, I noticed a sticker on a telephone pole near the memorial. It read, in English,

NO RAPE
NO BASE
NO TEARS

The island of Okinawa is long and skinny, about seven by seventy miles. The capital city, Naha, is in the south, with another large city, Nago, in the north. It's the main island of Okinawa Prefecture, the southernmost region of Japan. The chain of 160 small islands, most uninhabited, arcs between Kyushu and Taiwan, on the border between the Pacific and the East China Sea. At the northern tip of Okinawa Island, Cape Hedo, you can stand on the rocky ledge and watch the two oceans collide, the currents swirling and churning in teal and sapphire.

Often, the shorthand I use to describe Okinawa to Americans is "the Hawaii of Japan." This is because the chain of islands is far away—geographically, culturally, historically—from the rest of the country; because the islands were an independent kingdom taken over in the 1800s, a monarchy deposed; because the place is achingly beautiful, home to the turquoise and white beaches of postcards; because that beauty has turned the islands into a tourist mecca, its indigenous culture reduced and wielded for profit; because in recent years the indigenous culture and language have resurged, with local people working to revive what the government tried to erase; and because Okinawa has been made to house, depending on whom you ask, too many or too few U.S. military bases.

Okinawa hosts more U.S. military bases than anywhere else in Japan—the country that hosts more U.S. servicemembers than anywhere else in the world. These bases have their genesis in the tail end of World War II, when American forces landed on the island's beaches and, amid the nightmarish battle that ensued, started constructing runways in preparation for an invasion of "mainland" Japan that never came. After the Allied victory, the U.S. military occupied Japan for seven years, instituting a "peace constitution" that decreed the country would not remilitarize. Article 9 states that "land, sea, and air forces, as well as other war potential, will never be maintained." The 1952 Peace Treaty ended the occupation, and in 1954 American and Japanese leaders signed the U.S.–Japan Mutual Security Treaty, the start of the bilateral security alliance. Japan, without a military, would receive protection under the U.S. military umbrella. In return, Japan would host U.S. bases.

Today, Tokyo pays billions of dollars of the annual costs of U.S. military bases in Japan, to the point where the United States covers little more than troops' salaries. While most countries receive money from the United States to host bases, Japan and other "affluent but once-occupied nations with a tradition of bearing American burdens," as scholar Kent Calder puts it, pay the United States. These nations include Germany and South Korea, with Japan consistently paying the most. Tokyo's so-called sympathy payments are a great financial incentive for the United States to maintain bases in Japan, even if some have suggested otherwise. Presidential candidate and later president Donald Trump has repeatedly called on Japan to pay more for U.S. military bases.

American bases in Japan became concentrated in Okinawa because the 1952 Peace Treaty restored only the mainland's sovereignty. The U.S. military won continued rule of Okinawa, and over the next decade bases closed on the mainland and multiplied in Okinawa, where the U.S. military enjoyed total control. During the Cold War, as the United States built up its network of overseas bases, American soldiers seized Okinawans' land "by bulldozer and bayonet," displacing thousands of people to construct sprawling military facilities. Okinawa reverted to Japanese control in 1972, but, in what many consider a great injustice, the mainland didn't take back its share of bases. There are large bases in mainland Japan, like Yokota Air Base and Yokosuka Naval Base, both in the Tokyo region, and bases in Okinawa have been reduced since their peak, with some land being returned. But 70 percent of all bases in the country are still crowded in tiny Okinawa, mostly on the main island. They add about 50,000 American military personnel, civilian contractors, and family members to the island's population of 1.4 million. All four branches of service—the marine corps, army, navy, and air force—have a presence on Okinawa, with the marines making up the majority. The highest concentration of marine corps units in the Indo–Asia Pacific region is on Okinawa. Many anti-base activists focus on getting marines off the island because of their large numbers and because, activists argue, the marines' presence doesn't serve a real strategic purpose.

Whether 18,000 marines are needed on Okinawa hinges on questions of security and economics. Many believe U.S. bases need to be there for geostrategic reasons. The island's central location means servicemembers can respond quickly to natural disasters in the region and keep an eye on other threats. This is essential, they say, at a time when North Korea maintains nuclear weapons and long-range missiles and a rising China is flexing its power around Japan's borders. Others see China as an ally to cultivate and believe the U.S. bases make Okinawa a military target—less, not more, secure. They point out that marines use Okinawa for training, which they could do anywhere. In the event of a conflict with China or North Korea, the air force, not the marines, would be the ones to respond, and, in any case, with today's technology marines could get anywhere in the region quickly from mainland Japan or even the United States. The bases are in Okinawa not for regional security, but for the security of Japanese mainlanders, who want the protection of the U.S. military but not bases in their backyards. Whether Japan needs the United States for protection is also up for debate. Although the constitution dictates that "land, sea, and air forces . . . will never be maintained," Japan has had a military since 1950. The Japan Self-Defense Forces (SDF) is now one of the most powerful militaries in the world, with capabilities that have been expanding under Prime Minister Shinzo Abe. The constitution still limits the role of the SDF, but Abe seeks to change that with revisions to Article 9.

As for economics, in past years Okinawa depended on the bases for jobs and other income. Today, though, the U.S. military presence accounts for only about 5 percent of the local economy. Many argue the closure of the bases would give way to greater economic development in the islands, such as around tourism. But for locals who work on base, have base-related businesses, rent land to the bases, or are involved in projects funded by Japanese subsidies—compensation money for hosting the bases—a loss of U.S. bases would mean a loss of livelihood.

Whether one sees the U.S. military presence in Okinawa as necessary or not, it's indisputable that the prefecture shoulders a disproportionate share of bases for the U.S.–Japan security alliance, while those bases remain comfortably out of sight and out of mind for most of Japan. This invisibility is true for most Americans, too. The few dozen bases in Okinawa are a key part of the United States' global "empire of bases"—at least seven hundred military installments around the world, from Belgium to Honduras, Egypt to Mozambique, Colombia to Greece, Portugal, and Spain. The largest concentrations are in countries the United States gained access to through its World War II victory: Japan, Germany, Italy, South Korea. In the Asia-Pacific region, most bases are in Japan, South Korea, and the U.S. territory of Guam, but there are also bases in Australia and Singapore, and smaller ones in places like Thailand, Cambodia, and Hong Kong. All in all, these overseas bases cost American taxpayers as much as 100 billion dollars a year. While some politicians and military analysts say a "forward strategy" is necessary to maintain global peace and national security, others disagree, saying bases abroad make us less safe. For foreign host communities, American bases provide jobs but also eat up land and spew American soldiers, American families, and American culture; they fill the air with jets, the roads with tanks, the ground with toxic waste. The United States is the only country in the world to have this worldwide network of bases, and yet they remain largely outside the American consciousness. Americans unconnected to the military don't often think of them.

This seems especially odd in the case of Okinawa, which has a special place in U.S. military history. Some 12,500 American men died fighting to capture the island during World War II. Later, U.S. servicemembers deployed to Korea, Vietnam, the Persian Gulf, Iraq, and Afghanistan passed through Okinawa. The island became their last stop before war zones that could take their lives, a place to enact final desires. Since 1945, hundreds of thousands of American servicemembers, families, and contractors have made Okinawa their temporary or permanent home. American racial politics have bled into and shaped local communities. Formative American childhood memories have been built in Okinawa's humid, buzzing, overgrown terrain. Formative American sexual experiences have played out in the bars, brothels, and clubs outside the base gates. American histories permeate the island. But so many Americans hardly know a thing about the place.

I first traveled to Okinawa in 2002, when I was a college student studying in Kyoto and two friends and I flew there for fall break. Like any mainland tourist, we headed straight for the main island's narrow middle, its waist. There, beach resorts march toward Nago along the western coast. Hotel lobbies are filled with orchids and parrots, jet skis and banana boats cut the small inlets, and man-made lagoons house dolphins and manta rays. At Moon Beach, we lay on the sand and ate at the buffet, and when the weather turned drizzly the hotel concierge recommended we go south. He signed us up for a tour of the part of the island where the heaviest fighting had taken place during the Battle of Okinawa. In Naha, we boarded a bus with three other tourists, all Japanese men. The tour guide was a middle-aged Okinawan woman wearing a tight skirt suit and pillbox hat, both a screaming turquoise. She ushered us to a peace monument and a ramen shop, a glass-blowing workshop and a shrine commemorating children who had died. The World War II battleground had become a tourist trap, with chances to contemplate the hell of war and chances to buy souvenirs.

At the former Japanese navy headquarters, we saw pitted walls where officers had detonated grenades, committing suicide after learning of their defeat. I thought back to my Pacific War course, the shocking testimonies that had first pushed Okinawa into my mind. Okinawan families had been pressured by the Japanese military to take their lives, too, in an improvised frenzy of killing. Schoolgirls had begged soldiers for their own grenades, wanting to die rather than risk losing their virtue to American brutes.

Another day on that trip, my friends and I bused to the American Village, a kind of U.S.A. theme park erected near the beach where U.S. forces first landed in 1945. In a purple-lit club pulsing with hip hop, we sipped cups of watery awamori, the islands' distilled rice liquor, and danced alongside Okinawan women in camouflage hip-huggers and laughing marines. I wanted to know how we had gotten from those schoolgirls' wartime testimonies to here.

That summer, I returned to live on the island for ten weeks, researching my college thesis. Instead of the research, I remember hot sticky nights driving to the American Village, marines in the back seat clinking beer bottles. At the American Village, a giant red Ferris wheel with a Coca-Cola emblem at its center spun over clubs where servicemen segregated themselves by race and often assumed I was Okinawan or Japanese. Sometimes I played along, pretending not to speak English. That summer, I ate hamburgers at A&W drive-ins with blond bobby soxers painted on the walls. I talked to marines about the guns they thought were "tight." I saw the stars and stripes plastered on facades that advertised one-dollar well drinks and "hood" wear. I heard the American national anthem play over a PA system every day. I glimpsed an America I hadn't seen before, and I became someone else in its orbit.

After that, I couldn't get Okinawa out of my mind. Five years later, I went back to live on the island for a year. It wasn't just the history of the place that fascinated me. Life around the bases seemed to enact, in a dramatic way, questions I had about the United States, about what it means to be American, about the legacies of World War II, and about my own existence. On my mother's side, I'm fourth-generation Japanese American, with great-grandparents who emigrated from Hiroshima in the early 1900s. They farmed the California Delta, then lost everything when the U.S. government incarcerated them and their families in concentration camps during World War II. On my father's side, I'm descended from the nation's founders—white men and women who emigrated from Britain to escape religious persecution in the 1600s. In my paternal family tree is a man who signed the Declaration of Independence, others who established towns and companies and served as elected officials. In my family is the glorious myth of America, the America of the free and the brave, the land of opportunity. There's also the darkness of America, the xenophobia and racism and oppression of people of color. I saw that on Okinawa, too, these two sides had been playing out, in tandem and in tension, for decades.

Okinawa was different than mainland Japan. When I first traveled to the mainland in college, I experienced what many people do when they "go back" to the foreign lands of their families' origins. In the United States, I often answered questions about myself—"What kind of name is that?" "What are you?"—with the label *Japanese*. But to the Japanese I was only American. They didn't see me as having any claim to the country, as belonging in any way. Studying in Kyoto, in a sickening reversal of all the years I'd spent correcting pronunciations of my name in the United States, I found I couldn't properly say *Akemi*. "Candy?" Japanese people replied, stepping back with confusion when I insisted the name was theirs. In Japan, I found a country more obsessed with homogeneity, with myths of racial purity and hierarchy, than the United States.

Okinawa offered more space for someone like me. In his book of American night scenes on the island, Okinawan photographer Naobumi Okamoto writes, "The relationships between Okinawa, America, Japan and me. . . . Not sure what they are? I have been looking for the answer for this longest time." I had spent my adult life figuring out my identity in a triangulation with the United States and Japan, and on Okinawa I found an island of people doing the same. A *contact zone* is what Okinawa is called in academic speak—a place where ideologies, cultures, and politics collide. This is familiar terrain for a mixed-race person; in the melding and clashing I recognized something powerful. Instead of pollution or dilution, I saw creation. I saw people forging new identities, networks, and spaces—though the stories I heard told about Okinawa didn't seem to capture these shades of gray.

On the evening of April 28, 2016, Rina Shimabukuro put on her red sneakers and black parka to go out for a walk. Twenty years old, Rina was an office worker with long, dark hair and girlish bangs. She stood about five feet tall, and when she smiled, she showed off a set of straight teeth. One childhood classmate characterized her as friendly and good-natured, a girl who had been quiet in the classroom but broke out her singing and dancing skills when hanging out with friends.

Around 8 p.m., Rina texted her boyfriend that she was going walking and left the apartment they shared in Uruma City, on the island's central east coast. A river ran through the area where she walked. One side was both commercial and residential, filled with apartment buildings, restaurants, fishing shops, a Don Quixote mega-store crammed with discount household goods. The other side was more industrial, with warehouses and smokestacks, recycling centers and shipping companies. The roads were wide and cut by medians, where trash got caught in the weeds. A new-looking paved path ran alongside the overgrown river. A sign there warned walkers to pick up after their dogs, and a small pavilion offered a place to sit in the shade. The ground was littered with cigarette butts and bottle caps, and stray cats hissed from the underbrush.

A few hours after Rina went out, her messaging app showed she had read a text from her boyfriend. She didn't respond. She didn't come home. She didn't have her wallet. The next morning, her boyfriend reported her missing.

Over the next few weeks, Rina's friends posted about her disappearance on social media, and people speculated about what had happened. Some thought she had been abducted by a religious cult. Others suspected the boyfriend, who was Okinawan too. Meanwhile, the police worked the case. They circulated a missing-person flyer. They used GPS data to track her cell phone to its last location, the industrial zone near the river. They surveyed security footage of the area, combing through the hundreds of cars caught on camera. The breakthrough came when they brought in the owner of a red SUV for questioning.

Kenneth Franklin Gadson was thirty-two, an African American ex-marine who had been stationed on the island for a few years. The marine corps had sent him back to the United States in 2011, and after his honorable discharge he returned to Okinawa in 2014. He found a job on Kadena Air Base, working as a civilian contractor at a company that provided internet and cable TV to the U.S. bases. He married a local woman (who was "kind and very good looking," according to a neighbor) and adopted her last name, Shinzato. They had a baby and moved in with her parents a half hour's drive south of Uruma, in a small seaside town. "It looked like he was living a normal life," another neighbor said. But under police questioning, Gadson confessed that he had spotted a girl walking, pulled over, and assaulted her. He led them to her body in the woods.

When I traveled to Okinawa the next year, people were still talking about the murder. Gadson had confessed, but the grisly details of that night were still emerging, and his trial loomed. In the absence of facts and closure, rumors spread. Rina Shimabukuro and Kenneth Gadson were secretly dating, some locals told me; it wasn't a random crime. She was pregnant with his child. She was pregnant with his child, and his wife had found out, and his wife was the one who killed her. Gad-son had just disposed of the body, then taken the hit for his wife. The people who told me these stories tended to support the U.S. military presence on their island. Some seemed confident in their version (*every-one in Uruma City knows the truth*). Others were more uncertain (*that's just what I heard*) or indignant at the local media for distorting the truth (*fake news*). Anti-base activists, on the other hand, blamed the U.S. military for starting any rumors about a romance (*propaganda*).

I believed the news and didn't think the rumors were true, but I wanted to know why Rina's relationship to her killer mattered so much to so many people. So what if she had been dating the man? He killed her and dumped her body in the woods. Her dating him didn't lessen that crime. But to many people, it did.

NO RAPE NO BASE read the sticker at her memorial. NO RAPE NO BASE read the signs at many anti-base demonstrations. NO RAPE NO BASE read the sticker that appeared on an electric pole near the Uruma City home of an Okinawan woman I knew. Arisa was married to an American ex-serviceman who worked on base, and they had two young kids. "What does *rape* mean?" her eight-year-old son asked when he saw the sticker. Arisa was horrified, feeling like some-one had put it there for her family, making some nauseating commen-tary about her husband. She avoided her son's question, but he kept asking. Her husband tried to scrape off the sticker, but someone put up another one.

I became interested in Rina's story because it, like too many others before hers, came to mean much more than the crime itself. It came to mean something about the U.S.–Japan security alliance. In Oki-nawa, where there's a long-simmering tension over the U.S. military presence, stories about locals and Americans become allegories, and there's a war of stories going on. The pro-base side circulates videos of belligerent demonstrators outside the base gates to show the protest movement is driven by discrimination and hate. A video of marines cleaning up a local beach or visiting an Okinawan senior citizens' home means the U.S. military presence is altruistic. "If you get the community relations right, the politics fall in place," Robert Eldridge, a former military public affairs official, said in the wake of Rina's death. Eldridge called for more publicity of servicemen in Okinawa doing "good things." What he didn't say was that he also believed in publicity of Okinawan activists doing "bad things;" Eldridge reportedly had been fired from his position with the marines for leaking a tape of a prominent activist illegally stepping on base before being arrested. The tape ended up in the hands of Japanese neo-nationalists, the far right.

For anti-base activists, the most powerful story is a rape. A rape of an Okinawan woman or girl by a U.S. serviceman snaps people awake in ways a helicopter crash, chemical spill, bar-room brawl, or threatened coral reef can't. A rape captures the imagination of the public and media because it's a story in our bones—a metaphor we understand right away, without explanation. We're used to anthropomorphizing geography in this sexualized, feminized way. We talk about virgin land, Mother Earth, the rape of Nanking. When a U.S. serviceman rapes a woman in Okinawa, Okinawa becomes the innocent girl—kidnapped, beaten, held down, and violated by a thug United States. Tokyo is the pimp who enabled the abuse, having let the thug in. Soon, no one is talking about the real victim or what happened; they're using the rape as the special anti-base weapon that it is.

A rape has the power to assemble world leaders, spark mass protests, and shape global affairs. In 1995, the gang rape of a twelve-year-old Okinawan girl brought out more than ninety thousand people in protest. The swelling of public anger was so great that leaders agreed to close Marine Corps Air Station Futenma, dubbed "the most dangerous base in the world" because the homes, schools, and shops of Okinawa's Ginowan City push against its fences, in the path of the aircraft that take off and land there, day and night. The catch was that in return for Futenma's closure the U.S. military would build a new, bigger base on Oura Bay in the island's north. In 2017, when I returned to Okinawa, protest over this new base was raging, and activists were in need of new ammunition. Maybe what happened to Rina Shimabukuro could make a difference. It all depended on the details of her story.

Because the 1995 rape was so brutal, the victim so young (and a schoolgirl, the epitome of innocence and titillation in the Japanese imagination), that incident made the biggest political impact. Even a murder didn't trump it; there aren't any NO MURDER NO BASE stickers. For instance, a few months before the 1995 rape, a U.S. serviceman on Okinawa beat his Japanese girlfriend to death with a hammer. "He hit her head more than twenty times or something," veteran journalist Chiyomi Sumida told me. "It was such a vicious murder." But she said hardly any reporters attended the trial. The woman's death didn't mobilize tens of thousands of people. The woman's death isn't in Okinawa history books and museums. The woman was dating the soldier, and she was from mainland Japan. She wasn't a good symbol.

Sumida explained the general attitude toward cases like that: "If you don't want to get involved with trouble, then stay away from" U.S. soldiers. If you date an American and something terrible befalls you, "you asked for it." She said the media plays into this victim-blaming. "There's always a big, clear line," Sumida said. "If you are dating the person, and you get raped or injured, you don't get much sympathy from the public." That was why she thought people—she didn't know who—started "groundless rumors" online about Rina Shimabukuro dating Kenneth Gadson. If Rina was raped before she was murdered, people suggested—if she really was just walking down the street (*but why was she out alone after dark?*) and was randomly nabbed and assaulted—the incident was proof that the bases should close. But if she was having sex with the guy by choice, if she chose to interact with him, and he ended up killing her, her story wasn't a condemnation of the bases. It couldn't be used as a metaphor to represent the entire situation.

I started gathering my own stories of people in Okinawa because I was tired of hearing these crude dichotomies, wielded for political use. The pure, innocent victim and the slut who asked for it. The faultless activist and the rabid protester. The demonic American soldier and his savior counterpart. They're all caricatures, and if we're using them to understand the larger political, sociohistorical situation—the U.S. military in Okinawa, and by extension the U.S.–Japan security alliance and America's system of overseas basing—we're not getting anywhere. Dichotomies like these disempower and silence the real people involved with the bases, the full cast of characters who often inhabit ambiguous spaces.

As an allegory, a story like Rina's is incomplete. Her death is tragic and disturbing and representative of the widespread U.S. military violence against local women that stretches back to the American invasion. It taps into deep emotions concerning Japan and the United States that many Okinawans feel. But as a metaphor for the entire story of Okinawa and the U.S. military, it leaves out much of the vast, complicated reality.

What I found, as I traveled the island, is that most locals don't have a simple victim relationship with the U.S. military. Instead, since the end of World War II, Okinawan people have been actively engaging with the U.S. military empire, whether helping to enable or disable it. Local men and women—more often women, because of the predominantly male nature of the military—seek out relationships with the bases and their inhabitants, relationships that are often symbiotic, even if they're problematic. Many locals' motives center on love or money, but Okinawans also find community and new identities in the base world. As for the bases, connections with local people help the military installations run smoothly, boost the emotional health and built-up masculinity of soldiers, and make the bases harder to close. The bases may have arrived by force, but they have stayed because of the complex relationships formed with people living outside the fences. The truth is that when Okinawans choose not to cooperate, when they decide to challenge the U.S. military presence, their actions have the power to rattle the whole system.

During my stays in Okinawa, I spent time with locals, mainly women who live around the bases, in the contact zone. These are women who date and marry U.S. soldiers, who work on and around the bases, who have fathers or husbands in the military, who fight against the military. Even if not as obviously as the 1995 rape victim or Rina, these everyday women are players in the larger geopolitical game, influencing, challenging, and smoothing the way for the U.S.–Japan security alliance. Their stories reveal how deeply American bases abroad affect local communities, importing American ideas of race, transforming off-base cultures, shaping people's identities. Unlike the popular victim narratives, their stories paint a nuanced portrait of the U.S. military presence in Okinawa—how it persists, how it should change, and what life is like at the edges of the American empire, in all its darkness and glory.

2

EVE

WE DROVE SOUTH TOWARD NAHA AFTER ELEVEN ON A SATURDAY night. On the left, the base fences flashed, silver and barbed wire. On the right were convenience stores and used American furniture shops with names like Graceland and U.S.A. Collectibles. Camouflage and gas masks hung in the windows of thrift shops.

Eve turned up the American hip hop on the stereo. "Ladies' night," she exclaimed. Tonight she might meet her future husband.

Twenty-nine, Eve was an Okinawan receptionist who lived with her parents in Nago, on the northern part of the island. She had gotten her American nickname in college. Her friends used it, while her family and co-workers used her Japanese birth name. Eve was sleepy-eyed and cool, soft-spoken and sweet. Her skin was pale, freckled around her nose; her friends teased her about this whiteness, because Eve dated only black American men.

"Me, I like the black people," she'd told me. "I never had a Japanese guy."

She wasn't sure why. At first she had liked white men, but then she had switched to African American men, kokujin, and stuck with them.

They were just more attractive. When she went out with her friends, they went to places kokujin went.

That night in December, we were headed for Saicolo, a hip-hop club on Naha's International Street. In Japanese, the club's name meant "dice." Eve was dressed for the occasion in a flowy red top with cutouts along the sleeves, black lace-up pants, and heels. A pair of sunglasses served as a headband in her long hair. Her friend Maiko was behind the wheel; with her free hand, Maiko drank from a can and smoked cigarettes and toyed with her cell phone. She had a face that was at once pretty and hard, mean.

"Onegaishimasu," Eve pleaded, asking her friend to please drive carefully as we tore around a bend.

We stopped to pick up another friend, Ayako, who wore towering platform sandals and a messy bun of bleached hair atop her head. She worked on Kadena Air Base, like Maiko, and spoke English naturally. Amid a story told in Japanese, she threw in English phrases like "He damn ugly."

Camp Kinser passed on the right before the landscape turned urban, becoming more Osaka than American suburb. Crammed-together high-rises replaced the sprawl of fast food joints, used car lots, and boxy, one-story homes. In Naha, we parked off the freeway and headed to International Street. By day the area was crowded with tourists perusing tropical-themed souvenirs. By night, music thudded from bars, clubs, and izakayas. Saicolo was down a flight of stairs, subterranean. As we walked in, I overheard a white guy trying to convince a woman to leave with him. He was using all kinds of twisted logic, and she was smiling, not giving in, but maybe about to.

Inside, the club was terraced like a Balinese rice paddy and crowded with men. The DJ was playing Jermaine Dupri's "Welcome to Atlanta." Most of the patrons were black, like Eve had said, with a few white and Latino men here and there. I spotted one Asian American guy, identifiable with his military haircut, and a handful of Okinawan and Japanese guys, stylish in their caps and sneakers.

Among the female club-goers, Okinawan and mainland Japanese, some looked confident, at ease, striking in their dramatic makeup and tight outfits. Others were more casual, sticking to the perimeters, looking nervous but excited. Women like Eve, who only wanted to date American men, were common on the island, to such an extent that they had formed a subculture. One quality was a similar affectation and style. Women transformed their appearances, mannerisms, and speech to some approximation of the race and culture of men they wanted to date. With deep tans, gold jewelry, and slang they tried to creep toward a foreign world.

When I lived in Okinawa, women who favored African American men seemed the largest subset of this group by far. Local women's preference for black men was common knowledge among U.S. servicemen. "I heard Japanese girls like guys with dark skin," one Dominican American marine told me, his eyes sparking with hope. Conversely, a white marine coming from Saicolo said, "I want to drop a bomb on that club." He told me he had no chance of getting a girl there. In trying to untangle the relationships between locals and U.S. servicemembers, I found this phenomenon—and all the questions it raised about race and racism, history and desire—to be obviously fertile ground.

I waited with Eve and her friends to get drinks that were free but weak, then descended to an area above the dance floor cluttered with small tables. We swallowed our screwdrivers, which tasted like watered-down orange juice. Ayako agreed she needed a real drink. In line for the bar again, she told me she had lived in Arizona for a couple of years with an American boyfriend. They had broken up the month before because he couldn't come to Japan to live—visa issues. They still talked every day, but Ayako had moved on to meeting new guys.

The man in front of us in line turned and asked how long we'd been in Okinawa. He was short and white and young, wearing glasses.

"Two months," I said. "You?"

"One and a half."

He guessed we were marines or military wives. Ayako waited a moment to tell him, grinning, "I'm Japanese." She seemed happy he had thought she was American.

"Do you like Okinawa?" she asked him.

"Yeah, but it's haunted," he said. "Okinawa is haunted."

Ayako nodded. "It's true," she said. "There are so many haunted places."

At the bar, Ayako and I did tequila shots. She bought us glasses of Orion beer, speaking to the Japanese bartender in English. Back at our table, I asked Eve if she had seen any cute guys. She hadn't. "Let's dance," she said.

The dance floor, the bottom level of the club, was packed and sweaty. Towering above us was a flashing screen, the music pounding. Men came up behind Eve and Ayako, swiveling into their asses. When 2 Live Crew sang about wanting pussy, all the men shouted along.

With dawn not far off, we headed back north. In the car, Eve exclaimed something fast in Japanese—regret and frustration at not meeting anyone. Another night and no husband-to-be. I wondered if at times like these she thought about expanding her dating pool. Did she really want a partner, or was she chasing a fantasy?

I met Eve in 2008, when I was living in Okinawa for a year, renting an apartment in Ginowan. I'd tacked a map of the island to my wall, and one afternoon I realized what it was missing. Designed in mostly blues and greens, the English-language map featured roads and towns and golf courses, along with hotels, beaches, and resorts up the coasts. But the U.S. military bases were nowhere. The vast areas of land they occupied were marked only by expanses of beige, innocent as sand dunes. And in a way this was accurate, because to the tourists who picked up this map at the airport, the bases might as well have not existed. The bases weren't the reason they'd traveled to this paradise; the bases weren't what they thought about while lounging by the sea. The bases were off-limits—tourists couldn't get past those fences if they tried.

My other English-language map looked different. This one had been produced by a housing agency and given to me by an American used car salesman in a lot outside the marine corps base Camp Foster. It was obvious who this map had been created for. On it, each base was labeled with big red letters, a font larger than the one spelling out Okinawan towns. The bases were shaded with a patriotic, star-flecked pattern and lit up with icons—health clinics, libraries, fast food joints, bowling alleys. The bases bloomed to life on this map, which covered only the central part of the island, where the bases are concentrated. The southern and northern ends didn't exist.

In a 1969 *New York Times* article, reporter Takashi Oka distinguishes between "Okinawan Okinawa" and "American Okinawa." Okinawan Okinawa is the bucolic community of the prewar days, where "wiry, small-boned men and women with broad-brimmed straw hats or carefully knotted towels on their heads" work "the fields of sugar cane and sweet potato." American Okinawa "is much like United States military establishments anywhere else in the world, with offices, schools, clubs, barracks and neat bungalows surrounded by lawns— the whole enclosed behind high wire fences patrolled by sentry dogs." The two Okinawas are "inextricably interwoven" and yet apart: "In general, Okinawan Okinawa and American Okinawa go their respective ways, except in garish base-oriented towns such as Koza and Kin, Kadena and Ginowan." Four decades later, my two maps still delineated these two Okinawas, and many people on the island still lived in only one or the other. Either they were locals whose lack of base access relegated those large expanses to another world, or they were part of the U.S. military community and stuck to base and a few well-trodden off-base spots. But there was another world where those two overlapped, a third Okinawa the garish base towns had become. I was living in the midst of it.

Across the street from my apartment was Camp Foster. A half-mile down Route 58, the notorious Air Station Futenma was still squeezed into the middle of the city, as the 1996 deal to close it had been stalled due to opposition against the new "replacement" base in the north. This area was in the island's central part, known as chūbu, where most American bases are located. Chūbu has an identity distinct from the north and south. The south is dominated by Naha, which feels more like mainland Japan, a cityscape with tall buildings and a monorail. In the south, it's rarer to interact with the American military community. Residents can feel removed from the base presence, often against it but not directly affected (like gazing at a "fire on the other side of the river," as I heard it put once). The north is less developed, with expanses of dense jungle. The north hasn't been untouched by the U.S. military presence, and may soon become home to the large new base, but it hosts fewer bases and U.S. troops.

Every morning in my chūbu neighborhood, the reveille rang out from Foster, waking us with the jaunty bugle call. In the evenings, we were washed in the American national anthem, then the Japanese one, a song that seemed so slow, sad, and short that for a while I didn't know what it was. From the top-floor landing of my five-story apartment building I could see over Foster's perimeter fence, where the cramped streets of Ginowan gave way to rolling green lawns, wide roads, and low white buildings. On base, there was so much space, especially compared to off-base areas, which often felt claustrophobic, with either concrete or subtropical vegetation closing in.

At the foot of my building, traditional Okinawan homes clustered, their dark, peaked roofs fitting together like tiles. Among them were snapshots from another time: cisterns collecting rainwater, doors sliding open and shut. A stooped woman with her hair in an old-style topknot hung laundry on a line. Pairs of shisa, lion-dog statues, perched on rooftops to keep good spirits in and bad spirits out.

Two blocks away was Chichi's Gentleman's Club ("American Style"). Silhouettes of women with arched backs beckoned servicemen inside. Below that were Nashville Bar ("Mechanical Bull") and Pitsters Sports Bar & Grill ("50 Cent Chicken Wings"). Next door was Crazy Horse, and down the street was Pub U.S.A. There were Mary Jane's Rock Bar and La Pachanga Latin House, $1 Tube Shots and $5 Irish Car Bombs. There were boutiques with names like Sugar and Pink Dracula that catered to women who dated Americans. Their display windows showcased bright tube dresses, short shorts, and velour track suits—merchandise imported from the United States and drastically marked up. There was a Lawson convenience store, an unofficial staging area for journeys on and off base. At night, marines huddled around their souped-up rides in the parking lot, pregaming with cans of beer before sauntering over to Chichi's or driving up 58 to the American Village. Local women congregated there to meet whoever among them had the magic ID, the one that would get them through the base gate across the street.

A few blocks west was the ocean, suddenly, and sky, suddenly. The air smelled of fried food and garlic. On sunny weekends, old Okinawan fishermen in rubber boots and baseball caps waded in the surf. Tanned blondes in sports bras ran alongside Okinawan power-walkers hidden beneath track suits and towels, and middle-aged American men taught their kids to ride bicycles: "Don't stop, don't be weak." One early morning, I jogged past a group of local junior high school boys exercising in their gray and white baseball uniforms. For a moment, I was enveloped by the scent of clean laundry. Another morning, I passed an American woman in a sweatshirt walking a Chihuahua. She was videotaping the ocean, looking giddy. She must have just arrived on the island. She looked at me like, *Can you believe this?* The apartment parking lots along the water were filled with cars bearing the Y-lettered license plates of American military personnel. An ocean view was bought more easily with a U.S. military housing allowance.

On one of my first nights living in that neighborhood, I was at home when I heard a key in the front door, and suddenly it was open. In the doorway stood a middle-aged white guy wearing only a pair of boxers. "I should have knocked," he said, mortified. He had skinny legs and a beer gut. He stepped halfway behind the doorframe, saying he hadn't known anyone had moved in. His friend used to live here; he'd given him an extra key. I stared back and for some reason didn't feel alarmed. The next day, I would have the locks changed, but in that moment it seemed expected that this near-naked American man would unlock my door and appear in my apartment at 9:30 on a Sunday night. I was living in chūbu, after all.

Long ago, before the Americans, before the Japanese, Okinawa was an independent kingdom. The Ryukyu Kingdom was a thriving civilization built around international trade. Living on islands with not enough rich soil, forests, and fresh water, in a climate with regular typhoons and occasional tsunamis, Ryukyuans leveraged their central location to survive. In the fifteenth and sixteenth centuries, they served as middlemen in the transoceanic trade of luxury goods. From Southeast Asia Ryukyuan merchants brought incense, pepper, ivory, and rhinoceros horn. Routed through Naha, the goods sailed on to ports in China, Korea, and Japan. Peacocks and parrots stopped by the island on their way to the King of Korea. From China to Kyoto went glazed ceramics and coins; Japan shipped back swords and fans and folding screens. With the Ryukyuan merchants earning as much as a 1000-percent return on these dealings, the kingdom prospered. Its culture began to reflect the faraway places with which it traded. In Shuri, at the royal palace, elaborate court ceremonies were based on Chinese practices and architecture nodded to temples in Thailand and Cambodia. Textile manufacture was inspired by fine, gauzy weaving from China, Malaysian ikat patterns, and Indonesian tie-dye.

But what made the islands ideal for trading also attracted larger powers. The Ryukyu archipelago lies less than a thousand miles from modern-day Tokyo, Seoul, Taipei, Shanghai, Hong Kong, and Manila; it's long been eyed as strategic territory to command. In the early 1600s, the Japanese domain Satsuma wrested partial control of the kingdom and maintained that control for over two hundred years, benefiting from the Ryukyuans' lucrative tribute relationship with China. Then, in 1879, the kingdom lost all independence when Japan deposed its king and claimed the islands as a prefecture.

Leaders in Tokyo showed little concern for their new people. High taxes and limited social services helped poverty settle across the region. In the 1920s, the situation grew more dire when the price of sugar, the islands' main export, dropped. Facing famine, islanders subsisted on a diet of native, palm-like cycads (a time remembered as "cycad hell"). Thousands of Okinawans left in search of work elsewhere—in Osaka textile factories; in the fields of Hawaii, the Philippines, South America. Meanwhile, in Okinawa, the Japanese government taught people how to become Japanese. In what was known as "bad habit elimination," officials banned or discouraged traditional Ryukyuan customs. New generations of Okinawans studied the Japanese language in classrooms decorated with portraits of the emperor and empress of Japan. They dressed in Japanese-style school uniforms and cut their hair short, losing the traditional Okinawan topknot. Soon, Okinawans themselves were pushing assimilation. "We must even sneeze as the Japanese do," a local newspaper urged. In schools, students agreed to use "dialect cards," wooden signs hung around necks as punishment for speaking the local language. A student could remove the sign of shame only by catching another student in the act and passing it off to him or her. (The easiest way was to whack someone, eliciting an "Aga!"—*ouch* in Okinawan.) This assimilation game continued for decades, and now the native languages of the islands—rebranded as dialects—are dead or dying.

By the time hundreds of American warships gathered in the azure waters off Okinawa in the spring of 1945, Okinawans had effectively become Japanese. And, like their fellow citizens to the north, throughout the Pacific War they had been indoctrinated to serve as civilian soldiers. Young and old, male and female, Okinawans were mobilized into combat brigades and nursing corps, trained to brandish bamboo spears and sing war songs. They readied themselves to die for the emperor alongside mainland soldiers. They listened to the soldiers' warnings about what the invaders would do with captives: *The Americans will run over men with tanks. The Americans will rape women and girls. The Americans will cut off noses and fingers and ears.* The American men were "devil beasts." The fate better than capture by the Americans was death.

When the Americans invaded in late March 1945, landing on beaches and raining down artillery and bombs, unleashing what became known as a "typhoon of steel," Okinawa transformed into a battlefield. Outnumbered and outgunned, the Japanese military was aiming not to win, but to draw out the fighting in order to delay or discourage a mainland invasion. Okinawa was to be the sacrifice to keep mainlanders safe. By the end of nearly three months of some of the bloodiest fighting in the Pacific War, about 12,500 American troops, nearly 66,000 Japanese soldiers, and as many as 140,000 Okinawan civilians—one-third of the prefecture's population—had perished. Many Okinawans were killed in the crossfire between the Americans and Japanese. Others died from starvation or lack of medical aid. Some were murdered by American soldiers, and some were murdered by Japanese soldiers who didn't accept or understand how well their nation's assimilation polices had worked. In a devastating refusal of Okinawans' patriotism, Japanese troops still saw Okinawans as the Other: potential spies, liabilities, and competition for shelter and food. During the battle, there were reports of Japanese soldiers forcing civilians out of the caves where they hid, executing those who spoke the Okinawan language ("spies," some as young as toddlers), ordering whole villages to commit mass suicide, and raping local women or forcing them to serve as "comfort women" alongside the thousands of Koreans forcibly brought to the island. Okinawans' devotion to the Japanese empire, so carefully cultivated before the war, began to break down. "What's the difference between Okinawans and people from outside the prefecture?" wondered future governor Masahide Ota, when he saw Japanese soldiers tossing Okinawan mothers out of caves and stealing their food. "For the first time I began to be awakened to differences in our cultures. I began to see that I was an Okinawan."

The U.S. military encouraged Okinawans' distancing from Japan, too. In their hasty pre-invasion research, U.S. military analysts had determined Okinawans weren't really Japanese, and the Americans' arrival could be seen as a liberation of an oppressed people. Leading up to the battle, the U.S. military began its campaign for Okinawan hearts and minds by dropping on the island millions of leaflets promoting the ethnic and cultural differences between mainland Japanese and Okinawans.

The battle decimated the main island. Describing the postwar scene, an American navy doctor wrote that the "extent of the devastation is unimaginable. . . . Hardly a tree was left standing," and more than "95% of the homes were damaged or destroyed." Almost all farm animals died, and the agricultural fields were wiped out. The only remnant of the former Ryukyu Kingdom's great Shuri Castle was an iron fountain, a dragon that still spit water from its jaws.

Okinawans who had managed to survive discovered the Americans weren't the demons they'd been made to be. Rapes, killings, and atrocities did occur. But, as official protocol, U.S. forces tended to

civilian survivors according to international law, offering food, clothing, and medical care. One part of the invading U.S. forces, known as
the Military Government, was designated just for this task and began
taking in civilians as soon as the battle began. After a month, 120,000
Okinawans were in refugee camps. "Had it not been for this American
policy towards non-combatants," Masahide Ota writes, "Okinawan
civilians would have paid an immeasurably higher price during the
battle." The Military Government's main aim wasn't humanitarian;
civilians on the battlefield could interfere with American war efforts.
But once in custody, Okinawans received care not available elsewhere.
"American forces treated Okinawans just like their beloved children,"
a village mayor in northern Okinawa told a Military Government
commander after the war. "We are all profoundly moved by the depth
of your humanity. There are no words to express our gratitude." One
American veteran remembered an instance of Military Government
men venturing onto the battlefield in search of sewing machines so
they could make dresses for the Okinawan women in their camp.

As the fighting ended, the American victors confined almost all
Okinawan survivors in these refugee or internment camps, where they
received shelter, provisions, and aid, however meager. For a couple of
years, Okinawans eked out a living in tents and Quonset huts, eating
foreign foods like Spam, dried ice cream, and powdered milk. Often
there weren't enough K-rations to feed the overcrowded camps, and
some people resorted to desperate solutions like frying tempura in
motor oil. Others forged for seaweed, grass, frogs, and crabs. A few
thousand internees died amid these conditions, succumbing to starvation or malaria.

From the postwar wreckage and U.S. military scraps Okinawans
reconstructed their lost possessions. Airplane parts became pots and
pans. Used American fatigues became everyday clothing. Halved
Coca-Cola bottles became drinking cups, and tin cans and parachute
threads became stringed sanshin musical instruments. "We knew how
to make something out of nothing," remembered one woman who
was a high school student at the time. Everyone at her school wore
recycled U.S. military goods. The boys clomped around in combat

boots, and the girls sewed skirts out of parachutes and mosquito netting. In the early years, schools were held outside, without classrooms or desks or textbooks. During this time, Okinawans also consumed shreds of American entertainment, like one group that glimpsed a 1930s Hollywood film shown to GIs, "the actresses in barebacked white gowns."

After the Americans finally released them from the camps, many Okinawans returned home—only to discover their homes had disappeared. "As far as we could see, there were American military facilities," one villager from Yomitan described. "Trees were cut down; stone walls and hedges had been taken away; pampas grass and weeds were growing everywhere; wild birds from the mountains were nesting and mongooses were roaming in the midst of what used to be our village; it was sheer desolation." Another Okinawan, from a town farther north, glimpsed his former home from a distance, and "everything looked white like snow. We discovered that the village had been turned into an airfield. Every house had been burned down, and the fertile farms were buried under the runway." While Okinawans had been confined in the camps, Americans had taken tens of thousands of acres from tens of thousands of landowners.

Displaced Okinawans struggled to rebuild in new and unfamiliar spaces. Without other options, many took low-paying service jobs on and around the bases, working as cooks, gardeners, maids. Already scarce resources became scarcer as the local population tripled with the forced return of tens of thousands of Okinawans from Japan's mainland and former colonies. The initial postwar warmth toward the American occupiers waned, and locals' futures seemed bleak. "The students here are too puzzled to have any fixed hopes," said an Okinawan school principal. "Why bother to graduate from high school if the only job you can get is working on a labor gang for the American Air Force?"

Meanwhile, behind tall fences, Americans moved into gleaming new military facilities with movie theaters and yacht clubs. One Okinawan woman told me about her childhood in the late sixties and early seventies in Nishihara, a town east of Camp Kinser and south of Futenma. Mina remembered going up the hill with her friends to beg the American kids for things, communicating somehow through the language barrier. She remembered being let into American houses, where she marveled at the bathrooms. "All we had was a hole in the ground," she said. Once, an American girl gave her a small wooden doll, and Mina, who'd never had a doll, was overjoyed.

In an attempt to tamp down Okinawan discontent and longing to return to Japan, the U.S. military continued its campaign to revive Ryukyuan culture and pride. The occupying government, the United States Civil Administration of the Ryukyu Islands (USCAR), brought back the name Ryukyu and used U.S. public money to fund museums, libraries, and history texts on the Ryukyu Kingdom. It restored cultural and historic sites, ordered local broadcasters to speak in Okinawan, and attempted to establish a Ryukyuan flag and national anthem. At USCAR-built Ryukyuan-American Cultural Centers, locals watched Ryukyuan cultural programs, viewed Ryukyuan art, and attended lectures on Ryukyuan history, all for free.

At the same time, the Ryukyuan-American Cultural Centers taught American culture. Many locals were eager to learn. Hundreds of Okinawan women enrolled in a "Housewives' University" program, in which American women taught skills like cooking, cosmetics, and physical fitness. Other Okinawans took USCAR-funded trips to the United States. Local leaders toured sectors of American business and society. Young people received vocational and technical training at places like the University of Hawaii's East-West Center. Over a thousand students received scholarships to attend university in the States. When they returned, many took upper-level jobs connected to the American administration.

Despite these efforts, Okinawans grew more and more dissatisfied with the U.S. occupation. The Korean and Vietnam Wars further militarized the main island, as Okinawa became a key staging and "R&R" area, and American troops multiplied. B-52 bombers blasted off from Kadena Air Base on bombing raids over Southeast Asia. Outside the base gates, soldiers partied to hard rock played by Okinawan bands, not knowing what fates they'd meet across the sea.

The bodies of strangled sex workers began turning up. Military accidents killed civilians, and bases housed chemical and nuclear weapons. Pushed past their limit, Okinawans rallied to demand an end to the American occupation and a return to Japan. A "reversion," people thought, would bring Japanese standards of living and the closure of U.S. bases.

To quell this growing protest and to appease Japanese mainlanders who wanted a full return of their country from the United States, American and Japanese authorities reverted control of Okinawa to Tokyo in 1972. In the coming years, Okinawan standards of living did improve, the economy growing and diversifying. The prefecture's per capita GDP came to surpass that of countries like Italy and Canada, although income levels never caught up to those on the Japanese mainland. Year after year, the prefecture ranks first or last in a number of federal surveys: last in average per capita income; first in shotgun weddings, divorces, single-parent households, drunk driving, unemployment, non-full-time workers, and children living in poverty. Many locals I met could rattle off these superlatives, often with good-humored shame and weariness—not musing about the sociohistorical reasons for the disparities, but implying moral failing.

And, of course, with the reversion, in what many Okinawans considered a great betrayal, the bases remained. In this way, in 1972 everything changed in Okinawa—and also stayed the same. What affected Okinawans like Mina were things like the currency. Seven years old when the reversion took place, she remembered going to the corner store and struggling to count out the strange coins. She was used to American dollars, not Japanese yen. She also remembered shiny new Japanese buses where the old American ones had been. She remembered cars switching from the right side of the road to the left. Island officials ran a campaign called Think Left to prevent traffic collisions. It was the same kind of refrain I repeated while navigating the narrow streets.

"It was like everyone had culture shock," I said once to my friend Lily, a historian.

"The border crossed them," she replied.

In their history, islanders have been Ryukyuan, Okinawan, Japanese, and, to some extent, American. In recent years, there's been a resurgence of indigenous pride, with many referring to themselves as *Uchinaanchu*, "Okinawan" in the native language. But at the same time, many locals see Okinawa as a "champuru" culture, meaning a mix or blend. Champuru is the name of one of the prefecture's best-known dishes, a stir-fry that combines ingredients like goya (bitter melon), tofu, egg, and Spam. As a description of the prefecture, champuru is more like the "melting pot" or "tossed salad" metaphors of diversity in the United States than common ideas about the makeup of mainland Japan. In the social imagination, Japan has long been like the country's brand of white rice—superior for its purity—though national homogeneity is more myth than reality. In Okinawa, even when there's widespread protest against the U.S. military presence, the concept of champuru is celebrated with pride.

One night in Okinawa, my friend, an American named Kate, said to me, "I want to take you to a place that's like an inside-out sock." She led me through the seamy entertainment district outside Kadena Air Base in Okinawa City, down Gate 2 Street. The road that radiates from the southeastern edge of the base is nicknamed after the base entryway at its end. This gate—Gate 2—means the thousands of airmen stationed on the mammoth base spill out of this portal each day. The larger area is known as Koza, a name that lore says came from the Americans. After the war, the occupiers botched the pronunciation of either Kujaa, a local district with an internment camp, or Goya, a busy intersection, and the name stuck, becoming official in 1956—the only city in Japan written in katakana, the alphabet reserved for foreign words. Two years after Okinawa's reversion to Japan, Koza merged with a nearby town to become Okinawa City. Some say the new name was a rebranding, an attempt to distance the city from Koza's rowdy and violent past.

During the Vietnam War, the area was a notorious party zone for soldiers stopping over to "rest and relax." As one Okinawan musician recalls, Koza was a place where murder, sexual assault, and muggings "happened every day, though they were never on the news." Prostitution was legal then, and payday lines snaked out of brothels. In a reflection of American racial politics, the base town was unofficially but strictly segregated. White men hung around B.C. Street, now an arcade of shops and restaurants off Gate 2 Street, and black men frequented a nearby neighborhood called Teruya. Base commanders prohibited businesses from discriminating against customers based on race—if they did, they'd lose their official military endorsement—but still sanctioned these divisions in the name of maintaining the peace. When men mixed from the two areas, the racial tensions could explode into serious violence. White gangs battled black gangs, resulting in deaths.

Gate 2 had grown tamer over the years, though some storefronts looked like remnants from the past era, faded and run down. For sale along the street where Kate and I walked were hip-hop clothing and Asian souvenirs and Asian women ("GIRLS GIRLS GIRLS"). We passed a windowless establishment called 4Play, the facade stamped with silhouettes of big-breasted women. Another place, Amazonesu, had giant red lips painted around its windows. Often, when in areas like these outside base gates on Okinawa, I thought about a line by the writer Gloria Anzaldúa, in which she calls the U.S.–Mexican border an open wound "where the Third World grates against the First and bleeds." Okinawa was like that, too. All along the base fences, especially where they split in a gate, Okinawa grated against America, and a raw place opened.

Kate and I turned south from the main drag. As we entered a building on a side street, Kate said, "This is either the Okinawa in America or the America in Okinawa. Same thing, I guess."

The sign on the door read *Reverse*. She pushed it open, and inside, on a brightly lit stage, was a band in American 1950s costumes. They were either locals or from mainland Japan. The female singers wore poodle skirts and beehives, and the male crooner sported a silver suit and Elvis hair. I felt like I'd entered a David Lynch movie. The song "Can't Hurry Love" began, and a dozen middle-aged local women rushed to dance in front of the stage. A white man grooved at their center. The bar area was spotted with a few more grizzled Americans.

"He's probably been here since the Vietnam War," Kate said, pointing at one of them. Sipping cocktails at the bar, we watched the dance floor fill after the band broke into "La Bamba." When the Ritchie Valens hit had come out fifty years before, the island had been under American control. The 1950s and 1960s, per the history books, were a time of Okinawan poverty, racial and sexual violence, and land seizure and protest. Life under American rule had been difficult for Okinawans. But here in Reverse, the bar-goers swimming to "Surfin' U.S.A." suggested a different kind of memory, a nostalgia for that time. It was Kate's inside-out sock: a story inverted to reveal a hidden, messier side.

Around the island I noticed more paeans to America, many of which celebrated the occupation years. There were the ubiquitous A&W restaurants ("All American Food"), which had arrived in the 1960s and multiplied, remaining popular even after they had dwindled in the States. In the bar area outside Camp Hansen, benches were painted with classic American cars. In the American Village, a Statue of Liberty presided over shops selling yellowed *LIFE* magazines. Up Route 58, the restaurant American American, owned by a middle-aged Okinawan couple with a love of Americana, served steak, pie, and canned carrots and peas, using a logo with a 1950s housewife. At the new, ritzy mall, black and white photos of GIs playing golf and driving Chevys adorned the walls. One former U.S. military site—a neighborhood of squat, concrete family housing—had been repurposed as a "Stateside Town" of chic cafés and shops. The area announced itself with drawings of drive-in waitresses and more old-time Chevys. The streets were named after American states and decorated with retro touches—a rusted VW bus here, a red Coca-Cola bench there.

I asked an anthropologist, Hideki Yoshikawa, about this strange nostalgia for the occupation years. How could locals reminisce about a bygone America that invaded and snatched up their land? "For Okinawa, the U.S. is an enigmatic figure," Hideki explained. The 1950s and 1960s, when Okinawans first lived alongside Americans, were seared into the collective memory as a time of classic cars, Hollywood films, jazz, Coca-Cola, and hamburgers. Many remembered those years as the golden age of the United States, when the country's international image was one of a young, altruistic power. In Okinawa, memories of U.S. oppression coexisted with concepts of America as "the champion of democracy and freedom." "It's kind of ironic," Hideki said. Hideki was also an activist trying to stop construction of the new base on Oura Bay. In his work, which included bringing environmental lawsuits against the U.S. Department of Defense, he sorted through old American documents. In them, he found "they're referring to the idea of democracy, freedom, and U.S. values. [Americans] base their fights on these principles—just like I do." He laughed.

Eve started dating Americans at age nineteen, when she was studying English at Okinawa Christian University. Back then, she and her friends liked to hang around clubs, parks, and beaches and practice speaking English with American servicemen. The men struck her as more attractive than local guys—the way they looked, acted, dressed, spoke English, put ladies first. American men had big hearts, like in Hollywood movies. To her, they were movie stars, perfect and romantic and thrilling.

She realized the truth—that American men were "the real thing"— the hard way. In her early twenties, Eve became pregnant by her American boyfriend, a black marine. He wanted her to have the baby, but she had an abortion. She didn't want her parents to find out they were dating. Plus, she thought they were too young—he was only nineteen. After that, they dated two more years before he moved to a base in North Carolina. They managed another couple of years long distance, and she went to see him there, her first time to the States. The country seemed okay. The military base was big and boring. Then she discovered he had another girlfriend. She was devastated, and they broke up. That had been her longest relationship. Since then, she'd had trouble trusting men. "Why do they lie to us?" she wondered. "Maybe I have to be stronger."

Her experience hadn't deterred her from pursuing U.S. servicemen. Her single-minded goal was to marry one, and, approaching age thirty, she worried about it a lot. Pressure from her family didn't help. At first, her parents had been horrified that she liked kokujin. Now they didn't care. "Just tell us if you have someone to marry," they said. Eve's younger brother was about to get married, a reversal of order. "You have a boyfriend? You have a boyfriend?" he asked her. He wanted her to get married more than anyone. As an employee of Japan's Self-Defense Forces, he sometimes communicated with American service-members at work; he didn't care if she married one.

In Okinawa, there's a word for women like Eve: *amejo*, a woman who likes Americans. The term breaks into subgroups. Kokujo like black men, hakujo prefer white men, and spajo want Latinos. The words are all derogatory, mostly. The "-jo," though sometimes thought to mean "woman," as in "American woman," comes from the Okinawan word *jogu*. Jogu means to like or have an appetite for. The word "normally refers to one's food preference," scholar Makoto Ara-kaki points out, "and when the term refers to people, it carries strong sexual connotations. Therefore, 'Ame-jo' literally means a woman who favours an American man to whet her sexual appetite." A "sex-hungry military-man-eating machine," is how one twenty-two-year-old local woman put it.

I rarely heard anyone use the term to describe herself. An amejo was the other girl at the club—similar, maybe, but less classy or genu-ine or smart. An amejo was a rival. An amejo was a trashy bitch. An amejo was the opposite of a sexual assault victim. She was a woman who chose to engage with the known danger of the American soldier and therefore asked for whatever darkness headed her way. An amejo was beyond the sympathy of the public; an amejo could be silenced.

An amejo to one person was not an amejo to another. Everyone had his or her own definition—hard to explain, but easily applied.

"We can tell when we see that kind of girl," a twenty-one-year-old student named Reiko told me. "We can just say, oh, that's an amejo. It's clear."

"By how she dresses?" I asked.

Reiko laughed, not knowing how to explain. She and her two friends parsed it out, saying that spotting an amejo was something about the woman's personality (strong), her voice (loud), her eyebrows (bold), and her hair (permed). They joked they used to be amejo themselves—because of the tight clothes and heels they wore on weekends to bars around the bases, even though they were under-age; because of the free drinks they scored from marines; because of the way they worried their parents and generally acted rude. Since then, the women had "graduated from amejo," as one of them put it. They had focused on their studies, gotten boyfriends, started dressing more conservatively, and stopped going to clubs and bars. But they knew others saw them differently. Their boyfriends were American, therefore, as Reiko said, "From a different person's perspective, we are considered amejo."

Another couple of young Okinawan women who dated American servicemen told me amejo was a label that could be applied along with lipstick or eyebrow pencil. "When she wears her makeup, she is an amejo," one said about the other.

"Too much makeup," her friend offered in English. "I have eye-brows on fleek." When she had on her makeup, nose ring, and body-hugging dress, her family, friends, and co-workers called her an amejo. "I'm used to it," she said. "Like, okay. You guys can call me an amejo."

To Maki Sunagawa, who taught at Okinawa Christian University, where Eve and Reiko went, an amejo was a woman who dated Ameri-can soldiers without understanding the larger political and historical situation. "Some girls who are dating or get married to military guys are against the bases, and they want their boyfriends or husbands to leave the base and find another job," she told me. "For those girls, I don't call them amejo." Other women "don't really know their own history. They just see the positive side of American culture—movies, music." She said so-called amejo watch Hollywood movies, "see cool guys with beautiful actresses," and link the actors on screen to the soldiers on the island.

A local business owner named Mark, who was mixed American-Okinawan, expressed his positive spin on the term. "You know who gets a bad rap in Japan?" he asked me. Amejo. "But amejo are the coolest," he said. "They know what they want. And they're not consumed with what you think about them. . . . I think most women who make fun of amejo, it's rooted in jealousy, their own inability to be who they want to be." In Japan, he said, "you have to stay in your place. You have to be a good Japanese woman. For amejo to be so bold, that's kind of badass."

An amejo is the antidote to the stereotypical Japanese woman, the one known around the world: demure and white-faced and doll-like, a geisha. An amejo doesn't cover her mouth with her hand when she giggles, or smile and nod along with whatever she hears. She's not a ninja dragon lady either, red-lipped and disciplined. An amejo speaks in American slang and gets drunk and dances salsa and goes home with and fucks marines. An amejo says what she thinks and does what she wants, or tries to at least, hanging around Americans and hoping their can-do, individualistic attitude rubs off. As Mark said, this is a big deal in Japan, where conformity and collectivism rule and women are still expected to master the domestic arts, act with restraint, and cater to others. The country places third in world GDP rankings, but 114th in gender equality. Dating an American man can be a way out of Japan's traditional gender roles, and for some women the most extreme manifestation of that escape, the ultimate subversive act, is choosing a man who is black.

In Japan, there's a history of seeing African American people through the lenses of both Western and Japanese racism. Whiteness has been prized in Japan for centuries, signifying purity, beauty, and aristocracy. In the popular imagination, Japanese came to see themselves as white or light-skinned in relation to their "darker" ("less civilized") Asian neighbors. Western ideas of race became imported through early contact. In the sixteenth century, white Europeans brought along black servants on their visits to Japan. In 1854, Commodore Matthew Perry celebrated the "reopening" of Japan with an "Ethiopian entertainment" show for his Japanese guests. For the routine, his white sailors donned blackface. In the twentieth century, "Little Black Sambo" dolls and books were popular—until the international spotlight swung to Japan in 1986 with the prime minister's remark that American "intelligence levels" were lower than Japan's because of the "considerable number of blacks, Puerto Ricans and Mexicans" in the United States. Companies pulled Sambo products from shelves after an outcry from Americans, but later brought them back. Blackface, too, continued in the Japanese media. An American working in Japanese television and commercials in the eighties recalled how American extras were always white—unless the role was associated with crime. Then they'd cast a black actor. Some African American residents of Japan have said they're seen as more foreign than white Americans, the "Ultimate Other," and have reported facing slurs like "sambo, saru (ape), kaibutsu (monster), and kuronbo (nigger)."

Experiences, though, are diverse, and Japanese notions of blackness are not fixed. Many African American people have said they prefer living in Japan over the United States because they experience less discrimination there and are treated not as the "Ultimate Other" but as general gaijin, foreigners. After hearing warnings that the Japanese were racist, black American student Aina Hunter found a welcoming reception in Japan. She writes, "During my entire year in Tokyo I did not encounter a single demeaning image of an African or African American person." Moreover, she felt her race gave her an advantage over her white peers, enabling her to have closer relationships with Japanese students. "I came to understand that some students . . . saw me as more approachable because of my non-whiteness, in part because they viewed me as occupying marginal space in the U.S. power structure, which they quite openly expressed distaste for," she writes.

In the realm of sexual attraction, however, historical and persisting prejudices can manifest in fetishization. In the 1980s, author Amy Yamada capitalized off the idea that Japanese women who declare their love for black men are more transgressive than those who date whites, publishing explicit stories fetishizing black men. In Yamada's fictional world, Tokyo women date violent, hypersexual African American soldiers—one-dimensional men the female protagonists devour like the Hershey chocolate bars the postwar occupiers tossed to children. "I was totally in awe of his dick," says the narrator in *Bedtime Eyes*. "It was gorgeous, like a big chocolate bar." She describes her lover as "cooler than cool" and "looking like some kind of small-time gang-ster." She constantly sees his blackness ("It was the saddest color in the world, and yet it was the most beautiful color I had ever seen.") and uses him as proof of her own goodness ("As if by being assaulted by a dirty thing, I am made aware I am a pure thing. . . . His smell gives me a sense of superiority."). She is addicted to him, though he beats her—chokes her, knocks out her teeth, flings her against walls, drags her through broken glass by her hair. In one of the final images of the story, she is the one in power, the one who has been using him as a sex object all along. She imagines him naked, lined up and facing away with "loads and loads" of other men. "And in the same ceremonial way you might choose a Filipino hooker, I would shower his butt with champagne to call him over to me."

The novella won a prestigious literary award and became a bestsell-er in Japan. Anthropologist John G. Russell attributes this to the male character's race. He writes, "Had *Bedtime Eyes* depicted a relationship between a white GI and a Japanese woman, it probably would have gone unnoticed, certainly not receiving the sensationalized treatment lavished upon it by the Japanese mass media and literati."

In Okinawa, too, I saw women manipulating men like props. Unlike the typical stories of American soldiers in the erotic wilds of Asia—fraternizing with geisha girls, "me-love-you-long-time" hookers, and Madame Butterflies—these women were objectifying just as much as they were being objectified. "How about a Mexican?" I heard a woman ask Eve at a party, as if she were offering her a tuna-fish sand-wich. (Eve crinkled her nose in reply.) Another woman said she had been watching American television shows like *Desperate Housewives* to learn how white people talked. (Her findings: They used words like "awesome" and "freakin'," which, she said, black people would never use.) Others discussed the colors of white men's eyes as if surveying paint samples. (Such a selection!) "It's not like, 'Oh, the person I fell in love with just happened to be African American,'" scholar Makoto Arakaki told me. So-called amejo "are for black people or white peo-ple or Chicanos. They have a specialty." He said it's like saying, "I want a Chihuahua."

I saw this superficiality everywhere. During my first extended stay in Okinawa, when I was twenty, I felt as though American men and local women saw each other through an intoxicating haze of stereotypes and lies, Coronas and Hollywood movies. The same age as the servicemen, I spent a lot of sweltering nights that summer in the island's salsa clubs, tagging along with an American acquaintance who had amassed a posse of Latino marines. I saw how easy it was, through the haze, to get caught up in illusions. *Konnichi wa, kawaii*, men would say to me with beer on their breath. *Hello, you're cute*. I imagined them practicing the Japanese words like an incantation. Sometimes, I didn't answer in English, letting them mistake me for an amejo, feeling protective of my true self in this world of caricatures. Meanwhile, I let myself be wooed by the image of the macho, smooth soldier. I was undeterred by the men's bravado about fighting and guns; I believed their claims that they were single. I came from a place where boys went to college, not the marine corps; the culture of the American military seemed as exotic to me as that of Okinawa. In the salsa clubs, we all sang along to the summer's most popular track, "Obsesión" by Aventura, the perfect anthem for the scene. "No, no," the woman sings in Spanish at the refrain. "It's not love. What you're feeling, it's called obsession—an illusion in your mind."

But as I spent more time on the island, I saw not all cross-cultural relationships were built on illusions. Many so-called amejo used American slang they'd learned not from rap music or Hollywood, but from people they loved. If their altered appearances—the tans and acrylic nails and colored contacts—were like costumes, they were costumes they wore every day. Their goals seemed not so much to mimic, to impersonate, to appropriate, but to slip, half noticed, into a community that felt more open and right.

If what Aina Hunter experienced in Tokyo was a closeness with her Japanese peers due to a distaste of American racial hierarchies, this dynamic is even more heightened in Okinawa, where different racial structures are at play than on the mainland. The same type of Sambo doll with black skin, oversized lips, and grass skirt can be found with the word OKINAWA stamped on its chest. Okinawans—a minority group within Japan, struggling against prejudice and socioeconomic inequality caused by past injustices—have reason to identify with the African American soldiers they've lived alongside for decades. During the Vietnam War, when the American troops who flooded the island brought with them the turmoil of American racial politics, African American GIs and Okinawans sometimes aligned. In the midst of a Koza riot in 1970, when thousands of Okinawans were beating GIs and burning their cars, the crowd didn't target black servicemen. There was some unspoken bond between the Okinawans rallying against the U.S. military presence and the African American soldiers who had been drafted into service and segregated from their white counterparts. "We support the riot," airmen based on Kadena and associated with the Black Panther Party said in a statement the next day.

Koza isn't segregated anymore, but I still noticed servicemembers socializing by race. Latinos hung out at salsa bars, black men at hip-hop clubs, white guys at places with names like Nashville. If the bars Americans frequented were each filled with men of an array of races and backgrounds, the terms *kokujo*, *hakujo*, and *spajo* might never have been born. Women wouldn't be forced to choose a race when deciding which bar to visit. They could go to one and stay open to meeting whomever. The way some women in Okinawa identify based on their racial dating preferences is linked to the way race continues to order and separate people in the United States.

One afternoon I visited Okinawa Christian University, Eve's alma mater. Driving up to the campus, which is on a hill overlooking a small valley sliced into fields, I felt like I was approaching a castle. The architecture of the school is strange, with arches and towers built in stark gray cement. The university was founded after the war by Cho-sho Nakazato, an Okinawan teacher who regretted he'd fallen for the prewar militaristic fever and ushered his students to needless deaths. Nakazato was also Christian, a religion American soldiers and missionaries helped bring to the island during the occupation, when Okinawans were seeking solace from wartime trauma. In Okinawa, the percentage of Christians climbed higher than on the mainland.

Nakazato based his new institution on peace education, and decades later the university still has a peace mission and an official stance against the U.S. military presence. Many of the faculty are activists, involved in demilitarization scholarship and anti-base efforts. At the same time, the school has a reputation for turning out amejo due to its high number of female students who study English. Because its first teachers were Western missionaries, English education became the school's strength. And because it began as a two-year junior college, the school has historically attracted more women in the gender-imbalanced society. One faculty member I met estimated that at least half the female students studying English or tourism date American men. This creates some tension between the anti-base faculty and students, which sometimes is manifested in demeaning jokes. "That's amejo corner," one professor told another, pointing to a bench with an ashtray. Professors joke about the high number of Y-plate American cars in the parking lots—servicemen picking up their girlfriends or borrowed boyfriends' cars—and how the international couples who come to the campus café can't even communicate about what to order because of the language barrier between them.

I met Makoto Arakaki, a professor of intercultural communication, in the café, which was really just a handful of long tables in a corner of a lobby. No American men were around. Students streamed by between classes, and the cappuccino machine whirred. Makoto was in his early fifties but had a young air, with kind eyes and a joking, casual manner. He'd written an article on amejo. "Pretty much the everyday life I have here with my students," he said.

Many students, he told me, came to the school as "American wannabes," with the goal of speaking like a native American English speaker, not to use English as the global lingua franca that faculty like him had in mind. His students wanted to learn the language for narrow reasons: to get on-base jobs and meet Americans. In response, he and other faculty members were working to break out of the "post-colonial," "England/U.S.-worshiping" approach to English-learning that's popular in Okinawa and all of Japan.

But shaking the allure of America is difficult. In the school parking lots, along with the Y-plate cars, Makoto saw Japanese cars with stars and stripes stickers or "support our troops" yellow ribbons. On Facebook, he saw his students sharing U.S. military-produced videos and articles—the feel-good stories of helpful marines, the ones portraying anti-base activists as violent and hateful. "It makes them feel special to go out with the GIs and talk to them on their smartphones," he said. He mimicked a woman. "'Hi, honey, how are you doing today?' And everybody's like 'Wowwww! She's so cool!' That's the kind of atmosphere we have here."

In his own way, Makoto could relate. He was born in Okinawa in 1966, six years before the islands reverted to Japanese control. "As I was growing up here, wherever you drove you saw the fences," he said. The heavy presence of the American military bases—"like a colonial situation almost"—shaped him. "I didn't know about the politics, but I think I knew, subconsciously, the hierarchical relationship among Okinawa, mainland Japan, and the U.S." In that hierarchy, the United States was at the top, then came Japan, then Okinawa. That order dictated his tastes. "During my youth I never listened to Japanese music. . . . I just wanted to listen to American or English [music]. . . . In high school, I almost never studied and just played in a rock band, copying all this American eighties rock music." Sometimes, his band played in Koza—covers of Van Halen, the Rolling Stones. "We kind of sucked," he remembered, laughing. American soldiers used to throw beer bottles at them. "But we had some nice friends, too—marines. I still have a friend called Snake." He chuckled. "I never knew his real name. He used to get drunk and sleep on the staircase at the [bar]. We had fun back then. It was a crazy time."

When I'd talked to Maki Sunagawa, Makoto's colleague, she'd told me there were male amejo at Okinawa Christian University, too. "Not like as in dating, but they like to dress like marines," she said, and noted their "hip-hop style." "They work out, try to look bigger. They listen to the same music as marines do." They went on base to bars, movie theaters, and English classes and made American friends. Maki thought it was about identity. "They don't like who they are. They don't like that they're from Okinawa," she said. "They want to be just like Americans, because they are cool to girls."

Makoto sounded like he had been someone Maki would have categorized as a male amejo. "I wanted to get off this island," he remembered. "I hated it so much. Everything about this island. I thought
it was so backwards and lame compared to the kind of music I was
listening to." After he failed his college entrance exams, he decided to
attend community college in the States. "I wanted to go to the other
side of the fence, that kind of mentality." He ended up spending almost
a decade in California, eventually obtaining his bachelor's and master's degrees. "Of course I experienced discrimination being an Asian
American Studies student," he said. "So by the time I finished my MA
I didn't have the American Dream or the illusion [of the United States]
that I used to have."

He returned to Okinawa, but his grappling with the United States
didn't end. He learned that his new Okinawan girlfriend used to date
American GIs. "I had this strange feeling about that," he said. "I guess
it reminded me of some of the experiences I had when I was in high
school. Whenever we went to outdoor rock festivals in Koza, five or
six GIs used to pick on us, on the local boys." The Americans encircled Makoto and his friends and hit them. "Serious bullying going on,"
he recalled. Knowing his girlfriend had dated GIs sparked feelings of
jealousy toward those old adversaries. She also reminded him of his
grandmother. As an adult, Makoto learned his grandmother had been
raped multiple times by American soldiers in a refugee camp after the
war. She got pregnant and had an abortion. "When I found out about
that, that also had some effect on me. It's all mixed up with my experience as a boy growing up, admiring American culture."

I asked if he felt hypocritical judging his ex-girlfriend when he
too had been a fan of the United States. He thought for a while and
sucked in his breath. "I criticize her I guess because of the part of me
that was in the peace movement and also thinking about Grandma."
That girlfriend had been very "oblivious or unconscious of the history
and the political issues." He still hadn't figured out his feelings about
her. He paused, at a loss for words, then laughed with good-natured
embarrassment. Dating her, he said, "gave me a strange feeling, but,
yeah. . . ."

Many in Okinawa express the belief that once a woman dates an

American, she can't "go back" to dating local men, whether because of her changed preference ("American guys are like nicotine, once a girl smokes one . . . she'll be hooked," related one twenty-two-year-old local woman) or because of the stigma that follows her. An Okinawa Christian University student told Makoto she found a Japanese boyfriend after dating an American, but he "treated me as though I were a 'bitch.'" She said, "Whenever I told him I was going to a nightclub, he would say, 'There you go, Bitch! You just want to fool around with men.' It also really bothered him that I used to have an American boyfriend. Even his parents and relatives weighed in and felt compelled to label me as a barbaric Amazon. They almost treated me as if I were filthy. . . . Because of this sort of thinking, some girls are treated like kryptonite by Japanese guys."

Of course, there's an age-old conflict between local and occupying men, with the two groups viewed as being direct competition and women standing as symbols of the nation. Whoever boasts sexual access to the local women claims political control of the land. In her book *What Soldiers Do*, historian Mary Louise Roberts analyzes this in relation to U.S. troops in France at the end of World War II. She argues that beginning with World War I, wartime propaganda on all sides established "the 'enemy' [as] he who would ravage women as booty. . . . In this way, sex as a trophy of conquest became part of twentieth-century industrialized warfare," where "command of geographical territory signaled command of sexual territory." In 1944 France, Roberts tells us, French men were grappling with their defeat and loss of standing in the world, while the American liberators were beginning to see themselves as "giants." These new roles were symbolized and informed by intimate relations between French women and American GIs.

In modern-day Okinawa, similar symbolism and information is housed in relationships between local women and American soldiers. To local men, the amejo can suggest both the dominant foreign military still occupying their land and their own diminished manhood. The flip side of the myth about chivalrous, "ladies first" American men is deadbeat local guys. Many women cited Okinawan guys' supposed lack of romantic skill as a reason to date Americans. In his writ-ing, Makoto put it this way: "From an Okinawan man's perspective, these women who threaten their own masculinity should be punished and, thus, socially excluded. Use of this term [amejo] among men rep-resents their ongoing battle for domination and their inherent sense of possession of 'their' women."

In this way, the use of the term *amejo* is like the tonte ritual in lib-erated France, which Roberts describes. "Young women who had engaged in sexual relationships with the Germans were brought into a public area where their clothes were ripped and their heads shaved," she writes. Frenchmen then marched the shorn Frenchwomen through the streets in a spectacle of punishment and social exclusion. "The tonte was massively photographed by thousands of witnesses and bystand-ers," Roberts writes. These photographs, "widely distributed," "cre-ated the impression that collaborators could be easily identified and punished. The power of the image lay in its denial of the diffuse and profound nature of French collaboration."

A derogatory term like *amejo* can be seen as a less visceral way to punish and exclude women who date "the enemy"—suggesting they alone are the "collaborators," though the situation is far more "dif-fuse and profound." Scholar Ayano Ginoza argues that criticizing Okinawan women for their ignorance of history or acceptance of the bases ignores the real culprit—the larger "political economic system of militarism." She argues, "Usually, the militarization process is so naturally mediated in the landscape of Okinawa that many people, even politicians and critics of militarism, easily dismiss the process and blame Okinawan women." At the end of his amejo piece, Makoto writes something similar, that women labeled amejo are being scape-goated by "males in society who, like Ame-jo, remain hungry them-selves for the socioeconomic and political power that the U.S. bases bring to them."

I asked Makoto about this. "I was being a little sarcastic," he replied. "People are talking about 'amejo, amejo.' The real America jogu, wanting to be American, are the males running the politics, in conspiracy with the U.S. military to have the bases here and get what they want. . . . The males are the ones who criticize women for being amejo. My question is who created that—the political atmosphere, the social atmosphere? Who educated our kids like that? The people who are making the policies." He lowered his voice. "They are the ones who really want to fuck and be fucked by the military base."

When I asked Eve about the terms *amejo* and *kokujo*, she laughed. No one called her those names, she said, but they probably thought them, especially Japanese and Okinawan men. And old people. She didn't care.

Once, that night at Saicolo, I heard her use the term to describe herself. It was late, and we were collapsed onto stools by the bar. In a clearing, a couple of Japanese men were dancing, grinding against each other in some imitation of what the American men were doing with the women on the dance floor below. If these men were straight, there weren't any women in the club for them. The women had come to look for Americans.

"They like the music," Eve explained, nodding to the Japanese men. They were moving jerkily now, like robots. An American came over and danced with them, clapping his hands in a fraternal way. "They don't like amejo like us." As Eve said the word, she giggled. She seemed to be referring to herself, her friends, all the women in the club. It was the first time I had heard a woman wear the term with pride, a sense of belonging.

Eve wanted a husband, but only a black American would do. Her English was limited, and military life posed serious relationship challenges. The situation seemed destined for conflict and suggested a slew of issues—objectifying those of another race, abandoning the conventions of your culture, chasing after something foreign in an attempt to escape yourself. Maybe the men dancing before us would have dismissed Eve as an amejo—a contemptable woman, a member of a fringe group, an anomaly, a collaborator, a slut. But they, and so many others on Okinawa, were more like Eve than they wanted to admit.

3

ASHLEY

TO ASHLEY, LIFE ON OKINAWA WAS LIKE AN EXTENSION OF COLLEGE.
She explained this to me at a St. Patrick's Day party in 2009 at her
husband's squadron bar on Futenma airbase. Wearing a neon-green
wig and sipping a beer, she described nights she'd ridden a mechanical
bull, danced with lesbians, and drunk shots from a bottle of awamori
with a decaying habu—poisonous snake—inside. Sometimes, she,
her husband, and their friends went "slumming it" on Gate 2 Street.
That was fun, too.

Ashley was in her mid-twenties and had been on the island about
a year, accompanying her husband, an officer in the marine corps.
She worked on base organizing workshops and training for servicemembers. The daughter of a white American father and Asian mother,
she'd grown up attending international schools, then enrolled in an
elite American university. Just a few days into college, she met her
husband. Her plan hadn't been to settle down so early, but that was
what happened.

The squadron bar was a small, low-ceilinged room in a nondescript
building on the base, with a bar set up in one corner. Flags plastered

the ceiling, and the walls were decorated with portraits of past commanding officers, their heads pasted on incongruous bodies—the
Dalai Lama, a Native American chief, an eighties rock star. Around
the room, officers leaned against the foosball table or straddled stools,
gripping mugs of beer. Off to one side was the St. Patty's Day spread
of corned beef hash, green mashed potatoes, and green Jell-O shots.
Irish music played. The officers were all white men, their solid bodies adorned for the occasion with clown wigs and face paint. Most of
their wives, ornamented with green wigs and Mardi Gras beads, were
white, too. One woman, a doctor, wore a halter dress and glittering
green top hat. Soon she was tipping over, drunk, along with everyone
else. The current commanding officer—a tall, middle-aged white man
wearing a green garter belt pushed atop his blazer sleeve—posed in a
picture amid all the wives.

After a few hours, the group stepped into the cool, drizzly night and
headed by cab to Kadena Air Base. The Kadena Officers' Club (the
KOC, which, of course, was pronounced *cock*) had the feel of a mid-
range hotel bar, the space outside it like a lobby in Kansas City, with
orange carpet and potted ferns. The bar was big and dim, with a dance
floor and lots of men. Some wore polo shirts, and others wore khaki
flight jumpsuits with patched-on names like "Possum" and "Pukes on
Stewardess." Ashley informed me the uniforms were a unity thing—
and to attract ladies.

She hit the dance floor, her lithe figure and green wig attracting men
one after another. They didn't seem to mind her wedding ring, flashing in the light of the disco ball. The doctor wearing the top hat danced
close with her fiancé, a boyishly handsome pilot. By the bar, a serviceman told me he had graduated from the Naval Academy and never had
the stereotypical college experience—so this was it on Okinawa, now.

I had seen servicemembers out in clubs and bars on the island, but
was surprised they could regard their whole life here as a frat party. It
seemed like the U.S. military had built not a workplace but a fantasy-
land for young Americans who had never attended or couldn't let go
of college. I wondered at this choice in light of the political situation.

The U.S. military began reshaping Okinawa on its second day on the island. After landing on the central west coast on April 1, 1945, troops unloaded bulldozers, tractors, and cranes onto the beaches, then got to work widening roads and building new ones. The plan was to use the island as a base to launch an invasion of mainland Japan. "Okinawa glitters as [a] military prize," a *New York Times* article filed on April 4, 1945, proclaimed. "Okinawa will be one of the greatest acquisitions of the Pacific war." Military leaders who landed on the "green, neatly terraced" island marveled at its lushness, its flat expanses, its sheltered bays, its offerings of limestone and coral. In the imaginations of these officers, the flat expanses were runways, the bays ports, the limestone and coral material for roads. Okinawa offered "infinite possibilities for development," an American general declared—"limited only by political considerations."

At first, U.S. military installations on Okinawa were far from an R&R paradise. Just after the war, the U.S. government didn't know if it would establish a permanent presence on the island and held off rebuilding the ravaged landscape. While the occupiers on the Japanese mainland, under their separate administration system, pursued reform and reconstruction, Okinawa became known as the "forgotten island," "the logistical end of the line," and "the dumping ground of the Pacific." Three years after the war, an American Foreign Service officer remarked that "the southern half of the island still presented a scene of almost total destruction and desolation, as though the fighting had stopped only a few months before." The smell of burning tires, donated by the Americans to fuel salt plants, scented the air. Without permanent base structures, Americans lived in "hovels" and "run-down Quonset communities that look[ed] like hobo camps." For recreation they had "a few broken-down movie shacks and football fields."

Okinawa came to be seen as a place of exile within the U.S. military, "a dumping ground for Army misfits and rejects from more comfortable posts," as a 1949 *Time* article puts it. One veteran, writer M.D. Morris, remembers, "Only the worst were sent to 'The Rock'. . . . Anywhere in the Pacific, unruly troops were kept in check with the threats that 'goof-ups get shipped to Okinawa.'" Those on Okinawa were "of lower caliber than those assigned to Japan," noted a 1949 report from General Douglas MacArthur's headquarters. That same year, *Time* magazine reported that "more than 15,000 U.S. troops, whose morale and discipline have probably been worse than that of any U.S. force in the world, have policed 600,000 natives who live in hopeless poverty." According to the *Daily Boston Globe*, two thousand American women and children were also calling Okinawa home, trying their best to domesticate the place, "putting up white organdy curtains in rotting Quonsets." "It's like being sent to Siberia," the newspaper stated.

This collection of exiled and unhappy Americans "dumped" on the island reportedly led to an increase in crimes committed by U.S. military personnel against the local population. Morris attributes this delinquency to a simple lack of things to do. He writes, "Boredom set in. When outdoor movies or the occasional U.S.O. shows ceased to augment underground drinking, dice, and doxies, the troops again went after the Okinawans. In the first six months of 1949, American soldiers robbed and/or assaulted forty-nine, raped eighteen, and murdered twenty-nine innocent Ryukyuans." Many of these perpetrators faced no consequences because of their extraterritorial status.

Then came the Cold War. Seeking an outpost against communism, leaders in both Japan and the United States committed to entrenching the U.S. bases in Okinawa. Away went the Quonset huts. Along came the commissaries, churches, movie theaters, bowling alleys, golf courses, swimming pools, and yacht clubs. Off-base, the U.S. government began spending millions of dollars investing in island infrastructure, building water, power, and sewage systems; schools; hospitals; and roads. Soon, Okinawa became a choice destination among U.S. bases overseas. "Okinawa's charm and comforts make troops vie for duty there," the *New York Times* claimed in 1956. In its 1954 "Letter from Okinawa," the *New Yorker* reported that "living is so cheap that anybody earning the equivalent of a major's pay here should be able to save two or three thousand dollars a year. There are a number of inexpensive clubs for noncommissioned officers, and one of them, called Steak Haven, provides a floor show, featuring Mickey and the

Okinawan Young Star Band, and a dinner of chicken in the basket for seventy five cents." Also on offer at the clubs: bingo, rumba, garlic rolls, mint juleps. At the PX, for sale at discounted prices were mink stoles, electronics, "cocktail onions and hot pepperoni sticks," power lawn mowers and American-brand dog food. "The Commissaries . . . can supply practically any item of food available in large supermarkets in the States," boasted a military pamphlet. "Sports of all kinds are available, from ping-pong through tennis, baseball, football, basketball, to horseback riding."

U.S. military housing on the island soon contained all the amenities of home, plus colonial-style perks. The two- or three-bedroom concrete bungalows were well furnished and complete with "space for a maid's cot." In these homes, American families dined on imported American food "prepared by Japanese maids, who seem to be standard operating equipment for island-bound U.S. families," as a 1956 *Los Angeles Times* article states. "Aside from the fact that you're limited in scope," the article says, "life on a war-pocked Pacific island is much the same as it is in Southern California—with particular emphasis on water sports." Explaining the importance of these features, an American military leader in the early 1950s said, "This is a long way from home and you've got to give the people who come here or who are ordered here as pleasant a life as possible, with plenty of recreation."

As Ashley and her friends showed me, this is still the approach of the U.S. military on Okinawa. An assignment on the island is no longer a threat to hold over subpar troops; it's more like an imagined prolonged spring break. Chances to party and recreate on and off base abound, and on-base landscapes have persisted as simulacra of suburban America. There are wide roads, plenty of parking, cookie-cutter homes, and vast, manicured lawns. There are backyards and barbeques, and eateries with familiar tastes: Subway, Popeye's, Chili's, Pizza Hut. There are movie theaters and bowling alleys, gyms and military-sponsored jaunts to exotic off-base destinations like the grocery store. On base at the PX, the American-imported goods are cheap, and in parking lots elderly Okinawan men wait in taxis to drive servicemembers where they want to go. While outside the base fences Okinawan cities have grown crowded on an island with finite space, the military installations retain their sense of openness. Kadena Air Base is eight times less dense than its "host," Okinawa City.

But to some extent the United States has made off-base communities in its image. Before World War II, railroad lines connected Naha with a few other cities. The battle destroyed the Japanese steam-engine trains, and when Okinawans asked their American occupiers for replacements, like the monorails that were beginning to crisscross mainland Japan, military government officials said no. Instead, they built roads, part of the build-up of island infrastructure that was a benefit of the U.S. military's entrenchment on Okinawa. Highway 1 ran north to south along the western coast, a hub for U.S. military vehicles. A network of smaller roads spread from there, blood vessels flowing from an artery. During the occupation, locals called these new paved streets gun-do, military roads. When Okinawa reverted to Japanese control in 1972, Highway 1 became National Highway 58, an extension of roadways on islands to the north and a symbolic connector between Okinawa and the rest of Japan. Today, Route 58 is six lanes that, in central Okinawa, are often stalled with traffic. In recent years, Naha got its monorail, but much of the island remains a car culture. This also makes it a mall culture, with people wanting to drive to places with vast parking lots—a far cry from the urban centers of mainland Japan, where trains are the transporters and underground shopping arcades fan out from stations.

Eventually, the U.S. military presence even remade Okinawan bodies. Although older Okinawans boast some of the longest average lifespans in the world, younger generations have grown fatter and sicker than their mainland counterparts, thanks to Okinawa's car culture and embrace of American fast food.

As soon as servicemembers and their dependents arrive on the island, the U.S. military shapes how they view their new home. This is when the idea of Okinawa as a vacation paradise vies for space with warnings about the political realities. At mandatory day- or week-long orientations, speakers lecture about the people, culture, and history of

Okinawa. These briefings came under fire in 2016, when journalist Jon Mitchell obtained slides from a presentation called "Okinawa Cultural Awareness Training" that belittled the local anti-base movement. It characterized Okinawans as "more emotional than logical" and as trying to squeeze as much compensation money out of the U.S. and Japanese governments as possible ("it pays to complain"). The slides also explained that crimes by American servicemembers were a result of their special status as foreigners, or gaijin. "We get carried-away with our sudden 'gaijin power' (Charisma man effect) and tend to go over-board by doing things that is not [sic] acceptable to the majority in society," read one slide. In response to Mitchell's exposé, Okinawan governor Takeshi Onaga said the briefing was "a prime example of [the U.S. military's] arrogant attitude" toward local people. The head of the marine corps in Japan said they would "continue to review" the content of the training.

By the time I attended what's called Newcomer's Orientation Welcome Aboard (NOWA) the following year, organizers had reworked the presentations and cut the blatantly problematic remarks. But the lectures on Okinawa presented conflicting views of life on the island. On one hand, speakers sold Okinawa as a beautiful, exotic destination the U.S. personnel could enjoy and explore. This suggested a relaxed, vacation-type mentality centered on fun. To counter this, NOWA speakers also delivered stern warnings to behave with caution and restraint, along with frequent reminders that military personnel were "guests" and had to abide by a list of rules that grew stricter after each drunk driver or rape blew up into an international incident.

The one-day, weekly-run orientation was held on Camp Foster in a community center that looked like a high school gym in Anywhere, U.S.A. The temperature was frigid, despite the scorching summer day outside. (Utility bills are one of the many base expenses the Japanese government pays.) Fifty or so men, women, and children sat on red metal chairs around folding tables, dressed in T-shirts and jeans. Attending NOWA is mandatory for all accompanied marines, sailors, and civilians assigned to a marine corps or navy unit on Okinawa, plus their family members older than ten. Unaccompanied marines and sailors above a certain rank and unaccompanied civilians also attend NOWA. Single, lower-ranking servicemembers sit through a week-long orientation.

The 7:30 a.m. speaker, a man of color wearing fatigues, started his lecture by showing a map of mainland Japan and the Korean peninsula, with Tokyo, Mount Fuji, and Seoul circled in red. These were places people in Okinawa's U.S. military community could visit, along with destinations like Singapore, Australia, and Hawaii, thanks to free flights on military aircraft. Shouting, he talked up a marine corps resort on Okinawa's north coast and the island's subtropical beauty ("the best sunsets you've ever seen. Epic sunsets"). His lecture alternated between this kind of talk—selling Okinawa like a tour guide—and warnings about the precautions attendees needed to take because, compared to other military outposts, "Okinawa is different." He told the audience about off-limits places on the island and the dress code they needed to follow "out in town"—anywhere off base. He explained the "liberty order" that controlled the movements of servicemembers out in town. Those of lower ranks had fewer privileges, like earlier curfews and requirements to travel in pairs or packs. He warned against drinking and driving, as many speakers would. "Over here, because we're guests in this country, a DUI is front-page news and becomes an international incident," he said. This was part of his central message and that of later speakers: Okinawa is a tinderbox, where the mistake or crime of one person can explode into an international incident. But don't worry, there are a lot of beaches and cultural activities to enjoy at the same time.

The marine corps pushes off-base attractions partly out of concern for marines' mental health. "One of the things they worry about is marines staying on base and not doing anything, and then they get stressed out and want to kill themselves," Mike, a family readiness officer with the marine corps, told me. A civilian, Mike served as a resource for marines and their families. He said the risk of suicide was a "huge" problem on Okinawa, especially when marines stayed on base, feeling isolated and hiding out in the barracks. I'd seen the inside of some barracks on Foster. The living quarters were just as drab and industrial-looking as the outsides of the buildings, with beige cinderblock walls and bunk beds, somewhere between a dorm room and a prison. Mike said the risk of suicide escalated after incidents like Rina Shimabukuro's murder. Her death triggered tighter restrictions for marines, confining them more to base, and Mike and his colleagues grew more worried than usual.

But when I spoke to a higher-up in the marine corps, he downplayed this risk. "Suicide can affect anyone," said Colonel David E. Jones, the deputy commander of Marine Corps Installations Pacific. He cited the training they supply to help people identify someone at risk, as well as the Single Marine Program, which organizes group trips, sporting events, and community service. "For a lot of our young marines, this is their first duty station, and they're straight out of high school," Jones said. "For most, they may never have even left the state or town where they were born, much less come overseas."

For servicemembers who have little to no experience abroad, the newcomer's orientation can make an indelible impression. Later in the day at the one I attended, young Okinawan women played the part of friendly, attractive, and exotic locals, welcoming the attendees to the island. One wore a kimono, which local women don't wear in daily life. The other, dressed in a white blazer and yellow dress, described how a U.S. military family had "engaged [her] as a friend" when she was younger, introducing her to American culture. "I was mesmerized," she said. They encouraged her to study abroad, and she went on to graduate from a top American university. In a high, cheerful voice, she said, "So you see, I'm a good example of a great relationship between the marine corps and a local. . . . I'm merely asking you to be you—an American, nice, generous, and friendly, right?" The audience murmured agreement, and some people laughed. "My point is I want you to engage with the local people on a personal level."

Both women reinforced the first speaker's tour-guide spiel, describing local sites of interest, like castle ruins and beaches. They also summarized stereotypical aspects of Okinawan and Japanese culture, like karate ("Maybe you can find a Mr. Miyagi"), cuisine, chopstick etiquette, bowing, and superstitions.

In between the women, a white, middle-aged American named Ronald Appling covered more serious material. A civilian base worker, he wore glasses and an aloha shirt, his gray hair styled in a buzz cut. In contrast to the warm, smiling women, who spoke in sing-song voices on mics, Appling barked his script without amplification, like the man in the morning had. Appling seemed especially passionate about his material, causing the audience to perk up.

Appling's lecture was impressive in that it covered Okinawan history in depth, starting with the Ryukyu Kingdom and illustrating from an Okinawan perspective why Okinawans might oppose the U.S. military presence. Speaking about the Battle of Okinawa, he emphasized the high loss of life among Okinawans. "Clearly the biggest victims during the battle were the civilians," he said. "Memories of that victimization, if you will, have been cast down over a couple of generations since the war and serve as the foundation for some of the anti-base rhetoric that you may hear while you're here. Please understand: that is anti-base; it is not anti-American." He covered later history that might cause Okinawans to protest the base presence: U.S. military rule during the occupation, when locals lacked constitutional rights, and the taking of land during the Cold War with "bayonets and bulldozers." "Plus, during the occupation, U.S. servicemembers were not always held accountable for their actions," he said. "But because the military reigned [on] the island, there wasn't a darn thing the Okinawans could do about it. That raised the frustration bar even higher." This was an improvement over earlier trainings that had characterized the U.S. occupation as a time of public works and rebuilding, with no mention of crimes committed by U.S. troops.

Talk of "gaijin power" had been cut, but speakers did acknowledge that Americans in the military community on Okinawa have a special status that might make them feel immune to local laws. This special status is thanks to the Status of Forces Agreement (SOFA) between the United States and Japan that, among other things, regulates life for U.S. troops, civilian base workers, and dependents stationed in the country. Appling highlighted some of the privileges the people in the room had over the two Okinawan speakers as a result of SOFA. They could get a driver's license after a simple written test, without having to spend a couple of months and a couple thousand dollars obtaining one through the Japanese system. They paid cheaper road taxes; other taxes and fees they didn't pay at all. But, Appling emphasized, SOFA wasn't going to protect them if they broke Japanese laws. "We cannot go off base and make that bad decision and try to claim SOFA as a way of escaping responsibility," he said.

That wasn't quite true. To many Okinawans' indignation, the current SOFA still grants those it covers some protection from Japanese law. Japanese authorities can question accused criminals with SOFA status, but if the perpetrator gets back to base before local police catch him—like tagging home base—he can often remain in U.S. custody. There was an informal revision to this arrangement after the 1995 rape, with the United States giving Japan "favorable consideration" if it requested custody of a suspect accused of heinous crimes. But the two countries never officially revised the 1960 SOFA—something many Okinawans protest after military-linked crimes.

A type of colonial thinking lingers for many in the U.S. military community. It can come out in subtle ways, such as when I spoke to Colonel Jones. "Surprisingly, [even though] the military has been here . . . a while, intermingled with the population, there's still a good portion [of local people who] don't speak English," he said. This idea that locals should learn another country's language, instead of the visitors learning the local language, is a classic colonial mindset. More distressing have been reports of comments like those of the former U.S. consul general in Okinawa, Kevin Maher. In 2010 he allegedly made a number of disparaging remarks about Okinawans to a group of American University students, including that they are "masters of extorting Tokyo for money" and "too lazy to grow" goya, the bitter melon that's emblematic of local cuisine. These stereotypes are similar to what the marine corps had been teaching its newcomers ("it pays to complain") and echoes occupation-era thinking about local people. In his dissertation on the U.S. occupation of Okinawa, David John Obermiller writes, "The perception that Okinawans were permanent wards of the U.S. meant that [to] many soldiers Okinawans were lazy, stupid, and thus, if given the opportunity, would steal from Americans rather than work."

SOFA privileges, memories of the occupation, and a lingering colonial attitude can encourage those in the U.S. military community to feel they are above the law. I often think of a story the local papers reported when I lived on Okinawa. A group of American kids were caught throwing rocks at a man's home on the other side of the fence surrounding their military base. The rocks, some the size of large grapefruit, punched holes in his windows and caused nearly a thousand dollars' worth of damage. Actually, a succession of kids had thrown rocks—group after group—because this had been going on for ten years. For a decade, the children of marines had gathered on this edge of Camp Foster, inside, near their family housing area, and hurled rocks at the home of an Okinawan man. At one point, he asked the U.S. military to make the fence higher. He asked them to hang a sign that reminded kids not to throw rocks. Kids kept throwing rocks. He tried his own solutions—sheet metal over windows, his own fence, shrubbery. Still, American children launched rocks over the border and through his windows.

The U.S. military likes to refer to its relationship with Okinawa as one of "neighbors," or "guests" and "hosts." But those terms break down under scrutiny. The relationship between the local and U.S. military communities isn't so equal or polite; one of its main qualities is an uneven distribution of power. Maybe those kids would have tried the rock-throwing prank in the United States. But I imagine there it would have been stopped fast—by a parent, the neighbor, the police. On base in Okinawa, the kids learned they could get away with it. What did servicemembers feel they could get away with? After Rina Shimabukuro's murder, a sixty-three-year-old local who worked near Rina's home told a reporter, "When someone under the [Status of Forces] agreement commits a crime, it always gives me an impression that they know that they are protected by the agreement and that they have special privileges over us, as if Okinawa was their occupied territory." Rina's accused killer, Kenneth Franklin Gadson, had SOFA status as an on-base contractor.

Many Americans and base proponents cite a statistic that says Americans on Okinawa commit fewer crimes per capita than Okinawans. An earlier version of the newcomer's training stated, "SOFA status personnel make up less than 4% of Okinawa's total population. They account for less than 1% of the crime and traffic incidents on Okinawa." But as a defense of the base presence, this argument is iffy in a number of ways. One, anti-base activists would say that even one crime or traffic accident is too many; the number would be zero if the bases weren't present. Two, as Appling acknowledged at the training I attended, many consider each crime within the historical context. "When you start [adding up the crimes] over all the years we've been here since Reversion, you can start to see why things like that shoplifting or that DUI aren't individual, isolated incidents," Appling said. "Rather, they're the latest in a string of literally thousands of incidents involving SOFA status. So locally the question becomes, when does it end?" Three, local statistics tell a different story. Jon Mitchell cites numbers from the Okinawa Prefectural Police that say in recent years members of the U.S. military community have committed a higher rate of serious crimes than locals. Mitchell writes, "Between 2006 and 2015, members of the U.S. military, their dependents and military employees committed serious offences (murder, robbery, arson and rape) at a rate 2.3 times that of the local population." Four, all these figures don't include unreported crimes—which account for the majority of sexual assault cases—nor crimes committed on base and handled within the U.S. military system. At NOWA, one speaker acknowledged that on-base crime rates are high, especially compared to rates in local communities. "The crime rates of Okinawa are microscopic compared to the best, safest cities in the United States," the man in fatigues shouted. "The majority of the crime and low-level offenses are actually on the bases. . . . Out in town is extremely safe." Releases of crime statistics on other marine corps bases have shown a range of offenses, from theft and property destruction to violent crimes like physical and sexual assault, domestic violence, and murder. It's hard to imagine the many crimes committed on base don't spill over into Okinawa's safe communities. In a Starbucks outside a base on Okinawa, I overheard one servicemember say to another, "Americans commit all the crimes around here."

When servicemembers leave trainings like NOWA, what views of Okinawa do they take away? How do these differ from their initial ideas? One local set out to answer these questions. Nika Nashiro interviewed more than forty servicemen stationed on the island when she was an undergraduate and graduate student at the University of Hawaii. At a Starbucks outside a base on Okinawa, she chatted with GIs, asking them about their impressions of Okinawa and Okinawans. Her interest in the research was personal. Born and raised on the island, she was the daughter of a local woman and a Filipino man who had immigrated to Okinawa to work as an engineer. She attended international schools growing up, and because of her English abilities she worked on and around the bases as a teenager. Once she started interacting with servicemen, she started wondering how they saw her, what her petite figure and dark hair and eyes telegraphed to them. One customer made her uncomfortable when he came into the on-base store where she worked and said, "Hi, Sexy! Why are you so sexified? Is that your club clothes?" It was winter, and she was wearing a jacket over her plain shirt and jeans. She wanted to know how he could read such an outfit as sexualized.

When interviewing servicemen, Nika found that before coming to the island they associated Okinawa with stereotypical images of Japan and a tropical getaway: "cheap electronics, HONDA & TOYOTA, fast cars, beautiful beaches and sites, samurai, tatami mats, shōji (Japanese sliding doors made with bamboos and washi papers), bright neon, nice and kind girls, red light districts, and [a] leisure destination." Hardly any men had done their own research, relying instead on Hollywood and stories passed on from comrades. Then, once on Okinawa, they described their surroundings as "beautiful" and "heavily cultured," an island they loved, a place where they could relax. These perceptions echoed the way NOWA speakers talked about Okinawa as a travel and leisure destination.

Another parallel to the orientation was how many men told Nika they were stationed on Okinawa to protect the region from military threats and the aftermath of natural disasters. During the NOWA I attended, Appling stressed that the U.S. military was on Okinawa because of "location, location, location. . . . From this strategic location, the United States can respond quickly and effectively throughout the region, from the South China Sea to the Korean peninsula, be it a man-made disaster or a natural one." As if anticipating doubters, he went on: "That ability to respond quickly and effectively, that's not some bumper sticker, tattoo phrase. It's a fact." He said the marines had been able to "respond with life-saving assistance in short order" to places like Nepal, the Philippines, and Indonesia "based in large part on our presence right here on Okinawa." This viewpoint counters criticism from anti-base activists, who say the U.S. military presence on Okinawa causes more harm than good.

The men's exotified idea of Okinawa seemed to extend to local women. Lumping Okinawan women in with all Asian women, the men told Nika about colleagues who paid for sex in Thailand and called Okinawan women "'good care-takers,' willing to 'serve the [GIs],' very 'passive, held back and reserved' . . . 'very feminine and easy to flirt with' and 'short and tiny.'" One Latino soldier told her, "I love Okinawa, it's easy to flirt with people." He then demonstrated on a couple of local girls buying coffee. He and his friend, an African American soldier, boasted they had mastered the social cues and could read what women wanted. Large hoop earrings on a local woman meant she liked black men. Small earrings meant she liked white or Latino men. The African American soldier said he looked for women with big earrings and then told them whatever they wanted to hear.

Extending the idea of their role as protectors, men also talked about needing to rescue local women from backward local men. Women became less desirable and less in need of rescue when they had dated other American men. "The more English they speak, the more experienced they are with the American culture," one marine told Nika. "When a local girl speaks [a] good amount of English, it sometimes turns [me] off." A second serviceman shared, "[I] don't mind how many Japanese boys she was with, but do mind how many Americans she has dated." These servicemen weren't interested in Americanized women. They wanted to discover native women and go where no other Westerner had gone.

Nika's research suggests that the men retain certain aspects of the newcomer's training: the parts about the island's beauty and exotic culture, and the parts about being there to rescue locals in the region. The parts of the orientation that don't seem as memorable are the ones about the gravity of their actions—the way "Okinawa is different," a politically charged atmosphere where one incident can ignite. Instead, I saw at least one instance where this message had become a joke. At a bar frequented by marines outside Camp Hansen, a $10 cocktail that mixed shots of liquor with a fizzy, fruity Japanese drink was dubbed International Incident.

Of course, some servicemembers take their tour of duty in Okinawa seriously. There are a number, mostly men, who strive to leave the military community and enter local society in a meaningful way. They fall in love with local women, fall in love with the island, and never want to leave. This seems especially true for those looking to escape difficult lives back in the States. Okinawa is the poorest prefecture in Japan, but is wealthy compared to many areas of the United States. And in Okinawa, as in anywhere foreign, Americans can try to abandon whoever they were back home and be reborn into new "gaijin" identities. Because of the bases, they can leave the military and stay on the island, getting on-base contractor jobs and protection under SOFA. Because of the bases and the little Americas they create, American servicemembers can find a wormhole out of the United States.

This was the story of Kenneth Gadson. In Okinawa, he adopted his local wife's last name and planned never to return to the States. He didn't think America was a "caring society" and wanted to shield his wife from living there. After leaving the marine corps, he found a SOFA-status job on base and moved with his family to an Okinawan neighborhood. Until he confessed to Rina Shimabukuro's murder, his story resembled that of many American men on the island.

I met thirty-year-old Hernandez through his girlfriend of more than three years, a twenty-four-year-old local named Sayako. As is the military custom, he went by his last name. Hernandez had been in Okinawa for four years with the air force and seemed open and sincere. We talked one night at Rycom Mall, the giant new shopping center built on a former U.S. military golf course. What struck me right away was how the couple resembled each other. Both looked racially ambiguous, with dark hair and eyes, the same shade of tan skin. They were even dressed alike, in black tops layered over white undershirts, with jeans. When I pointed this out, they laughed, saying they hadn't realized.

Hernandez worked in the air force security forces, the military police. Part of his job was responding to off-base crimes involving Americans. For a SOFA-status person, the U.S. military "protects you to a certain degree," he explained. "But if the Japanese already have you in their custody, we can't do nothing about it." Therefore, the goal of Hernandez and his colleagues was to get to the perpetrator before the Japanese police did. "If we arrive at the same time as the Japanese, we have to make sure to get them quickly before the Japanese do. . . . We have to say, 'No, he's our people.'" In the case of a serious crime, like murder, the Japanese police could take the suspect into custody.

Hernandez's days started at 3 a.m., when he woke for a shift that started at four. His body had gotten used to as little as four hours of sleep a night. His schedule made it difficult to see Sayako, especially because he had to abide by a curfew and return to the barracks before it got too late. But the two were making it work. When they could, they explored the island together, visiting beaches, parks, castle ruins— just like military officials hoped. For Hernandez, the life was the fulfillment of a long-held dream.

"When I first got to Okinawa, I was ecstatic," he said. He had loved Japan since childhood, when he escaped into the world of the Japanese anime series *Dragon Ball Z* and *Pokémon*. Hernandez grew up in a Mexican American family in a rough area of San Antonio, where gun violence was the norm. "You would always hear helicopters in the air or gunshots at night," he remembered. His parents often confined him to the house for his safety. But the violence wasn't just in the streets. According to Hernandez, his father—a "cheater" who drank too much and did drugs—physically abused his mother. Eventually his mom divorced him, but his sister wasn't able to leave her own abusive relationship. Her husband killed her and then himself in a murder-suicide. Hernandez felt like domestic violence was a curse upon his family.

Amid all this, he started learning about Japanese culture and saw the country as somewhere he could live a "healthier lifestyle." Unable to relocate on his own, he looked to the U.S. military. "The military was literally the only option," he said. He had seen the path work for his older brother, who had joined the army. "He showed me a better direction, because it changed his life, too." At age twenty-five, Hernandez became an airman. A year later, he was flying to Okinawa.

At first, his ideas of Japan collided with reality. "When I first got here, no offense to the Japanese, I thought I was going to hear that anime high voice." He thought all Japanese women spoke in a cheery falsetto and was surprised to hear many with deep voices, normal voices. He also thought all women would dress and act overtly sexual, like in anime pornography. But, again, the women seemed just normal.

The idea of a healthier lifestyle did appear to be true. Gone was the constant threat of violence. Even the fast food restaurants were improved, the burgers made with more care, the fries not drenched in salt and oil. During his early days on the island, Hernandez yearned to enter that longed-for world, but had a hard time leaving base. Not knowing Japanese, he felt nervous and afraid of being inadvertently rude. He saw others succumb to culture shock and depression, like a guy who stayed in his room on base and let it fill with trash and roaches. People gossiped he kept a rat as a pet. "This place does affect people like that," Hernandez said. Servicemembers who stayed inside playing games or watching TV went crazy. It was harder for people without cars, like marines without a high enough rank or special permission.

Life improved for Hernandez when he met Sayako and started studying Japanese. Now he was like a military poster child for embracing the local culture. As Mike, the Marine Corps Family Readiness Officer, said, "My biggest thing is if you make Japanese friends, you're going to act like Japanese, and then once you get to know the culture a little, you're not going to want to dirty your face by getting in trouble. . . . I've never heard of anybody that got involved in the culture getting in trouble." Hernandez had gotten involved in the culture to the point where he reveled in being mistaken for a local, which he thought he could pull off with his appearance and language and cultural skills. "I try blending in as much as I can, and it kind of works out," he said. His Okinawan male co-workers even anointed him with an Okinawan nickname. "They said, we're going to call you *Higa* because you kind of look Japanese. They say, are you sure you don't have any Japanese or Asian blood?" Sayako's family also had accepted him, often asking when he was coming over to the house.

When it came to anti-base protesters, Hernandez said, "I want to sympathize with the locals as much as I can. But I have to have them understand that we can't all just leave. I know a lot of them want us to leave, but what can I do?" He thought on one hand it was unfair so many bases were on Okinawa. But on the other hand, the island needed the U.S. military to protect it from other countries that wanted the prime real estate.

Hernandez was scheduled to leave Okinawa the following year, but didn't want to go. "I want to make Japan my new home," he said. "I've grown so much in love with the people and the culture that I see back home is not going to be the same." He didn't want Sayako to live in a place like his old neighborhood in San Antonio—"to feel unsafe everywhere you go." He thought the Japanese were healthier and more respectful of each other than people in the United States or Mexico. When his contract ended, he planned to join the military reserves so he could keep some of his benefits, get retirement one day, and stay on the island. Then, he planned to look for a contract job on base, where he could obtain SOFA status. Without that, he'd only be able to stay in the country a few months at a time, on a tourist visa.

Looking back, Hernandez thought if he hadn't joined the military, he "probably would have been six feet under," like a few of his friends. He mentioned the possibility of marrying Sayako. Later, speaking about the history of violence in his family, he said, "I told her I'll never do what my father, what my sister's husband [did]. She can hit me"—the couple laughed—"but I'm not going to be the one to strike back at her. I'm too scared to do it. I don't want to feel how my dad or my sister's husband" felt. Later, he tweeted at me about an article on Rina Shimabukuro. "This breaks my heart so much still hearing about this," he wrote. "I can't even imagine ever doing this to the people here I have grow[n] to love."

For marines and sailors on Okinawa who did decide to marry, there was another military-run training, the premarital seminar. The mandatory event was another way the U.S. military dictated the lives of servicemembers on Okinawa. As scholars have argued, this type of control over personal lives reinforces the military's efforts to reprogram soldiers as loyal, selfless fighters. As the military would have said, seminars like this equip servicemembers with the tools they need for success.

As part of her job, Ashley helped organize the two-day seminar. On a spring morning in 2009 she met me outside Camp Foster to escort me to the training.

"Nice weather," she said as we waited at the guard booth. She looked up at the clear sky, an achy shade of light blue. She looked stylish that morning, with her sleek bob and bright orange shirt, which was tucked into black slacks worn with a slim belt and heels. As we walked back to our cars, she told me that at today's seminar there would be plenty of guys marrying local women—for better or for worse.

We drove to the Globe and Anchor, a hotel-conference-room-like space with framed photographs of Marilyn Monroe and other old movie stars on the walls. About seventy seminar attendees, all early, were sitting at round tables, drinking coffee and eating muffins. Like at NOWA, most couples were dressed in jeans and T-shirts, although some men wore fatigues, and some Japanese or Okinawan women donned form-fitting dresses and heels. I found a seat at a back table with an American couple and a blond woman in a sweatshirt who couldn't have been much older than twenty. As a whole, the attendees seemed disengaged, just wanting to get through this.

"Are you marrying Japanese?" a white man asked, walking around the room. He handed over a special packet if someone said yes, along with one written in Japanese for his fiancé. At the front of the room, he introduced himself as the vice consul from the U.S. consulate. The audience welcomed him with half-hearted applause. "Raise your hand if you're marrying a non-U.S. citizen," he said, and more than a third of the audience raised their hands. Through more questions we learned most couples were Americans returning to the States to wed, or Americans marrying Japanese citizens.

Next, he shouted along to a PowerPoint presentation, going over different scenarios—what to do if the woman was Filipina, how to apply for immigration, how to get a proxy marriage. He covered international parental child abduction, emphasizing that if your Japanese wife absconded with your kids, the United States had no recourse to get them back. Later, in 2014, Japan would sign the Hague Abduction Convention, requiring officials to enforce international custody orders, but at that point, nothing yet required them to intervene. And Japanese courts didn't recognize dual custody. In a divorce, the mother usually got the kids. The vice consul cited one couple who had joint custody of their son in California, but the wife returned to Japan with the kid. He was three years old now, and the father, stationed in the United States, had no way of seeing him.

"We deal with this every day," the vice consul said. "It's a big issue. Think about it." People didn't like to think about their marriages falling apart, he said, but 50 percent did. The rate was even higher for military and international marriages.

This was the somber core message of the day: Be careful. Are you sure you want to marry this person beside you? It's not going to be easy, especially if you're marrying someone of another culture and language. Throughout the day, only one speaker offered her congratulations. Everyone else punctuated their presentations with warnings. A military lawyer said three out of every five of his clients were getting separations. Sometimes he saw a couple from a premarital seminar just a few months later, getting a separation. "Just think twice," he warned.

This stance wasn't new for the U.S. military in Okinawa. After the war, the occupying force discouraged fraternization with "natives," and interracial marriage was still illegal in parts of the United States. In the first few years after the war, the U.S. military alternately allowed and banned marriages between its troops and local women, vacillating between trying to change and accepting the reality of the situation: the men and women were interacting, dating, and falling in love. Eventually, military leaders permitted the marriages, but institutionalized warnings against them remained in the newcomer's orientation and literature. An Okinawan woman who worked on base from 1951 to 1964 remembered, "The company commander told them it was all right to play around with the girls in town, but never to get serious. Not only did they hear this in their initial 'orientation,' but it was also printed in their 'information pamphlet.'"

At the Globe and Anchor, a Japanese woman did a short spiel in Japanese for "women who don't speak English that well." About six women followed her to the back of the room during one of the frequent breaks.

The next speaker worked harder to capture the audience's attention. An animated chaplain, young and blond, showed a clip from *The Princess Bride*—the scene in which the minister at the wedding of Buttercup and Humperdink speaks with an unbearable lisp. *Mawage. . . .* "Hopefully you won't have that sort of experience," the chaplain joked.

"I don't get it," the couple at my table said to each other. They looked even more annoyed by the seminar.

"Look at the person you're here with," the chaplain said. "Remember what you think about them right now. Because there will be bad times."

He handed out a booklet from the Prevention and Relationship Enhancement Program (PREP), developed for couples at the University of Denver, and led them through various activities. These included rating their relationship using a point scale, practicing effective communication, and role playing. The attendees without partners present just sat, doing nothing. Many of the couples did the same. The chaplain didn't seem to notice, remaining upbeat.

"Guys and girls are wired differently," he explained. "They just work differently." He showed a PowerPoint slide about it. Men were "Mr. Fix-Its," wanting to fix everything without asking for help, programmed like that since childhood. Women were "pursuers," wanting to make a connection with their partners "at all costs." His message was that men and women were biologically different, leading to inevitable inequalities and conflict.

On screen he showed a cartoon of a woman standing at a bathroom sink, her wet hair obscuring her face. She reached behind her, hand outstretched. The caption read, "Hand me the hairdryer."

The room rumbled with low male laughter. Horror crawled through me. The man standing behind the woman in the cartoon was about to pass her a handgun.

It wasn't until the Cold War that the U.S. military started bringing servicemembers' spouses and kids to overseas bases. As with all decisions, the one to deploy families was about ensuring the smooth functioning of the military installations. Families—along with the reproductions of America on base—help boost troops' morale. (Though not for all men. "Out here I have to live with my wife, and I don't see any reason you should get out of living with yours," one serviceman in Okinawa said to a group of unaccompanied officers in 1957.) Families also help limit soldiers' relationships with local women—and the problems that might ensue. For the local community, families serve as a domesticating presence, neutralizing some of the tension of living alongside thousands of war-trained troops. One Okinawan journalist I met likened the American families to hostages. The presence of spouses and children make servicemembers more likely to defend the island in the event of a conflict. For the U.S. military, family members like Ashley also bring a valuable labor pool.

During the premarital seminar lunch break, Ashley took me to a café on the water nearby. She and her husband lived off base in the same neighborhood. In Okinawa, military regulations vary about who can or can't live off base, but, generally, unaccompanied servicemembers can leave the barracks if they achieve certain seniority, and military families can—or have to—live off base if on-base housing is full. Many servicemembers opt to live outside the fences because they receive generous housing allowances and can rent big new homes that sometimes come with ocean views.

At the café, I asked about the cautionary tone of the speakers. "You seem like you're trying to scare people away," I said.

Ashley laughed. Cross-cultural relationships were hard, she said. Both sides had to extend effort, or the chance for success was low. Usually, in the successful relationships she saw, the man learned Japanese or the woman learned English. In the failed ones, neither learned to speak to the other. Communication was most important after that initial honeymoon stage, which many of the seminar couples were in now. Through PREP they tried to orient couples, provide tools, and warn them to be careful, to think it through.

"Does the seminar ever change people's minds about getting married?" I asked.

"Oh, yeah," she said. "Sometimes people don't come back the second day." Ashley didn't say it, but it seemed like she and the other speakers would consider that outcome a success. Better to prevent a marriage than have it end in divorce.

Ashley stabbed at her lettuce and said that people got married for the wrong reasons. As she explained it, many men stationed on Okinawa were lower-ranking and on their first tour of duty, away from home for the first time. Living in the barracks, without a car, a guy like that was faced with "not a very good selection of females" around him. Life wasn't so great. So he started dating Okinawan women and found a girlfriend who loved and cared for him. Marriage became attractive because it allowed him to move off base, get a car, and receive a higher salary and housing allowance. Listening to Ashley, I remembered one twenty-year-old Okinawan who'd told me her fiancé, a twenty-year-old marine, had been pressuring her to marry him so he could "get paid."

Ashley chewed thoughtfully. In her opinion, she said, a lot of guys getting married were too young. They hadn't matured or worked out their personal issues. The average age of the men in the seminar was early twenties, she guessed. Often, the Okinawan women were older—maybe the guy was twenty-two and the woman was thirty-six with two preteen kids. "That's an awkward situation," Ashley said. She couldn't guess at the older women's motivations, but thought the men wanted someone to take care of them, being away from their mothers for the first time.

Another big reason people got married was that the woman was pregnant. Those couples went downhill fast. Soon, the woman didn't want to have sex anymore, and the man got antsy and turned to someone else. He lost interest in his wife and kid. He didn't want to support them financially, and it became a legal issue. Ashley saw that kind of scenario more than she liked.

A different common problem began when, after a couple married, he got a tour conversion and added three years to his stay on Okinawa. By the end of that, he was ready to return to the States, but her family and friends were in Okinawa. So he left, she stayed.

Ashley pushed away her plate and wiped her hands. "One thing I hate," she said, "is that story about the American as the bad guy." She was alluding to a popular perception on the island that American servicemen were prone to committing offenses like cheating and abandoning pregnant girlfriends. "It's not the whole story. Women scam men all the time." She drank some water. "Tag chasers," she said— a term for women who only want to date military men. She told me about a marine who fell in love with a Thai woman. After knowing her only a couple of weeks, he wanted to get married. The woman told him, "Buy me a big diamond ring first," and he did, and she took off.

"Just when you think things are calming down," Ashley said. "We hear crazy stories."

Later, I spoke with the vice consul from the U.S. consulate, and he echoed Ashley's defense of American men. He described what he thought was a typical situation in Okinawa. A twenty-year-old Okinawan woman meets a twenty-two-year-old American serviceman at a bar. Neither speaks the other's language, but they're "in love." They get married, have a couple of kids, and after two years the guy's tour of duty is up. They go to the States—Arkansas, let's say. There are no Japanese restaurants, no one who speaks Japanese, and the woman grows homesick. She takes the kids back to Okinawa for a long visit. After six months apart, the couple decides it's best to get divorced.

"This is how it happens," the vice consul said. A lot of Okinawan women didn't want to leave Okinawa—that was how they ended up single mothers. The father wasn't this evil guy, a bastard. Some American fathers paid thousands of dollars in child support, without the right—because of Japanese law, because of Japanese mothers—to even call their kids on the phone. That was the side of the story people didn't often hear. "The American man is not evil," he said.

Back at the seminar, everyone looked sleepy and even less attentive. People gathered at the refreshment table, eating cookies and ignoring the chaplain, who continued to talk about issues couples should discuss pre-marriage, like kids and checking accounts. He played a Berlitz commercial that featured a German coast guard hearing on his radio, "We're sinking!" The coast guard replied, "What are you thinking about?"

"Improve your English," the tagline read. As Colonel Jones had implied to me, the idea was that the onus was on Okinawan women to develop their foreign-language skills to communicate with their American partners, and not the other way around.

The seminar ended an hour early. The next day, I sat again with the solo, bored-looking blond servicewoman. I asked what she thought of the seminar.

"Stupid," she said. She'd already talked to her boyfriend, who was back home in the States, about all this stuff. But if the seminar got her out of work, she was happy to be there. "I'm counting down the chapters," she said, jabbing the PREP book. "I can't wait until the end."

The chaplain continued his lectures, covering sex (generally, women were more sensual, he said, and men were more sexual). At a coffee break, I talked with a young-looking white guy wearing a red Billabong T-shirt and cargo shorts. He liked the seminar, he said. It was covering some things he and his Okinawan fiancé needed to work on, like communication. She spoke good English, and he had learned some Japanese, but language became a problem during arguments, when she "forgot" her English. The seminar had shown her how to be more structured in their conversations when there was conflict.

I asked about cultural barriers.

He shook his head, grinning. "Her family loves Americans."

Listening to the chaplain, I watched Ashley at the side of the room, whispering to a colleague. Throughout the seminar, she'd been mostly backstage, sometimes announcing speakers or instructions. Ashley, too, had married a serviceman and married young. They'd attended the same college but had different cultural backgrounds. Was her marriage more likely to survive than these? Had part of the reason they'd married young been so that she could come with him overseas? They seemed to be in a honeymoon period, too, divorced from reality on this island far from home.

That following September, as the humidity lessened and the light shifted—the edges of fall—I went to a wine-tasting event on base called Okinapa. In the crowd of dressed-up servicemembers and their spouses, I ran into Ashley. She took hold of my elbow and steered me away from the crowd. Her friend had been killed in Afghanistan, she said. I'd met him that night at the squadron's St. Patrick's Day party.

I remembered. His fiancé had been the hot doctor in the green dress who'd been all over him on the dance floor. She had told a story about the two of them taking off each other's clothes in the kitchen of their apartment, mad with desire. I learned that after that party, they had gotten married, and three weeks later he'd volunteered to fight in Afghanistan. He was killed during a rooftop firefight.

"We still can't believe it," Ashley said, hugging herself and staring into the throng of drunk couples. She looked pale and haunted. Not long ago, she'd been dancing in a green wig, declaring Okinawa an extension of college, a party. But Okinawa wasn't like college. The U.S. military played up the beaches and familiar foods, the parties and scuba diving, so servicemembers didn't dwell on the real reason they were on Okinawa: to train and prepare for battle. Servicemembers stationed on the island were regularly deployed to the Middle East. There was a direct line between this world and far-away fighting. No matter how pleasant and safe—a paradise—Okinawa seemed to men like Hernandez and couples like Ashley and her husband, the U.S. military presence on the island was about war.

Ashley said she'd been bringing the widow bottles of wine, which was bad, she knew, but it helped for a moment at least. "What else can I do? I don't know what to do." She looked at me. "How could this have happened?"

4

SACHIKO

WAR FIRST CAME TO OKINAWA NOT ON THE MAIN ISLAND, BUT ON THE smaller ones scattered to the west. One of the Kerama Islands, Toka-shiki is an oasis of jeweled forest, turquoise water, and sand the color of sun-bleached bone. Just six miles long and one mile wide, it lies about twenty miles off the southwestern coast of Okinawa Island. I visited once, on a day trip. A tour company promising relaxation fer-ried us to the island and deposited us on a beach so bright and hot we could barely see. We squinted at arrows that darted in the clear surf. We took photographs that would come out overexposed. At one point, I stumbled off the beach, into the jungle, and up a small hill. The foli-age pulsed with cicadas. I stood in a stone tower and looked at the sea, dragonflies swerving by. Everything felt muffled, tamped down with the heat. Only later did I connect that day to the stories that had sparked my awareness of, and my obsession with, Okinawa.

Sachiko Miyagi grew up on Tokashiki before the war. Born in 1927, she was the third youngest of nine children born to Jitsui and Nae Makiya. Her mother was known as a kind and gentle caregiver, while her father was a community leader, a teacher who had gone on to become principal of the primary school, then mayor of Tokashiki, then president of the bonito fishery union. He was known as a cheerful man who loved and was loved by the people of Tokashiki. He cut his children's hair himself, lopping the girls' locks into the traditional okkapa style, a bob with blunt bangs. He cut theirs shorter than other girls', above the ears, and when Sachiko complained, he assured her she looked very cute.

Food could be scarce on the island then, but life was rich with community. Fishermen worked the sea, and when they hauled in a big bonito catch, they raised flags on their boats, signaling the village. People came down to the beach and awaited the fishermen, who chopped off fish heads and passed them around for free once ashore. Women stewed soup with the heads, a treat for their families. Sachiko worked for her family gathering food, but the chore was an adventure. With her friends she explored the mountain, walking amid the clear air and evergreen trees, searching for edible plants. There was still time to play—jumping rope, spinning tops, tossing balls, picking watermelons and chilling them in the well.

Like her older siblings before her, Sachiko left this tranquil life after middle school to continue her education on Okinawa Island; Tokashiki didn't have a high school. She moved to the bustling urban area around Naha and attended Shuri Girls' School, where students learned the arts of sewing, weaving, and dyeing. As across all Japan, education was also in service to the emperor, training students to serve him with filial devotion. Since Japan had plunged into war in 1931 with the invasion of Manchuria, the indoctrination had intensified. Okinawan students like Sachiko lined up in their dark uniforms to bow low to the northeast, where, far away, the Imperial Palace stood. In the mornings they made offerings to Amaterasu, the goddess that the emperor was said to have descended from. Before meals they thanked the emperor for their food. They believed Japan was waging a holy war for Greater East Asia, the natural leader of other Asian countries and their protector against Western imperialism.

The government pushed this wartime propaganda on all Japanese citizens. The mass media became the mouthpiece of the state and broadcasted fabricated news of military victories and brave troops who died praising the emperor. (Witnesses testified most soldiers' actual last words were calls for their mothers or wives.) Those who died were referred to as "smashed jewels" (gyokusai) and fallen cherry blossoms. The enemy were the white imperialist "fiends" and "savages." Japanese military defeats and atrocities overseas were censored. People who voiced their doubts, even in their diaries, were labeled traitors and hauled away by the secret police.

As war drew closer to home, Okinawans became increasingly militarized along with all Japanese. Fed a diet of jingoistic propaganda, citizens trained for war. Able young Okinawan men were drafted and sent off with cheers of "Banzai!" to battlegrounds across Asia and the Pacific. Men, women, and children who stayed behind practiced air-raid drills and formed neighborhood associations to manage the shrinking food rations and nightly blackouts. Housewives joined defense associations, seeing men off to war with Okinawan dance and senninbari, belts with a thousand red stitches sewn by, supposedly, a thousand women, to keep them safe.

For older Okinawan students like Sachiko, who turned seventeen in 1944, education became focused on military preparation—air-raid drills, bamboo spear practice, day-long marches to build endurance. Sachiko and her classmates traded their coveted sailor-collar uniforms for monpe, baggy work pants. By 1944, all classes on the island stopped. Schoolhouses became outposts for the Imperial Japanese Army, and students as young as middle schoolers became construction workers and food scavengers. In her fourth year of school, Sachiko was sent to a district in Naha to help build an airport, removing stones from the runway. She also worked digging a cave. Okinawa is honeycombed with natural limestone caves, which in earlier times played sacred roles for Ryukyuan people. They were seen as the homes of deities and served as tombs, precursors to the man-made ones that line the island's hillsides. In war they were to become bomb shelters, and the Imperial Japanese Army wanted to build more.

In the summer of 1944, Japanese military leaders decided some Okinawan women, children, and elderly should evacuate the islands.

Their concern wasn't safety; they were counting mouths to feed. With incoming Japanese troops, the military wanted civilians who couldn't contribute to the war effort to leave. The evacuation was half-hearted, though, and by then the waters around Okinawa had grown treacherous with American submarines and warplanes. When the opportunity arose for Sachiko's youngest brother, Sanetomi, to evacuate to Kyushu by ship, their father Jitsui refused. Sanetomi was the baby of the family, the one Jitsui had spoiled with sweets when he was young. Jitsui thought the journey was too dangerous, but Sanetomi's teachers implored him to reconsider. He'll be safer, they said. Jitsui relented. Watching his youngest disappear on a boat from Tokashiki, Jitsui waved and waved, until he was sure his son could see him no more. It was the last time he'd see any of his children.

Sanetomi and two of his older sisters, who were teachers, were joining thousands of Okinawan children evacuating the prefecture. Their ship traveled in a convoy with others, including one called the *Tsushima Maru*, which carried more than eight hundred school children. On the ships' second night at sea, in the waters off Kagoshima, a U.S. submarine torpedoed and sunk the *Tsushima Maru*, killing nearly all of its seventeen hundred civilian passengers. Sanetomi's ship was spared.

Back in Okinawa, more and more civilians were mobilized to make up for insufficient Japanese troops in the islands. One contingent, the Home Guard, was comprised of men up to forty-five years old, who were ordered to serve as soldiers without receiving military training. Eventually, the sick, the elderly, the young, and the disabled joined the Home Guard's ranks, as Japanese forces dwindled further. The military also mobilized all students from the main island's twenty-one junior and senior high schools. Girls aged fifteen to nineteen joined nursing corps and learned to deliver medical aid and helped prepare makeshift hospitals in caves. Boys aged fourteen to nineteen became the Emperor's Blood and Iron Student Corps and Signal Corps. Their duties would be delivering messages and supplies and repairing bridges and telephone lines. Sachiko and her sixty schoolmates began their medical training in January 1945 and in mid-March became the Zuisen Student Corps, named after a spring.

Because of their educations, the mobilized students believed the Imperial Japanese Army was unparalleled and American soldiers were "devil beasts" who would show no mercy as invaders, ripping apart children, flattening men with tanks, and ravaging women and girls. Japanese soldiers who related these tales were perhaps inspired by their own military's atrocities across Asia. Some recounted to Okinawans the brutal rapes, torture, and slayings the Imperial Japanese Army had committed in China, suggesting the same was in store for Okinawans if Americans took them captive.

The Imperial Japanese Army forbade its soldiers from surrendering or being taken as prisoners of war—upon penalty of death. As the war went on, state propaganda extended this policy to all citizens. In slogans, the Japanese people became united as the "one hundred million Special Attack Force," or suicide unit, and "one hundred million shattering jewels." Okinawans might have been even more willing to lay down their lives because of their years of being treated as second-class Japanese. They wanted to prove their patriotism, their identities as Japanese subjects. "We were consumed by a burning desire to offer our lives in defense of the nation," said one Signal Corps member. "We had no fear of death whatsoever. This is how we had been educated and we accepted this without question." A Blood and Iron student corpsman recalled that he was afraid, but resigned to die: "The militarist education had affected every sinew of my body." Girls also fantasized about dying in battle and being immortalized with other war heroes at Yasukuni Shrine in mainland Japan. "Give your life for the sake of the Emperor, wherever you may go," the girls, in their bobbed haircuts and pigtails, sang. Confident in their mission, they went off to war with their school supplies and toiletries, imagining themselves helping soldiers in between catching up on their studies. Under the safety of the red cross, they would tend to Japanese soldiers with calm benevolence, wrapping wounds in white bandages and murmuring reassurances.

On the night of March 27, 1945, Sachiko and her classmates gathered for a makeshift graduation ceremony outside the man-made cave where they would work, the field hospital of the 62nd Infantry Division. The

setting was a candlelit tent on a patch of grass; in attendance were the
school principal and a few others. The girls received tags labeled with
the infantry division and became civilian employees of the Imperial
Japanese Army. During the poignant ceremony, the girls began to feel
despondent, missing their parents and sensing the oncoming terrors.
"We sang the school song, but halfway through everybody started to
cry and you couldn't hear the words," one graduate remembered. "We
all felt that there was just no hope." The officer in charge of the hospital confirmed their fears when he declared, "You girls will all die with
me in battle." Another graduate remembered the ceremony differently.
They sang a military song, she said, with lyrics like "If I go through the
mountain, I will be a corpse on the grass. It's my earnest desire to die
at the Emperor's foot." Mid-song, the girls were cut off not by crying
but by U.S. bombs exploding, close enough that sand rained down on
the tent.

Five days later, on April 1, 1945, U.S. forces landed on Okinawa.
Sachiko and other student nurses across the island were thrown into
war. Injured soldiers began pouring into the hospital caves. "They
petrified us all," remembered one woman. "Some didn't have faces,
some didn't have limbs. Young men in their twenties and thirties
screaming like babies. Thousands of them." The students were tasked
with tending to these men, stacked in crude bunk beds. Sachiko and
her friends were shocked at their new jobs, immobilized until their
superiors ordered them to move. Girls picked bucket loads of maggots
from pus-filled wounds and carted away bedpans, mortified by the
men's exposed bodies. In surgery areas, they held down soldiers who
received operations without anesthesia. The girls were left holding
still-warm, sawed-off limbs. Sachiko watched strong soldiers break
down, screaming and blubbering under the knife. She noticed the
most excruciating pain came during eye surgery. Other dying soldiers
screamed out for food and water, sometimes so starved they demanded
the broiled arm or leg of a comrade. Some men shared memories of
their homes, while others directed their anguish at the girls, calling
them idiots if they faltered, slapping their faces, shouting that they'd
come all the way from the mainland to defend Okinawa and *this is how*

you treat us? Some men snarled, "I hear that Okinawan girls are hook-ing up with the Americans now that they've landed. Maybe you girls should get out there with them too."

The military also ordered the student nurses to do the perilous work of venturing outside the caves to bury bodies and limbs, transport messages, wash bandages, and haul in supplies. Every time they did so they risked taking fire from guns or bombs. Girls died this way. Oth-ers were blown up or asphyxiated when Americans hit the caves with bombs or gas attacks. At the Nageera Cave in Haebaru, where the Zuisen Student Corps worked, three girls died, two from disease, one from shrapnel wounds sustained while collecting water outside. Soon, Sachiko lost her fear of death, every day wondering *maybe today is my day to die*. All she hoped for was a quick end, without suffering. Mean-while, food supplies dwindled. The students and soldiers survived on a rice ball a day, ones so small they could easily be enclosed in a girl's hand. The combs, mirrors, and toothbrushes the girls had brought along became useless, with no time to groom or water to bathe. Their faces grew caked with dirt, their scalps crawling with lice, their bod-ies with fleas. The caves became overcrowded, and when girls had a chance to sleep, they slept standing up. Bodily functions like men-struation and defecation stopped. Recalling the battle, one woman remarked, "I felt more dead than alive."

Sachiko's daughter Chie took me to one of the hospital caves where girls like her mother had worked and died during the battle. It was a humid, windy, clear-skied day in 2009. Chie was in her early fifties, a high school English teacher and peace activist who, years later, would take me to the protest site on Oura Bay. Known for her colorful outfits, that day she wore a shirt and jeans that were both bright pink. Her hair was styled in a side ponytail adorned with fake hibiscus flowers. We drove to the south of the island, where the fighting had culminated, and outfitted ourselves with hardhats and flashlights. At the mouth of the cave, Chie translated a placard, which related the terrors of war matter-of-factly. During the Battle of Okinawa, the placard read, the island's many natu-ral caves became hiding places for the Japanese military and Okinawan civilians. This cave served as a hospital, sheltering hundreds. It was organized by injury, with different areas for people with brain damage, in critical condition, and so on. It had a bathroom area, a kitchen area, a bed area. Doctors conducted operations without anesthesia. At one point, the healthy people had to leave the wounded behind, so they injected them with poison to give them quick deaths.

Overall, Chie said more than once, the cave saved people. It was heaven in the cave, compared to what was going on above ground.

We descended into the earth. I was thankful for the hardhat and flashlight. The path was slippery and steep, and a few times I hit my head on the rock. Inside, the darkness expanded, the temperature dropped, and we found ourselves in large caverns, water dripping on our arms and bats streaking overhead, caught in the beams of our flashlights. On the ground were broken pieces of pottery and bottles—one bottle from the 1970s, Chie said, examining a label. Sometimes we heard voices echoing from other groups, but most of the time we were alone.

Chie asked me to turn off my flashlight. The blackness rushed in. She spoke about the war and what people endured—the smells, the screams, the dark. And still, it was better down here than up there. She talked about her father's sister, her Aunt Fumi, who'd worked in this cave or another as a student nurse. Chie didn't know the details, because her aunt had died at the end of the war.

"People still find bones in this cave," she said.

As we made our way through the caverns, I tried to imagine, as Chie had instructed. The stench of rotting flesh, of excrement. Men screaming out in agony. The bulk of a warm body meeting yours in the dark. Blood, slick and iron-smelling. As things worsened, more unusual sounds: the munching of maggots, blooming like white blossoms in a shaft of moonlight. The short cry of a child, muffled by a Japanese soldier, maybe for good. The decomposing of bodies, which one survivor described as "the kind of sound you hear when something is simmering in a pot." Explosions from above shaking loose a rain of rocks. The exhaustion, the hunger, the fear of death so protracted and pronounced it felt like a full-body numbness. And all the while the Americans were walking the island above, waiting to rip off your clothes and rape you, mutilate you, murder you.

Back in the daylight, we blinked in the sun, the heat and humidity claiming our bodies again. We walked through the visitor's center, where there were articles about a World War II bomb that had detonated recently in a construction site. A power shovel, digging a trench for a water line in Itoman City, bit into the earth, and a crater, fifteen feet wide and five feet deep, burst open. The blast blew out more than a hundred windows in a nearby senior citizens' home and took the helmet off the head of the construction worker operating the machine. He sustained serious facial injuries but survived, and one senior citizen was harmed. No one knew where the next blast would hit. "All of southern Okinawa has the same problem; we don't know where unexploded bombs are hiding," a mayor of a nearby town remarked. Over the years, accidents had included one outside a Naha kindergarten in 1974, when construction workers were installing new water mains during a school celebration. Some four hundred parents and kindergartners were assembled outside when a pile driver met a bomb. The explosion killed four construction workers and flung kindergartners into the air, burying them in sand.

Across the island, it was common to find all kinds of weaponry in the earth: rockets, shells, artillery rounds, hand grenades, flares, machine gun ammunition, land mines. Over 2,500 tons of unexploded ordnance remain on Okinawa, leftover from the 200,000 tons of explosives dropped on the island during the battle. Schools teach kids to identify and leave alone the rusted bullets, bombs, and grenades, and the Japanese Self-Defense Forces is regularly called to dispose of findings. Chie told me people in Okinawa wanted the national government to pay for this recent accident in Itoman, to take responsibility, but leaders in Tokyo had refused.

The strategy of the Imperial Japanese Army was to draw out the Battle of Okinawa for as long as possible. From the start, military commanders knew they would lose—American forces outnumbered them five to one. In fighting, they wanted to inflict as many Allied casualties as possible and delay what came next. U.S. forces wanted to take Okinawa Island as a base for their mainland invasion, and Japanese leaders were willing to sacrifice the lives of Okinawan civilians to put this off, waging a war of attrition so mainland forces had longer to prepare. Japanese troops dug in to caves in the south of the island, waiting for the Americans, who landed on the central coast, cutting the island in two. The GIs who trekked north met little resistance. The ones who moved south were confronted with fierce fighting. Okinawan civilians were also lucky or unlucky depending on which end of the island they chose for their escape. The U.S. military had firebombed Naha months before, but some Okinawans reasoned being close to the Imperial Japanese Army headquarters in the south offered greater safety. As U.S. forces began shelling the island, some Okinawans fled north, some south. This decision often determined whether they would live or die. In the north, the U.S. military quickly took in civilians and brought them to refugee camps, where they received sustenance and remained out of the line of fire. In the south, civilians were caught on the battlefield, exposed to bombing and gunfire and put in competition with Japanese soldiers for shelter and food. The armed soldiers usually won. Okinawans wandered from place to place, in constant search of water to drink, scraps to eat, and places to hide, praying a random shell or rain of bullets wouldn't hit them. Families became separated or watched each other die.

Toward the end of May 1945, Japanese forces on Okinawa had lost some two-thirds of their 110,000 men and began retreating farther south, bringing the student nurses with them. Cave hospitals were abandoned, and the men and girls too injured to travel were left behind or given poison or grenades to end their lives. Some patients were resigned to this fate, while others fought desperately against death. Medical staff held down struggling men to give them lethal injections. Other patients found new strength. One student nurse watched with horror as a soldier who had lost both legs dragged himself after them through the mud.

The journey south was a new hell, the roads reduced to a muddy slog by bombs and rain, pitted with craters, strewn with bloated corpses, and crowded with battered soldiers and civilians alike. Children clung to the lifeless bodies of their parents and called out "Sister!" when seeing the students, who could only continue on, hauling their classmates on stretchers and trying not to get hit with shells. The girls saw sights that would haunt them forever: babies suckling from headless mothers, blasted soldiers with dangling eyeballs, people stuffing their intestines back into their bodies, classmates whose faces, buttocks, or limbs were blown away. The girls became numb to this type of death. "The thing that frightened me most was myself," said one student nurse. "It was as though I'd become some sort of hard-hearted person who couldn't cry even when I saw a dead body. I felt that I'd turned into a cold human being." A Zuisen Student Corps member remembered, "I felt nothing at all. No human feeling remained in my mind."

Some 30,000 Japanese soldiers and 100,000 civilians became squeezed into a smaller and smaller area on the southern tip of the island, the ocean on one side, American forces on the other. Most civilian deaths occurred during this time, after the Japanese military chose to retreat to prolong the battle, instead of surrendering or taking their last stand at their headquarters in Shuri. As Japanese forces (and their nurses) arrived in the south, they kicked out civilians from their hiding places in caves, condemning many to deaths on the battlefield. When Sachiko watched Japanese soldiers order locals to leave Ihara Cave so they could take it over, she knew those people were about to die. She started forming what would become her lifelong belief: The military doesn't protect people. The military harms people.

In mid-June, the situation became more chaotic after the U.S. commander, Lt. Gen. Simon Bolivar Buckner, was killed in an artillery strike, and the Japanese commander, Lt. Gen. Ushijima, announced, "The battlefield is now in such chaos that all communications have ceased. It is impossible for me to command you. Every man in these fortifications will follow his superior officer's orders and fight to the end for the sake of the motherland. This is my final order. Farewell." A few days later, Ushijima committed suicide without formally surrendering, drawing out the battle even further. American forces began "mopping up" the battlefield, disposing of soldiers and civilians with a ferocity some say was revenge for their fallen commander.

Under the burning June sun, the student nurses roamed the southern coast, facing U.S. military ships at sea and men with flamethrowers at their backs. The girls who had survived to this point were presented with a choice. American soldiers called out for civilians hiding along the coastal cliffs to surrender. "Americans will protect you," the GIs broadcast from their boats. "We have food. We'll rescue you!" But the indoctrination against the enemy had been a success. "Never live to suffer the disgrace of being captured," the girls recited. They saw Japanese soldiers shoot their own comrades who tried to surrender. While some Japanese officers did encourage students to live, others enforced the official line to "fight to the end." One Japanese soldier taught Sachiko how to kill herself. Detonate a grenade close to your heart, he said, so death will be instant.

No one believed the Americans' promises of protection. "We thought we were hearing the voices of demons," one student nurse, Kikuko Miyagi, recalled. "From the time we'd been children, we'd only been educated to hate [the Americans]. They would strip the girls naked and do with them whatever they wanted, then run over them with tanks. We really believed that. . . . So what we had been taught robbed us of life." Instead of surrendering, Kikuko's classmates begged their teacher to kill them. He eventually obliged, pulling the pin on a hand grenade when they came under fire, killing himself and nine girls. "We were simply too terrified of being stripped naked," Kikuko said. "That's what a girl fears most, isn't it?"

During the war, mainland Japanese cities endured catastrophic fire-bombing, and Hiroshima and Nagasaki experienced the cataclysm of the atomic bomb. On the mainland, some 300,000 to 400,000 civilians lost their lives. Okinawa, the only Japanese prefecture to suffer through ground combat, sustained a much higher per capita rate—some 140,000 civilian deaths in a prefecture with fewer than 450,000 residents. As a result of the ninety days of fighting, nearly one in three Okinawans died. Civilians forced to serve in the Japanese military died at an even higher rate. Sixty percent of the 22,000 untrained Home Guard "soldiers" died, as well as perhaps the great majority of the Koreans the Imperial Japanese Army had brought and forced into battle, labor, or sex work.

Of the sixty-one girls who had entered the Zuisen Student Corps with patriotic optimism, thirty-three were lost. Sachiko was one of the survivors. She managed to stay alive in Ihara Cave, watching her classmates die one by one, every day thinking it would be her turn. A military doctor helped save her from suicide by telling her she must live in order to let mainland Japanese know what had happened in Okinawa. Although for years afterward she would keep her story locked inside her, protecting herself against the memories, eventually she would speak out, sharing the anti-war beliefs born during her ordeal.

Sachiko's time in the cave ended when U.S. soldiers discovered her and others hiding there and took them captive. Sachiko was surprised to find that the Americans in uniform seemed kinder than the Japanese.

Sachiko's younger brother Sanetomi and her older sisters who had evacuated to the mainland survived the war as well. All in all, two of her eight siblings perished: her eldest brother, who had been mobilized to fight on the mainland, and an older sister, who became a battlefield nurse and died of malnutrition. Soon, Sachiko learned her parents back on Tokashiki also hadn't been lucky. Before the battle on Okinawa had even begun, they had died in a scene that was perhaps the most horrific part of a battle filled with horrors.

American forces showed up at the Kerama Islands a week before their invasion of the main island. On Tokashiki, a Japanese captain named Akamatsu commanded a squadron of one hundred sailors whose mission was to attack the American fleet in one-man speedboats on suicide missions. His stance toward Okinawans was unmerciful. No one was to surrender or cooperate with the Americans, even civilians. As American battle ships drew near at the end of March 1945, Akamatsu ordered the islanders to relinquish all their food to him and his men, then gather in a designated area.

Up to a thousand villagers traveled to a place near a military camp and the Onna River. Some walked all night through a downpour lit red by American tracers. Sachiko's parents were among the group that assembled. All their children were off the island, evacuated to the mainland or mobilized into service.

Even though the villagers shared a sense of doom, that morning women took care in dressing and fixing their hair. They waited maybe minutes, maybe hours, and then received their order from the soldiers: commit suicide. The troops passed out hand grenades, but only had about thirty for everyone. Some failed to detonate, while others exploded, killing the men, women, and children huddled around them. American forces, hearing the explosions, began unleashing a torrent of artillery and shells, and a mad contagion swept through the people of Tokashiki. What came next is hard to grasp. The scene seems incomprehensible, unimaginable. The villagers of Tokashiki became animated by some deadly mix of military indoctrination, terror over what the Americans would do, threats from Japanese soldiers, and the madness of war. The villagers thought the Japanese soldiers were embarking on their own suicide mission. They thought what they were about to do was the most humane and loving act. They thought the only way forward was to do what the state said was honorable: shatter like jewels.

Family members turned, crazed, on one another. The grenades gone, they used what they could find: razor blades and hatchets and scythes, sticks and rocks and lengths of rope. Sons plunged kitchen knives into their mothers' necks; brothers cracked rocks against their sisters' skulls. Fathers beat their wives and children with branches.

"As if by chain reaction, it spread from one family to the next," a survivor, Shigeaki Kinjo, said. "We must all die that way. Everyone seemed to think so. People began to raise their hands against their loved ones." Kinjo, sixteen at the time, was with his mother, older brother, and two younger siblings. "My memory tells me the first one we laid hands on was Mother," he said. "We might have used a string. When we raised our hands against the mother who bore us, we wailed in our grief. I remember that. In the end we must have used stones. To the head. We took care of Mother that way. Then my brother and I turned against our younger brother and sister. Hell engulfed us there."

When the killing subsided, 329 people, including Sachiko's parents, were dead. The stream ran red. Survivors were stunned to find the Japanese soldiers hadn't perished on their suicide mission. The speed-boats had never launched, and the men were still alive. "I just couldn't believe it," Kinjo recalled. "We'd chosen to take our own lives because we thought [the soldiers] were all dead. That was when our sense of solidarity with the military came crashing down around us." After that point, he said, "the Japanese more than the Americans became the object of our fears."

When student nurses emerged from caves at the end of the battle, they were blinded. They hadn't been outside during daylight in weeks. As their eyes adjusted, for the first time they got a good look at the enemy, the American men who had been incinerating their island for the past three months. To the girls, these men were the devil, hardly human, known as Goat Eyes, because Okinawans had come to believe the invaders lacked night vision, like (supposedly) goats. The girls steeled themselves against what came next: the rapes, the mutilations, the slaughter. "I'm not afraid of dying," said one girl, pulling a GI's rifle muzzle toward her chest. "Kill me now, please! You may kill me." Instead of shooting her, the GI smiled and treated her leg wound with disinfectant. Girls refused American canteens, thinking the water was poisoned. The soldiers chuckled and drank from the canteens, show-ing they were safe. The girls accepted sips. Slowly, they realized the future wasn't going to look the way they had imagined.

5

ARISA

WHEN ARISA WAS A GIRL IN THE 1980S, HER FATHER DEVISED AN unusual game. He challenged her and her sister to walk all the way around Kadena Air Base with him. The family lived in Okinawa City, close enough to the base that the Japanese government paid for double-paned windows and an air-conditioning unit in each room to muffle the noise of the aircraft. In her father's game, the three of them would set out from their house and begin walking along the tall fence topped with barbed wire. "I think my dad wanted us to know how big Kadena Base is," Arisa said. Kadena is the biggest U.S. Air Force base in all of Asia, swallowing chunks of Chatan Town, Kadena Town, and Okinawa City. Its two runways stretch more than two miles each. When anti-base demonstrators joined hands in protest around the base in 1986, forming a human chain, they needed more than 20,000 bodies.

Arisa, her father, and her sister would start at the northeast end of the base in Okinawa City, following the fence south through the entertainment district of bars and clubs. They'd break for lunch at an A&W, then rest again at McDonald's after reaching Route 58 in Chatan, on the base's western side. They'd continue north into the town of

Kadena, where residents received even higher subsidies from the Japanese government, since they were closer to the runways. After four or five hours, the circle would be complete, and Arisa's father would reward his daughters with ten-thousand-yen bills, a considerable prize for a kid.

Arisa's parents were both busy professionals, her father an engineer, her mother an elementary school teacher. Although they didn't discuss their political views of the bases, Arisa knew her mother voted for anti-base candidates and sometimes protested outside the bases as part of a teachers' organization. The prevailing attitude at Arisa's school, too, was against the bases. Perhaps with his game her dad was trying to engender some sense of injustice in his daughters, showing them viscerally how much land Kadena Air Base occupied. The impression on Arisa, in any case, was positive. She would remember those walks with fondness, not only because of the cash she earned, but also because of the adventure and the way they etched the base into her imagination.

On an overcast November day in 2008, Arisa drove me onto the base she had spent her childhood circling. At the Kadena Air Base gate, an Okinawan guard examined her ID and waved her minivan through. The once off-limits world unfurled around her. The roads doubled in width, and neat green lawns stretched to the feet of neat white buildings. The dense concrete cityscapes of central Okinawa and its snakes of traffic gave way to quiet.

Arisa had grown up to marry one of the men behind the fence. She was in her early thirties now, a beautiful woman with bright eyes and freckles. Her husband Brian had retired from the military and worked as an on-base contractor, granting the family SOFA status and access to the base. That day, she was headed with their one-year-old son to an international festival, where Brian was performing with his dojo. The festival was off base on Gate 2 Street, but Arisa was using the base as a shortcut. Driving around it would have taken much longer.

Wet met Brian near Gate 2 and left the base. Gate 2 Street had been blocked off for the festival, and vendors were selling cups of beer and greasy Japanese food. The aroma of sizzling meat mixed with an underlying stench of urine. "If you want to see homeless people, go to Gate 2 Street," a friend had told me. Nearby communities struggled with poverty, and older local men in tattered clothes had come, hoping to collect a few bucks or a plate of food. Also intermingled with the American military families and young servicemen were women who could have been labeled amejo, dressed in man-catching outfits of booty shorts and heels.

Brian, dressed in his black-belt karate uniform, lifted his son into the air, swinging him around, and then handed him off to Arisa. Forty years old and white, Brian was from Michigan but had lived in Asia, mostly Okinawa and South Korea, for eighteen years. He told me he never wanted to leave. I watched American guys yell hello to him, inviting him out, saying they'd missed him at the bar. He strode down the street, a lion on the savannah. I saw why he never wanted to leave.

Arisa and Brian had first met in this area. Arisa had hung around B.C. Street when she'd been single and worked at a housing rental agency that catered to military servicemembers. "Yes, I was an amejo," she told me later. "But I was not a playgirl." She said she hadn't been set on which nationality she would marry; she had been open to anyone. She'd studied English at Okinawa Christian University and spent time living in Canada, Oklahoma, and Oregon as a student. She had dated a few other Americans before meeting Brian through her job at the housing agency. Initially, she thought he was too old for her—nine years older. He pursued her for a year before she realized she felt comfortable around him, and his age stopped being an issue.

We watched Brian's performance, which mixed karate with Eisa, Okinawa's traditional dance for the dead. The music was that melodic island tinkling over the deep beat of drums. Brian jabbed and kicked as a shaggy purple dragon snapped at the crowd.

Arisa bounced her son on her hip, looking thoughtful. "I wanted to get married so bad when I was young and single," she said. Once she did, though, marriage wasn't what she'd imagined.

"How?" I asked.

She searched for the words. "Forever," she said. "It's forever."

The first marriage between an Okinawan woman and an American serviceman was reported in August 1947, two years after the end of the war. The local community nicknamed the woman "American Hatsu"—a play on her first name, Hatsuko, and the character in it that also meant "first." Like women decades later, she took on the identity of her American partner, becoming the "first American" of Okinawa.

Before the Battle of Okinawa, unions with the enemy "devil beasts" would have been unthinkable. But as civilians were taken captive, they were astonished to find American soldiers weren't making a policy of raping, torturing, and killing them. They were providing food, water, and medical aid. This treatment was in stark contrast to both the pre-invasion horror stories of Americans and the way the Japanese military had dealt with Okinawans. As one girl in a student nursing corps said, even her Okinawan comrades couldn't help her the way U.S. soldiers did. "I hated and feared those Americans," she said, "but they treated me with great care and kindness, while my classmates, my teachers left me behind." In the devastated postwar landscape of stripped forests, demolished homes, and bombed-out farmland, the conquerors doled out little luxuries like chewing gum, candy, and lotion, items that would linger, potent, in imaginations. "Half a century later," one Okinawan woman recalled, "I still keep Jergen's soap and lotion to remind me of that moment of joy during my wartime teenage years living in poverty."

To Okinawans who were starving, sick, wounded, and shell-shocked, the American men who provided the necessities of life appeared like bizarre, startling saviors. "What a strange race with noses two or three times bigger than ours, and blue eyes!" a teenage girl thought the first time she saw Americans up close. The soldiers patted her head, gifted her chewing gum, and called her "cutie" as they drove her to a refugee camp. She wondered, "What made their eyes that color and their hair golden. . . . The soldiers were white and black, and some of them looked Japanese, yet they were communicating easily with the others. What kind of country was America, anyway?" Later, the woman married an American soldier and moved to the United States.

Another woman recalled that she was attracted to her American husband because his odor wasn't like the Okinawans'. He smelled like soap. Other local women reported being won over by American chivalry, the same "ladies first" behavior that would charm Okinawans decades later. "When I was carrying boxes through the hallway, an officer behind me rushed ahead to open the door," said one woman who worked on base in the early 1950s. "Would a Japanese officer open the door for a girl? Never! I couldn't believe there were such kind men in this world." The Americans were also the ones to bring one form of gender equality to Okinawa. Just after the war, when locals were still in refugee camps, they granted women the right to vote. For the first time, and seven months earlier than women in mainland Japan, Okinawan women could run for office and cast ballots. They exercised this right in elections for the new local governments set up under the occupiers.

Two weeks after announcing Hatsuko's marriage, the Japanese-language paper reported she was not alone: "The new story is of passion blooming like deigo flowers between Okinawan girls and American boys in a love that knows no borders, and of courageous young women marrying men from a foreign land." Locals celebrated the first international marriage in one village, in 1950, as a symbol of "Okinawan-American friendship." By the mid-1950s, according to one account, marriages between Okinawans and Americans numbered more than two hundred a year; in the sixties, they climbed to more than five or six hundred a year.

Couples' love may have known no borders, but soon the reality of language and cultural barriers and the difficulties of military and transnational life challenged many unions. In 1958 an organization formed to help cross-cultural couples with common problems. International Social Assistance Okinawa (ISAO) received funding from the local government and private donors like American wives' clubs, and was staffed by local women who solved issues by any means necessary. Masayo Hirata, who served as an ISAO social worker for thirty years, beginning in the late 1960s, told me one service the organization offered was on-base counseling in partnership with the Marine Corps Family Services Center. She and an American counselor advised couples two on two, explaining basic cultural differences. For example, Masayo said, "Americans say, 'What's wrong? Tell me.' And Japanese feel that you should know without me telling you. You should know why I'm mad." She also remembered marital disputes over Okinawan customs like taking expensive photos on a baby's hundredth day, or giving 50,000 yen to a close relative getting married. One couple came to ISAO because the husband had bought spare ribs for a Sunday barbeque with his friends. Before Sunday, his wife boiled them with seaweed. Masayo laughed heartily. "He was so mad."

Other situations were thornier, and social workers had to improvise. Tasked with finding long-lost American fathers, they resorted to laborious tactics like combing American phone books and contacting every man by a certain name. When an Okinawan wife and mother in the States wanted to get divorced, they encouraged her to return to Japan, where the courts were more likely to give her custody. Later, that advice might be considered encouraging international parental child abduction, but at the time, Masayo said, the ISAO social workers were just thinking about what they deemed best for the children: to be with their mothers and extended families in Okinawa.

After forty years of operation, in 1998 ISAO closed as a result of diminishing funds. With it disappeared help for the women who needed it. "The work we did, we were the only ones," Masayo said. Today, even though relationships between American soldiers and local women in Okinawa are increasingly common, and the stakes are high—with negative incidents having the potential to blow up into international news—resources to prevent and solve relationship problems are hard to find. On the servicemen's side, there are attempts like cultural sensitivity trainings and counseling. Women who date Americans are often cast out on their own. Japan isn't a culture of therapists and airing personal problems, and in Okinawa there are persisting stigmas against dating American servicemen. Women who confide in family and friends may find them disapproving or unsympathetic, with an attitude of "What do you expect?" Any resources offered by the military are accessible only to military spouses, not to girlfriends who lack the ability to go on base. Local government offices don't deign to deal with women's relationship issues. Lawyers for international divorce or child-support cases are scarce. When I lived in Okinawa, only two off-base attorneys, both American women, were known for that kind of work. Many women end up frustrated, shut out, alone.

So, within ten years of ISAO shutting its doors, a new organization sprouted up to help women dating or married to American servicemen. This one was even more improvised, a team of volunteers—including Arisa—who seemed an unlikely group to help others. Many of them were dealing with problems of their own.

"Having trouble in a relationship with an American?" the flyer asked, above a cartoon of a couple. The hulking man wore fatigues and faced away, while the slender woman, half his size, faced forward, midriff bared and hip cocked. She looked pensive—or pissed off.

The flyer listed the following possible troubles:

Unplanned pregnancy
Placing a child for adoption
Divorce
Looking for a child's father who has returned to the States
Child support and other legal issues
Feelings of isolation and rejection
Having problems you can't share with Japanese family or friends

A Tokyo transplant named Atsumi had founded the support group in 2007. Arisa joined after her son was born and she quit her job. She thought the volunteer work could be a meaningful use of her free time. The twenty or so group members, all volunteers, were mostly women who were married to or dated American men themselves. Lacking training, they did their best to provide advice, support, information, and referrals to "clients," the women who called seeking help. The members attended regular meetings, usually held in one of the island's many A&Ws, and discussed client issues over root beer and curly fries, often relying on their own experiences to guide the way. More-serious issues, like physical or sexual assault, were referred to an American volunteer who worked as an on-base counselor at the marine corps' Family Advocacy Program, which supports domestic-violence victims and treats offenders.

Eve, who was searching for an African American husband, was also a member. She had joined because she wanted to learn how to help herself one day, once she achieved her dream of marriage.

One night in November 2008, I attended a group meeting held at Atsumi's Okinawa City apartment. Barack Obama had just been elected president of the United States, and many islanders were optimistic that the change he'd promised would extend to Okinawa. Activists hoped his presidency would mean a base reduction. Atsumi hoped he would listen to Okinawan women's grievances about American servicemen. She planned to write him a letter.

In Atsumi's apartment, the lights were low and the scent of cinnamon was strong. A turtle tank glowed red from the floor. Atsumi's husband, a black marine, and her eight-year-old son sat on the sofa watching television, two shaved heads united against the flow of women through the front door. When I arrived, Atsumi appeared, unsmiling. I'd heard a lot about her. Other women who dated Americans respected her for her toughness and determination in standing up to the U.S. military. And there were her appearance and mannerisms. "You've got to meet her," an American friend had told me. "You can't believe this person is Japanese. She's so far from what she must have started as."

Whoever Atsumi once was, by the time I met her she had become someone new. She had darkened her skin and lightened her hair, so that both were hues of gold-brown. She had veiled her eyes with hazel-colored contacts and crowned them with penciled-in eyebrows where hair had once grown. Her earlobes and neck were adorned with gold, and her nails were dressed with acrylics that extended an inch and a half past her fingertips and were painted with flowers and palm trees and glitter. Her speech played tricks on people. "When you talk to her on the phone," my friend said, "you'd bet all your savings that she's black. But she's not!" Atsumi was Japanese. An Okinawan friend of hers, Eri, told me the same thing; Atsumi sounded like a kokujin, a black woman, on the phone. The first time I spoke to her on the phone, I thought she sounded like a parody, some exaggerated idea of black American speech.

She ushered me and the group's members to a small, wood-paneled room off her kitchen. A dining table and chairs filled the space. I squeezed into a chair at one end, while Arisa, Eri, and six other women fit themselves around the table. They looked unified, not only in the matching group polo shirts they wore, but also in their over-all style. Many of them sported glittery acrylic nails, lightened hair, and browned skin, like versions of Atsumi. One woman cradled a two-month-old baby. He was half white and had lots of brown hair curling up in waves.

According to Atsumi, the group had helped sixty to seventy clients since its inception a year and a half earlier. When I asked about the reason most women called, she tapped the words "unplanned preg-nancy" on the flyer. The busiest time for hookups was the summer, she said, when locals, soldiers, and tourists spent the sweltering days and nights at beaches and clubs. That whole situation was a recipe for unplanned pregnancies. A lot of servicemen were young, away from home for the first time, in a locale that could feel more like a spring break destination than a workplace. "Them boys feel like they on vacation for two years," Atsumi said. "And girls, they don't speak much English. But they just love, *love* to go out and mess with a lot of active-duty guys. Next thing they know is they pregnant. But they don't know those guys' names, where they stationed at, what they do." The group tried to help by tracking down men—sleuthing out names, Social Security numbers, wives in the States. It was a version of what ISAO counselors had done decades before, flipping through American phonebooks. Despite the group's efforts, Atsumi said, most unplanned pregnancies ended with abortion. In Japan the procedure is generally uncontroversial, without the same religious debates as in the West, but Atsumi didn't like the option ("It kills the baby"). Still, she understood the women were young and didn't want to be single mothers.

"I really want you to meet my members," she had told me. One was pregnant, and the father, her American military husband, had just been killed in Iraq. "She been through a lot," Atsumi said. "Not too many people can go through this." Another woman, a college graduate who spoke fluent English, had just returned from the States, where her husband had been cheating on her. She had been through a lot, too. I started to understand that in Atsumi's group of women, hardship was worn with pride. The more shit you had endured and survived, the more respect you commanded.

At the meeting, Atsumi ordered the women, "Explain why you joined the group. In English." Then she left.

The women looked around nervously. The one to my right began. "I joined this group because I lived in the States for two years and saw women there mistreated by their husbands." The woman's name was Yoko, and she had soft curves and long, buttery hair. She had lived at 29 Palms, the marine corps base east of Los Angeles, while her husband had been stationed there. Back then, she couldn't help the women around her, because she didn't have any knowledge. Now she did.

An accountant with a sharp, fox-like face chimed in. Two years ago, she had suddenly lost touch with her American boyfriend, a serviceman on the island. She'd called Atsumi, who figured out everything in two hours. The boyfriend was married. He had kids. And he had gotten into an accident and died.

"Make me go nuts to learn about the wife," the accountant said. She had been too naïve to read the signs and realize he hadn't been single. She never wanted to make that mistake again. She didn't want other girls to make that mistake. She patted her belly. She'd grown stronger since then and was determined to make a good life, to work hard, for her "half baby," as she said in English. She meant half American, though didn't mention the father.

Eri, the oldest group member, took her turn. At thirty-four, she commanded a certain space, if not respect, from the other women, who were mostly in their twenties. She spoke in a deep voice with a dramatic gravity and rhythm—short, emphatic sentences and long pauses— as if this was a church sermon she had been waiting to deliver.

"Where should I start?" she began, producing chuckles around the table. "I have three boys with my husband. When I got pregnant with the first, I didn't know anything about him. I just fell in love." She asked if he had a girlfriend in the States. He said no. To be sure, she did her homework, researching his Social Security number, American address, phone number. No other woman surfaced. She felt reassured. Then one day during her pregnancy he announced his time was up in Okinawa; he couldn't extend his tour of duty and had to return to the States. "Okay, I trust you," Eri told him. She planned to join him later. But soon after he left, Eri received a phone call—from his wife.

Eri gave birth to the man's baby in Okinawa without him—without child support, without a job. She didn't have anyone to talk to and was always hungry, worried about buying baby formula and diapers. When her son was two years old, his father returned. This time, he promised to marry Eri—even though, Eri later learned, he was still married to his American wife.

"I can't even count how many times he betrayed me," she said. "How many times he lied. I almost went psycho. I almost killed myself. But my baby boy helped save my life. If I didn't have the baby boy I might not be here."

Eri had been hearing stories lately: "Abortions. Babies without daddies." She swept a hand toward the group member cradling a new-born; she didn't seem to understand English. The father of that baby, Eri announced, was a twenty-three-year-old married serviceman. He had left the island after the baby's birth, without telling the mother. Now, she was trying to track him down to get a paternity test and claim child support, but had hit a dead end. She'd been holding on to hope that he might come back—that he wanted to see his baby, that he really did care—because he had contacted her once on social media.

Eri knew why this sort of thing happened so often between local women and American men. Women didn't understand the cultural dif-ferences, she said. If a Japanese guy was kissing, having sex with a woman, they were dating. If a Japanese guy got a woman pregnant, he asked her to marry him.

"Responsibility," called out one member.

"Even if it's a one-night stand, the guy is going to marry her," Eri said.

After the baby was born, the couple might divorce. But first they did the right thing and got married. In Japanese, there was slang for "shotgun wedding"—"dekikon," something like "oops-we-already-made-a-baby marriage." But, the women pointed out, there was no Japanese slang for "baby daddy."

American men had no sense of responsibility. All the group members agreed about this.

"Americans are cold," Eri said. She wondered if American men felt anything at all for their babies.

Over the years, Eri had learned to be more American, more up front. She tried to say yes if she meant yes, no if she meant no. But communicating with the father of her children—he eventually divorced his wife, she took him back, and they had more kids—was still hard work.

"We always disagree," she said. She had to explain basic things like how in Japan parents don't show affection for each other in front of their children. Or why they needed to spend $300 on a traditional leather backpack for their school-age son. "I have to let him know about Japanese culture," she said.

"Does he want to learn?" I asked.

"He say he don't have a choice."

Arisa said sometimes when she did something nice for her husband, he questioned her sincerity and accused her of being Japanese, too polite. She felt like she couldn't win.

"Sometimes you have to give up," Eri said. "Follow the American way."

"If you wanna date Americans," Yoko said, "you gotta know how they treat you."

In Japan, the concept of chivalry is largely absent. When a woman approaches a doorway, a man is more likely to shoulder past her than hold open the door. Lovers are less vocal about their love; the common phrase to express "I love you" in Japanese is "I like you." So when a local woman dates a man who opens doors, picks up the dinner tab, and declares his adoration—"ladies first" behavior—jumping to conclusions is easy.

"We think we're being treated so nicely," Eri said. "We think: He's got to be so into me to do things like that." But, to American men, those words and gestures might mean nothing. "They're just made that way."

Dating an American serviceman, the women explained, was a detective game, a test of investigative skill—because you sure as hell couldn't trust the guy to tell you anything. Young women couldn't read the signs, so the group's members taught them. The military ranking system indicated a man's pay grade, education level, and dedication to work. The base at which he was stationed hinted at whether he was single or married. A guy on Camp Hansen, the women explained, had a greater chance of being single—and he might be more aggressive in pursuing you, even if you weren't interested. Kadena meant probably married. If he was single, a guy in the air force could be smart and respectful, but sometimes those ones were as bad as marines in the shit they pulled. The women studied the numbers and trends of the U.S. military like analysts, informing themselves to avoid ending up alone with a newborn.

Even marriage, though, had its dangers. With an active-duty husband came the possibility of his getting injured or killed in action. This had been the fate of the husband of one member of the group, Hotaru. Her story was especially wrenching because they had been married only a month, with a baby on the way.

The weekend after the meeting, Arisa hosted a baby shower for Hotaru at her Okinawa City home. Arisa's house was bright and spacious and outfitted with American-sized furniture and appliances, which looked new and expensive. The cavernous refrigerator had been bought on base, and the tall dining table, surrounded by black leather bar chairs, was filled with food. Grinning from frames on tables and walls were square-jawed Brian and their cherubic son. Looking around, the baby-shower guests seemed envious. Arisa had won the American-marrying lottery. Sensing this tension, Arisa rushed to explain it hadn't always been like this. For a few scary months after Brian retired from the military he was without work; they were eating up their savings and had a newborn. Then he found work on base, and the family moved from their small, Japanese-style home to this one.

Hotaru took her place at the head of the table. Twenty-five years old, she was fresh-faced and striking, with undyed black hair and faint glitter around her eyes, which were large and intense. Someone pointed out how skinny she still was, and she said she'd gained only ten pounds since conceiving. She was due in less than two months.

"Sorry more people aren't here," Arisa told her.

Hotaru smiled weakly and told Arisa please don't worry.

Four other members of the group had shown up: Eve, wearing large silver hoop earrings and heavy eye makeup; Yoko and Eri, who had been at the meeting at Atsumi's; and Satomi, who looked like she was in her early twenties and wore dramatic eyebrows and black yoga pants. She stayed glued to her cell phone for most of the party, texting.

Hotaru presided over the plates of sandwiches and bowls of cheese puffs with one hand on her belly. Her expression looked at once knowing and uneasy. It had been only three months since the incident. *Stars and Stripes*, the military newspaper, had reported the whole story.

Hotaru and her husband had first met at a party on Camp Schwab. She was a local girl, and he was a sergeant in the marines—tall, good-looking, white, from Tennessee. When he asked her out, she replied no; because of their cultural differences, she thought it wouldn't work. But he persisted. "We discussed the different environments and cultures we grew up with and the difficulties we may face," the paper quoted Hotaru as saying. "After a good talk, we both were convinced that we would be able to overcome any differences."

On their first date that spring they visited the Nago aquarium. By the holidays, it was serious. Hotaru traveled to Tennessee with him for Christmas. He was from a small rural town that Hotaru "instantly liked." The "countryside environment" reminded her of where she had grown up in Okinawa. "I knew that I would fit in the town," she said. "And more than anything else, his family and relatives all accepted me so warmly." Back in Okinawa, he decided to extend his reenlistment another four years. He had first joined the military right out of high school, at seventeen. His mother told the newspaper he had said "he had not done his job yet. He said he was a team leader and he had to go with his men." By extending, he knew he would be deployed to Iraq.

Hotaru remembered his attitude about the deployment had been "strange." Before he left the island, he talked about last chances— his last chance to see a friend, his last chance to view a scenic spot. "And then . . . he told me he wanted me to have his baby—to leave his DNA." In May, a month after he'd left for Iraq, Hotaru learned she was pregnant. He pronounced the baby a miracle and wanted to marry as soon as possible, by proxy. Hotaru doubted they could while on opposite sides of the globe, but he had planned ahead. Inside a suitcase he'd left with her was a file with all the required documents, already filled out. He rushed her through completing her end, although she was slowed by morning sickness. He had a scheduled mission coming up and wanted it finished before then.

In July, the couple wed. In August, he was killed in a firefight while clearing abandoned houses in the desert north of Baghdad.

Now their baby was on a cake. I stifled a gasp. In blue, black, and gray frosting, an ultrasound rendering decorated the top of the sheet cake. The portrait was monstrous—a bulging, bruised head; alien eyes; uncertain limbs. Only from afar did it start to look like an unborn child.

"4-D," explained Yoko as Hotaru passed around the original photo. Through the marvels of medical technology we could see the contours of the baby's face, imagine what he looked like inside his mother.

"He looks hafu," Eve remarked. The others agreed.

I frowned. Did this watery, from-the-future image look biracial? We could hardly identify it as human.

Arisa retrieved a knife from the kitchen and handed it to Hotaru. "I can't cut the baby," she said. "Only the mother can."

Hotaru sliced us squares of cake. She was planning to move to rural Tennessee to live with her in-laws after the baby's birth. She'd told the *Stars and Stripes*, "I want our son to know how much his father was loved by so many people. I realized that it was best to raise him in the environment where his father grew up, so that he would feel his father's presence and be proud of him." His parents planned to come to Okinawa a month or two after the birth and bring them back. They were a young couple, she told us. And her father-in-law had built her a separate living space attached to their house. She and the baby would have their own entrance and bathroom and living room.

As we ate the cake, she admitted the move terrified her. She was scared to live with near-strangers. She was scared she'd miss Japanese food. She was scared of the language barrier; she didn't speak much English. *Stars and Stripes* hadn't mentioned these fears, which echoed her initial concerns about being in a cross-cultural relationship. The paper had reported that Hotaru's mother had "mixed feelings" about the move, but Hotaru was steadfast. She had been portrayed as strong and selfless and sure. Now, around the food-filled table with other Okinawan women, she seemed shy and uncertain. I wondered if the paper had taken liberties with her story. *Stars and Stripes* was a propaganda vehicle during World War II, though since then had become editorially independent and often covered crimes committed by servicemen and anti-base protests in Okinawa. Certainly, its version of her tale was patriotic and inspiring: her husband's passionate service to his country, including his ultimate sacrifice; her alleviated worries over their cross-cultural relationship, which hinted at the alleviated worries of all Okinawan people over the American bases; the swell of support from the military community. "I have received tremendous support from the Marine Corps," Hotaru was quoted. Later, the paper reported the wives of the men in her husband's battalion also threw her a baby shower, a surprise. "They offered so many gifts that they [hardly fit] in my car," she said. "I was overwhelmed by their warm thoughts."

While the paper might have depicted her as more confident and certain than she was, her loyalty to her husband and his identity as a marine seemed genuine and unwavering. She told us the baby was going to take his father's name, and she was thinking of getting a memorial tattoo to honor him—a smaller version of the "recon jack" that had spanned the inside of his bicep. The design was a melding of military images into a patchwork skull and crossbones. Half a skull joined with half a parachute over a cross made out of a scuba diver, a knife, a paddle, and a wing.

She didn't know how long she could legally stay in Tennessee. To get a U.S. green card, a non-citizen had to be married to an American for two years. Hotaru would probably travel to Tennessee on a six-month tourist visa, leave the country, and then return for another six. That might be the extent of her time there. I wondered how much this limitation enabled her to go. A year in a foreign place was manageable, imaginable. Forever wasn't so easy.

"I don't want to die in the States," Arisa exclaimed. With Hotaru's upcoming move, the challenges of living in the United States were on the minds of the other women, too.

Yoko agreed. In Florida, her husband had pointed to a military cemetery and said they'd be there one day. "But I'm not going there," Yoko told us. She'd already asked her dad if she could be buried in his family tomb. In Okinawa, patriarchal rules dictate who gains entry to the family tomb, said to resemble a turtle shell but meant to evoke a woman's womb. In death, you return to the place from which you came. Custom says women are buried in their husbands' family tombs. If they don't marry, or marry a foreigner, they're left out alone.

"In the American military," Yoko said, "husbands and wives are buried on top of each other, in the same grave. Not side by side."

"So romantic," Hotaru said. "Like they're sleeping." I wondered if she imagined being buried on top of him, if she thought there wouldn't be another man for her. She was moving in with his parents on the other side of the planet. She was only twenty-five.

I tried to imagine the "good talk" that Hotaru and her husband had had after she had voiced her concerns. Had his words really convinced her, or had it been his smile, his dimples, his Tennessee twang? If he had lived, would they have overcome their differences? She would never know. With him, she'd be forever in that starry-eyed, honeymoon phase. He'd only become more perfect with time.

Years later, I reconnected with Arisa. It was 2017, and we met for breakfast a couple of times, once in a Hawaii-themed pancake house, once at a trendy new café in the American Village. Her son was now ten, and she had a daughter who was almost six. She and Brian were still married. At times, she said, the cross-cultural differences had almost driven them apart. The key to their success had been Brian. Throughout everything, he had remained committed. "I think the reason we aren't divorced is my husband never gave up," Arisa said. "I almost gave up."

Through her work with the support group, she knew that other women who dated or married Americans didn't have such happy stories. "To be honest, when I was in that group, I was kind of sad," she said. "All I heard were sad stories." There were domestic violence cases, and lots of women with unwanted pregnancies. Many couldn't find the fathers and ended up getting abortions. "I didn't hear any happy endings," she said. "A happy ending was she got over it and had the baby and then worked as a single mom." Arisa had felt helpless and didn't stay in the group for long. She wasn't the only one. Without funding or trained counselors, the group had broken apart, although the founder, Atsumi, still did the work on her own.

Arisa considered herself lucky, not only because of Brian's commitment. Unlike her friends who'd moved to the States with their active-duty husbands, she and her family had been able to stay on the island, thanks to Brian's civilian job as a security manager on base. Financially, they had enough so that she didn't work, their kids attended international schools, and they took family vacations to places like Hawaii and Florida. Having an American husband had also come with perks that had made her life easier. "My husband is really supportive doing the housework," she said. In comparison, she cited her friend's Japanese husband, who worked from 8 a.m. until 10 or 11 at night, rarely seeing his kids and dumping all the housework on his wife, who worked, too. In addition, Arisa didn't have to deal with obligations around Okinawan in-laws, like preparing food and visiting ancestral tombs on holidays to honor the dead.

While Arisa enjoyed escaping some aspects of her culture, she was proud she had retained others, like the Japanese way of thinking about others. She thought her personality hadn't changed, though marrying an American had affected her world view. Making a life with someone of another culture had opened her mind to different perspectives, a practice she was teaching her kids. This way of thinking extended to the base issue. When she was younger, during those days of walks around Kadena Air Base, having an anti-base attitude was normal. She said she still understood Okinawan anti-base protesters, and agreed it was unfair that a small island hosted such a large number of American bases. The island was crowded, and she was aware of her privilege in being able to cut across Kadena Air Base to avoid traffic. "Some bases have to go to the mainland," she said. But Arisa felt like she could never get involved in the anti-base movement. "After marriage I can see the other side of view as a wife of an American," she said. "Now I cannot choose which side I should go on." For one, without the bases, her husband wouldn't have a job. They'd have to leave the island. "I cannot support people who are against the base because of my situation," she said. "I cannot say 'No more base!' that loud. . . . Before marriage, I could do that if I wanted. But now, no." Her parents had been affected, too. "Because I married an American, my family changed," she said. Now her parents had more positive experiences with the base, which balanced out the negative stories in the media. Her mother, who used to protest the bases, now thought differently because of Arisa.

"When I hear taiko drumming, I can feel my spirit is of Okinawa," Arisa said. But over the years she had become more and more entwined with the American bases, a duality that lived inside her. On a recent trip north, she had driven by Camp Schwab, where Okinawans were demonstrating against the building of a new base. Approaching the protestors, she grew nervous—"because I'm Japanese, Okinawan, but driving a Y-plate car." She knew why they were protesting, she could understand why they were protesting, but there she was with her U.S. military plates and Okinawan face. She imagined they would see this and turn on her, yell at her, brand her a traitor. When she passed the gate and the line of elderly Okinawans waving signs, however, nothing happened. The drama was all in her mind.

6

SUZUYO

AT FIRST, THE INCIDENT THAT CHANGED EVERYTHING WAS JUST A
mention in the local news. Details were vague. Three suspects
"appearing to be foreigners" committed "an act of violence" against
an elementary school student. In a place like Okinawa, people read
between the lines. Suzuyo Takazato learned of the story nearly a week
later at the Naha airport, just returned from an international women's
conference in Beijing. Her friend was there to meet her, surprising
Suzuyo. She handed her a newspaper clipping. All the positive energy
of the conference, where Suzuyo had exchanged concerns and ideas
with other women from around the globe, evaporated.

This is what Suzuyo and the world would come to learn: On the
evening of September 4, 1995, a twelve-year-old Okinawan girl was
walking home from school in her neighborhood in Kin, a town on
the island's northwest coast that hosts the marine corps base Camp
Hansen. The girl wore her school uniform and carried a book bag. She
stopped at a stationery store to buy a notebook, and when she came
out, a white car pulled up. Three American men inside spoke to her,
appearing to be lost. She moved closer.

In Okinawa, it was a normal Monday, but for U.S. military personnel it was Labor Day, a holiday. Earlier that day, two marines, a navy seaman, and a fourth serviceman had rented a car to cruise through Naha on their day off, hoping to pick up women at the bars and clubs along International Street. They wanted to "get a girl," but had no success. They discussed their options. They could buy what they wanted, but the seaman, twenty-two-year-old Marcus Gill, complained he didn't have money to pay a sex worker. He suggested another idea. "Let's go rape a girl," he said. "It was just for fun," he later explained. The fourth serviceman bowed out once he realized they were serious—there were duct tape and condoms.

Gill and the two marine privates, Rodrico Harp, twenty-one, and Kendrick Ledet, twenty, drove in their white rental car through the town of Kin. Harp and Ledet were both from small towns in Georgia; Gill was from a small town in Texas. All three were black and, in the eyes of their communities back home, "well-mannered young men." As the *Los Angeles Times* later reported, Ledet "was a Boy Scout and church usher; Texan Gill took advanced-placement English and won a football scholarship." Like so many, the men had joined the military looking for escape, for better lives. "He always wanted to go into the Marine Corps," Harp's sister said. "That was his way out of this small town, his way to make something of himself."

According to Gill, Harp was the one to pick out the girl, spotting her as she went into the stationery store. When she came out, the men feigned to ask directions. Then they grabbed her, hit her, threw her into the backseat of the car, taped her mouth, and bound her arms and legs. When Gill complained that she kept looking at him, Ledet covered her eyes with duct tape.

They drove her to a deserted spot amid sugarcane fields. Gill climbed into the backseat. He was a six-foot, 275-pound "tank." According to Harp's attorney, Gill "violently" beat the girl, saying, "Let me do what I want to do." He punched her face and stomach and raped her. The other two men later denied taking their turns after Gill, saying they faked it after noticing how young she was (it "didn't feel right"). Gill disagreed, testifying that Harp and Ledet had been enthusiastic participants. "Let's do this!" Ledet exclaimed at the outset, according to Gill. In court, describing the rape and how they had joked about their victim, Gill made the court interpreter weep.

After the assault, they dumped the girl, bleeding and unconscious, from the car. Into a trash can they threw her new school notebook and their own underwear, covered in her blood. The girl managed to crawl to a nearby house for help. Unlike after so many other sexual assaults, she and her family decided to report the crime to the police, reportedly because the girl wanted to ensure the men wouldn't harm anyone else. She wanted to "lock the bad soldiers in the jail forever, so that they can never get out." With a wealth of physical evidence, police had little trouble tracking them down. "It almost makes it more arrogant, more insulting that they made no attempt to cover their tracks," one local said in the aftermath, "almost as if they had a right to this girl." She spent two weeks in a hospital recovering.

News of the incident hit Suzuyo Takazato especially hard following the women's conference. She wondered, "Why were we so empowered and excited there, but at the same time here, a twelve-year-old girl was in so much fear and pain and isolation?" She sprang into action, calling the other local women who had attended the conference and telling them to meet at the vice governor's office the next morning. The vice governor was a woman who had gone to the conference, too. Together, the women wrote a statement and scheduled a press conference. They took the news brief and turned it into an international firestorm.

I met Suzuyo more than twenty years later, in her cramped office-apartment in a Naha high-rise, stacked floor to ceiling with papers and books. She was seventy-two years old, with short, caramel-dyed hair and smiling eyes. She was quick to laugh and easily talked for hours in a calm, methodical, friendly way, until she realized she was late to lead a protest rally or give another interview. Suzuyo had become one of the best-known activists working to close U.S. military bases in Okinawa. She was the co-chair of Okinawa Women Act Against Military Violence, an advocacy group that fights for women's and human rights and demilitarization. One of their main projects was documenting

all cases of U.S. military violence against local women since the end
of World War II. The group combed through memoirs, newspaper
archives, local histories, government documents, police reports, and
personal testimonies, compiling accounts. The 2016 edition the group
published, its twelfth, details at least a few hundred crimes, many
involving multiple victims and/or multiple GI assailants. Reading
them gives the sense of everyday horror, of a place where gang rapes
were as common as collecting sweet potatoes. In the "Settlement" col-
umn, most cases are categorized "No charge filed."

> *April 6, 1946: Around noon, [a] 19-year-old woman returning from
> work in her potato field in Urasoe Village is threatened by 4 GIs carry-
> ing guns, who carry her into the tall bushes nearby and gang-rape her.*

> *April 7, 1946: A 26-year-old woman returning home after the potato-
> digging work is carried off in a GMC military truck to an air-raid shel-
> ter, where she is gang-raped by 6 GIs.*

> *April 7, 1946: A 28-year-old woman in Shuri City is talking with her
> husband after dinner when 3 GIs break into the house, hold down the
> husband, and gang-rape the woman.*

Suzuyo and other female activists had founded Okinawa Women
Act Against Military Violence, along with the first rape crisis center
on the island, after the 1995 rape. The group and center came about
in large part thanks to Suzuyo. In fact, you could credit Suzuyo with
setting off Okinawa's third major anti-base movement, which uses as
its fuel U.S. military violence against women.

One of the first known sexual assaults by an American in Okinawa was
in 1853, when Commodore Matthew Perry stopped by the Ryukyu
Kingdom with four warships. He was on his way to Japan to try to
force open the isolationist country. In the Ryukyus, Perry strong-
armed his way into establishing a short-lived American military base
on the main island, the first of many that would follow one hundred
years later. During this visit, one of his men, the sailor William Board,

broke into a private home, drunk, and raped a woman. Ryukyuan men heard her cries and rushed in to seize Board; he escaped and ran toward the waterfront. A rock-hurling crowd pursued. At the water's edge, Board was hit or tripped and fell into the sea and drowned. When Perry found out, according to the expedition's official account, he "soon became convinced that the man's death, though unlawfully produced, was probably the result of his own most gross outrage on a female, and, in such case, [was] not undeserved."

This story of vigilante mob justice defies the popular image of Okinawans as a peaceful, happy-go-lucky people largely unbothered by the U.S. military presence. For instance, a 1946 pamphlet written by the U.S. military government in Okinawa states, "The average Okinawan is a docile, rustic citizen who passively accepts the changes that have come to his way of life since [the] American occupation." A "picture of contentment and simplicity" is how a navy souvenir booklet characterized "the native Okinawan" just after the war. General Douglas MacArthur, in 1948, called Okinawans "simple and good-natured people" who could "pick up a good deal of money and have a reasonably happy existence from an American base development." A couple of decades later, describing the sometimes chaotic occupation scene, M.D. Morris wrote, "Fortunately, life is more peaceful than would be reasonably expected, due mainly to the placid nature of the Ryukyuans and the deep regard by all for the serious reasons behind the continuing American presence there." More recently, U.S. military and U.S. government workers have expressed beliefs that the anti-base movement is motivated by Okinawan greed—a calculated effort to extract more federal subsidies ("it pays to complain")—or laziness—collecting secret payments from China instead of working real jobs.

These stereotypes ignore the history of resistance among Okinawans. Since the arrival of the U.S. military bases, citizens have organized and spontaneously gathered, time and again, to fight against unjust treatment by the American and Japanese governments. In many cases, these movements have had the power to affect the U.S.–Japan security alliance—though not to the end activists want.

The first major anti-base movement took place in the 1950s in the context of all-powerful U.S. military rule. The United States Civil Administration of the Ryukyu Islands (USCAR) was a U.S. government regional office that took over control from the U.S. military in 1950. But USCAR wasn't so different than its military predecessor. The administration was headed first by Douglas MacArthur and then by a series of other generals known in Okinawa as high commissioners. These men reported to Washington, commanded all U.S. forces in the islands, and reigned over civilians with total authority, gaining monikers like "The King."

To American military leaders, colonial-type control of Okinawa seemed natural. The U.S. military had paid for the territory in blood during the war. But overt colonialism was out of vogue and contradicted the postwar image of the United States as a liberator and harbinger of democracy. This led officials to dance around stating what Okinawa really was. The American consul general to Okinawa in the mid-1950s wrote, "It may be denied by some who are skilled political scientists that the United States position in Okinawa is a 'colonial' one; but in the eyes of most of the world our status here is close enough to colonialism so that the label with all its opprobrium will stick and be used. It is, then, an anomaly that the power in the world most against the basic philosophy of colonialism should find itself ruling a foreign area and its inhabitants." In 1957, the *Saturday Evening Post* reported the "island is actually controlled by the military as a prize of war, although official circles avoid the term."

Unlike in mainland Japan, where the U.S. occupation had operated under a "demilitarization and democratization" agenda of political, economic, and social reform—"so that the will to war will not continue," as the U.S. assistant secretary of state remarked—U.S. policy in Okinawa prioritized the U.S. bases. Considerations for rebuilding Okinawan society and ensuring people's rights were secondary. Under USCAR, Okinawans were neither Japanese nor American citizens. They lacked constitutional rights and participated in a sham democracy (a "prenatal form" with the "color" of self-government, "if not its reality," said the *Saturday Evening Post*). They needed USCAR-issued passports to travel to the Japanese mainland. Anyone suspected of participating in communist activities could be denied travel, and any material USCAR deemed anti-American or communist could be censored or subject to official reproach. Potentially subversive items like cameras could be confiscated.

The bases were at the center of the local economy. By the mid-1950s, as many as one in three employed Okinawans worked in base-related jobs. On-base service positions like cooks, gardeners, and maids paid little—far less than the salaries of co-workers of other nationalities. In its hierarchical pay structure, the U.S. military paid Japanese workers three times as much as Okinawans, Filipinos ten times as much, and Americans eighteen times. Many Okinawans couldn't afford basic conveniences like electricity and running water. When Bolivia offered four hundred Okinawans the chance to immigrate in 1953, four thousand people applied.

Meanwhile, on the Japanese mainland, the country regained its sovereignty in 1952. With the enactment of the U.S.–Japan Mutual Security Treaty, which permitted the hosting of U.S. bases in Japan, mainland anti–U.S. military base demonstrations that had begun during the occupation intensified. Farmers, students, politicians, labor unions, and left-wing groups banded together from across Japan to fight against the same grievances as in Okinawa: the loss of land, the dangers of living around military bases, and the remilitarization of the country, seen as unconstitutional. They held mass rallies and sit-ins and tangled with local police outside U.S. bases, their skulls cracking under police batons. They took their movement to court. In the 1957 "Sunagawa incident," a Tokyo district court ruled in favor of seven protesters who had been arrested for trespassing on a U.S. base. The court decreed the activists weren't breaking the law. Under the nation's peace constitution, it was the U.S.–Japan Mutual Security Treaty that was criminal. "It cannot be said that the stationing of the United States armed forces in our country is permitted under the Constitution," stated the presiding judge. Although the Supreme Court overturned the ruling, the case helped galvanize the mainland's anti-base movement and paved the way for the massive demonstrations against the re-signing of the security treaty in 1960.

Mainland demonstrations proved so successful they helped push the U.S. military to look elsewhere for its base-hosting. American officials realized continued anti-base sentiment could jeopardize their position in Japan. As then Secretary of Defense Charles Wilson said, they needed to "scotch the idea so prevalent in Japan that that country was still occupied. If we could not succeed in destroying this idea, we stood to lose our entire position in the Japanese islands." This came at a time when, as historian Dustin Wright explained to me, aviation advancements were making the exact locations of military bases unimportant. "They were building planes that could fly farther," Wright said. "So having air bases on the mainland was not necessarily so important anymore. Couple that with anti-base activism on the mainland, and this sort of anti-American sentiment that was festering on the mainland, and they began to slowly think about moving to Okinawa." Okinawa was far away, geographically and psychically, from mainland Japan—and the U.S. military still controlled it. The occupation government in Okinawa didn't have to go through time-consuming legal processes to confiscate land; they could just take it. They could also quash local protest against the bases by enacting anti-protest laws or ordinances and prohibiting Okinawans from taking legal action. And Okinawans didn't have the benefit of a large, connected citizenry. Cut off from Japan by an ocean and USCAR travel restrictions, Okinawans could only rally the small number of people within its borders.

So, in its 1950s Cold War build-up of bases, the U.S. military turned to Okinawa, ramping up its seizures of private property. In many places, Okinawans resisted, but the military responded with force. One Okinawa Prefecture account describes a 1953 incident in which 1,200 residents tried to block U.S. military bulldozers from razing their land. More than a dozen American armored vehicles with

machine guns rolled up, and 350 GIs "in full battle gear" surrounded the Okinawan resisters. "The somewhat surreal atmosphere at
first gave the impression that it was all being done just for show," the
account describes, "but as the circle tightened and the bayonet points
began to touch flesh, many began to fear the day would end in a bloody
massacre." Finally, the American servicemen began beating the Okinawans, hitting them "with their rifle butts, kicking them with their
combat boots, and throwing them into drainage ditches."

In these violent land seizures, Okinawans lost more than their
homes and livelihoods. In traditional Okinawan culture, land repre-
sents a connection to one's ancestors who inhabited and farmed the
same soil. "It is not a commodity, something that can be considered
an object for buying and selling," Governor Masahide Ota explained
in 1996. "If I may paraphrase further, land is an irreplaceable heritage
graciously bequeathed to us by our ancestors or a spiritual string that
ties us to them." In another severing of ancestral ties, the U.S. military
seized burial grounds. The curved-top stone tombs would come to be
scattered throughout the military installations, requiring descendants
to submit official requests to go and pay their respects.

By 1955 the number of displaced Okinawans reached a quarter million. The next year, pockets of local resistance organized into an "All-
Island Struggle." In June, some hundred thousand people gathered
in a Naha schoolyard in protest. Demonstrators spilled onto nearby
rooftops and into neighboring venues. A local newspaper described
the crowd as in "a state of feverish excitement," shouting "yes!" amid
"a storm of hand-clapping." Protesters listened to the speakers with
such rapt attention they didn't even fan themselves "in the stifling air
of packed people." The main complaint of the crowd was the lump-
sum payments the U.S. military wanted to offer in exchange for seized
land. Landowners demanded instead annual payments calculated
using fair market rates.

Sexual violence by U.S. troops also mobilized protesters at times.
In 1955, a six-year-old Okinawan girl named Yumiko was raped and
murdered by a U.S. airman. The "Yumiko-chan" incident helped

foster anti-base attitudes that led to the All-Island Struggle. Other incidents, not all reported, occurred that year, too:

September 6, 1955: A U.S. soldier enters a house where a 32-year-old woman is sleeping, and he rapes her.

September 9, 1955: A 9-year-old girl from Gushikawa City is abducted from her bed by a U.S. marine and is seriously injured.

September 14, 1955: 3 U.S. soldiers enter a house, attempt to rape a 24-year-old woman, but her husband seizes them, and he [is] cut by [a] knife. When they are running, they cut in the stomach area of a 27-year-old woman.

By many accounts, the occupation years were a time of widespread sexual assault. The exact number of rapes following the Battle of Okinawa is unknown, as most cases went unreported or ignored. But the chronology put together by Suzuyo and others, as well as personal testimonies, passed-down stories, and U.S. military policies, suggests the severity of the problem. In May 1945, the U.S. commanding general in Okinawa, in an attempt to reduce assaults, instituted the death penalty for those found guilty of rape. It didn't seem to be effective. Witnesses recounted the "girl hunts" American soldiers conducted in civilian refugee camps, where Okinawans were confined after the war. Men went tent to tent looking for women to rape, sometimes in broad daylight. In villages, locals adopted a system of ringing a bell, often a discarded U.S. military oxygen cylinder, to warn everyone when U.S. soldiers approached. "The Americans are coming! Hide!" people screamed. One Okinawan woman recalled, "There were so many cases of rape in those early postwar years that whenever we spotted an American on our streets, we thought for sure he was a rapist." She said the bell clanging usually scared away Americans, but not always.

U.S. military policies attempted to protect women, especially their own. In hospitals, off-duty medical corpsmen served as special police who patrolled the sickbeds with rifles, looking for GIs who sought to sneak in and assault nurses and patients. The few American women on the island—dependents and nurses—were forced to live almost like prisoners. M.D. Morris, who was on the island at the time, describes the situation for nurses: "Because they were female . . . they had to live inside a stockade, surrounded by a high barbed-wire fence, with a sentry at the only entrance-exit. They could come and go freely from this convent-like sanctuary to go to work in the wards, or recreation within the confines of the hospital grounds. But to leave the station to go to a PX, or movie, or sightseeing they had to go in groups of three in a vehicle, and in daylight hours only. At night there had to be an armed male escort, and curfew was midnight with no exceptions." Another postwar U.S. military order required American women to carry firearms. Director of Public Safety Paul Skuse wrote the sidearm rule wasn't to "protect our women from the poor docile natives—but to protect [them] from our own troops." If stopped by military police and found without a weapon, a woman would receive a ticket. Going out to look for flowers, an officer's wife holstered her .32 Colt automatic in her jeans. Dining at the on-base club, women first checked their hats and their pistols.

With American women removed as targets for sexual assault, "the natural attention of the vast majority of enlisted men was turned upon the Ryukyuan girls," Morris writes. Morris uses the word "natural" often in describing GIs' thirst for women. "Naturally sports and movies were not enough," he writes. "Regardless of regulations or consequences, the men had to find women." Moreover, they harbored the "idea that all female Okinawans were fair game for the conquering heroes." Morris describes one incident in which twenty soldiers in a moving truck grabbed a local "girl," gang-raped her, and threw her back off the truck without stopping. Victims of sexual violence included Okinawan men, such as one sixty-two-year-old who was sexually and physically assaulted in a shack for hours by an American soldier in 1949.

In response to the rash of rapes, the U.S. military found a scapegoat: the segregated units of African American troops. Reportedly, Okinawans complained to the occupation government that black soldiers were committing a high number of crimes. Military leaders responded by recommending all black troops leave the island. In 1946 the director of general affairs for military government, Lt. Commander James Watkins, wrote to the commander that "extreme ill will" had grown between Okinawans and African American soldiers on the island, and the "fear of cruelty, rape, and violence replaced respect for American authority." Black GIs were "by no means the only offenders," he wrote, but thought they were enough to blame that he urged their withdrawal "to avoid further compromising the American position in the eyes of the Okinawans." Over the next year, most African American troops were sent away from the island—to be replaced by a new group to accuse. Units of Filipino men known as the Philippine Scouts arrived in Okinawa, and soon islanders were blaming them for violent crimes. Director of Public Safety Paul Skuse agreed, later saying that bringing the Scouts to Okinawa was the army's biggest mistake during that time, for, he claimed, the Filipinos committed more crimes than their African American predecessors had.

It is unknown whether these units really did commit a higher proportion of sexual assaults than white units. Many have tried to explain why that was the case: because black soldiers were concentrated into fewer units, the influence of bad apples couldn't be dispersed and diluted as with whites; the Filipinos were enacting revenge for the wartime atrocities committed against their people by Japanese troops; men of color brutalized Okinawans because they had found someone lower on the oppression totem pole ("Black troops, some at least, saw in the Okinawans, the 'gooks,' a people they could feel superior to and treat as they were used to being treated," writes a veteran who served in the military government at the time). But perhaps the issue wasn't with these troops—it was with the Okinawans and U.S. military officials who were more likely to blame them. In her study of American forces in France during World War II, historian Mary Louise Roberts shows that in France, too, locals accused black soldiers more than whites for the crime of rape. She writes, "It is impossible to determine whether a disproportionate number of black men did, in fact, commit rape." What she argues is that "in many cases . . . charges against black soldiers were based on hearsay and 'sightings' produced in an atmosphere of racial hatred and fear." Racism also caused the U.S. military to be more likely to take rape accusations against black GIs as truth, without sufficient investigation, and convict them—including executing African American soldiers at a rate staggeringly higher than for white soldiers. This "cooperation between French civilians and U.S. military authorities in the prosecution of sexual crimes . . . created a proliferation of charges against black soldiers," Roberts writes. The two groups became "deadly allies in racism." In Okinawa, where there were Japan's historical racism against dark-skinned people and the same U.S. military that harbored prejudices in France, it is easy to imagine similar "cooperation" between civilians and authorities in blaming African American and Filipino troops.

For whatever reason, a disproportionate number of high-profile rapes in Okinawa have involved black men as the accused. There is the 1995 rape, as well as others in 2001 and 2008. There is Kenneth Franklin Gadson, who confessed to assaulting Rina Shimabukuro. Each incident compounds the specter of the predatory black GI. "When a suspect is black and from the military, people here assume he must be guilty," said Annette Eddie-Callagain, an African American lawyer who represented the serviceman charged with rape in 2001. "Meanwhile, whenever something happens, the rest of us think, Oh, please, don't let him be black." One legendary story is from the postwar period, when a village of Okinawans—far from being the "poor docile natives" military officials imagined—banded together to retaliate against a string of rapes, then kept their retaliation secret for more than fifty years. As locals tell it, at the end of the Battle of Okinawa, three black marines terrorized the mountain village of Katsuyama, in the island's jungled north. Every Saturday, the men, sometimes armed, sometimes not, abducted local women and raped them. The villagers formed a plan. One weekend, they hid and ambushed three men they took to be the rapists. A couple of Japanese soldiers assisted, firing from the bushes, and the villagers beat the three Americans to death. They threw the bodies into a cave. Around town, people took to calling the spot the derogatory name for black people: "Kurombo" Cave. The murders became local lore, hidden from authorities until

1998, when bones were excavated and identified as those of three nineteen-year-old black marines who went missing in 1945. With the statute of limitations passed, the prefectural police didn't investigate their deaths. "You know, that is why so many Okinawans are afraid of black men," said one local woman, remembering the story.

Despite the pervasive sexual violence and racial issues of the postwar time, the focus of the earlier anti-base movement remained on land issues. And, after a couple of years, the U.S. military succeeded in fracturing the island-wide movement, though not before granting some concessions. The U.S. military agreed to increase its payments to landowners and enacted collective bargaining rights for local laborers. Mass resistance simmered down—until it swelled up again during the Vietnam War.

Suzuyo Takazato emerged as an activist later in her life, but the seeds were planted early on. She was born in 1940 in Taiwan, then a Japanese colony. Her Okinawan parents lived there a total of fifteen years, her father working as a civil servant. The family survived the war there, then, along with all Okinawans in Japan and its former colonies, was ordered to return to Okinawa. The family settled on Miyako Island, one of the smaller islands of the Ryukyu archipelago, where Suzuyo's grandparents lived. They would stay five years, until Suzuyo was ten, before moving to Naha on the main island. Those were the difficult postwar years, but Suzuyo recalls a happy childhood on Miyako. Her mother was a teacher who heaped love upon her family. "She raised four children, and each of us [now] has a strong confidence I was loved most," Suzuyo told me, laughing. Her mother was also a talented singer, a passion Suzuyo inherited. As a girl, Suzuyo would visit the sweet potato field behind her house at night. Alone in the field, she belted out songs her mother had taught her.

During those pleasant years on Miyako Island, there was one trial Suzuyo endured. She was left-handed, which her mother labored to change. "Although she loved me so much, she trained me to switch to write with my right hand," Suzuyo said. This small difference, being left-handed, engendered in young Suzuyo a fiery awareness of injustice, of how society's arbitrary rules and conventions unfairly disadvantaged some. "I was so angry," she said. "I was always rebellious."

Years later, Suzuyo was employed as a social worker in Naha. It was the 1980s, and she started hearing a chilling, recurring story from clients. Sex workers told her U.S. servicemen had almost strangled them to death. Suzuyo realized this had been a collective experience during the Vietnam War. The violence in Southeast Asia came back with the soldiers who stopped over on Okinawa for R&R, frequenting the bars and brothels around the bases while shattered with PTSD. Later, Suzuyo learned that GIs had killed one to four women a year in Okinawa during the Vietnam War—often sex workers they strangled and then dumped, naked. Those murders were the tangible evidence of countless other sexual assaults and near-killings. "Women kept silent, but dead bodies showed the real violence," she said.

February 22, 1969: A 21-year-old hostess is murdered in Koza City and her nude body disposed of by a private second-class in an artillery regiment.

February 22, 1969: A 19-year-old woman is strangled to death in Koza City by a U.S. private second-class who works at Machinato supply base.

February 22, 1969: A 20-year-old woman is strangled to death in Koza City by a soldier who belongs to the 15th Artillery Unit.

But the murders of sex workers weren't the Okinawan public's main source of anger during the Vietnam War. In those years, the whole island became militarized, as the U.S. transformed Okinawa into a storage area and launching point for fighting across the sea. "Okinawa is to be one huge depot for the materials of warfare," the *Los Angeles Times* reported as American troops began to be deployed to Vietnam. "The blunt fact is that on Okinawa the military does take precedence over everything else, including the lives of the Okinawans who farm their vegetable patches right up to the limits of the bases, and who swarm into firing ranges in quest of expended brass, to the dismay of range safety officers." M.D. Morris makes this point repeatedly in his account. "In effect, all Okinawa is one tremendous American base," he writes. "Literally, there is no place in the islands where the ubiquitous soldier, sailor, marine, or airman—or his base—is not conspicuous."

Living amid a giant weapons depot subjected Okinawans to accidents—like when a trailer tumbled from a military aircraft onto an Okinawan girl, killing her, in 1965—and contamination. Unlike U.S. bases in mainland Japan, those in Okinawa were unregulated; the U.S. military could use them as they wished, including as storage for chemical and nuclear weapons. In 1969, a deadly nerve gas leaked from a military storage facility in Okinawa City, sending a couple dozen U.S. servicemen to the hospital. That same year, the presence of U.S. servicemen on the island reached its highest postwar number, eighty thousand troops.

Increasingly fed up with their second-class status, with the bases, with the weapons and accidents, with the traumatized soldiers who acted above the law, and with the island's part in killing other Asians, Okinawans demanded an end to the American occupation and a return to Japan. This became the second major movement against the U.S. military bases, organized around the "reversion" of Okinawa. Reversion, Okinawans thought, would bring removal of the U.S. bases as well as Japanese constitutional rights and standards of living. Teachers and students played a central role in the movement, and in the 1960s over 90 percent of Okinawans agreed returning to Japan was the best course. Many on the Japanese mainland agreed, wanting all of their country back from the Americans.

In 1969, Okinawans learned that the United States and Japan had reached a deal and that reversion would occur in a few years' time— but it wasn't the victory people wanted. Okinawa would revert to Japan, but the U.S. military bases would stay. Outrage over this and all the other ongoing grievances erupted one Saturday night in December 1970 on the streets of Koza, ground zero for partying and mayhem during the Vietnam War. The trouble started when a carful of American GIs hit an Okinawan pedestrian. The Okinawan man wasn't severely injured, but the U.S. military police's arrival to escort the servicemen back to the safety of the base helped set off the growing crowd. A couple of weeks earlier, the U.S. military had acquitted a serviceman of killing a local woman—who had been on the sidewalk—in a hit-and-run while he had been intoxicated. No one was getting off so easy that December night. Not long after the night's first accident, another American-driven car rear-ended a local one, and bystanders encircled the U.S. military car, breaking its windows. Soon the neighborhood's bartenders and bar hostesses, drunks and rock bands, schoolteachers and government workers were hurling bottles and rocks at the U.S. military police, who shot into the air, only inflaming the scene further. The mob started pulling Americans from their cars and beating them. The cars were overturned and lit on fire, with female bar workers supplying the fuel in the form of gasoline-filled cola bottles. Some Okinawans cheered, some sat and watched the flames in silence, some broke into traditional dance. "It felt just like a festival," one Okinawan man remembered. "This was the first time we'd stood up to the Americans. The first time we all came out and made our feelings known." He likened the moment to the tearing down of the Berlin Wall: "Anger and elation mixed with a sense of doing something right for once."

As the crowd reached as many as five thousand Okinawans, hundreds of local and military police tried to quell them. U.S. military helicopters rained down tear gas. Water cannons fired. A faction of the mob turned toward Kadena Air Base's Gate 2, rolling the burning cars toward the security guards. They broke through the gates. School windows shattered, and Molotov cocktails set more cars ablaze. The riot—some say uprising—lasted through the night, leaving dozens of Americans injured and some eighty American vehicles burned.

Even extreme acts of resistance like this didn't change the deal between the United States and Japan. On May 15, 1972—what some protesters dubbed "the day of humiliation"—the islands once again became Okinawa Prefecture. And for the sake of "deterrence," Japan agreed to the U.S. military's staying in Okinawa. In fact, Tokyo paid a high price for it. As scholars Gavan McCormack and Satoko Oka Norimatsu point out, it wasn't so much a "reversion" as a "buyback." Japan paid about $685 million to the United States to resume administration of Okinawa and began footing much of the cost of the U.S. bases.

In the 1972 "buyback," only some of Okinawans' demands were

met. Japanese citizenship meant the return of political and legal rights—but also a return of pressure to assimilate. In some places, for instance, school kids who spoke Okinawan again had to wear a sign of shame. Crimes committed by U.S. servicemen decreased—but, of course, didn't disappear—as they were held more legally accountable and as the dollar–yen exchange ratio decreased their spending power and ability to frequent off-base entertainment areas. The islands' economy got a boost—though local income levels continued to lag behind those on the mainland—and the Japanese government began injecting billions of dollars into Okinawan public works projects. These roads, community centers, and schools were an attempt to subdue local protest over the bases. But after 1972, on top of the existing U.S. military presence, Japan's Self-Defense Forces further militarized the island by setting up a new presence there. For many Okinawans, the fight was just beginning.

In 1989, Suzuyo Takazato ran for Naha City assembly and won. She began to distinguish herself as a leader and advocate for women's rights, gaining supporters. As a politician, she drew on her experiences as a social worker to highlight military violence against women and the lasting psychological damage it inflicts. "As a social worker and counselor, I spent 10 years listening to the heartbreaking stories of Okinawan women whose lives were destroyed and disrupted by the violence of militarism," she wrote in 1994. "The real wounds of war are not the destroyed buildings, rather the destroyed human hearts of Okinawans and Americans." She often told the story of one woman she counseled, who had been gang-raped by three U.S. servicemen at age twenty-one. The attack plummeted the woman into a downward spiral: into work as a bar hostess and dancer outside the base gates, then into sex work, then into psychiatric hospitals. One day, she told Suzuyo, "I stopped being a human at the age of 21, but I really am a human. Don't forget this." The woman felt "dirty," but Suzuyo knew the issue was society, not the woman. "She and I were the same age," Suzuyo said, "and the only difference between us was whether we had been lucky or not."

By 1995, Suzuyo was in her second term as a Naha City assembly member and was leading a contingent of seventy-one women from Okinawa to the Fourth U.N. World Conference on Women, held in Beijing. At the conference, Suzuyo presented on structural military violence against women. That was around the time she started researching Okinawa's past and discovering an untold history of pain. "Looking back, I realize that the reversion movement and reversion itself totally overlooked the problems of women," she wrote in 1994. "Okinawan women who survived the battlefield assault faced a new battle in postwar years: the sexual assault that continued throughout U.S. military occupation and the U.S. civilian administration." She wanted to bring these problems to light. And when she and the others returned from Beijing on September 10, 1995, she found an opportunity to do so.

September 4, 1995: An elementary-school girl is abducted and raped by 3 U.S. military personnel.

According to Suzuyo, the prefectural government didn't want the rape publicized at first. Officials were content with the four to five lines in the newspaper, that sketchy account that didn't even make clear when the incident had happened. But whether or not Governor Masahide Ota wanted a big news story initially, once Suzuyo and other women publicized it, he began using the rape to boost his anti-base platform. He held his own press conferences and issued demands to the Japanese and American governments: to release the suspects from U.S. military custody to local police, to apologize, to close all bases in the prefecture. With his position as governor as well as his being a historian, war survivor, and former Fulbright scholar to the United States, Ota became the face of the protest in the Japanese media.

The female activists received more air time internationally than domestically. Suzuyo organized one of three women's rallies that September, which she says drew significant media attention, especially from foreign reporters. Correspondents from major American, British, and Australian news outlets traveled to Okinawa to cover the protest. Suzuyo was often the one representing the women's groups, appearing on CNN and other media outlets. At a rally in Tokyo at the end of September, she highlighted again how sexual assault was left out of the base discussion. "When demanding the withdrawal of the U.S. military, when asking for the revision of the SOFA, when protesting against the U.S.–Japan Security Treaty, do we all remember that violence against women and girls has [happened] and continues to happen today?" she asked. "Why is this threat not listed—alongside helicopter crashes, airplane engine noise, and bullets accidentally whizzing over fences—as damages to Okinawans' lives?"

Talking to foreign journalists, Suzuyo fielded the same questions over and over. How many other sexual assaults by the U.S. military have taken place in Okinawa over the years? Where is the data? But the U.S. military government hadn't kept official numbers during the occupation. After reversion, the prefectural police started tracking crimes, but their statistics included only reported incidents. "It's a very small number compared to the reality," Suzuyo explained. So she started leading an effort to come up with a more accurate number. She and other activists began checking past newspapers and assembling a chronology of assault. The first version was six pages long. They translated it to English and brought it on their multicity "Peace Caravan" to the United States, where they connected with academic, student, and activist allies; presented on Okinawan history and the ongoing issues of U.S. military sexual violence; and issued their demands to the American people and government. These demands included investigating all past crimes committed by U.S. military personnel in Okinawa, establishing a plan to close all bases in the prefecture, and improving the military's newcomer orientation and sensitivity trainings. When the women returned to Okinawa, they kept researching sexual assaults, combing through more archives, looking for witnesses. The list grew longer.

Despite Suzuyo's efforts, public discourse quickly moved from the story of the rape to the story of Okinawa. This occurred in part because of the Japanese media's tradition of not covering rape in order to protect the victim's privacy. "Rape is only reported when it leads to murder," explained one Japanese reporter, Hideki Yuii. In the case of the 1995 rape, Yuii convinced his superiors at NHK, Japan's public broadcaster, to let him write about the apprehension of the suspects because he connected it to a larger debate about the U.S.-Japan Mutual Security Treaty and police jurisdiction. The rape of the schoolgirl became useful as an entry point into other issues and as a symbol to represent the rape of all Okinawa, especially its land. In the weeks following the crime, Governor Ota refused to sign by proxy the leases of local landlords who had been forced to rent to the U.S. military and were now refusing to renew out of protest. Scholar Michael Molasky writes that this particular crime was especially effective as a symbol "because the victim was young, innocent, and female—and because the crime was rape. No single act, not even murder, surpasses rape in its ability to dramatize the fear and humiliation of life under foreign occupation. And no victim better symbolizes the vulnerability of the social body than does a young girl. . . . The fact that she remains unknown by name while her fate is known to everyone only heightens her allegorical value."

The 1995 rape/allegory proved powerful. The incident has been cited as a turning point, the marker of a new era in Okinawa's history. "Nothing was the same after that," one ex-serviceman on the island told me. "That was the rape that changed everything," another said. Publicized by Suzuyo and others, it tapped into an undercurrent of anti-base anger that had been flickering for two decades. In 1995, the atmosphere was especially charged after summer events commemorating the fiftieth anniversary of the Battle of Okinawa and calling for world peace. As Suzuyo had experienced returning from the conference, the contrast between those ideals and the reality of continued violence made the incident feel more egregious. Joining the women's groups and governor in protest were organizations that included teachers' associations, labor unions, and political parties. Everyday Okinawans got involved, too. The rally that activists organized in October brought out 85,000 protesters—91,000 including protests on the outer Okinawan islands of Miyako and Ishigaki. Even conservative politicians and business leaders who had been silent on the base issue participated. The target of protest was not only the U.S. military base presence, but also the Japanese government for its role in keeping the bases in Okinawa.

This mass protest pushed Japanese and American lawmakers to reexamine the U.S.–Japan Status of Forces Agreement. They also agreed to close Marine Corps Air Station Futenma—although any promise of change was soon snuffed out. In September 1996, Governor Ota succumbed to pressure and signed the land-lease renewals. A few days later, the Japanese prime minister revealed that Futenma would close only on the condition of building a new base in the island's north. Political deadlock ensued, as activists rallied against the new base. Futenma remained where it was, and people went back to their lives, until the next horrific crime that would pull them into the streets.

Suzuyo didn't step away from anti-base activism, even when public anger died down and the group of women who had gone to the Beijing conference dissipated. She didn't shift her focus from sexual violence against women and children, even when the media and other leaders did. She went to work co-founding Okinawa's first rape crisis center and the advocacy group Okinawa Women Act Against Military Violence. At the first Okinawa Women Act Against Military Violence meeting, over one hundred women joined. They were stay-at-home mothers and retirees, university students and elected officials, teachers and local government workers. They elected Suzuyo and a prefectural assembly member, Keiko Itokazu, to serve as co-chairpersons. In the following months, the group organized sit-ins, delegations to Tokyo, and a trip to the United States, all to raise awareness of and protest military sexual violence. They joined other groups in demonstrating against the new base in Okinawa's northern district of Henoko and started holding international meetings with activists from other countries hosting U.S. military bases. In June 2017, the International Women's Network Against Militarism held their ninth meeting, twenty years after their first. Representatives from the Philippines, Guam, Hawaii, Puerto Rico, South Korea, and the mainland United States flew to Okinawa, where the women swapped updates and toured the island, learning about the legacy of the war and the ongoing struggle in Henoko.

One of the network's goals was to raise Americans' awareness of sexual assault around U.S. military bases abroad, in the same way that sexual assault within the U.S. military had gained national attention. According to the U.S. Department of Defense, there were 6,172 reported cases of sexual assault within the U.S. military in 2016, up slightly from the previous year and almost double the number reported in 2012. Meanwhile, the total number of sexual assaults according to an anonymous survey was 14,900, a decrease from the last survey in 2014. Some said these numbers showed progress. More men and women in the military felt safe to report, and the total number of assaults was dropping. Others said serious problems remained, including the fact that nearly six in ten victims who reported said they experienced retaliation. According to Gywn Kirk, a scholar and founding member of the organization Women for Genuine Security, Suzuyo connected numbers like these to what happened off base in Okinawa. "Suzuyo-san said, you know, if they rape or commit acts of violence against their own colleagues, no wonder they do it against women in communities outside the bases," Kirk said. Political science professor Manabu Sato told me something similar. The U.S. military has difficulty preventing sexual assault on base, he said. "How can you prevent every crime outside the base? That's not possible." If American soldiers "come out into Okinawan society and nothing happens, that's a miracle."

Suzuyo's interest in connecting with women outside Okinawa had its roots in her two years studying abroad in the Philippines as a young woman. Once, a classmate invited her to Olongapo City, which hosted the massive U.S. naval base at Subic Bay. "I was shocked because I thought: I'm back in Okinawa," Suzuyo remembered. The area around the base looked just like Koza. Suzuyo began to realize Okinawa's issues extended far beyond the island.

In the Philippines, Suzuyo also learned about the atrocities the Japanese military had committed in other Asian countries during the Pacific War. Visiting her classmates' homes, she heard families talk about killed and missing loved ones and the brutality of Japanese soldiers.

She learned about the women Japanese soldiers had kidnapped and used as sex slaves. "I don't condemn only U.S. soldiers, but also Japanese soldiers—the military system itself," she told me. She said she also holds society accountable, including traditional Okinawan society, which was patriarchal and condoned the selling of young girls into prostitution when families needed money. As long as a society ranked people based on the circumstances of their birth, Suzuyo thought, a society supported violence.

March 13, 2016: A Japanese tourist in her 40s gets drunk and she is sleeping in the hotel hallway when a 24-year-old Marine corporal 1st class rapes her.

May 19, 2016: A 20-year-old woman, who has been missing since April 28th, is raped and murdered by a 32-year-old former Marine, who is working [on] Kadena Air Base. Her body is found on May 19th.

In March 2017, I met three Okinawa Christian University students to talk about sexual assault and Rina Shimabukuro's death. We sat outside at a Starbucks on Route 58 as Friday commuters inched along. On the other side of the roadway used to sit the U.S. Naval Hospital on Camp Lester; then, some of the land was returned. Now there was a McDonald's.

The women sipped their frothy coffee drinks. Erika was twenty-one, about to graduate and start working in hospitality at a new international resort hotel in the American Village. Reiko, also twenty-one, had grown up outside Futenma Air Base and studied in New York City. Mei was twenty-three and from Naha, and had an infectious, hearty laugh. The three friends had been born around 1995, into this new era of Okinawan history. But that hadn't made them wary of U.S. soldiers. All three spoke English and had American boyfriends, two of them in the military.

Recently, Kenneth Franklin Gadson had revealed that part of the reason he had assaulted Rina Shimabukuro was because he knew women in Japan rarely report rape to police. A 2014 Japanese government survey found that fewer than a third of rape victims nationwide had spoken to anyone about the incident, including family and friends. Only 4 percent had reported it to the police. This falls far below the number of police-reported rapes in the United States—about a third of the total, according to one survey. In the 1995 rape case, too, the men had admitted that knowing these odds contributed to their decision to commit rape. I asked the university students about this. Why didn't women in Japan report rape?

"If we tell the police, we need evidence," Mei said. One of her friends had been raped by a close Japanese friend and didn't go to the police, because she thought she had no evidence. "If I was raped," Mei said, "I wouldn't tell, because rape is body abuse, so it's kind of difficult to find the evidence." Other reasons she wouldn't report were to protect her parents ("I don't want to see their sad faces") and to avoid intrusive questions she might be asked in court, like "Did you spread your legs?"

Erika had reported sexual assault, once. She had been in junior high, walking home, when an Okinawan man on a bicycle rode up behind her and touched her breasts. Then he sped away. "I was really scared," she said. "It was right in front of my house. I told my family, and they called the police." Warning notices were put up at school, but they never found the man. "I don't even know who touched me." She said it would have been different if she had known the man. If a friend sexually assaulted her, she wouldn't tell the authorities. "He did bad things, but I would feel sorry for him," she said.

"I guess people don't want to break their relationship," Mei explained. "They want to keep that relationship, like before." If a total stranger raped her, she wouldn't care about him, so maybe she would report the rape. If a friend raped her, she would keep it secret to maintain social ties.

Erika agreed. "My boyfriend's friend was a marine," she said, "and he raped a co-worker on base. She was American. She told the police, and he's in jail now. He's actually my friend. . . . So I'm sorry for him. Even though he did bad things."

"You don't think he should go to jail for that?" I asked.

"Hmm," Erika hummed. "Well, it's difficult." She laughed nervously.

"It's really difficult," Reiko agreed. She had been quiet and now spoke in a passionate voice. "But I wouldn't care if I know him or not."

"You would go to the police?" Mei asked.

"Yeah, because I'm the only one who can tell the police. Maybe the same thing will happen to another girl, and she'll get hurt more than me." Reiko back-pedaled a bit. "I'm not going to say arrest him or something. . . . But you should keep your eyes on him."

I asked if they thought American servicemen committed sexual assault more often than Japanese or Okinawan guys did. Reiko said no. She started speaking slowly.

"Sometimes it's not only the guy's fault," she said. The other two murmured sounds of agreement. "Girls should be careful . . . when they go to the bar, or when they walk in the middle of the night. We know normal people don't usually walk around at 2 a.m. or something." She said a man who committed rape definitely did a bad thing. "It shouldn't happen, but . . . I think it's not only the guy's fault." Erika and Mei agreed. They talked about girls who wore tight skirts and got drunk at the club, looking for a bad boy. Those kind of girls set themselves up for rape, they said.

None of them thought what happened to Rina Shimabukuro was her fault, though.

"She was running at 8 p.m.," Mei said. "Around her house. She was familiar with that area."

Later, I talked to Suzuyo about victim-blaming. She said Japanese and Okinawan society, including the local newspapers, often say a victim of sexual assault was careless, or tempted her attacker, or didn't defend herself. That is why many women are reluctant to report. They've seen how society treats victims, so they try to protect themselves by remaining silent.

Suzuyo cited a 2008 rape case involving a fourteen-year-old girl. This one hadn't been wearing her school uniform or walking home from a stationery store. She had been hanging out with her friends on Gate 2 Street. When a thirty-eight-year-old marine approached them on a motorcycle, she accepted his offer of a ride home. Later, she testified that instead of taking her home, he raped her—but the case didn't stir up mass protest like the one in 1995. While trying to organize a demonstration, Suzuyo received phone calls from people asking why the girl was wearing what she was wearing. Why was she in that neighborhood? Where was her mother? For a sexual assault to resonate as widely as it did in 1995, the public needed a "purer" victim.

This victim-blaming was evident time and again, like in the aftermath of an alleged rape in 2001. A local woman said a U.S. airman raped her on the hood of a station wagon in a parking lot in the American Village, after she had left a night club there. He said she wanted it. Predictably, some dismissed the woman as an asking-for-it amejo. The (female) Japanese minister of foreign affairs remarked there must have been "something wrong with the girl, going out so late at night."

Even the #MeToo movement, which is bringing global attention to the issue, hasn't had an effect on Japan the way it has on other countries like South Korea. The few Japanese women who have spoken out about sexual assault have been met with media silence and criticism. "The worst comments seemed to come from older women who for decades have lived in a male-dominated world," said Shiori Ito, who went public with her account of being raped by a prominent journalist. "They felt I wasn't behaving the way a Japanese lady should. I was told it was wrong to have the top button of my shirt undone during the press conference. If I had cried they would have been more sympathetic." Even when Ito received death threats, she remained determined to tell her story and seek justice in order to try to move social attitudes forward. "It was tough, but I couldn't let it defeat me as then I would have become an example of why people shouldn't speak out about these crimes," she said.

The issues extend to the ways sexual abuse is legislated, investigated, and tried in Japan. Sexual harassment isn't criminalized and is widespread in workplaces, and rape laws are problematic, despite some recent advancements. "Japanese law regarding rape is very backward," Suzuyo told me. For more than one hundred years, antiquated sex-crime laws upheld a narrow view of rape as vaginal penetration by a penis. In 2017, the national legislature finally made some revisions to the laws, such as including forced oral and anal sex as rape and raising minimum sentences. But activists cite remaining issues like the prerequisite for "violence and intimidation" in convicting sexual assault, which leaves no room for psychological or emotional coercion. The age of consent is still a mere thirteen, and there is no law against spousal rape.

When police do investigate cases, they are notorious for discouraging victims from pursuing legal action, interrogating them at length, and making them reenact their abuse, risking secondary trauma. They may ask inappropriate questions about the attack and the victim's sexual experience, like "Do you think the accused thought you were attractive?" and "Have you ever had anal sex?" They may warn that, if the case goes to trial, defense attorneys will ask even more humiliating questions. Knowing about these practices helps deter victims from reporting.

The issue of under-reporting is why Suzuyo doesn't focus on the number of assaults in her chronology. "The number is not important," she said. "We cannot just count and say three hundred, four hundred, because this is inadequate still." She thought the low reporting of rape in Japan and Okinawa—the "deeply rooted sexual discrimination" in society—enabled the bases to stay. "If we had a society in which anyone could complain about suffering sexual violence, could the U.S. military have remained stationed here this long?" she asked. How could the bases survive an avalanche of headlines crying out *rape*?

In 1996, three Naha District Court judges convicted Marcus Gill, Rodrico Harp, and Kendrick Ledet of rape and abduction. They sentenced Gill and Harp to seven years of hard labor in a Japanese prison, and Ledet to six and a half. Ledet received a shorter sentence because the judges believed he hadn't followed through in raping the girl. Ledet's sister told the press the three men had been made "scapegoats" in the larger anti-base movement. "I think it is inhumane to sacrifice life in exchange for land," she said. The president of the Okinawa chapter of the NAACP said the men's race or nationality had caused them to receive longer sentences than what was typical for Okinawans. "I'm not sure whether it's because they are American or African American," he said.

The men served their time in jail on the Japanese mainland, forced to make cell phones and car parts, and then moved back to the States. Three years later, in August 2006, Ledet's body was found in the apartment of a twenty-two-year-old college student outside Atlanta, Georgia. The two had been former co-workers at a pizza parlor, and she was dead, too—sexually assaulted, strangled, and bashed in the head. Ledet's wrists had been slashed. Police said it looked like a murder-suicide.

In Suzuyo's view, there is an inalienable connection between military training and sexual violence. "That's because if you don't have the perception of discriminating against others, and making them comply with your will by force, then you can't make it as a soldier," she said. She explained her views further after the 1995 rape, at a rally in Tokyo. "Education does not help because the military itself is a form of structural violence," she said. "A soldier may be a good son to his mother or a good husband to his wife. However, once he is integrated into the military, he learns the imperative of killing the enemy before the enemy kills him. . . . The soldier is trained to inflict violence. In fact, this is the whole purpose of military training. Teaching humanity in the military is a gross contradiction. The military is a place for teaching brutality."

At the 2017 meeting of the International Women's Network Against Militarism, Gywn Kirk expressed a similar view, with a caveat. "It should be said, it must be said, that of course not all U.S. soldiers are involved in acts of sexual violence," she said. "But there is a pattern that keeps repeating, and so it's important for us to look at the relationship between military beliefs and ideals, being trained to kill an enemy, and attitudes toward women, especially women of color—in your case, Asian women."

Some within the U.S. military community in Okinawa agree, with many calling out the marines. "The problem is mostly with the marines, and it has to do with the way they are trained," said one former airman.

He described the "intensive jungle warfare training" that marines do in northern Okinawa—"set loose in the woods by themselves for three months at a time," deprived of sleep and food. Once, on a drive through the north, this veteran and his family came across a group of marines: "They were filthy. They looked like a bunch of wild men. Well, you take a bunch of guys that have lived like that for three months, and you get them back to camp, and you give them the weekend off and send them out into town, to the bars in Chatan and Naha, and expect them to act normal. It's not going to happen."

Another factor people cite is the short-term nature of many service-members' stays on Okinawa. The Unit Deployment Program (UDP) sends marines stationed in the United States to train in the Pacific for six to ten months. As the newcomer's orientation explained it, they "sea bag" at Schwab or Hansen, "get acclimatized to the weather, and they're gone." They may spend a month on Okinawa, and then they're off to train at marine corps installations in other countries. Some argue because these marines are focused on combat training—developing their physicality and aptitude for violence—and they're on the island for a short time, they are more likely to assault local women. A bar manager in Kin told me the troublemakers around there, in the enter-tainment area outside Camp Hansen, were always the "UDP assholes." One instance where this recipe led to violence was in 2012, when two sailors deployed to Okinawa for a couple of days violently raped an Okinawan woman outside her apartment building, hours before their scheduled departure from the island. This timing "raises the suspicion that they timed the attack to minimize their chance of getting caught," the *Asahi Shimbun* commented.

In 2012, Rodrico Harp, one of the men convicted in the 1995 rape, said part of the reason Marcus Gill had proposed raping a girl that eve-ning was because he was leaving Okinawa soon. "He said this was his last tour overseas and he was going back to the United States," Harp said. He thought Gill had raped women in Okinawa before, though. "It was like he did it all the time or something. That's what he was saying."

As the highest-profile female activist in Okinawa, Suzuyo has fielded criticism. Male anti-base activists have accused her of focusing too narrowly on women's issues, which they deem non-political. "You!" a man shouted at her once during a meeting of Okinawan activists. "You always only raise the violence against women issue. That's not political. That's not what the U.S.–Japanese Security Treaty is about!" Suzuyo shot back, "You know only one-half of what security means if you don't think military violence against women is part of this issue!"

Scholars, too, have taken aim at Suzuyo. Chris Ames argues that her "oft-quoted remark" that "the bases themselves are pollution" sets up a good/evil binary in which the bases and everything and everyone associated with them—including Okinawans who work on base or who have relationships with members of the U.S. military community—are polluted as well. Ames also brings up her beliefs about how the military breeds violence in its soldiers, both at work and at home. This view, Ames says, "sting[s] Okinawans with a U.S. military husband, father, or friend." Annmaria Shimabuku goes a step further, saying this view prevents Okinawan women romantically involved with American servicemen, as well as the offspring of such unions, from participating in anti-base protest. "Okinawan activism has come to the point where individuals who experience the most impact by the U.S. military are precisely the ones who find difficulty in participating in 'the movement,'" she writes. Linda Angst has criticized Suzuyo for "disturbingly" using patriarchal language in her rhetoric, such as calling Okinawa "the prostituted daughter of Japan." In response, Angst wrote, "Referring to the 1995 rape victim as a sacrificed or prostituted daughter both enshrines and subordinates her within an existing nationalist patriarchal discourse that consistently tropes women as helpless victims." Without naming Suzuyo, Angst also calls out "protest leaders" for idealizing Okinawa's traditional society as one of peace and equality and for ignoring the issues of "the real prostituted daughters of Okinawa"—the base-town sex workers.

When I spoke with Suzuyo, I didn't see evidence for most of these criticisms. She and others in her group made a convincing case for the link between the military and sexual violence, and that women's security should be included when talking about overall security. If the bases were there to protect civilians in the region, how could officials account for the large number of women harmed by their presence? Suzuyo also made a point to say she didn't let Okinawan or Japanese society off the hook—there was no idealized past. In addition, she hadn't forgotten "the real prostituted daughters." She had a history of outreach to sex workers and included them in the discussion during the 2017 network meeting.

But I did think something wasn't working in the overall rhetoric about the bases, something maybe Suzuyo was contributing to. The 1995 rape warranted ninety-thousand-plus protesters taking to the streets. But an American serviceman's bludgeoning to death of a Japanese woman with a hammer, four months earlier, had also deserved public outrage. While military training undoubtedly promoted violence, many American servicemembers lived in peace with their families. The extreme, selective nature of the discussion did polarize and silence; it left out the ambiguity, the gray spaces and the people who lived in them. Even women most at risk of military violence—women who worked in the bars and brothels around the bases—weren't always the victims Suzuyo made them out to be. Some of these women had chosen this work and managed to walk away with something they wanted.

7

DAISY

DAISY WANTED A BETTER LIFE FOR HERSELF AND HER MOM—FOR HER mom, especially. When Daisy was young, her family lived in a rural area of the Philippines, a "simple life" where candles lit the night and banana leaves served as umbrellas. Daisy remembers enjoying herself, unaware of any other way to live. But she also watched her mom work herself ragged, raising seven kids on her own. To put food in their mouths, Daisy's mother managed orchards of banana, coconut, and cacao trees, hauling produce to market twice a week. She'd come home late at night, drunk. She'd wake at four in the morning for another day of work, sometimes still drunk. If Daisy didn't hear her stir, she would check that her mother was breathing. She prayed to God for her mom's life.

There had been too many tragedies. When Daisy was a toddler her father died from colon and liver cancer. A couple of months later, her baby brother died in a fire. Daisy doesn't know how it happened. Her mother was at work, leaving the kids home alone. Daisy remembers fire licking across their roof, but the house didn't burn down. The flames took only her brother. After that, her mother never left them alone again.

Daisy was the second-youngest child but took on the responsibility of caring for her mother and younger sister when the family left the southern island of Mindanao to escape guerilla fighting. Her oldest sister had her own problems: ten kids and a husband who beat her. Her older brothers had left for work on Luzon. So at age sixteen Daisy dropped out of high school and started working to support her mother and sister. First, she served as a live-in maid for a wealthier family, making two hundred pesos, or about five dollars, a month. Whenever she could, she snuck in time to read English-language magazines, studying on her own what she couldn't in school. After that, she worked a stint as a nanny, cut short because the boss was "not good." The next job that she found, one at a bakery, paid double the one as a maid. The owner, a pharmacy student, was kind and loaded Daisy with bread, cheese, and candy when she went home to visit her family. Then, Daisy moved on to a printing factory in Manila, where she silkscreened T-shirts. That paid the best of all, thirty-five pesos a day with room and board. Daisy had brought herself a long way—but still it wasn't enough.

As a kid, Daisy had visited her cousin, whose father was an American soldier. Daisy's aunt had met him during World War II. Looking around their house, Daisy thought, "Oh my God—they're millionaires. One day I want to have this." She started clipping pictures of houses from magazines and promised her mom that one day she would build her a house like that.

To fulfill her promise, she needed to earn more money. So when Daisy was twenty-one, she decided to go to Japan. She knew what she was risking. She had heard stories about other girls who had gone on entertainer visas, stories about girls murdered around the U.S. Navy base in Yokosuka. She knew what everyone thought when you said you were going to work in Japan: you were going to sell your body. Daisy had never even been on a date, avoiding men because she feared they would derail her dreams. Her mom begged her not to go, to stay at her job in Manila. But Daisy was determined. She could earn far more in Japan than in the Philippines. She told her mom she was unafraid, even of death: "If it's your time, it's your time." With her oldest niece, she applied for and got a six-month entertainer visa to work in Japan. Officially, the visa was for cultural dancing, but Daisy didn't know what awaited her across the sea.

The promotion agency decided where each girl would go within the country. Daisy's niece, who was tall and beautiful, got sent to mainland Japan. "They said mainland Japan is first-class," Daisy told me, laughing. "I'm probably not that pretty." Daisy was assigned to Okinawa.

Before leaving, she asked God for an angel to guide her. "Please don't let me sell my body," she prayed.

As long as U.S. bases have existed in Okinawa, so too have sex workers to serve the troops. For both the Imperial Japanese Army and the U.S. military, sex work has been seen as a natural and necessary complement to soldiers in order to keep them in fighting shape. What has varied over the decades has been the women's backgrounds, their working conditions, and their degree of agency. During the Pacific War, the Japanese military notoriously set up a "comfort women" system in which they enslaved thousands of women from Japan and its colonies and occupied territories to supply sex to Japanese soldiers. These Korean, Taiwanese, Filipina, and other Asian and Pacific Islander women endured systematic rape and abuse wherever the Japanese military went, and Okinawa was no exception. Before the battle, the Japanese military forcibly brought thousands of Korean women to the southern islands and established some 130 "comfort stations" across the prefecture. The kidnapped Korean women and a small number of Okinawan women were made to serve dozens of men a day. Most of the women died during the battle. Some who survived continued working, now servicing American soldiers.

Following Japan's surrender, Japanese authorities rushed to establish new "comfort facilities"—these for the American occupiers. They reasoned the men would need sex, and without such a system they would take what they wanted from the public. In Tokyo, the Japanese government and police forces worked with brothel owners, doling out direction and government funds. "A hundred million yen is cheap for protecting chastity," a Ministry of Finance official said. Impoverished women were recruited to work for the good of the nation, a sacrifice to protect more affluent women from harm. "To New Japanese Women," a sign in Tokyo's Ginza district announced. "As part of urgent national facilities to deal with the postwar, we are seeking the active cooperation of new Japanese women to participate in the great task of comforting the occupation force." Soon there were "recreation and amusement" centers across mainland Japan, segregated by the race and rank of customers, where a dollar bought a GI sex. Servicemen poured into the centers, until after only a few months the U.S. occupying government shut them down, trying to stanch the explosion of venereal disease. Officials continued to permit prostitution, however, now confining it to certain city districts. In the postwar devastation, tens of thousands of Japanese women supported themselves and their families with this work.

Under the separate U.S. administration of Okinawa, the story was similar but different. Both the U.S. military and Okinawan leaders condoned prostitution, and thousands of Okinawan women were pushed into sex work to survive. With the loss of male providers in the battle and the loss of farmland in the building of bases, they didn't have other options. A key difference was that in Okinawa the drawn-out occupation meant state-sanctioned prostitution lasted longer.

In his firsthand account of occupied Okinawa, veteran M.D. Morris writes that "for the common good" U.S. military officials organized a prostitution district after the war, and before they made it legal: "some wiser, saner heads worked out an off-the-record arrangement whereby all interested girls were assembled in a single area in which drinking, money, medical examinations, and an orderly movement of actually thousands all were controlled closely." Military buses took troops to this area after-hours, until "some chaplains and others" banned the buses from stopping there. Instead, the buses "slowed down to a low-gear crawl," and men jumped on and off the moving vehicles. When the "crusaders" finally got their way and shut down the prostitution district, the sex workers scattered. The U.S. military became unable to enforce medical examinations, and "the island-wide venereal disease rate skyrocketed." Fees for sex also increased, and troops resorted to stealing cars to reach brothels. Or, bored again, they became generally drunk, disorderly, and dangerous. "Once again innocent Okinawan girls, instead of their more willing sisters, fell victims to the inevitable violent prurience," Morris writes. Just as for Japanese authorities, for Morris and others in the U.S. military community on Okinawa, there was a dichotomy between "innocent" local women and "their more willing sisters." In their minds, depending on the regulations surrounding sex work, one group of women or the other was going to field the American soldiers' "inevitable" and "violent" lust.

With the unofficial prostitution district shut down, Okinawan women started renting rooms in residential areas to see customers. In one town, now a part of Okinawa City, local leaders rallied to kick out these women so American soldiers wouldn't be prowling their streets looking for sex. The locals brought their grievances to Major General Alvan Kincaid of Kadena Air Base, but he brushed them off, saying, "They're just healthy, red-blooded young GIs, so there's nothing we can do. Soldiers' sexual affairs are none of our business." Later—after the conflict between local residents and U.S. soldiers escalated, with GIs threatening to torch the mayor's house if he intervened—Kincaid decided it was his business. He presented the local leaders with a solution: build a "special district" on the edge of town.

In this way, Okinawan officials began collaborating with the U.S. military in building prostitution districts around the bases. The public debated whether these "dancehall[s] and facilities for recreational sex" would be a boon to local society—bringing in money, limiting the spread of venereal disease, and protecting "innocent" women and girls—or whether they were immoral and harmful to the women who worked there. Female activists protested the districts, citing the latter, but didn't succeed in stopping them.

In these new entertainment areas, the U.S. military instituted an "A-sign" system in an attempt to control sexually transmitted diseases. Beginning in 1953, GIs could only frequent establishments officially "approved" by the U.S. military and displaying a big red *A*. Bars, restaurants, and clubs got this stamp of approval when they passed sanitary inspections and subjected their employees to medical testing. Still, STDs remained a problem. In 1957, one marine corps division reported that a quarter of its troops had been incapacitated by venereal disease. The next year, the number was more than a third. In 1964, the *Washington Post* reported the VD rate among all marines on-island was "so high" it had "been 'classified' by the command."

M.D. Morris describes one of these areas as "a neon-lit nirvana for Neanderthals" patrolled by military police and "teem[ing] with enlisted service personnel of all branches, colors, and sizes." Pawnshops offered quick cash to GIs looking to pay a bar worker's "out fee." The two could "then retire to one of the 'hotels' in the area, after which he [would] sweat out the next two weeks hoping he [hadn't] gotten VD." In the *Saturday Evening Post*, establishments selling sex were "joy palaces"—"more than 1000" with names like the "Venus, the Butterfly, the Cinderella and the Chatterbox . . . each advertising with gaudy neon the presence of 'many-beautiful-hostesses!'" The 1957 article reported Okinawan women were "delighted" by their new profession because they had a tradition of selling their bodies to soldiers: "Okinawans were used to Japanese troops before the war and accepted marriages of convenience. They are now delighted by what Americans are willing to pay for company and entertainment."

Needless to say, not all the women were delighted. Suzuyo Takazato explained the debt-bondage system that kept women indentured to brothels during the occupation. In a typical example, the daughter of a poor family agreed to (or was coerced into) sex work, and in return the brothel gave her family a sizeable loan. This allowed the family to eat, but the woman became indebted to the brothel, carrying a high-interest loan that was nearly impossible to pay off, no matter how many U.S. soldiers she serviced a night. Suzuyo said the fee for sex in those days was five dollars a person. A whole night, one veteran told me, cost twenty. These earnings could be cancelled out by the penalty fees the brothel imposed: Twenty dollars for missing work on a U.S. military payday. Ten dollars for missing work because of illness or menstruation. Other high fees were for room and board and personal products. The fees added up, along with the loan's high interest rates, so when a woman got paid at the end of each month, her debt had only increased. According to Suzuyo, the average loan a sex worker carried was $2,000. "Too much," she said, "because in those days, a teacher's salary was $100 a month." The highest loan reported was $17,000.

Some Okinawan women were able to operate outside the debt system. "Honey" was a postwar term for a woman who secured a longer-term relationship with an American soldier, who might put her up in an apartment and buy her nice things. Okinawans adopted the English word after noticing the GIs' nickname for women. Among locals, honeys were disdained for their perceived immorality, while also envied for their material advantages. One Okinawan woman remembered honeys who enjoyed "gifts of chocolate, soaps, and face creams" and donned new clothes, while everyone else wore "coarse and drab" things, "torn at the seams and worn in the seats."

In this postwar landscape—with so many women in sex work, and prostitution sanctioned by the U.S. military, and a great economic disparity between U.S. soldiers and locals—the purchase of sex became commonplace for GIs. Marine corps veteran Douglas Lummis said that when he arrived on Okinawa in 1960 the base commander told his men, "On Okinawa the number of prostitutes is approximately the same as the number of U.S. military [soldiers]. There's just about one for each of you." Lummis recalled that hiring a prostitute became "just something that one could do. And virtually everybody—with some exceptions—virtually everybody availed themselves of that service. And that's part of what made Okinawa exotic in the Marine Corps imagination."

The number of sex workers in Okinawa peaked during the Vietnam War. A 1967 police survey determined some 7,400 women were working as prostitutes. Another source estimated the number was double that—which meant about one in every twenty to twenty-five women between the ages of ten and sixty was involved in sex work. Together, their labor generated more money than any other local industry—more than pineapple and sugarcane farming combined. One Kin club owner recalled how much money GIs spent during the Vietnam War at his establishment, which employed twenty "hostesses." The cash was literally overflowing: "We stuffed [the bills] into buckets, but they still overflowed, so we had to stomp the piles down with our feet. . . . Dollars were raining on us."

Suzuyo Takazato told me that in 1970 the Ryukyuan government had the opportunity to enact the Japanese mainland's Prostitution Prevention Law, which had prohibited sex work since 1958, but decided to wait until the official reversion. "Here is the twisted feeling of Okinawan people," she said. Lawmakers knew the dire situation of many indentured sex workers, but were afraid that if they banned prostitution, U.S. soldiers would commit rape. They also wanted to keep that money in the economy. "In a way," Suzuyo said, at that time Okinawa was "economically supported by individual women who worked as prostitutes." These women were the ones who pulled their families— and all of Okinawan society, really—out of postwar poverty. But in society's eyes their hard work and sacrifices weren't selfless or noble or admirable; they were shameful.

When Okinawa reverted to Japanese control in 1972, prostitution became illegal and women were freed from their debt bondage. Some continued to work, with local police often looking the other way. Those who wanted to leave the profession received financial assistance and access to temporary living facilities, thanks to the Japanese government. Suzuyo said the government also helped some brothel owners become hotel owners. But in a way Tokyo also authorized the next wave of sex workers by issuing entertainer visas to overseas workers. Soon, Filipinas replaced Okinawans in the red-light districts outside the base gates.

Stepping off the plane on Okinawa, Daisy was careful to touch her right foot to the ground before her left. That way, she would head in the right direction. It was March 1992, and she was twenty-four years old. Her first impression of the foreign island where she would live and work the next six months was that it was clean. After the close chaos of Manila, a megacity, Okinawa seemed small and quiet and so very clean.

She moved into a house in Kin outside Camp Hansen, where she would live with the other Filipinas working at the club. In those days, Kin was crowded with clubs and women from the Philippines. The place Daisy was sent to was run by an Okinawan woman, the mama-san, who owned three bars in one building, two downstairs and one upstairs. Daisy learned she would rotate among them, talking with customers and dancing on stage. The pay proved impressive. Even just her new food allowance—10,000 yen a month, plus rice—was more than she had made at the printing factory.

Women like Daisy replaced Okinawans in the entertainment districts around U.S. military bases because of economics. When Okinawa reverted to Japan in 1972, the dollar gave way to the yen as the islands' currency. The new exchange rate raised prices on American servicemen. Meanwhile, as part of Japan and no longer a de facto colony, Okinawa enjoyed an economic boost, with women's economic power increasing, too. Presented with better opportunities for education and employment, many no longer had to turn to sex work. Soon, the primary way local women and American servicemen interacted was through dating—mixing in the island's clubs and shopping centers. Often, the woman was now the one paying for the man. I heard many stories about Okinawan women buying their younger military boyfriends clothes, meals, electronics, cars. "Every time he said he wanted something, I bought it for him," said one Okinawan woman, who had dated a twenty-year-old marine when she was thirty-two. "Once he mentioned seeing a beautiful thirty-inch TV set that he couldn't afford. 'How much is it?' I asked him. 'Seventeen hundred dollars,' he answered. 'Oh, that's cheap,' I told him, and bought it for him. I guess we used each other for different reasons." A veteran named Mitch told me in the early nineties, his friend had dated an older Okinawan woman they'd nicknamed "ichi man yen," or ten thousand yen, for the high-value bills she shelled out. "When he'd go out with her she always paid for everything," Mitch said. "He thought he was having a great time. He didn't think of himself as being a pet. I didn't either. We didn't know." U.S. servicemen had become the "honeys."

This new set-up may have been lucrative for GIs, but it wasn't good for boosting what scholars call militarized masculinity. In order to be effective soldiers, the thinking goes, men need their stereotypical masculinity reinforced, and this happens in relation to women who are stereotypically feminine—sexually available, submissive, weak, in need of protection. Having a woman pay for things doesn't build the type of manliness needed to charge a battlefield. The U.S. military needed a new pool of laborers to do this work—ones who were less economically powerful than Japanese and Okinawan women.

Meanwhile, in the Philippines, the problems of excess labor and foreign debt caused the government, as part of its economic strategy, to encourage women to migrate overseas as domestic help and entertainers. Throughout the 1980s, the number of Filipino contract workers migrating to Japan rose steadily; in 1981 there were 11,656; in 1987 there were 33,791. The vast majority were female entertainers. On the mainland, many went to work in hostess clubs serving Japanese customers. In Okinawa, they were concentrated around the bases. Though the Philippines had its own U.S. military bases, women could make more money in base-town entertainment areas in Japan.

By the mid-1980s, an estimated four thousand Filipinas worked in the bar areas outside U.S. military bases in Okinawa. Okinawan women who stayed in the business moved to areas that served mostly Okinawan and Japanese men—at higher prices. According to Suzuyo Takazato, Japanese tourists paid $50 for sex, while outside the bases what had cost Americans $5 during the occupation now cost $20. Women from other countries like Thailand may have migrated to work in Okinawan bars and clubs as well, but the vast majority were Filipina because the governments of Japan and the Philippines made it easy for them to migrate. While legal, the entertainer visa system was largely yakuza-controlled, including the promotion agencies in the Philippines. A bar owner in Okinawa paid a yakuza-run promotion agency a fee, and the promotion agency recruited women for the bar and paid their salaries, taking big cuts for themselves. "My salary is $400 a month, but I only receive $290 because $10 is deducted for insurance and $100 for the manager in the Philippines, at the promotion agency," explained one Filipina working in Kin in 1989. The women's travel to and from Okinawa was also deducted.

The women were legally in Japan as "overseas performing artists," meant to sing or perform cultural dances in groups. So some were shocked when, on their first night, they learned they'd have to dance alone, wearing little to no clothes. One woman, Rowena, cried her first time onstage, while her "papa-san" shouted, "Take off your bra." He said if she lost her panties, too, she would be "number one." Along with performing, women were required to sell a certain "quota" of drinks per month. At one Kin club in the late 1980s, the quota was four hundred. Each drink cost an inflated $10, and the woman received a $1 commission. The penalty for failing to make quota was receiving just half the commission. Doing this work, most women received only a couple of days off per month.

Life in the clubs was about luck—or, as Daisy saw it, providence. Women had no control over which club the promotion agency sent them to, and clubs differed according to owner. Some had high drink quotas and would send women back to the Philippines if they didn't meet them. Others forced women to dance naked and perform sexual acts on customers in "dark corners." Some places controlled the women's movements outside the club, going so far as to lock them inside their rooms. In 1983, a fire raged through one Kin establishment, and two Filipinas died because they were trapped behind bars.

Before Daisy's first night of work, she repeated her prayer: "God, please, *please* send an angel to guide me." She learned she would have to "sexy dance" and felt mortified, with no clue how to do that. But Daisy's co-workers proved to be supportive. Knowing how inexperienced she was, they took her under their wings, showing her how to dance. On her first night, they let her take her turn onstage when the club was empty. Her mama-san also turned out to be kind, giving them another chance if they didn't make their monthly quota but had regular customers.

That night, Daisy's first customer was a middle-aged African American marine. Sitting with her, he asked if she was new and had a boyfriend in the Philippines. "No," she replied to the second question.

"Yeah, right," he said, teasing. "That's what everybody says."

The next night the man came back to see her. And the next. And the next. The other girls told Daisy he had never visited the club that often. His name was Thomas, and Daisy sensed he had a good heart. Thirty-eight years old and from Virginia, he had joined the marine corps right out of high school. Like Daisy, he had started working at age sixteen. Now he was separated from his wife and supporting their three kids. Talking with him, Daisy noticed he was patient and polite, never ordering her around like other men. He grew devoted to her, asking her at the end of the month how many more drinks she needed to meet her quota. Then he bought the rest. He took on a second job to pay for them. Daisy began to think he had been sent from God. He was her angel.

Daisy felt God was watching over her, but she was making her own destiny, too. She quickly figured out how to navigate the high-stress environment of the clubs in a way that worked for her. She abstained from drinking and smoking because she had grown up watching her mom escape through those substances. She developed an outgoing and friendly manner of talking to customers, steering talk away from sexual territory and focusing on putting them at ease. "You don't need to be fluent in English to have a good conversation," she said. She thought about it like the servicemen were visiting her home. She needed to make them feel welcome; like a true hostess, she needed to entertain. She strategically chose her conversation topic: their families. She asked about parents and siblings back home, if they were married. She asked to see photos of their mothers and sisters. Like Daisy, they were foreigners in a strange land, pushed to take a career risk in search of better lives. She sensed when they were lonely and wanted a cheerful conversation with someone who cared. Many customers liked her approach, and she grew a list of regulars.

"Most people say you're going to sell your body because you're working in the club, but it's not true," she told me. "It depends on you." If women wanted, they could go on "bar fines," negotiating $100 to $150 to leave with a customer, presumably, but not always, for sex. Daisy said their mama-san never forced them. "It's up to them. It's personal. If I wanted extra money or big money one time, I could do it." She said she heard of an entertainer being forced to go out with a man only once, and that was years later, when someone told her it had happened to his girlfriend. Daisy said the sale of sex didn't happen in the club in part because of immigration services. Japanese officials would drop by regularly, undercover but obvious with their questions: How much is your salary? What do you do here? How old are you? Is that your real name? Legally, entertainers weren't supposed to even sit with their customers; they were supposed to perform together on stage, physically removed. Some women reported that club owners would receive a tip when immigration officials were going to pay a visit. The owners would then close for the night or make sure women were dancing modestly in groups.

Rob Oechsle, an American army veteran, likens the entertainers' work to "the bargain-basement version" of the Japanese geisha. A Filipina bargirl sat "with the customer for the purpose of chatting him up, pouring his drinks, lighting his cigarettes, stroking his ego, and all else that goes with the territory," he writes. Like a geisha, she wasn't a prostitute. Their work differed only superficially: "While the Geisha offers you her 'cultured' samisen music, the Bar Hostess offers you Karaoke. Where the Geisha offers you her gorgeous kimono, old hairstyle (actually a WIG in most cases) and a face that has been dipped in a bucket of white paint, the Bar Hostess offers you a more modern look, and can pour your drink and chat you up just as well as any Geisha." Their main job, he writes, is "titillating and building up the male ego, while . . . separating him from his hard-earned money." This is the work of helping make militarized masculinity. As one U.S. serviceman in South Korea said of the Filipina bargirls outside the base, they liberated him from the fear of rejection. "Back in the States, when I go to a bar, I have to get up and go to a girl," he said. "Here, I just have to sit down and they come to me. And they are mostly very beautiful women."

But most servicemen didn't see the women as artists, skilled in their craft of boosting the male ego. Many saw them as sex workers, through a lens of racism and sexism and militarism. Around the time Daisy was working in Kin, U.S. servicemen could be spotted wearing T-shirts emblazoned with the form of a woman and the letters LBSM—"little brown sex machine." The acronym played on the military one for submarine-launched ballistic missiles (SLBM) and alluded to the Filipinas working around the bases. A bar-area poster told the story of a GI's night with a woman using phrases like "Two slanted eyes look into mine." The woman asks, "You come, GI?" and the man, leaving the next morning, says to himself, "Did I fuck 'that'?????!!!!!" Rob Oechsle told me that in these bars he'd hear American men come in and say, "Hey, bitch, how much do you cost?" Some women, in response, would cry.

Daisy was thankful her mama-san acted as their protector, intervening when men became too drunk or aggressive, trying to push past a woman's boundaries. Daisy said her sole bad experience in the club was with a drunk guy who, when Mama-san told him it was time to buy another drink, fumbled with his zipper. "Touch me," he told Daisy. Daisy refused and left for the bathroom. He got mad, asking Mama-san where she was. When Daisy explained, Mama-san kicked him out.

The option to make extra cash through sexual services was always there, and sometimes Daisy felt tempted, thinking about her dream of building a house. Once, a Japanese man offered her 100,000 yen for sex, "big money," but she declined the offer, not wanting to develop a habit. "If you go out and make a lot of money one time, you might do it again," she said. "You will get used to it."

Falling in love was another story. "Working in the club was fun but at the same time scary because you never knew when you might fall in love," she said. She saw other women get dumped and heartbroken. Despite being cautious, Daisy found herself falling in love with Thomas. She loved his sense of humor, his patience, his respect for her. Having grown up without a father, she liked that he was older, paternal. He took care of her. She thought, "He was the one sent from heaven."

At the end of her six months on the island, Thomas asked her to marry him. But Daisy didn't believe in marriage. Not after she had watched her sister struggle as a "battered wife." Daisy returned to the Philippines thinking that if Thomas showed he was serious about her, she would change her mind and marry him. She applied for another six-month visa and returned to work in Okinawa.

I confess I had imagined a different story for Daisy. The year I graduated college, *human trafficking* became a buzz word, and I reported a story about women trafficked from South Korea and held prisoner in a neighborhood not far from my campus in Providence, Rhode Island. Later, in Cambodia, I worked at a foundation that awarded grants to anti-trafficking NGOs. I retold heart-wrenching testimonies from girls lured to the city with promises of jobs cleaning hotel rooms. In Phnom Penh, they were forced into brothels. Meeting Daisy, I kept looking for that type of narrative. *Were you ever pressured to . . . ? Did you hear about other women being forced to . . . ?* But she refused my storyline over and over. *No, it's up to them. It's personal.* Other accounts from Filipinas who worked in Kin echo Daisy's. An entertainer chose whether to engage in sex work.

The work of renowned Okinawan photographer Mao Ishikawa also suggests that working in bars was empowering and not about the sale of sex—not only for Filipinas but also for Okinawan women before them. In 1975, when Mao was twenty-two years old, she took a job at a bar in Koza so she could photograph GIs. The establishment was a Black Panther hangout and the biggest club in Teruya, the black part of segregated Koza. The Vietnam War had just ended, and customers were always reuniting at the club, bumping fists and embracing, discovering who had made it back alive. Working there, Mao found she felt more comfortable with black men than with Okinawan men. She thought they treated her and other bar workers as equals, like the women did for them. Later, she realized her bond with those men was about their shared struggles. Okinawans faced discrimination from Japanese mainlanders, while African Americans were in the same position relative to white Americans.

I heard this sentiment about black servicemen and bargirls from others, too. It was the opposite of postwar speculations that black GIs were more likely to assault local women because they had found "a people they could feel superior to and treat as they were used to being treated." Instead, African American soldiers were said to exhibit more empathy toward locals compared to white servicemen, who were the ones who felt superior. One Okinawan woman who had worked as a bartender outside Kadena Air Base said, "White customers who came to the bar tend[ed] to look down on Asians. I think they feel superior to Asian women and treated us in the way they think we deserve. . . . Many of them think it's okay to touch Asian women's bodies when they [are] drunk. I mean, they touched our butts. . . . They were rude, haughty, and disrespectful." In an entertainment district outside a U.S. military base in South Korea, a Filipina entertainer said when she lied that she was a virgin to gain sympathy, she chose black servicemen because they had "good hearts." Mitch, an African American veteran who came to Okinawa with the army in 1991, told me a story about a business trip he took to the Philippines. It was the early 2000s, and he had left the military but stayed in Okinawa, selling cars on base. On the trip, he and other sales guys went out one night in Angeles City, to a notorious brothel area near the former site of Clark Air Base. "What was shocking was I saw the white guys were much more comfortable treating the Filipina women as objects," he told me. "The black guys were uncomfortable. . . . We didn't like it." The white men were drunk, with their guards down. "I saw a side of white people I had never seen before." Observing the scene, Mitch shared an uneasy, knowing look with the other two men of color. "That's how they see black people. That was like an insight. We saw that and we said *okay*. We never spoke of it. We just knew." He thought that dynamic extended to Okinawa. African American men didn't fetishize local women like white men did, he said. "There was never a sense of superiority or a sense of entitlement."

Before long, one of the Teruya men became Mao's boyfriend. "He was very kind," she told me. "But ugly. Not my type. So soon I found another guy." Mao and I were meeting in 2017 in Ginowan. In her mid-sixties now, she wore her hair colored a rusty brown and permed into a cloud. In her ears were gold hoop earrings, and an oversized red aloha shirt hid her colectomy collection bag. Recently she had been diagnosed with Stage 4 cancer, but seemed in good spirits, telling her story in her coy, charming, animated way, widening her eyes with surprise or closing off her features in disapproval. Mao had become one of Okinawa's best-known photographers, often wrestling with issues of the U.S. military presence. For one project, she walked the perimeter of every base on the island, taking photos. "You can see the real Okinawa when you walk around the fences," she'd said.

Back in the 1970s, Mao quit the club and moved in with the second guy, his friend, and his friend's girlfriend, the four of them sharing a small apartment near Futenma. Mao started photographing their lives. In her black and white images, Okinawan women with delicate eyebrows and voluminous Afros wear bell bottoms and halter tops, show off their breasts and tattoos, smoke and drink, lounge and laugh together. The walls behind them are decorated with pictures of black men and women. The GIs in the photos are dressed in suits and hats, slacks and button downs, short shorts and white athletic socks. Everyone is smiling and posing, draped across each other, goofing off or relaxing, snazzied up for the club or disrobed at home. They look happy.

Mao had started out wanting to photograph American soldiers, but realized the Okinawan women working in the bars were more interesting. On a small island that could feel socially claustrophobic, these women managed to be free-spirited, uninhibited. They didn't care when prejudiced family and friends judged them for hanging out with, dating, loving black men. The women enjoyed their lives, enjoyed their bodies, enjoyed sex, unapologetically. In this, Mao recognized a more extreme version of herself, and she felt overwhelmed by their way of life. To her, these women were like akabana, the beautiful red flower that grows everywhere on Okinawa, the one you picked if you didn't have money to buy a bouquet when you visited a grave. She decided to follow their example, care even less what others thought. "There are those who look down on women who work at military bars," she writes in the 2017 collection of these photos, *Red Flower: The Women of Okinawa*. "They assume that the women are prostitutes. That is a total misconception. . . . The bar girls were living their lives to the fullest."

With the Vietnam War over and Okinawa again a part of Japan, GIs emptied out of Teruya, heading back to the States. Bars and clubs shut down. Mao's co-workers told her the action had moved to Kin, where there were still racially segregated bars around Camp Hansen. Having grown tired of her second GI boyfriend, Mao left him and went north, where she worked in another bar, taking more photographs. That life came to a close in 1977, when she married a soldier in the Japan Self-Defense Forces. When she returned to Kin a decade later, she found the women working in the bars were Filipina. At the place Mao used to work, she found the mama-san and six Filipinas sitting around, "just killing time," without many customers. On stage, one woman danced. When Mao explained she had been one of them ten years earlier, the Filipinas invited her into their lives—back to their "dorm," into their workplaces, even back to the Philippines to renew their visas. In the black and white photographs Mao took, the hostesses snuggle together on bunk beds, sleep backstage on sofas, dance topless or in high-cut bikinis and leg warmers. Back home, they're reunited with their kids, the "stars" of their villages because of the gifts they brought, the money they sent. The style has changed—now the women sport blown-out bangs, blazers, and acid-washed jeans— and in their Okinawa apartments there are rosaries, not "black is beautiful" posters, on the walls. But many of the images are similar to the ones of "akabana." The Filipina women flash their breasts for Mao, grinning; they embrace GIs in their beds and on the streets of Kin; they hang around cluttered apartments, affectionate with each other, eating and laughing and primping. They look happy.

It's hard to know if Daisy's experience is atypical or perhaps made rosier with the passage of time. Certainly, other Filipina women who were placed in more restrictive or abusive clubs, felt more financial pressure, or weren't so lucky with their customers would have had a harder time. Women with darker tales might be less likely to share their experiences. And even if sex work was an entertainer's choice, she was still vulnerable to abuse. Going off alone with a serviceman on a bar fine could be dangerous—and when things went wrong for a Filipina entertainer on Okinawa, her story didn't ignite wide-scale sympathy or protest against the bases.

One example is from 2008. Twenty-one-year-old "Hazel" had been in Japan only a few days on an entertainer visa, working at a Gate 2 club called Mermaid. She was a petite woman, just five feet tall and one hundred pounds, who said she'd come to Okinawa to earn money for her family. At the Naha airport, a Filipino broker had taken her passport, assuring her it was for safekeeping. Her first night, she was disturbed to find that instead of dancing, she was to mingle with military customers. She had heard about bar fines but thought they meant leaving the club with a man to eat or hang out. Her third night on the island, she left Mermaid with a twenty-five-year-old Kadena soldier named Ronald Edward Hopstock Jr. and a group of ten other Filipinas and servicemen. They ate at Wendy's and sang karaoke. Hazel found Hopstock kind, and at around 3 a.m. agreed to check into a nearby hotel with him, not knowing her way back to the house where she was staying.

At 8 a.m. the next morning Hazel appeared in the lobby of the hotel, pale and bleeding profusely. After nearly dying from blood loss, she was hospitalized for a week. Hopstock told police he'd paid the $200 bar fine to take her to the hotel, with the understanding that they'd have sex. Hazel said she'd had no notion about such a deal and never received any money. She'd thought she'd come from the Philippines to dance, not to sell sex. Hopstock said the two then engaged in consensual sex, stopping when she started bleeding. She said she went to sleep in her clothes and awoke to find him ripping off her pants and penetrating her.

The case received some media attention, but the Naha prosecutor's office dropped the charges against Hopstock, citing insufficient evidence. "Three points at issue were the place where the alleged act took place, the relation of the two individuals and the circumstances before and after the alleged event," said the deputy chief of the Naha District Public Prosecutor's Office. The U.S. Army took over the investigation. Local Filipino residents and women's activists in the Philippines protested. One Filipina activist and lawmaker, Liza Maza, voiced her concern that Japanese prosecutors were declining to exercise their jurisdiction in cases involving U.S. servicemembers and were making a habit of passing off such cases to the U.S. military. She questioned whether the U.S. military would fairly prosecute the case: "I believe there will be some legal action, but probably not a charge of rape. I have some reservations because the perpetrator is one of their own."

The U.S. Army did charge Hopstock with rape, along with not bringing a "liberty buddy" that night off base and paying for sex on other occasions. But then, during the military hearing, Hazel admitted she had worked as a hostess in Hong Kong before coming to Okinawa—to some, an admission she wasn't so innocent—and a doctor revealed Hazel was genetically male. She had something called androgen insensitivity syndrome, which had caused her to develop female genitalia but no cervix. Her condition was the reason for all the bleeding from sex. It also appeared to be a reason the Okinawa prosecutor dropped charges. At that time, Japanese law still defined rape only as forced male-female, vaginal penetration.

The U.S. military ended up dismissing the rape charge, too. Hopstock pled guilty to the other charges, admitting he had hired a prostitute twenty times in Okinawa, after men from his unit had introduced him to a sex district called Hooker Hill. Filipina activist groups protested the dismissal, but there was no such movement among the Okinawan public.

In 2004, the U.S. State Department, in its annual Trafficking in Persons (TIP) Report, called out Japan for issuing entertainer visas, which it claimed were used "to facilitate the movement and exploitation of trafficking victims." "Thousands of women," the report read, "are granted these temporary visas in the expectation of legitimate employment in the entertainment or hospitality industries. . . . On arrival at their destination, victims are stripped of their passports and travel documents and forced into situations of sexual exploitation or bonded servitude." Of the 55,000 Filipinas who came to Japan on entertainer visas in 2003, the TIP Report stated, "many" were "suspected of having become trafficking victims."

Embarrassed, Japanese lawmakers responded by stopping the flow of entertainer visas. Over the next two years, the number of Filipina contract workers in Japan plummeted from more than 80,000 to about 8,600. The 2006 TIP Report noted Japan's "remarkable progress," and many celebrated an anti-trafficking triumph. Others, however, maintained the women were not victims and the legislative changes disregarded their agency and removed their ability to migrate legally for better opportunities abroad. Entertainers weighed the benefits of the work against the risks and chose to come to Japan, these people argued. Even with the promotion agency's deductions and other fines, the pay surpassed what they could make in the Philippines—much more than the salaries of, say, a department store clerk or a teacher. For most women, one six-month contract wasn't enough. Like Daisy, they left and decided to return again. But after the TIP Report, the privilege to migrate abroad became one for men. In 2007, for the first time in twenty years, more males than females left the Philippines for work. Women who wanted to work as hostesses in Japan were now more likely to migrate illegally, overstaying tourist visas and becoming more vulnerable to abuse due to their undocumented status. In 2007, the Japanese government estimated there were some 19,000 undocumented Filipinas in the country, while nongovernmental organizations reported the actual number was higher.

Today, there is no longer a vast population of Filipinas working around the U.S. military bases in Okinawa. Since the Japanese government stopped issuing entertainer visas, no other large-scale migration of women from abroad has taken place. Most Filipinas who remain in Okinawa migrated illegally or through marriage. Romeo Medoruma, an Okinawan-Filipino retired base worker who volunteered at the Philippines' consulate, told me that recently many Filipinas had been coming to the island on tourist visas and marrying Japanese men or U.S. servicemen. Before, he said, a Filipina had to have established residency in Japan to marry in the country, but the Japanese government had changed the requirements. "The funny thing is the word spread so fast," Romeo said. A three-month tourist visa was fairly easy to get, and soon brides started arriving. Now he saw one or two a week coming to the consulate on tourist visas to get married. Most were marrying American servicemen they had met on the internet or while the men were training in the Philippines. Romeo thought those were love marriages. But the women marrying Japanese men were driven by economics. Twenty years earlier, they would have come on entertainer visas instead. These women were in their twenties, marrying men aged sixty-plus. "It's a chance for them to get out of poverty," Romeo said. "And it's a chance for the Japanese guy to have someone help." The marriages were business arrangements, set up by a professional broker or friend. The woman acted as a caregiver to the man, and maybe worked in a bar.

These days, Romeo said, women working in the remaining Filipina bars outside the bases were probably married to Japanese men. The bar owners themselves were often Filipina wives of locals. "But as you know, the business over there is dead right now," he said, referring to the Gate 2 area. "So most of them are closing." High-profile crimes had led to tighter restrictions on U.S. servicemembers, like earlier curfews. He said the women working there would probably move to places with Okinawan and Japanese customers, if they could speak Japanese.

One Wednesday night in June 2017, Romeo took me to one of the hold-out Filipina bars around Gate 2 Street. Walking the street, we passed shuttered Indian tailors, strip clubs, and chicken stands. Romeo, who was in his late sixties and had a full head of white hair, had a grandfatherly kind of energy and said he didn't normally come out here. He pointed out one club that still employed entertainers— some Filipinas and a rock band of Filipino guys.

One of Romeo's missions was to dispel the myth that all Filipinos on Okinawa were linked to bars and prostitution. "Filipinos are now teachers, healthcare providers," he said. All kinds of people of Filipino descent lived on the island, including some whose roots stretched back to the Battle of Okinawa, when the U.S. military brought thousands of men from the Philippines to fight alongside Americans. Later, men from the Philippine Scouts worked on base and married local women.

Turning down a side street, we came across an abandoned Filipina bar called Club Hawaii Night, which had once announced itself in neon. Now it looked eerie under the streetlight, arrested in time. There was something about the Gate 2 area and its run-down or forgotten buildings, like something living that should be dead.

We arrived at Silky House, a complex of small bars with a love hotel on top. Inside, a dark hallway with black and white checkered floors housed rows of closed doors. The sounds of karaoke echoed. Above each doorway, a box announced the bar's name: My Place, Angeles City, Boracay Beach, the Spot. If the box was illuminated, the bar was open. We opened the door to Angeles City. A bar ran across one side of the room, with enough seats for maybe six. Pleather chairs furnished the rest of the space. The purple walls were decorated with a Hawaii state flag and screens playing karaoke videos. The music blared. At the bar, two American servicemen were singing karaoke, beer bottles lined up in front of them. Behind the bar stood a Filipina woman, maybe in her early fifties, wearing a low-cut pink tank top and denim shorts. Reading glasses were perched atop her head. She seemed bored, staring at her phone. She told us she had arrived in Japan more than thirty years earlier, working in Tokyo as an entertainer. Then she had met and married an American GI, who was later stationed in Okinawa. This establishment, she said, was owned by a Filipina who didn't come around much. On weekends it got packed with American and Japanese customers. The marines were supposed to leave at midnight to make curfew, but sometimes they didn't. "They don't care," she said.

Back on the deserted streets of what used to be Koza, Romeo and I passed vacant storefronts lit by fluorescent lighting and in various stages of decay. New York Restaurant, once a popular purveyor of heaping plates of American food, had been gutted, and its windowpanes were veiled with grime. "Empty. Empty," Romeo said as we walked down B.C. Street. "These all used to be bars," he said, gesturing to apartment buildings and a call center. About thirty years earlier the city had tried to erase the street's seedy history by erecting a roof over the sidewalks and painting the storefronts white, hoping to rebirth it as an attraction for tourists and locals. City workers tried to market the American base town as an exotic international destination. A 1994 Okinawa City guidebook boasts, "As you walk along Gate [Two] Street, you have the feeling of being completely in a foreign country." These ploys didn't work, though, partly for the logistical fact of limited parking. On car-centric Okinawa, everyone now goes to the American Village or Rycom Mall, which offer expanses of free parking. "Okinawa City is a dying city," Romeo said. "There's nothing here anymore."

Red-light districts still exist in other areas of the island. Rob Oechsle, an American veteran who came to Okinawa with the army in 1973, married a local woman, and never left, told me Japanese and Okinawan women work at the Naha "soaplands." These are legal businesses that together employ a couple thousand women, who service mostly Japanese and Okinawan men paying $200 for a "bath." Another famous prostitution area is Yoshihara, not far from Gate 2 Street in Okinawa City. Until about five years earlier, when the city instituted a "clean up" campaign, a thousand women sold sex there, Rob said. Once, he cruised through with an air force buddy, and girls were everywhere, calling out clichés like "love you long time." The street was packed with guys. Half the doors posted "Japanese only" signs, but GIs used to frequent Yoshihara—calling it "whore corner," I'd heard—until the U.S. military declared it off-limits.

The U.S. military may have come to adopt an official stance against prostitution, but sometimes its unofficial stance is revealed. After the 1995 rape, the commander of the U.S. military in the Pacific, Admiral Richard Macke, told reporters the crime was "stupid"—only because the three men should have hired a prostitute instead. "For the price they paid to rent the car they could have had a girl," he said. Japanese lawmakers also continue to expose their thinking that prostitution is a necessary and natural complement to soldiers, and to take that away would mean more sexual assault. In 2013, the mayor of Osaka, Toru Hashimoto, defended the Japanese military's enslavement of comfort women during World War II, saying, "When soldiers are risking their lives by running through storms of bullets, and you want to give these emotionally charged soldiers a rest somewhere, it's clear that you need a comfort women system." Hashimoto's outlook extended to the U.S. military in Japan. He said he told a senior marine corps official in Okinawa that marines should buy sex more often because, of course, their lust cannot be contained. "We can't control the sexual energy of these brave marines," Hashimoto said. "They must make more use of adult entertainers."

On her second entertainment visa to Okinawa, Daisy found Thomas just as loving and devoted as before. This time, she accepted his proposal, and decades later the married couple lives in a new-looking three-bedroom apartment in Okinawa City with their two teenaged kids, a son and a daughter. Their home is inviting, decorated with display cases housing Daisy's treasures. She likes to collect flowers and angels made of ceramic and glass.

After Thomas completed his second stint in Okinawa with the marines, he retired with thirty years of service. He found work as a government employee on base so the family could stay on the island that they loved. Daisy left the clubs and worked at the Futenma U.S.O. for fourteen years, cooking food for the marines, a stress-free job she enjoyed. When the couple's first child was one, Daisy convinced her mother to come to Okinawa, telling her, "I want you to remember I promised you: when I have my better life, I want you to experience it also." Daisy's mom moved into their apartment on Camp Kinser, and Daisy showered her with new clothes and meals out, anything that might make her happy. Daisy was overjoyed to finally be delivering her promise. For six years they lived like this, her mom staying nine months of the year in Okinawa, three months in the Philippines. Daisy continued sending money back, paying school tuition for her nieces and nephews. She also helped bring two of her sisters and one of her cousins to Okinawa. That was how her younger sister met an American airman, married him, and moved to Arizona. Her other sister and the niece Daisy had first come to Japan with both married Japanese men and lived in Nagoya. Daisy put the finishing touch on her dream when she built a new house for her mom in the Philippines.

She said she was grateful for how her life had turned out. Thomas was a kind, loving husband and good provider, and they had two wonderful kids. Her daughter had just graduated high school and wanted to move to California and become an optometrist. Daisy hoped she would join the U.S. Air Force and pursue higher education that way. As for Okinawa, Daisy loved living on the island. "I'm free," she said, laughing. "This is my home."

That summer, I ventured out again onto Gate 2, this time on a Saturday night during a payday weekend. My friend Yuki and I headed to a club called Black Rose, where a wet T-shirt contest was happening. The prize was a hundred dollars. In the crowded club, the event manager jumped on top of the bar and invited all the finest women to claim a white T-shirt and enter the contest. One woman came floating through the crowd, carried aloft by a bunch of servicemen. She looked glassy-eyed. The song "Everyday We Lit" came on, and men raised their glasses, shouting along: "Every day we're lit/you can't tell me shit." I was surprised not to see many Okinawan or Japanese women in the crowd. Nearly a decade before, when I had gone to Saicolo in Naha with Eve, local women had been out in full force.

The show began. The first contestant was an African American woman wearing black booty shorts along with her T-shirt. The DJ played Nicki Minaj's "Anaconda" and she smiled, grabbing her ample breasts and moving them in circles under the showerhead on stage. Men shoved past me to get closer. They pressed record on their cell phones and held them up.

The second woman was white, with glasses and a tattoo sleeve. She pulled the T-shirt taut against her breasts, sticking out her tongue, looking delighted. When Nicki sang, "I came just to kill," she made a gun with her hand and shot from her hip. A guy in the crowd shot back.

The third woman was racially ambiguous, with cropped hair and ripped abs. On her feet were Air Jordans and Chicago Bulls socks. She raised her arms, shouting along with the men. One guy in front turned around to look at his friends with surprise and rapture. She bounced up and down with a cool confidence. Men screamed.

The last contestant was the woman who had been carried up there.

On stage, she laughed, seeming bewildered. She looked Latina, with a black bandana tied around her head. When the music started, she put her breasts under the stream of water and moved her face away from the spray. She opened her mouth and looked like she was just focusing on not falling down.

The show ended, and guys clapped each other on the backs, laughing and yelling. At this club on this night, Okinawan and Filipina women were no longer the ones working to boost militarized masculinity. With females making up more and more of the U.S. military—more than 16 percent in 2017—American women had taken their place.

The contestant with the six-pack won the contest, the others claiming runners-up bottles of champagne. As midnight approached, men and women spilled onto the sidewalk outside. They had to be out of the bar by twelve, back on base by one. Managers at Black Rose and other bars had complained to me about these restrictions, which hurt their businesses. To me, they seemed locked in a self-defeating cycle. The bars, clubs, and brothels promoted the excess drinking and dehumanizing of women that helped lead to the drunk driving and sexual violence, the crimes and accidents that became international incidents and got the servicemembers confined to base. The base-town businesses lamented the loss of their customers, downplayed or dismissed the incidents, and waited for the soldiers to return. Then the cycle started again.

Men and women milled around outside Black Rose. A couple of military police officers stood watch. "All these bitches out here hoes," one guy announced. My friend Yuki asked a different serviceman what everyone was waiting for. "We're trying to fuck these bitches," he replied.

"We're waiting for honchos," said the woman who had won the contest, using the local military slang for taxis. A hundred dollars richer, she had changed into a baseball jersey and was holding the hand of a woman with a U.S. Marine Corps tattoo on her shoulder. A taxi pulled up, and the women left the men standing in the street.

8

MIYO

LIKE DAISY, MIYO CONSIDERED HERSELF LUCKY—THOUGH MANY IN Okinawa might have been surprised to hear it. "I'm fortunate," she told me. It was a cool December night in 2008, and we were at a beachside burger place in Chatan, just south of the American Village. Beyond the outdoor tables, Araha Beach looked clean and deserted in the streetlights.

Miyo was the daughter of an African American veteran and an Okinawan woman. She'd lived on the island since she was five, after stints with her family in New Mexico and on Yokota Air Base outside Tokyo. Now twenty-six years old, she worked at an American contracting company on base. She considered herself lucky because as a kid she'd attended an on-base American school as well as a Japanese "cram school" to learn to read and write Japanese. She became bilingual, and when she switched to a local public school in fourth grade she was able to keep up academically. That was why other kids hadn't bullied her much.

She ate a French fry. "Still, though, wherever you go you're going to get it."

"Get what?" I asked.

She looked toward the ocean, adjusting her crocheted headband and teasing out tendrils of curly hair on either side of her face. "People are always going to think you're a gaijin," she said. A foreigner. She was quiet, then brightened. "Around here, though, there are a lot of mixed people. Like us!" She swept her arm through the air, even though we were the only ones around.

Okinawa was the only home Miyo knew, but many other Okinawans didn't recognize her claim to the island. When she visited the countryside, people freaked out when they heard her speak Japanese. They couldn't reconcile her face with the words. She said she didn't take it personally. "I've learned to have fun with it," she said. For example, she had a friend who was half Filipino, half Chinese, who looked Japanese, but couldn't speak the language well. When she and Miyo went out, waiters assumed her friend was Japanese and Miyo was the foreigner, although it was the other way around. Once, when a waiter brought them one English menu and one Japanese menu, they switched right in front of him, to his surprise.

Miyo's interactions with Americans raised questions about her identity, too. People stared at her in Mississippi when she went to visit her father's family at age twenty. At the mall, a guy came up and grabbed her arm. He said something she didn't understand.

"What's going on?" she asked her cousin, terrified.

"He's hitting on you."

Another time on that visit, she had her hair down—so much depended on how she wore her hair—and a guy at a shopping center approached her and touched it. "Are you Indian?" he asked. "Hawaiian?" She couldn't believe that in America strange men approached women and touched their hair.

Even at home with her relatives there were issues. Every night on that trip, she took a shower and washed her hair.

"Why are you doing that?" her cousin asked.

"Doing what?"

"You don't have to wash your hair every day. You're black."

"I didn't know I'm black!" That was the first time that idea had occurred to Miyo.

The workings of race and ethnicity in the United States confused her. "I'm not used to the race issue, being here," she explained. "It's just you're Japanese or not. That's about it."

Growing up and living in Okinawa, Miyo had thought a lot about whether she was Japanese. She didn't think she looked Japanese, but the food she cooked, the food she liked, her attitude, the way she thought: all that was Japanese. "But of course I'm not 100 percent," she said. Miyo had dual citizenship, which isn't technically legal in Japan after age twenty-two, but many dual nationals get away with it because the government looks the other way. Miyo was in the process of transferring everything to the United States, though, because her company had offered to cover her under the U.S.–Japan Status of Forces Agreement, which meant a salary cut but a free college education. She planned to start taking one course at a time on base.

"For me, the only question is am I Japanese or not?" She pushed away her plate and reached for her headband again. Adjusting it seemed to be a nervous tic. *So much depends on how I wear my hair.* She fixed the curls around her face. "I still don't know whether I'm Japanese."

She said in Okinawa she was careful not to wear too much makeup, because if she did other locals saw her as the wrong kind of girl. "Like one of those snack bar girls," she said. She meant a bar hostess who was paid to flirt with customers, and maybe do more, for the right price. Some bars liked to employ mixed-race women because they could speak Japanese and customers found them exotic. "My face is too loud," Miyo tried to explain. "Maybe I need new makeup."

We finished our burgers and walked toward the beach. Old anger toward Japan and its delusions about racial purity bubbled up inside me. The country harbors a longstanding myth of homogeneity, even though people everywhere have always been mixing and migrating. Japan contains ample diversity—native groups like Ainu and Okinawans, Korean Japanese, Chinese Japanese, Brazilian Japanese, Filipino Japanese, multiracial and multiethnic Japanese. But in the "Japanese or not" model, people must "pass" if they can, or be labeled gaijin, "outside people." I had come to expect this dynamic in mainland Japan, but thought Okinawa, with its multicultural history and minority status within the country, allowed more room for diversity. As I learned, though, Okinawa has its own hang-ups about racial mixing, especially when it comes to locals and U.S. servicemen.

After the war, mixed American-Japanese people entered the social imagination, in both Japan and Okinawa, through stories of unwanted babies. On the mainland, the media reported on infants, with their telltale black or white features, discarded on train cars and in trash bins. In Okinawa, a local newspaper announced a trend of unmarried women who were getting pregnant by U.S. soldiers and seeking illegal abortions. One twenty-two-year-old had resorted to infanticide: "When she realized it was an illegitimate child with the skin of a foreign race, she was arrested three days after delivery for suffocating and murdering the child in her underarm as she breastfed it." Questioning the women who had gotten abortions, police assumed they worked as prostitutes. According to the *Okinawan Times*, which like all Okinawan media then was subject to U.S. military censorship, the women denied the assumption indignantly: "The women were outraged at the investigator's assertion that they exchanged their chastity for material goods from the military and instead proclaimed they were living in pure love." The reason for the abortions, the newspaper reported, was the young, single women "thought of the reality of childbirth" and "didn't know what else to do."

Anxiety continued to permeate ideas about children born between Okinawan women and the occupiers. These men included GIs and the thousands of Filipino workers the U.S. military brought to the island to construct the bases and then staff them. In the mid-1950s, the local Okinawan government moved to legalize abortion to control population numbers, but also to "strengthen the Ryukyuan people" and prevent their "deterioration," an allusion to the mixed-race children being born. Meanwhile, media and government surveys reported on the absence of these children's fathers. Of ninety-four biracial children living in the Naha area in 1949, most were being raised by single mothers, a local newspaper found. Just two couples were married under local law, and twenty-eight women said their children's fathers had left the island. Six years later, the first government survey of mixed-race children on Okinawa found a slightly higher, but still low, rate of children living with their dads. About half the kids lived with single mothers, 30 percent with other Okinawan family members, and 10 percent with both parents. Two-thirds of the fathers were absent and paying no child support.

Although there were mentions of "pure love" and, in one article, "the welcome fruits of love across international borders," many Okinawans came to associate mixed-race children with runaway fathers and mothers who were sex workers. One Okinawan woman described this stigma when she recalled how many single mothers sent their biracial children to rural towns to live with grandparents while they worked in cities: "Commonly, you would see grandmothers walking around with small blond children in villages like Motobu and Nakijin. Older folks, grandparents, were ashamed of the children because it was generally assumed that most of them were conceived by mothers who were involved in prostitution."

Another common assumption was that mixed-race children were the product of rape. The women's rights group Okinawa Women Act Against Military Violence illustrates this assumption in their chronology of sexual assault. Alongside the descriptions of violence, they list the birth of biracial babies.

January 1946: From this month, ten months after U.S. forces land on Okinawa Island, many Okinawan women give birth to biracial children.

September 23, 1949: The number of biracial children total 450.

While sexual violence was widespread following the war, it seems fair to say these 450 mixed kids reported in the *Uruma Times* weren't all the result of rapes by U.S. soldiers, as Okinawa Women Act Against Military Violence suggests. As we know, many postwar women chose intimacy with American soldiers, whether out of "pure love" or economic necessity or some combination of both. And while many American fathers were absent, not all these men chose to leave their families.

Some Okinawan women left the men, and during the occupation the U.S. military was often the culprit, discouraging or outlawing international marriages.

The "occupation babies" of Okinawa weren't so tragic, but thinking about them that way made their lives more difficult. For many Okinawans, seeing the multiracial features of a kid on the street could roil the same anger and despair as passing a red-light district or hearing about a rape. Like the innocent, violated woman, the biracial person became a symbol of Okinawa's subjugation, helping make them unwanted.

Stereotypes about American-Okinawans persisted past the occupation. Associations between mixed-race Okinawans and rape happen to a greater degree after high-profile sexual assault cases, like the one in 1995. During that media frenzy, one mother told reporters, students at her son's school taunted him, saying his mom had been raped by U.S. soldiers, just like the headlines in the news. Another student recalled her public school teacher giving a lesson on the Battle of Okinawa and explaining, "In Okinawa, Americans raped Japanese women . . . and there are now a lot of cases of an international marriage [sic]." Her classmates soaked this in and asked the biracial girl, "Was your mother also raped by an American GI?"

Related to this devastating stereotype is one of the tragic mulatto, the offspring of Madame Butterfly, "the plight of the Amerasian children." The media, academics, and activists often fall back on this trope. One *New York Times* article that is referenced a lot was published while the island was hosting the 2000 G-8 Summit and international eyes were trained on Okinawa. In "A Hard Life for Amerasian Children" Calvin Sims echoes the narrative put forth by the Japanese media, which in their summit pre-coverage "reported widely on the racial discrimination, poor education and financial distress that many of these biracial children endure in Japanese society." Japanese reporters did so to provide a vivid "example of the social ills caused by the many United States military bases" in the prefecture. In his piece, Sims writes about the struggles of the single mothers of the approximately "4,000 Okinawan children abandoned by American servicemen."

A few paragraphs later he cites "the local government['s] [estimate] that about 200 Amerasian children are born in Okinawa annually." This math—two hundred kids a year, times eighteen years—means *all* children born to Okinawan mothers and American fathers end up being left behind by their "deadbeat" dads. Just as Okinawa Women Act Against Military Violence does in its sexual assault chronology, Sims writes one tragic story for all mixed-race people. The only child he quotes is a twelve-year-old whose public school experience was "sheer torture" because her classmates bullied her and called her "half," a term Sims defines as a racial epithet. A *Time* magazine article, published a day after Sims's, features the same girl and states Okinawa's "thousands of Amerasians" serve as "subtle signs of the uneasy union of cultures" on the island. The author, Tim Larimer, also mentions the term *half,* "a none too subtle reminder that they can never be completely Japanese."

What Sims and Larimer didn't realize is that the Japanese term *hafu,* derived from the English word *half,* emerged on the Japanese mainland in the 1970s and 1980s as a neutral or positive identifier for mixed-race Japanese people. It became divorced from the English meaning and came to connote international glamour, like the white-Japanese models who were showing up in ads. "How to look like a hafu," proclaimed makeup tutorials in Japanese women's magazines. *Hafu* was unlike derogatory terms of previous years, like *ainoko.* Most people I met used and preferred *hafu* to self-identify, even if outsiders didn't understand, thinking it reduced them to fractions.

As for bullying, mixed-race children's experiences differ greatly, depending on where and when they grow up and whether they are part white or part black. With larger issues of racial discrimination, hafu who are part black often face more prejudice than their part-white peers. One contributor is the idea that looking more Caucasian, with whitened features, is desirable, whereas looking mixed Asian-black is not. An Okinawan woman who dated black American servicemen explained to me her kids were going to be ugly. "Black-Asian kids are never cute," she said, wrinkling her nose. Half-white Asians, however, were beautiful, she said. So many of them were models. Her friend was pursuing white men just to have cute babies. In recent years, these racist beauty ideals have been challenged by famous hafus in the Japanese entertainment industry, like black-Japanese beauty queen Ariana Miyamoto, who claimed the title of Miss Universe Japan in 2015.

Bullying of all mixed-race kids was especially brutal in the postwar period. Okinawan peers hurled taunts of "half-blood," "Yankee," "American," and "ainoko," along with, often, actual rocks. One biracial woman told me her Okinawan mom, who later married an American, threw rocks at mixed kids when she was young. It was just what everyone did. Another woman, Hana, told me kids in the Okinawan countryside in the 1970s chucked rocks at her and her sister. The pair thought it was a game and flung the rocks back. Only years later, when one of those former kids apologized, did Hana realize their malicious intent.

"I don't think it's physical bullying anymore," an American-Okinawan man named Kento told me. "Maybe emotional bullying. And that emotional bullying could be direct, it could be indirect, or it could be unconscious." For Kento, it happened when he transitioned from an international school to a local public middle school in Okinawa. On his second or third day at the new school, someone said, "You look like John," and that was it. Everyone started calling him John and continued to do so through high school. He hated the nickname, though the kids weren't trying to be mean. "It was neutral," he said. "I think it was just because of how I look. Maybe they thought it was appropriate for me to have a Western nickname." Still, the name was a blow to Kento, who was trying to assert his Japanese identity and prepare for a life in Japan.

Even when mixed-race people don't have negative experiences growing up, their narratives can get twisted by others who have the tragic mulatto story in mind. One mixed Okinawan woman related her experience talking to a Japanese reporter in a focus group: "She didn't understand that we were telling her that we were fine. And then she wrote up something so strange about us kawaisō [poor], confused halfies. I don't like interviews. They never get it. They always switch up our words. All of us are so different and they make us the same."

Again, a well-meaning outsider insisted on one tear-jerker tale for all mixed-race people in Okinawa.

To address the real problems facing multiracial families, a couple of social welfare organizations operated in Okinawa. International Social Assistance Okinawa (ISAO) started out in 1958 brokering adoptions of mixed-race kids to the United States, but staff quickly realized that wasn't what most Okinawan families wanted. When parents were unable to care for a child, extended family members stepped in. If that wasn't possible, ISAO helped mothers put their children in foster care. "Many people are under the impression that many biracial children were sent to the States, but it's not true," former ISAO social worker Masayo Hirata told me. In any one year, fewer than ten kids would be adopted to the United States. Most of ISAO's work was supporting families with counseling or legal aid, including to deal with the statelessness problem. Until 1985, under Japanese law, citizenship was passed down only through the father, unless he was "unknown or possesse[d] no nationality." A baby with an American father and Japanese mother was not a Japanese citizen, unless his mother was willing to immortalize in the family registry her child's status as "illegitimate." American citizenship was also hard or impossible to obtain for babies whose fathers had left, didn't report the birth to the U.S. consulate, or didn't meet a U.S. law that said an American could pass on citizenship to a baby born abroad only if the parent had lived in the United States "at least five years consecutively after age fourteen." A U.S. soldier under age nineteen didn't meet this requirement. His child born in Okinawa would legally belong to no country.

In 1979, the International Year of the Child, ISAO helped raise awareness of the statelessness problem, and journalists, attorneys, and concerned others descended on Okinawa. Masayo pointed out that in 1975, the International Year of the Woman, the public hadn't mobilized to end discriminatory practices like this nationality law. "But when it came to children, everybody got together," she said. With national and international pressure, Tokyo changed the law. "It was a big help to the women's movement," Masayo said. "Only after this nationality law was amended, legally, men and women were equal in Japan."

Another organization that helped biracial kids and their families was the Pearl S. Buck Foundation. The writer Pearl Buck, who grew up between countries and cultures in an American missionary family in China, invented the term *Amerasian* and had a passion for helping the mixed-race children she could identify with. In 1964 she established the Pearl S. Buck Foundation to aid Amerasian youth across Asia, and over the next six years opened up offices in South Korea, Okinawa, Taiwan, the Philippines, Thailand, and Vietnam. In 2008, I met the longtime director of the Pearl S. Buck Foundation office in Okinawa, which had since closed. Betty Hoffman, an older white woman with big sunglasses and a beige skirt suit, explained the foundation had paired mixed-race children with Okinawan caseworkers, who helped them obtain healthcare, counseling, and job training and placement. Children also received sponsors in the United States, who sent modest monthly stipends and letters of encouragement. The kids and sponsors established long-term relationships, with some eventually meeting, and some kids going to the United States to live. Like ISAO, the foundation wasn't an adoption agency, though; the goal was to prepare kids for lives in Okinawa. "They were strongly advised to be educated in the Japanese system," Betty said.

At its height, the foundation worked with more than four hundred kids in Okinawa. That number gradually decreased with the increasing social acceptance of biracial people. "In the early days, any child who was different would stand out and feel teased and embarrassed," Betty said. "But now it seems like young people are trying to emulate their look." She seemed to be referring to the white-Japanese beauty standard and also, maybe, to the local trend of "kokujo" women trying to look African American. Even during times of less social acceptance, kids who had done well academically had been able to climb out of poverty. Betty told foundation success stories with pride: children who had gone on to prestigious American universities and established successful careers, who lived international lives or happy, middle-class family ones in Okinawa. They were far from the tragic cases portrayed by the media.

Miyo and I fell into an easy friendship. We were the same age, and she lived half a block from where I was renting an apartment, across the street from Camp Foster. For Christmas, she invited me to the home of her father and stepmother for dinner. Her parents had divorced when she'd been an adolescent, and each had remarried and still lived on the island. She was closer to her father and stepmother, often spending time with them.

Frank and Fumi lived in a condo nearby. Holiday smells enveloped us as Frank welcomed us in: roasting turkey and onions sautéed in butter. Frank, who had just turned fifty, was a paunchy, gregarious guy wearing shorts and a red Tommy Hilfiger shirt. "I'm a short-pant man," he said. Fumi was Okinawan and in her late thirties, warm and thoughtful. The couple, who had met through work, had been married nine years.

"A relationship needs to be 50/50," Frank said as Miyo and I settled on the plush couch. "Of course I iron my own shirts—they're my clothes! It would be different if Fumi didn't work."

"He's the perfect man," Fumi said, not facetiously. She beamed.

"No such thing as perfect," Frank said.

"Don't even try, girls, to find a man like him, because you can't."

The love and affection between Frank and Fumi was obvious. They built off each other and cracked each other up.

Over dinner Frank told us how he'd come to Japan. When he was growing up, Mississippi never felt like home, mostly because of the racism he experienced as an African American boy. He knew he had to leave. "All my classmates who stayed? They're either dead or in jail now," he said. And something about Japan tugged at him. "Starting in high school, I had this fascination with Japan," he said. "I had chopsticks. In high school in Mississippi, I ate with chopsticks." Part of the allure was Yukio Kasaya, a skier in the 1972 Olympics. "He was just so cool. He got the gold medal for doing that ski-jumping thing." Like much of the world, Frank was also enthralled by a country that could pull itself out of the nuclear ashes: "They didn't stay down."

Frank first arrived in Okinawa in 1977, a security police officer in the air force. Since 1987, he'd lived on the island continuously. The place felt like home, the way some places just did. "I feel comfortable in Japan," he said. "In the States, you got to look over your shoulder all the time. Here, I don't worry about my wife or daughter being safe when they go out." He had left behind American racism, though still encountered subtle tensions in Okinawa.

"Remember that lady," Frank began, turning to Fumi, "when I used to go running down Convention Center Road?" Every evening, running along the sidewalk, Frank had encountered a local woman walking toward him. Seeing Frank, she stepped into the street until he ran by. "That used to bother me," Frank said. "And then one day she couldn't step off because there was a shitload of cars. She had to stay. So she stopped and moved to the side and stood there. When I ran by I said, 'Konbanwa.'" Frank made his voice soft, respectful. *Good evening.* "I gave her a nice smile. And she smiled back. After that when we passed she never went into the street again."

"How can you speak to people you don't even know?" Fumi asked.

"I don't want people to have negative feelings about me, even though I might not ever see them again." He didn't go on, but he implied he wanted to leave a good impression because he wanted to change their minds. He wanted Okinawans to start seeing black men in a different way. He wanted to quell their fears and disprove their stereotypes. Every minor interaction was a chance to do that.

Frank planned to stay in Okinawa, but it wasn't entirely up to him. Every three years he had to renew his spouse visa. And there was the question of the bases. "Without the bases, I ain't got a job," Frank said. "Without the bases, I got to leave." Frank managed an automotive center on base, employed by a Japanese company contracted by the U.S. military. If the bases closed, Frank would legally be able to stay in the country, since he was married to Fumi, but he wouldn't be able to earn a living, not easily. He didn't speak much Japanese. And his link to the United States would be lost. No bases would mean an end to this life that was an ideal mixture of Japan, Okinawa, and the United States.

The family, I soon learned, lived on and off base, in English and Japanese, among Americans and among islanders who'd never pass through the fences. Spending time with them, I found more of the Okinawa that resonated with me as a biracial person. Courtside at basketball games, we cheered for the Ryukyu Golden Kings, reflecting the diversity of the team, who were Okinawans, Japanese, and white and black Americans. Frank yelled in Japanese at the American visiting players, trying to throw them off their game. Miyo feigned embarrassment, and locals around us laughed. One afternoon, when I mentioned I missed American cereal, Miyo said, "Let's go get some." She drove me across the street from where we lived and signed me on to Camp Foster. Within ten minutes I was at the PX, where the shelves were stocked with familiar American-brand foods. Miyo pushed her shopping cart confidently down the aisles of browsing military families. Elsewhere on the island, in local cafés and shops, I watched her switch effortlessly between talking to me in natural English and using formal Japanese with servers and cashiers.

To me, Miyo belonged here, to this whole island. She was Okinawan. In many ways, the experiences of mixed-race Okinawans who wonder "Am I Japanese or not?" aren't so different from those of locals who also grapple with blended identities and questions of belonging. "I feel myself to be a Japanese, but the people from Japan proper did not look on Okinawans as real Japanese for a long time," a young Okinawan journalist said in 1969. "They considered us not quite Japanese, and not quite Chinese, sort of half-and-half. Many Okinawans feel they have to prove they are real Japanese, not just to the Americans but to the Japanese also." In a society of people considered "half-and-half," Miyo should have fit right in. But I knew others didn't see it that way. And for mixed American-Okinawans who didn't live in both the on- and off-base worlds, the question of belonging could be even harder to answer.

In October 2008 I walked through a residential neighborhood in Ginowan, at 8 a.m. already sweating in the humidity. I passed concrete houses and apartment buildings until I saw the sign: "we are all STARS!" above the words *AmerAsian School* in rainbow letters.

There, next to an empty lot full of weeds, was the two-story building that housed the school.

At 9 a.m. the school assembly began. Students lined up under the overhang outside, youngest to oldest. They seemed rather tough, with a defiant air. A teacher pressed play on a stereo, and on came a recording of a choir singing the school song in Japanese-accented English.

What do I see?
Happy hearts all day
All the children
Work and play every day

At first, no one sang along. Some kids mumbled, while others just stood there.

We're happy
No matter what people say
We follow our hearts.

After a verse in Japanese, the chorus began, and the kids' voices grew louder.

AmerAsian School is treasure
AmerAsian School with wonder
We're happy with who we are, Yes we are
And never will give up forever

At the next English verse ("No matter what people say / We are proud of this AmerAsian School"), their voices softened again, until the final rendition of the chorus. Then the energy swelled into something semi-inspirational, with about half the kids clapping to the beat, belting out the words. Some performed half-mockingly, twisting their mouths too big, pulling faces at one another.

In Okinawa, one of the biggest decisions for mixed-race children is where to attend school. That choice will likely determine a child's dominant language, peer group, and future on the island and beyond, charting her life course. For a long time, the choices were limited to three types of schools. First are the local Japanese-language public schools, which are free and enroll mostly "full" Okinawan and Japanese students. Second are the on-base Department of Defense Dependents Schools (DoDDS), where the instruction is in English and the curriculum is American. Free admission is granted to children of Department of Defense personnel, and many American-Okinawan kids with parents who serve in or work for the U.S. military attend. One woman, Jackie, told me that when she went to Kubasaki High School on base in the late 1980s and early 1990s, the "half" kids had been the cool clique, envied by other students, partly for their ability to navigate the off-base party scene. In that environment, Jackie had worn brown-colored contacts to hide her blue eyes because she thought she looked too white, uncool, not half-Okinawan like she was.

The third type of school is private English-language international schools, many of which are Christian. Christ the King International School operated from 1953 to 1989 and enrolled many Filipino-Okinawan students, as well as American-Okinawans and others. Okinawa Christian School International, established in 1957, still exists today and teaches a Bible-heavy, American-style curriculum. Students don't have to be Christian to attend, although the goal of the school is to convert them. The missionary teachers conduct all classes in English, except for the Japanese-language classes, which are required for all middle and high school students. Tuition is high by Okinawa standards, but lower than the DoDDS cost for non-military families. The majority of students at Okinawa Christian School International are mixed American-Okinawan.

In 1998, five Okinawan mothers of biracial children decided none of these options were suitable. At public schools, they said, their kids faced too much bullying and couldn't develop their English skills. DoDDS were too expensive if a child's parent had left the military—or his family. Okinawa Christian School International was also pricey, especially for single-parent households, and in 1997 parents were hor-

rified to learn the school's new site was a former industrial waste facility. Fed up, the women set out to create a fourth choice: the AmerAsian
School in Okinawa (AASO), an institution specifically for American-
Okinawan kids. "I'm sure we had fears, concerns," one of the founders told me. "But we felt we had no other choices. We just had to do
it." The women started their makeshift school in a leased conference
room, with just over a dozen students, then moved to a dilapidated
house nearby. Their mission was to provide a bicultural, bilingual education for their children who were not half, they said, but double.

In 2003, I spent a summer volunteering at the K–9 school, intrigued
by a place where almost all the students were mixed American and
Okinawan. It seemed like the kind of place I would have dreamed of
attending when I was a kid, hating feeling different from my mostly
white peers. Articles had praised the school as a bold solution to the
terrible situation of mixed-race kids in Okinawa. "The 48 students
have found a haven where kids who have always been different can
now be just like everyone else," *Time* magazine reported in 2000. The
New York Times indirectly quoted the school's founder and principal,
Midori Thayer, in saying the AASO "provided a nurturing atmosphere where children could learn in both English and Japanese and
did not have to feel ashamed of their dual backgrounds." Japanese-
language articles conveyed similar messages, including catchphrases
like "double education," "double pride," and "not half, but double."
"Dream School," proclaimed a national paper, the *Asahi Shimbun*,
back when students were meeting in the conference room.

By its fifth anniversary, when I first arrived, the school enrolled
sixty-two students and had moved to a larger building gifted by the
city, where it would remain. Midori Thayer told me about 70 percent
of the students had divorced parents, and about half had fathers who
had left the island. Thayer was the school's driving force and public face, helping secure funding from organizations like the United
States–Japan Foundation, the Okinawa Women's Foundation, and
the American Legion. Along with international media attention, the
AASO regularly appeared in local and national news. With pride,
Thayer told me the school had reached the point where local news

outlets regularly called her to ask if anything was going on. "Now we can choose what media coverage we want," she said. When one AASO graduate, William, told his Japanese high school classmates where he had gone to middle school, they said, "Oh, you mean the one that's on TV all the time." At the school's fifth anniversary celebration, students were unfazed by cameramen and fuzzy microphones on booms, thrust inches from their faces as they munched on pizza.

Volunteering at the school, I quickly saw its story was more complex than the one in the media. Instead of a "double" education, the school's emphasis was on teaching English. Students, teachers, administrators, and promotional materials all conveyed this message. And many students told me they hadn't chosen the AASO to escape bad situations. One white American-Okinawan middle school student named Yumi said most of her friends, including her best friend, were classmates at her former public school. She showed me pictures of them laughing, crowded into sticker photo booths. She missed them. But she had left that school and came to the AASO to learn English.

I soon realized why these kids felt pressure to learn English. On Okinawa, visibly multiracial people who don't speak English meet that set of well-worn assumptions: their fathers abandoned them. Their mothers are sex workers, amejo, or rape victims. The easiest, quickest way to dispel these stereotypes is to display English abilities, implying a different narrative: happily married parents and the close, consistent presence of an American father who passed on his native tongue. Without English, a mixed-race Okinawan is relegated to a shima hafu, an "island half," the disparaging term for a hafu who attended Japanese schools and speaks only Japanese. Thayer has noted the hit this takes on the child and his family. She writes, "If an Amerasian child goes to a Japanese school and cannot speak English, the child will be labeled an 'Illegitimate Base Child.' This is not only painful but also mortifying for the mother." University of the Ryukyus professor Naomi Noiri, who also has been instrumental in shaping the AASO, said English skills are *the* determining factor for whether an American-Okinawan is labeled positively or negatively in society. "Amerasians get lumped into two categories depending on whether they have a good command of English," she writes. With English skills, one becomes "a Double to emulate." Without the language, an American-Okinawan is reduced to "a native 'Island' Double," "a kid abandoned by an American father . . . with no ties to America."

This is the binary for American-Okinawans. On one side is the stigmatized shima hafu—monolingual, monocultural, with a single mother and sketchy life story. On the other is the enviable "Double to emulate"—bilingual, bicultural, with two married, international parents. Most mixed-race people I met alluded to this distinction, with some calling the two groups the more neutral "Okinawan halfs" and "American halfs." The implication is that you grew up either more in Okinawan society or among Americans, which usually means the U.S. military community. Your dominant language is either Japanese or English. And what decides which kind of "half" you are is the school you attended. This dynamic differs from that in mainland Japan, where, without the lingering omnipresence of U.S. military bases, a more universally positive hafu image has emerged. Mixed-race people there are more likely to be linked to the idea of cosmopolitan professionals and celebrities than GIs.

In Okinawa, some American-Okinawans have worked to subvert the shima hafu stereotype into a positive identity, choosing to master the dying Okinawan language over English. In 2009 I saw educator and entertainer Byron Figa speak at the University of the Ryukyus. He was dressed in a traditional Okinawan outfit, the top wrapped shut and clipped in place, the fabric's blue ikat pattern like paint-brushed zigzags. Byron had chiseled, handsome features that looked Caucasian, and when he came on stage speaking deep-voiced Uchinaaguchi, the Okinawan language, and played Okinawa's banjo-like instrument, the sanshin, people laughed, delighted at the contrast. He wasn't the first to play on people's expectations this way. "When you hear my name, Denny Tamaki, and see my face, you think that I am an American," writes an American-Okinawan politician in his memoir. Prior to running for local office, Tamaki worked as a popular radio host in the 1980s, switching between Japanese and Okinawan on air. "However, if you listen to me talk, I'm definitely an Okinawan. You might enjoy the gap."

During Byron's presentation, he told us, in Japanese, that his face was American, but as for English, "I don't know!" He exclaimed the English words with a heavy accent and waved his hands, playing on the sympathy of the audience members who shared the national anxiety about not knowing the language they had studied throughout school. Later, when I visited Byron at his home with a friend, I found his English skills were much better than he had let on. His performance had been an act to demonstrate that physical appearance doesn't tell you anything about a person's language or identity. Byron was tired of people asking him whether he spoke English, or complimenting his chopstick skills. He was trying to popularize a new way of seeing mixed-race people in Okinawa, including use of the term *Amerikakei Uchinanchu*, American-Okinawan. He wanted a clean label, without baggage, one people could understand right away.

Byron told us that when he was a kid, other Okinawan kids bullied him, calling him American or generic American names like Johnson, instead of using his Japanese name. By high school, he took matters into his own hands and christened himself Byron, after the middle name of James Dean. In his early twenties he moved to the United States for a couple of years, but didn't feel he belonged there. Back in Okinawa, he joined a movement to revive traditional Okinawan culture and eventually became the self-proclaimed "Mr. Okinawa." He taught others the disappearing language and connected with Okinawans in their eighties and nineties, increasingly the only ones who spoke it fluently.

Byron saw the gulf between American-Okinawans who could speak English and those who couldn't as being immense and uncrossable and crippling to those on the no-English side. He called them on- and off-base hafus, and said for a long time he had assumed those on base had no identity problems. Later, "American halfs" echoed this dynamic to me. One woman said she thought Japanese halfs were self-conscious and tried to hide their American sides, ashamed, while American halfs were well-adjusted and curious about their Japanese identities in a healthy way. A man told me he had attended a talk by Byron and learned Japanese-speaking halfs don't like English-speaking halfs. "There's some kind of rivalry going on that I was oblivious to," Mark said. "They were jealous of me because I got to live out my American side—and my Japanese side, and speak both languages. They would see kids like me on the bus and be jealous."

Talking to Byron, I started to feel like the AASO was necessary, an inevitable outcome of this situation for mixed-race people in Okinawa. With its low tuition fees, the school was trying to be a rickety bridge over that canyon, allowing the no-English kids to cross to the other side.

The problem was in the process the school inadvertently disparaged non-"double" Amerasians. As the AASO was beginning to be featured in the media, it drew the attention of local adult Amerasians, including Byron, who were moved by its cause and wanted to help. Byron and others offered their time, thinking they could serve as role models for the students. Most were quickly alienated and soon disassociated from the school, however. These adult American-Okinawans, most of whom were not bilingual or bicultural, felt the school was using them as examples of what *not* to be.

School leaders became adept at putting this dual narrative into the media—on one side the tragic Amerasian, on the other the bilingual global citizen—often for the purpose of fundraising. A school promotional brochure I came across in 2003 was titled "Trouble in Paradise . . . The Plight of the AmerAsian children in Okinawa." The children's plight, it said, was the inability of fatherless Amerasians to attend base schools. This was presented in contrast to Amerasians of two-parent households, who were seen as valuable contributors to society. "The majority of [Amerasian] children were raised in loving households," the brochure read. "They are now becoming the future bridges to East and West in our ever-globalizing society. Unfortunately some of these Amerasian children were not so lucky. Due to severe economic hardship brought on by broken marriages, many are now being treated as the cast-offs of Okinawan society." The brochure described a "typical example" of a girl whose father had "fled" to America and didn't pay child support. She was forced to attend a local public school, where she was "bullied and harassed for being 'different' . . . paying a high price in psychological trauma." "These children need your support," the brochure implored. "There are an estimated 4000 AmerAsian children in Okinawa proving that this school answers a long, unaddressed need. These children are the solution, not the problem." A photograph showed about a dozen mixed-race students sitting outside on folding chairs, unsmiling and squinting in the sun.

The notion that Japanese society is unwelcoming to racial others is important to the AASO because the school isolates the children from their Okinawan peers. In order to gain support, they must prove this type of segregation is necessary. One result has been, as AASO graduate Travis told me, students often feel well-wishers' pity. Arriving on this subject, he grew passionate. We were meeting in a McDonald's near the AASO in 2009. He had graduated years before, but spoke about the AASO in present tense. "We're getting pitied," he said. "Why are we being pitied? We're regular. We're like everyone else. Why are we being pitied? I never understood that. I'm a person, you know? And I just look like this, and people are pitying us? Thinking that we're less—or more. I think that . . . gave the wrong message." He remembered people interviewing students and saying "poor kids, poor kids." "But I never thought that way," he said. "I always thought it's a blessing that we're both, that we could speak both languages." He paused. He was nineteen, but seemed older, wearing a Bluetooth earpiece and speaking with confidence. "You know, I really thank God for all their support," he said, alluding to the school donors. But he always thought there were needier children than the AASO students—students without families or homes. Why give all those donations to mixed kids? What was the big deal? "Because we're in Japan? In the States it would be like a regular thing."

A former AASO principal, an American, told me the visibility of the school in this way was needed to make people care. He liked to use a metaphor about a girl who comes home and says, "Mom, I found the cutest kitten at the park." The girl wants to bring in the kitten, but her mom says no, she doesn't want to see it, because if she does she'll start to care. When Okinawan friends got drunk and told him they thought the AASO shouldn't exist, he responded, how many Amerasian children do you know? "It's like shutting the door before you see the kitten." He was aware of the negative side of likening kids to stray kittens. He said one of the school's biggest problems was the "ghetto effect," the "these poor kids" attitude. If you put kids on TV enough, he said, it happens. Every year at the school he had seen the ghetto effect increase. It was "an easy card to play." He remembered times they'd shut down classes to herd the kids outside, so some visiting official could talk to them. He thought the school should focus on academics, how well the students were doing, not on generating pity for them.

After establishing the kids' "plight," the AASO argued that investing in the students was investing in Okinawa's future. As the brochure described, with financial support they could become bilingual and bicultural, "the future bridges to East and West in our ever-globalizing society." They could become "the solution, not the problem." They could take on the burden of cross-cultural, international understanding, relieving larger society of the task. This idea that AASO students were linked to internationalism was successfully projected to people on the island and mainland Japan. I watched school visitors congratulate the students on being "international children" despite the reality that many had never been to the United States or even outside of Japan or Okinawa. Many did not have fluent English skills and struggled through ESL classes.

Naomi Noiri, the professor who has been credited with shaping the school's philosophy, has argued that Amerasians are also useful because they are "people who can assist Okinawans to overcome their own identity disruption." In Noiri's thinking, Okinawans should care about mixed Okinawans because they can help reveal a more nuanced, diverse picture of larger society—as opposed to the simplistic concept of Okinawans as a unified, "pure" ethnic population, the "gentle southern islanders" popularized in recent years on mainland television programs and by Tokyo-based Okinawan singers. In this way, again, the value of mixed-race people lies in what they can do to aid the majority population.

All in all, this vision of the tragic Amerasian being transformed into a useful citizen has been effective in getting people and organizations to open their pocketbooks. The school's former principal told me about some of the donations the school had received—$10,000 from the U.S. consulate, $3,000 from a singer named Coco who featured the kids in one of her songs. An Amerasian who had modeled in the seventies spent tens of thousands of dollars flying the students to the mainland and putting them up in hotels so they could visit her elephant park. One person in the community marveled at how much money the school was able to raise, and then wondered where all of it went.

As I spent time at the AASO, volunteering as a teacher in 2003 and again from 2008 to 2009, I saw it wasn't quite the mixed-person's utopia I had imagined. Aside from the problematic narratives it put forth, the school struggled with a lack of consistent funding and teachers. Many teachers were military wives who cycled in and out with their husbands' changing duty stations. I heard the first grade class had never had a teacher for more than a few months. At one point, administrators tried to pressure me to become the first grade teacher, even though I had no experience with early childhood education. According to staff members, the educators were woefully underpaid, earning a third of what teachers usually made, just "one step above volunteers." I also heard about a lot of cross-cultural misunderstandings between the local and American staff—at a place that claimed to specialize in biculturalism.

The AASO was not immune to bullying. Yumi, the student who had left her friends to attend the AASO and learn English, told me her new classmates mocked her limited English abilities, calling her dasai, or lame. They had internalized the idea that biracial people who were less than "double" were inadequate. Another middle school student, Jenny, told me a clique of older girls had bullied her at the AASO. Jenny thought these girls had been tormented by others for being half black when they were young, then took the chance to become the bullies at the AASO. Jenny said the experience, though, had made her stronger.

One big challenge came when students graduated. The AASO ended with middle school, and almost all the graduates went on to local Japanese high schools. The transition could be hard. First, students had to pass the grueling high school entrance exam, which took a load of extra studying. Yumi told me that during her last year at the AASO she crammed every day after school from four to six, then again for hours after dinner. When students passed the exam, they had to move from the sheltered "haven" of the AASO, where all the students were like them, to an all-Japanese environment. For Yumi, that shift was smooth because she had attended Japanese school before, but for others it was difficult. Travis explained that he went from knowing all his classmates to being in a school of 1,400 strangers. "Being thrown into a Japanese high school" was a "big culture shock," he said. Everything was different, and he felt "pushed around" by students who teased him, calling him an American, a foreigner, and expecting him to be more outgoing and loud, like Americans in movies. Travis didn't feel like he had a strong foundation for who he was, or that he was prepared to deal with criticism. He also felt like he didn't know how to interact with people who were different from him. When an American pastor approached Travis his freshman year, Travis gladly followed him to the church. He became a devout Christian and forged a new identity based not in race or nationality but in faith.

Looking back, Travis thought the AASO could have prepared him better. "I heard once they said they want to protect us [at the AASO] from the outer people trying to criticize us or stuff like that," he told me. "But I think maybe that's the wrong way to see it, because we're going to have to get out anyway, someday. We can't be protected by the school forever."

Betty Hoffman, the former director of the Pearl S. Buck Foundation in Okinawa, said something similar. Her one objection to the AASO was its isolation of biracial kids. "I feel isolating them . . . is an injustice to the children," she said. "I feel they should be a part of this society on a broader scale because I don't feel they're getting the best of either [American or Japanese] education this way." She thought the goal should be integration into public schools and larger society, as the Pearl S. Buck Foundation had advocated, not segregation at "a special school." "The local education is excellent and it's free. That doesn't make any sense to me," she said.

For another AASO graduate, attending a Japanese high school was difficult at first, but soon became enjoyable. William was nineteen years old and mixed Okinawan–African American. He said his first year at the high school, he fought to adjust to a totally Japanese environment, where he attracted a lot of attention from his peers. He was the only part-American at the school, and the other students regarded this as cool, a point of respect. "Everyone wanted to talk to me," he said. "I was like 'Back up off me. I'm not talking to you.' But then it got better. I made friends." Part of the reason, he thought, was because he could speak English. Even if he only spoke it with the American English teacher, everyone knew he could. "If you're in Japanese school and you don't speak English, they'll be making fun of you," he said. By William's second year he got used to speaking only Japanese and joined the basketball team. "After a while it was pretty fun."

Despite its issues, the students and staff I interviewed said they supported the AASO overall. The students had figured out how to extract what was useful for them from the school. Travis said studying English at the AASO helped him realize his "potential to go around the world. It helped me see myself as global." When I met him, he was working at an international preschool and planned to attend a bible school in Singapore. He thought if he had attended only Japanese schools he'd still be struggling with his identity "because I look like this but I only speak Japanese. . . . There would always be something battling inside." William was planning to use his dual languages in his career, first in the marine corps, then maybe as an interpreter. He had joined the marines out of high school, following his dad's footsteps, to pay for his higher education. He didn't exactly feel "double" Japanese and American. "I know I'm not Japanese when I look in the mirror," he said. Instead, he had forged his own flexible identity that suited him in different situations. One time in high school he was driving in the bus lane to avoid traffic and the police stopped him. He handed over his American license and acted like he didn't know any better. They let him off with a warning. "They're more lenient to Americans," William told me, smiling.

For Yumi, attending the AASO had been worth the extra work. She had accomplished her goal of learning English and felt her two sides, Japanese and American, were more integrated. She had used the opportunity to become more open-minded and friendly than she would have at a Japanese school. And now she could have deep conversations with her father, who before had felt like a roommate, on the other side of the language barrier. She was about to attend Okinawa International University, a school she had chosen in part because of its proximity to the AASO. Yumi planned to volunteer at her former school so she could give back and be a friend to the students, someone consistent in the midst of revolving teachers. She wanted to study marketing so she could sell Okinawan products to the world. "I like Okinawa, so I want other people to know about Okinawa," she said. She planned to live on the island forever.

Through her "lucky" combination of base school, Japanese school, and cram school, as well as her close relationship with her father, Miyo had achieved what the AASO touted—a fluency between countries. She had an impressive cultural agility, the ability to switch back and forth between the United States and Japan, between languages. But was she living the dream, riding a rainbow between cultures? It wasn't so simple. Her skills had landed her a stable job working between the off- and on-base communities, coordinating with Japanese suppliers to outfit the bases. She provided for herself and spent her disposable income on trips to the mainland, a car, her apartment. She kept in touch with local friends and made new ones who rotated through the military community. One group had been American military spouses of diverse backgrounds. "I'm the mixed one," Miyo said. "One is Japanese. One is Mexican. Two are black." They had all moved back to the States, though.

When I caught up with Miyo in 2017, nine years after I'd first met

her, she said she was restless, in need of a change. She had been taking online business classes in Japanese, but otherwise her life had
remained the same since I'd last seen her. She lived in the same apartment, worked the same job, hung out with her dad and Fumi, was still
single. Looking back on the past decade, she wondered what she had
achieved. She mused about relocating to Tokyo, using her skills in a
new setting, but hadn't taken any steps toward a move. She still didn't
feel totally a part of Okinawan or Japanese society. She said her dream
was to win the lottery and "buy an island, live on my own, and surround myself with books."

For the most part, mixed-race Okinawans who learn English and
stay on the island become involved in the bases in some way. Like
Miyo, they work in between the on- and off-base communities. Some
work in the borderlands outside the military facilities, like Mark, the
son of an Okinawan woman and Mexican American veteran. His parents ran a local chain of Mexican restaurants, which Mark took over
and revamped. He saw his taco restaurant as a place to build community, especially between the U.S. military and locals. "I'm thinking if
you can get Americans and you can get Japanese into the same building and have them brush up against each other," he told me, "that's
sometimes enough to help educate." At one monthly event he held
at his restaurant, he invited people on stage to tell a story around a
theme. If you make yourself vulnerable, Mark explained, the community becomes stronger. The theme one evening in 2017 was "kandō
shita"—"I was moved." A white serviceman talked about sitting on
the beach after work and feeling sad, though he didn't know why. He
went to Family Mart and bought cigarettes, though he didn't smoke,
and smoked one. His wife was living the civilian life in Boston. Eventually, he came to muster some feeling of a universal life force tying
everything together. A twenty-two-year-old African American woman from Louisiana told us she had never been outside the States before
coming to Okinawa. She had been so afraid. But on base she had found
a community, people who offered her and her husband money when
they couldn't pay their bills. "Pay it forward," they said. "Someone
did it for me, now I'm doing it for you." Receiving this generosity,

she sat in her living room and cried for hours, the dog looking at her funny. For the Okinawans in the audience, it was a window into the fragile human lives of those wearing the U.S. military uniforms.

Other mixed-race Okinawans helped bring together the local and U.S. military communities on base. Forty-six-year-old Hana, the daughter of an Okinawan mother and white American father, managed a large store on base. There, she was always brokering miscommunications, often stemming from the language barrier, between her military customers and local national staff. In staff meetings, she had to explain everything twice, once in English, once in Japanese. Other managers were Americans from the United States who had a harder time and relied on Hana for help. Jackie told me about one American-Okinawan friend who worked for the marine corps and liaised between the bases and Okinawan community in a very specific way. She was the only person Jackie had ever met who was truly bilingual, advanced in reading and writing both languages. She used this rare skill to smooth over crimes committed by U.S. servicemen. Jackie called her the "gomenasai" lady, the "I'm sorry" lady. "She's the one who's on TV apologizing every time there's an incident," Jackie said.

These bilingual, bicultural people weren't the tragic aftermath of deadbeat dads or rapists. They weren't exactly the "bridges to East and West in our ever-globalizing society" either. If they were helping anyone by being human bridges, they were helping the U.S. military. These hafu had surveyed the local landscape and forged the best lives for themselves, flexing ambivalent identities, establishing base-related careers. And in the process they worked to help the bases remain—not unlike many Okinawans.

9

KIKI

ON A MUGGY SPRING AFTERNOON IN 2017, KIKI DROVE ME AROUND HER workplace, Marine Corps Air Station Futenma. Kiki was Okinawan and in her late forties, with a warm smile and side-swept brown bangs. That day, she wore jeans and a gray sweatshirt decorated with turquoise ties. She worked at the chaplain's office doing administrative work and was taking a break to drive me through base. With a kind of pride, Kiki told me that access to this base was more restricted than to others. This was a rare view into a place at the center of international controversy. It was my first time on Futenma since that St. Patrick's Day with Ashley and the officers, and in the intervening eight years the dispute over the base had only grown.

Futenma has been called the most dangerous base in the world because its busy flight line is crowded on all sides by Ginowan City homes, schools, and businesses. Fighter jets and, since 2012, twin-propeller Ospreys—dubbed "widowmakers" because of their crash record—take off from Futenma and fly low over dense neighborhoods. In recent years, aircraft accidents have only narrowly avoided killing or injuring local students. In 2004, a helicopter crashed into neighboring Okinawa International University, miraculously harm-ing no one on the ground. In 2017, a helicopter window fell from the sky onto an elementary school playground bordering the base, miss-ing the nearest child by just fifteen feet. Schools hold drills in which students run to take cover from imagined U.S. military aircraft. These hazards were supposed to have ended, per the 1996 agreement to close Futenma in an attempt to calm the public after the schoolgirl rape. But for more than twenty years the agreement had been stalled because of the condition of Futenma's closure: building the new base on Oura Bay. Okinawans wanted a reduction of bases, not a relocation. Con-struction in Henoko had begun to inch along after years of protest and political gridlock, but fierce opposition still threatened to derail the project. Until the new base was built, Futenma wasn't in danger of demolition, though the protesters who set up outside its gates were reminders that some Okinawans were working to close all U.S. mili-tary bases on the island. A triumph for them would mean an end to Kiki's job.

I studied the scenery as we drove, feeling strange to be somewhere I'd spent so much time thinking about and staring at from the other side of a fence. On maps and in aerial photos, Futenma can appear small—not like sprawling Kadena, only a fraction of the size of Schwab or Hansen. It looks like a modest oval carved out of a city, maybe its smallness highlighted by the way buildings squeeze against it. But as I toured Futenma with Kiki, the base seemed enormous, infinite. The city of Ginowan was all but invisible, and, like on other bases, there was so much space. Wide parking lots harbored just a few cars. Expanses of grass unfurled between buildings. To Kiki, the spa-ciousness reminded her of when she'd lived in Los Angeles, the great sprawl of America.

An irony is that base land, in some sense, has been preserved by the U.S. military. While much of the island has become swathed in asphalt, within the fences are open spaces and protected pockets of nature. On some edges of Futenma, the base side of the fence is a thick blanket of green, alive with birds and butterflies, while the Ginowan City side is all concrete apartment buildings. People who lived on the bases as kids have reminisced to me about the magic of these over-grown areas. An American poet who resided on Kadena in the 1970s wrote that "at 6, 7, 8 years old [the base] was a tropical paradise to me." He remembered "that parts of the base were weirdly sylvan, lots of uncleared brush & forest & old fortress, lots of weird insects." An American-Okinawan woman, Jackie, who grew up on Kadena in the 1980s remembered the base as "this jungle that you could explore. It was amazing." The jungle began next to her family's house and looked impenetrable, "like this tangled mess." Jackie and her friends spent their afternoons in the trees, traveling well-worn paths carved by little feet. They played Tarzan, trying to swing on vines, forged for berries, and waded across streams that seemed like rivers. Jackie now worked on Kadena and still appreciated its vegetation. "You know why I like Kadena?" she asked me. "Kadena has beautiful trees." She said toward the middle of the base are old gajumaru trees, which are like banyan trees, with dramatic aerial roots. "Whenever [the U.S. military] gives land back, I feel like the Okinawans tear down every-thing green," she said.

"And build a mall," I added. Many bases that have closed have become shopping centers—the American Village, Rycom Mall, Shin-toshin in Naha. These commercial areas may be successes for the local economy (and for big-box stores from the mainland), but not for the environment. Parking lots and retail shops have swallowed up any natural spaces that had been left on the bases. Gazing at Futenma, with its buildings that looked like remnants from the occupation era, squat and beige, I wondered what this base would become if the politicians and protesters ever ended their stalemate. The strangest idea I'd heard was to build a Disneyland here. Some Okinawans wanted a mainland-grade amusement park to generate jobs and tourism. One anti-base demonstrator in Henoko, who was waving a sign urging protection of native animals, told me she favored a Disneyland. Would that do any-thing to save the red-footed Okinawan rail? Trading the American military for American capitalism didn't make much sense to me. Why not keep some of these natural assets?

But the wild greenery on the bases isn't as idyllic as it looks. In recent years, journalist Jon Mitchell and others have exposed the high levels of contamination found on and around U.S. military installations on Okinawa. Military documents show that hundreds of accidents have leaked contaminants like jet fuel, antifreeze, diesel, hydraulic fluid, and raw sewage into the ground, rivers, and storm drains by the thousands of gallons. Barrels of chemicals have been unearthed by Japanese builders after land has been returned. Water testing around the bases has shown unsafe levels of carcinogens, and American families have reported cancers and other serious maladies after moving to the island. But neither Japan nor the United States has made any official inquiry into the possible widespread health effects on Okinawans and U.S. military personnel that might result from these toxic chemicals seeping into the earth and waterways.

Kiki and I drove near Futenma's runway, where a big-bellied chopper hovered. I asked Kiki if it was loud working here, and she answered no, a little defensively. Noise pollution is one of the main complaints from locals around the bases; some say the sound of aircraft causes headaches and prevents students from learning and people from sleeping. But Kiki said the noise didn't bother her. She was used to it.

We arrived at the chaplain's office, located in a one-story building with fluorescent-lit hallways decorated with generic motivational posters ("Communication," "Team Work," "Vision"). In the bathroom, the faucets cried rust stains. Officials had held off on needed improvements to the base—some critical—in anticipation of tearing the whole place down. As the years ticked by and infrastructure aged, they approved some repairs despite knowing locals might see them as an admission that Futenma wasn't going anywhere.

As Kiki settled into her large office, she told me she hadn't known about on-base jobs for locals until her late thirties. As part of the Status of Forces Agreement (SOFA), the Japanese government hires and pays base workers like her, who are then supervised by U.S. military personnel. One type of full-time position known as a Master Labor Contractor (MLC) is open to permanent residents of Japan who are unconnected to the U.S. military; another, Indirect Hire Agreement (IHA), is open to permanent residents of Japan who are non–U.S. citizens. People who work as MLCs and IHAs represent a small fraction of Okinawa's workforce, and most Okinawans who secure these jobs grew up around the bases and hear about the opportunities through word of mouth. Kiki, who was born and raised in Naha, learned of this hidden world when a friend recommended she look for a job on base—because she spoke English, after taking college courses in Santa Monica, and because she was going through a divorce and needed a new career to support herself and her four kids. Kiki was able to secure a six-month temporary job on base, which turned into a permanent one, and she'd worked for the U.S. military as an MLC ever since.

Entering the base world, Kiki discovered she preferred an "American-style" workplace. The pay was good, and she could take leave whenever she wanted. She felt less stress. Japanese employers, she thought, wanted to control their workers too much. "And women always have to get drinks for men," she said. At age nineteen, she had worked part-time for the prefectural government and, along with other young women, had been expected to make tea for her co-workers. Some men asked her to do their personal errands. This rankled Kiki. Was serving tea and making bank deposits in her job description? Was using her time like that a good use of taxpayer money? She quit after six months.

"I was always uncomfortable working at a Japanese place," she said. "The woman is under the man, always, in Japanese society. Still." Although she saw younger Okinawans making progress in terms of gender equality, she thought her marriage to an Okinawan had been typical of what older women endured. Though Kiki had been working and raising four kids, her husband hadn't contributed to household work. "He didn't cook rice or anything," she said. Her frustration grew until one day she shocked him by saying she wanted a divorce.

Working on Futenma, she found that her male co-workers treated her as their equal. American couples she met seemed to practice mutual respect. "That's why I feel so comfortable here," she said. "And because I'm Christian." Kiki had been raised Christian by her great aunt, then returned to the religion after her divorce. In Japan, Christianity, with its history of persecution and small number of followers, remains on the margins, and off base Kiki felt judged for her faith. On base, she felt surrounded by people who shared her beliefs and respected all religions.

Her duties at the chaplain's office were easy: receiving phone calls, making chapel reservations. She'd had the time and energy to develop a new project that was outside her job description. Kiki was licensed to teach secondary school English, and in November 2015 she started organizing a weekly English discussion class on Futenma, bringing together locals and marines. Other U.S. military bases on the island already offered free English classes, but they were more structured, like school. Kiki's vision was to create a class that didn't feel like studying. It was informal, with no teacher or agenda. People formed their own small groups, and Kiki just supplied discussion questions, many intended to spark cross-cultural exchange. Examples were "What's Obon? Japanese folks, please explain to Americans," "Who's a better basketball player, Michael Jordan or LeBron James?" and "What was the most disgusting food you ever ate?"

The class was open to all locals, but Kiki didn't advertise it off base, fearing anti-base people would hear about it. "People who hate the bases, I don't want them to come," she said. Okinawans who attended learned about it through word of mouth, while marines saw ads about the volunteer opportunity. For locals, the class was a chance to practice English with native speakers, which might have cost 5,000 yen elsewhere. For marines, it was a chance to collect letters of appreciation, which helped them earn promotions. Some men came looking for dates—not Kiki's intention, but out of her control—and international couples had emerged from the class, including some who got engaged. Other marines, Kiki thought, just wanted to mingle with locals or practice speaking Japanese. More than anything, Kiki saw people at the class enjoying each other's company. The number of participants had been growing, moving the event to larger and larger spaces. Currently, about one hundred people—half U.S. servicemembers, half locals—showed up every Tuesday night at the Futenma U.S.O.

In addition to the English class, Kiki had started coordinating community-relations events off base. A couple of Saturdays a month, she or another staff member took marines to volunteer at local senior citizens' homes. Twenty to thirty servicemembers would spend an hour washing cars, cleaning windows, and visiting with the elderly. I asked what Okinawan war survivors thought of these American soldiers, and Kiki said it depended. Some homes didn't return her calls after saying their residents complained about Americans.

This type of extra work fulfilled Kiki. "I always wanted to be like a bridge between Americans and Japanese," she said. "I love helping people. That's my nature. So me? By doing what I want? Then I get paid? Wow, I'm lucky."

Everywhere we went on base that afternoon, Kiki greeted people cheerfully. She explained only twenty MLCs worked on Futenma, so they all knew each other, and it was "cozy." Clearly outgoing, a self-proclaimed people person, she also chatted with marines she didn't know. I saw how her personality meshed better with an American environment than a more reserved Japanese one. We stopped at a food court, where the Pizza Hut and Subway looked like any in America, except the workers were Japanese and the other customer was a man in fatigues. Kiki purchased soup and sandwiches, chatting with the cashier. Living off base and spending time with anti-base activists, I had come to see the bases as so loaded with meaning. But once I got on one, up close, it could seem so banal: the stuff of Subway sandwiches and small talk.

Later, I met with Okinawa Christian University instructor Maki Suna-gawa, who also talked to me about amejo. Maki said some of her students attended a free English conversation class on base, either the one on Futenma or another like it. Maki was twenty-seven years old and from Naha, poised and deliberate with her words. We were at the campus café, and Maki cupped her coffee. As an English-language instructor, she said, she was glad her students were practicing, but she was troubled about how the weekly experience affected their views of the bases. "It makes it hard for them to see other points," she said. They formed "really positive opinions" of the U.S. military presence and didn't want to consider other perspectives.

Maki had written her master's thesis on propaganda—papers, advertisements, videos—that the U.S. and Japanese governments as well as Okinawans produce to sway public opinion in favor of the bases, especially the new one in Henoko. The materials she analyzed touted the benefits of the new base and how marines helped Okinawan society with beach clean-ups and other volunteering gigs. "Their point is because they clean beaches once a week or once a month, and because they say hello to local Okinawans . . . they're good. They can be here," she said. Locals who consumed these media, sharing videos on Facebook and liking U.S. military posts, saw only the surface of the issue, she thought.

A military official had confirmed to me that volunteering was a strategy the marine corps used to strengthen ties with locals. "Volunteering is a huge method that we use . . . to reach out to the local community," said Herbert Corn, deputy assistant chief of staff of the region's Marine and Family program. "It's a big deal." Programs like one for single marines organized trips to visit local orphanages or clean up trash. Critics like Maki would claim these activities benefit the U.S. military more than they do the local populace, boosting the bases' image. Maki implied the free English classes on base were another calculated effort by the U.S. military to win over local opinion and keep the bases on the island.

"I met a woman who started one of those classes," I told her. The English class on Futenma was the invention and pet project not of U.S. military community-relations specialists, but of an Okinawan woman from Naha—someone with a background like Maki's. This wasn't what Maki expected. She laughed, at a loss for words.

To get another local's perspective about working on base, I met Naomi one evening in summer 2017 in a Starbucks on Route 58. We'd only previously communicated online, but she greeted me like a friend. She wore a loose black and white striped top, and her long, auburn hair was tied half up. As we settled at a table and began to talk, she maintained eye contact and smiled a lot. She was perceptive and thoughtful, having reflected at length on her experiences.

Thirty-four years old, Naomi had grown up on the island, in love with the United States after a childhood trip there. As a teenager, she took English lessons on base, and after high school she enrolled in an American community college outside Palm Springs. She spent more than seven years in California, attending school and working. After moving back to Okinawa, she knew she wanted to work in an international environment, in part to maintain her English skills, in part because she didn't think she could survive in a Japanese workplace. "I was Americanized," she said. "The way I talked, the way I thought, what I wore was completely different from the Japanese." She explored work at an international university and a beach resort on Okinawa, but those job offers hadn't clicked. The best fit seemed to be on base. So, like Kiki, she became an MLC. For the past six years, she'd worked at the U.S. Navy Hospital, doing contracts and administrative work.

Naomi said the bond was strong among MLCs in her office. Together, they formed the lowest rung of the chain of command, below American active duty and civilian personnel. Unlike the Americans, MLCs didn't cycle out every few years; they were the continuity that kept the place running. A military official, Colonel David E. Jones, implied to me that any difficulty local workers had with this setup wasn't logistical, but cultural. He trotted out generalizations about Asians I had never heard before. "I know in Asian culture you want to know somebody forever," he told me. "But every three years or so, sometimes longer, a good chunk [of base personnel] leaves . . . and it's a newness. Change is not something within Japanese culture that from my understanding is dealt with very easily. They don't like change too much."

Naomi put it another way. "We are the ones who know everything, but we don't have any authority," she said, sounding not unlike Okinawan base workers of earlier eras. "We Okinawans were placed at the bottom, yet we did the hardest work," testified one former base worker from the 1950s.

Naomi also had frustrations with the MLC pay-grade system. She said it didn't financially reward workers enough when promoted, leading to a lack of motivation for advancement. Meanwhile, she saw active duty and civilian workers benefit from more substantial pay raises, along with the promise of retirement, which Naomi also didn't have.

These inequities seemed heightened by the fact that Naomi and other MLCs like her were essential to the functioning of the bases, and not only for their continuity. Naomi was especially important in her office because of her fluency in English and Japanese and her familiarity with different cultures. "Language is the most difficult wall, I would say, because it's easy to cause misunderstanding," she said. "Sometimes one word creates bad decision-making or even can trigger [someone] to get fired." She had heard about an instance when one local said, "I'm going to kick your ass" in Okinawan to his boss. Someone translated the phrase into Japanese as "I will kill you." To avoid debacles like this, an interpreter needed to understand the cultures and languages of Okinawa, Japan, and the United States. "Three different cultures, three different languages are involved," Naomi said. In her office, Naomi was the one moderating communication to ensure no one misunderstood. The other MLCs had varying degrees of language ability, with most being weak in one of the languages. Her Filipina co-worker, for instance, was married to a Japanese national and spoke English and Tagalog but not Japanese. Naomi had to serve as her interpreter. It was difficult, essential work. "Bilingual people are the oil that makes two gears work at the same time," she said. In the on-base work environment, "without bilingual people, it's not going to operate."

Over the first four to five years on the job, Naomi had learned a sophisticated system of code-switching to thrive in her multicultural workplace. "Once I go through the fence, I become chotto, a little bit, American," she said. On base, she shifted her mindset, ready to say "no" if she meant "no" instead of the "Hmm, let me think about it" she'd use off base. She had to be ready to adjust depending on whom she was talking to, something she excelled at because of her experience living in both the United States and Okinawa. "I can imagine how they tend to think," she said of Americans and Okinawans. She knew with a local, middle-aged man who worked on base, she had to joke with him, talking to him casually, with an Okinawan accent. When she spoke to her contractor from mainland Japan, she switched to a Tokyo accent, which she'd learned from having Japanese roommates in the States. With her American supervisor, she had to use clear and professional English. If she messed up, the stakes could be high.

"If I talk to an Okinawan ojichan [grandpa] with a mainland accent, he'll block me right away. Boom! 'I don't talk to you anymore.'" If she talked to him the correct way, he treated her like family. "That's how I figured out how to survive in that environment. I like it, actually."

Any frustrations Naomi felt were outweighed by the positives of her job. Compared to local Okinawan pay, she said, hers as an MLC was better. On the mainland, that wasn't true. The U.S. military bases there were continually posting job vacancies that locals didn't want to fill. But on Okinawa, securing an MLC position was competitive. In 2003, the *Okinawa Times* reported that 550 full-time jobs on base had attracted more than 20,000 applications. In the eyes of many locals, an on-base job was prestigious and sought-after, thought to provide stability, good pay and benefits, and the gloss of internationalism.

For Naomi, working on base allowed her to express a part of herself—the English-speaking part—that she couldn't off base. "I have to speak English sometimes," she said. "I have to speak Japanese sometimes. Sometimes I mix the two languages if I want. That's who I am." Looking back on her experiences, Naomi thought it was easy to label the different roles she had played: Okinawan, international student, adult professional. But those labels didn't adequately describe her. "The inside is more difficult," she said. "I'm a blend of so many factors: Okinawa, United States, California, and on the base. . . . It's hard to categorize me right now." She thought if she hadn't gone abroad or experienced American culture, she wouldn't have been happy. "My personality fits to the American culture sometimes." She valued this flexible self she had cultivated. "My perspective changes almost every day," she said. "I'm creating my own style." She was grateful to live in Okinawa and have this chance because of the bases, unlike her study-abroad friends who had returned to mainland Japan, gone to work for Japanese companies, and lost their ties to their international lives. "As long as I'm working with the Americans, civilians and military, I'm happy," she said.

Okinawan women like Naomi and Kiki have a long history of working on the bases. In the aftermath of World War II, many local women sought on-base jobs to provide for themselves and their families. Ones who secured this work were often seen as lucky to tap into the affluence of the bases. In contrast to the still-ravaged, destitute off-base realm, the bases boasted plentiful provisions and shining domestic spaces, even when they were little more than dirt encampments of tents and Quonset huts. Ceilings were lined with electric lightbulbs, and men ate on white tablecloths. On American holidays there were feasts with shrimp cocktails, roast turkey, pumpkin pie, and tables overflowing with fresh fruit. On-base jobs as maids, clerks, typists, and restaurant servers provided women a chance to earn money, learn English, and escape into this "dream world." Entering private homes on base, Okinawan maids marveled at their employers' roomy living quarters, which were outfitted with washing machines, televisions, and stoves. "I'll never forget stepping inside that house for the first time," remembered one Okinawan woman who worked as an on-base live-in maid. "There were thick carpets, soft sofas, and big appliances everywhere. The greatest sight, though, was the stack of bath towels in the bathroom closet. Towels in every color of the rainbow!" Entering an American family's on-base home in 1955, another live-in maid wondered at the "flush toilet, shower, and running water in the house! No Okinawan had [running] water in [his] house at that time."

The types of jobs women could secure were sometimes determined by superficial reasons. U.S. military employers were known to hire women based on appearance, with the "glamourous jobs" going to Okinawans deemed more attractive. "I wanted to work at the PX, or in one of the shops or clubs on base, but those jobs were already snatched up by the really pretty girls," one Okinawan woman said. "I used to watch them heading out to work wearing lipstick and all sorts of makeup. I didn't get one of those positions on base, so I had to settle for a job as a maid." Some Okinawans, especially men, imagined that these local women, ranked by their looks and working (and sometimes living) in the homes of American servicemen and their families, were at the sexual disposal of their employers. Female base workers had to battle a stigma about their supposed virtue, sometimes becoming synonymous with those who dated GIs. They were derided as immoral "honeys" who dressed in garish clothes and were off-limits as respectable marriage material for Okinawan men.

During the occupation, there were major downsides to working on base for all Okinawans: a lack of workers' rights and constitutional protections, and a nationality hierarchy that positioned Okinawans on the bottom. Immediately after the war, Okinawans weren't even paid in money for their work cutting grass and carting supplies; they received compensation in material goods like food and clothing instead. In 1946, workers began to receive wages, but conditions still weren't fair. "In the military, Okinawans are always at the short end of the stick," Tsuneo Oshiro, who supervised other local workers on a U.S. Navy base, told the *New York Times* in 1969. "The military issues regulations and orders: you obey or lose your jobs. We receive no protection from either the Japanese, American or Okinawan Governments. And about the best you can be in the military as an Okinawan is a supervisor for several other Okinawans, like me." Oshiro acknowledged his relatively high pay—$154 a month, while Okinawans in civil service and private business earned an average of $115 a month—but he pointed out that he enjoyed no job security or opportunity for advancement. "How can you have a hope for the future when you have little chance for promotion and no security in your job and when you may be fired at any time?" he said. Another Okinawan man, who worked as an on-base electrician, recounted the abuse he endured at his job, which included "the humiliations of separate toilets, of being refused service in the military base cafeteria." He said his American boss forced him to test live wires and "kicked [him] like a dog when he refused." "I just wanted to be recognized as a human being," he said. These were the situations that caused Okinawan base employees to organize throughout the occupation, demanding fair wages, humane working conditions, and—when the U.S. military tried to suppress their organizing—the rights to bargain collectively, strike, and picket. Demonstrators faced off with U.S. military police who brandished bayonets.

But women's postwar accounts of working on base are often positive, perhaps an indication of the type of work they did and how they had more to gain, given the relatively fewer employment options off base. Women also weren't contending with crushed male egos, struggling with their military defeat. "I just didn't like being bossed around by young GIs," explained one Okinawan man, who later chose to emigrate to Bolivia. A scholar's interviews with other male emigrants to Bolivia revealed two commonalities: "(a) nearly all of them were employed at one time or another by the U.S. military bases . . . and (b) they developed a strong sense of humiliation and resentment as a result of that experience." Rather than tolerate this humiliation and resentment, the men risked emigrating to an unknown land.

Today, both men and women talk about the benefits of working on base, even if women perhaps still have more to gain due to the heightened sexism often found in local workplaces. Forty-six-year-old MLC Daisuke told me his base job had its roots in his mother's postwar employment. She worked as an on-base housekeeper, and when Daisuke was growing up he visited the other side of the fences often. "I met a lot of military personnel," he recalled. "That's why I wasn't scared of them." He remembered hanging out near an airfield, where GIs gifted him candy and he gaped at the military aircraft. From these experiences, his family formed a positive impression of the U.S. military. One of his sisters married an American serviceman, and Daisuke attended university in Illinois, then started working on base at age twenty-four after returning to Okinawa. He'd gone from an initial gig as a forklift operator to positions that ranged from administrative specialist to supply-stock control assistant at an on-base school.

"I don't have any stress," Daisuke told me, laughing. An extroverted guy, he said he hadn't experienced any culture shock working on base. "I think my whole life is like American," he said, still laughing. "I have a lot of Japanese friends, but every time I talk to them, I feel different. They are looking at me saying, you're weird." He called himself a straight talker, someone who dispensed the truth, a trait he'd picked up on base. "I've been dealing with Americans more than Japanese," he explained. Unlike Naomi, Daisuke didn't recalibrate his behavior when he drove through the base gates. With locals, he didn't engage in tatemae, what he described as the Japanese practice of hiding your true thoughts and feelings in public. His friends said he hurt people that way, but Daisuke shrugged it off, urging them to be more upfront too.

While Okinawans report many benefits to working on base— including a more open and equal culture, where men are gentlemen who wash their own dishes—some women do talk about sexual harassment, even if they don't use the term. Over dinner, my friend Miyo and her friend Sachi, who'd lived in Australia, recounted stories about American men they worked with on base. A married guy had pursued Sachi, presenting her with a pair of Marc Jacobs heels one Christmas, hoping she'd give him something in return. The women watched Americans openly cheating on their spouses, and asked me if that was American culture or military culture. Both Miyo and Sachi fielded sexual comments and sometimes unwanted touching from male co-workers. They said men only treated Japanese and Okinawan women that way because they thought Japanese women were enculturated to stay silent or brush off sexual harassment. Indeed, Miyo and Sachi didn't seem angry about the dynamics they described, but instead seemed resigned, as if that was what one had to expect when working with Americans.

Nika, an Okinawan-Filipina who'd attended international school on the island, hadn't sat by when facing sexual harassment in her on-base workplace. When an enlisted guy came in to the hardware store where she worked and made inappropriate comments, Nika dialed her manager. "I didn't want to let this go, because I hated the guy who thinks he can get away with it," she told me, and added that other local women who weren't as Westernized might not have spoken up. Her manager reported Nika's complaint to the man's boss, and the man received a warning and never returned to the store.

Women with experiences like these don't necessarily think of themselves as victims. Continuing to work on base is a decision they make after determining that the pros outweigh the cons. Nika catalogued her experiences—"juicy stuff"—to use in her graduate school research. Sachi found she preferred working on base because of what other women had cited: no unspoken rules, like in a Japanese office; more freedom; less judgment. She could talk to her boss as a peer. It was a good place to work while she prepared for her next stint abroad, this time to Cuba to study Spanish. After that, she planned to move to Mexico and work for a Japanese company there. Base work was helping her get where she wanted, which was ultimately far from the U.S. military.

A couple of weeks after meeting Kiki, I returned to Futenma to attend one of her English discussion classes. This time, walking on base in the twilight, I inhaled the scent of fresh-cut grass and felt transported to a Midwestern summer. Young guys in twos or threes strolled by. The air was warm and close; there was a tranquility to the scene, even though not far away two Ospreys hung in the sky, roaring. The change was jarring just minutes after inching through snarls of traffic on streets where I couldn't read the signs. As always, entering base, I also felt the thrill of going somewhere I wasn't really meant to be, somewhere off limits. In that way, I could imagine how locals might feel when they crossed the fence line to attend the class.

Outside the U.S.O., an elderly Okinawan taxi driver, skinny and in shades, was dumping a pile of dry cat food on the ground for two strays. A local girl who looked like she was ready for the club was talking on her phone while her marine boyfriend looked on, beaming. Inside, there was a rec room–like space with cheap carpeting, brown pleather couches, beanbags, and a couple of televisions playing sports. Locals and marines trickled in and chose their own groups, many reuniting with people they'd talked to in past weeks, others nervously meeting for the first time. They formed circles on the floor or around tall tables, and the space buzzed with chatter and laughter. The locals spanned all ages, from retired Okinawans down to a baby. The marines were almost all male, wearing jeans and button-down shirts or T-shirts. Every so often, a bored-looking Asian American serviceman in a hoodie came by with a suggested question for discussion. Snippets of conversation floated around: "I support the Oxford comma"; "Cheese, sausage, and kale." On one side of the room people played ping-pong and pool, the ping-pong ball bouncing around the room. In another area, an American named Mike was teaching an Okinawan woman how to play the sanshin. A white man with a buzz cut, Mike was a veteran and civilian worker on Futenma who helped Kiki with the class. He'd lived on the island twenty-eight years, becoming fluent in Japanese and adept at cultural traditions like the sanshin. "With the instrument, I get to teach Okinawans their own culture," he'd told me. "That really freaks them out.'"

I joined a group of four older locals, seated around a high, round table. One woman, maybe in her forties but with grayed teeth, was a divorcée from Tokyo who worked at an international university on the island. The others were Okinawans who were part of an English club: two retired women and a junior high school English teacher, a man who didn't speak much English. They showed me their textbook, which was teaching them phrases like "different strokes for different folks." They said they'd started coming on base to practice English a year earlier because there was nowhere else to go. They all lived near Futenma, in Ginowan.

Completing the circle were two young white marines. The shorter one, who had a piercing gaze, was from Redding, California, and the taller, bespectacled one was from Pennsylvania. They both had been on the island about a year, with one or two more left. Sitting with the locals, they seemed nervous and polite, even though this group met together each week. One of the retired women turned often to the marine next to her, bending her head close to his and asking him questions. She recorded his answers carefully in her notebook, looking at him with earnest respect. I wondered if that look was part of the reason these men returned week after week, along with getting their letters of appreciation.

That night, the conversation prompts were "What is the weirdest dream you ever had?" and "If you won a million dollars, what would you do? Would you donate some of it to charity?" No one shared any dreams. The marine from Redding said he would buy a Ferrari with his million dollars. The other said he would start a private defense contracting company and fight Somali pirates. The Okinawans talked about using their winnings to travel and buy or remodel homes. They listened as the marines strayed from the prompts, talking about their lives: how they loved Okinawa, where they had learned to scuba dive, which was relaxing, just like shooting—shooting at a range in the snow, all alone, that was the best. Just you and the sound of the bullet hitting the target. They talked about caves beneath the bases, rumored to be booby-trapped ("like *The Goonies*") and serving as makeshift tombs for Okinawans who had committed suicide or gotten torched with flamethrowers during the war. They talked about this lightly, but no one seemed offended. One marine recommended living in Kentucky, because it was green and mountainous and the Mississippi was as good as the ocean.

Later, a young woman who worked at a Naha travel agency joined the table and tried to teach the marines some Japanese words. They dutifully repeated them, though I could tell nothing was sticking.

When the group broke up after a couple of hours, many others were still lounging around the room, talking, the atmosphere crackling with energy. That night the class was so big it spilled into adjoining spaces. Later that month there would be a record number of participants, about 175. The popularity of the class was still growing. When I dropped by other small groups, I found they had warm atmospheres too, with no one seeming to judge one another and everyone striving to communicate. Many of the marines seemed sincere and lonely. Earlier, Mike had told me the class was a great resource for servicemembers newly arrived on the island. "They come here and have a blast," he said. "They meet new friends; they're learning Japanese as they're teaching somebody else English." They learned about local places to go, directly from Okinawans. "They wouldn't get that [information] for at least another year, probably, if they tried it on their own," Mike said. I listened as one Okinawan woman recommended a local fast food place to a marine, who said the only off-base spot he'd visited in his couple of weeks on the island was the American Village.

I chatted with one marine from Alaska who brought up the protesters outside the base. They were there every weekday, waving their signs and yelling. They were paid to do that, the marine said. They worked it just like any job, with weekends off. He said their employer was a Japanese ultra-right group that drove around in a black van flying imperial flags. I knew the van and had seen its passengers harass anti-base protesters, but he insisted they were on the same side. The black van group wanted the foreign military out, he said, and the Japanese military to rise to power again.

Before I left, I found Kiki in the eating area, hanging out with her son and daughter. During the class, she had stuck to the perimeter, looking content and proud and talking with anyone who stopped by. "I think the program thrives because of Kiki," Mike had told me. Her passion, her knowledge of both local and American cultures, and her relationships with people on and off base were instrumental to the program's success. "Without all that, something is going to break down," Mike said. When I said goodbye, Kiki hit me playfully and told me her son had decided he wanted an American girlfriend. Now he wanted to learn English and had come to the class for the first time.

Outside, I walked past the pile of cat food the taxi driver had left. A black cat bounded away, leaving the base still and deserted in the streetlights. Driving away from the gate, maneuvering my car through the low cement blocks that made you zigzag slowly, I thought about how activists would label Kiki's English class pro-base propaganda. The locals who attended the class probably did develop more positive views of the bases. Was that the result of a sophisticated hearts-and-minds campaign, or just what happens when you put people of different backgrounds together in a room and get them to talk to each other? As much as I empathized with the activists who bemoaned U.S. military propaganda, I also felt moved by what I had seen in the class. No matter the politics, wasn't it better if locals and U.S. servicemembers came to see each other as human? Wouldn't that move the debate forward in a more nuanced and productive way? As for Kiki, in doing her extra work she was certainly aligned with higher-ups in the marine corps. Whether they had explicitly told her their strategies, or she had sensed them, or she had happened to echo them and been encouraged to pursue her ideas, I didn't know. As a base worker, Kiki herself had received pro-base conditioning.

Like the English classes and community service, hiring locals to work on base is a strategic move for the U.S. military. When I spoke to him, Colonel David E. Jones acknowledged the pro-base ripple effect of Okinawan base workers: "All of the Okinawan and Japanese who work here on the bases take their positive interactions back home into their communities and say, 'Hey, I work there. This is what goes on.'" One thirty-five-year-old Okinawan secretary, discussing the U.S. military presence, described how her employment had changed her views. "I have to admit that my remarks might be biased because I work on base," she said. "It's probably easy to be brainwashed by working there." She cited everyday conditioning like having to stand when the American flag was raised or lowered and working beneath photographs of the U.S. president and military officials. "Those sorts of things remind me that I work on a U.S. base and probably shouldn't criticize the American presence here," she said. "But, I try not to be influenced by such things. I mean, I could easily be affected the opposite way by reading the local newspapers here, which are critical of the bases."

The supposed anti-base biases of the two local newspapers, the *Okinawa Times* and the *Ryukyu Shimpo*, were favorite subjects of the Okinawan base workers I met. When I brought up this sentiment to Tomokazu Takamine, the former president of the *Ryukyu Shimpo* and a longtime reporter, he said U.S. military accidents and crimes weren't a topic they wrote about by choice. Ever since Takamine started reporting in 1970, he said, he wanted to tell stories of ordinary Okinawans unconnected to the U.S. military—stories of fishermen, farmers. When he became an editor he had the same desire to publish happy stories about Okinawa's beautiful nature and culture. But he rarely got the chance, he said, because crimes, accidents, and issues associated with the U.S. military or the Japanese Self-Defense Forces were constantly happening, taking precedence in the news cycle. Takamine and his colleagues prioritized these stories because of public demand and their larger political and historical implications. At the same time, Takamine said he used to drink with U.S. military officials, his frequent interview subjects. At his wedding, American servicemen had celebrated alongside Okinawan members of radical leftist groups. Takamine's son, Chota, also a journalist, told me he couldn't imagine such friendships existing between Okinawan reporters and American military officials in the current climate. The situation had become much more polarized.

I did hear one generous view of the local media on base, from Rebecca Garcia, a marine corps public affairs director. She pointed out that the media everywhere tends to report on bad news more than good. "I don't necessarily believe they're against us," she told me. "When it comes to news, if it bleeds it leads, right? . . . What's more exciting? Hearing about the DUI or hearing about a beach cleanup?" The consensus among those who worked on base, though, seemed to be that the papers exaggerated any crimes or accidents committed by American servicemembers on the island, in order to incite anti-base sentiment, while downplaying incidents involving locals. The newspapers gave the impression that everyone in Okinawa was against the U.S. military presence, they told me. "That's bogus, man. That's bullshit," Daisuke said. "The U.S. military is part of our Okinawan society." He thought the local newspapers were playing a political game and had stopped reading them five years earlier.

Kiki also didn't trust the local papers and explicitly worked against the image she saw in them, that "Americans are very mean and of course evil or something," as she put it. To plant in locals' minds another picture, she agreed to host a couple of Futenma tours for elementary school students and their parents. Unlike the Okinawans who came to the English class, these families didn't have a prior interest in English or Americans. She thought they came scared of the base, linking it to war. "But no, very pleasant people work here," Kiki said. After they saw that, meeting friendly base workers, with Kiki acting as their interpreter and guide, their image of the U.S. military changed. She transmitted their positive feedback to the colonel, who was thrilled. "I try my best to help make a good relationship between America and Japan by doing these things," she said.

After Rina Shimabukuro's murder, Kiki redoubled her efforts, leading marines on off-base volunteer excursions to combat the articles in the newspapers. "Last year was very bad," she said. "The Okinawan newspapers tried to find any small incident and make it bigger." She cited cases of Americans drunk driving as an example—"small stuff."

In that atmosphere, post-murder, the base community had to keep a low profile, but Kiki continued her work. "I still had to keep doing the same thing, like I do, to make the image better and better."

In this way, Kiki was in direct opposition to other Okinawans whose mission was to expose a negative view of the bases. These were the anti-base activists trying to stop construction of the new base in Henoko and, ultimately, close all bases on the island. But Kiki didn't believe they were Okinawan. Like others on base, she believed the protesters outside the Futenma gates were paid employees from other places. Daisuke told me they came from the Japanese mainland and from South Korea, where people hadn't forgotten Japan's colonial rule. "Our people are really fed up with it," he said. He explained why he thought Okinawans weren't protesting outside the gates: "Most Okinawans are laid back. They are quiet. We don't do that. Because we have a history. We've been working with the Americans over seventy years." Kiki told me the protesters were violent and attacked small American children, cursing at them. "I always try not to look at them," she said. The demonstrators left her alone when she drove through the gates because of her Japanese license plates, but harassed the "Yankee" plates. She felt bad for those Americans because they were individuals who were incapable of controlling the outcome of international geopolitics. "None of us has the right to change anything, right?" she said. She thought the protesters should gather outside the Japanese Self-Defense Forces offices, not the U.S. bases. "They are not smart, I think," she said, chuckling.

Kiki echoed what Daisuke had told me about friendly, laid-back natives. "Not so many people show hate to American people," she said, "because Okinawan people are very friendly. People who do the protest? Most of them are not from Okinawa, but from the mainland or hired from other countries. Like Taiwan or I don't know, Chinese, or something like that." She laughed.

I understood why Kiki wanted to promulgate a positive image of the bases. She loved and needed her job and didn't want to lose it. She genuinely liked her co-workers and U.S. servicemembers and thought more locals should see they were good people. But in Kiki's stance toward the protesters I saw a great irony. She spent so much time working to bring together locals and U.S. servicemembers so they could move past stereotypes and know each other as individuals. But she wasn't doing the same with her fellow Okinawans outside the base gates.

Naomi was different. Unlike Kiki and Daisuke, she couldn't imagine the protesters as mercenary foreigners. Naomi knew anti-base protesters. They were members of her family. Naomi's whole family, except her, was against the U.S. military presence and sometimes protested in Naha or outside the base gates. Her parents had tried to stop her from working on base. "They don't like it because of the political reasons, historical reasons," she said. Sometimes her aunt joked about seeing Naomi at the Camp Schwab gate, where her aunt went to demonstrate and Naomi went for work. "It's half joke, but half serious," Naomi told me. Like military spouse Arisa had described, passing the protesters outside Camp Schwab, where the most intense protest had been taking place, roiled in Naomi complex emotions because of her blended identity. "I have to go there as a representative of the naval hospital," she said. "But I am Okinawan. So it's really difficult. I was scared at first, but now it's more sad."

Men similar to her grandfather demonstrated outside the gates, she told me. They waved signs that read, "Get out of Okinawa." "They don't say it to me, but I feel like I'm their enemy," she said. Without locals like Naomi, the bases would suffer—how would they function?—and Naomi was afraid the protesters would figure that out and come after her. Whenever she drove by them, she donned big sunglasses, sometimes a face mask. If they saw her features, she feared, they might recognize her at the grocery store and confront her.

She hated seeing Okinawans fight each other like this, in conflict over the U.S. military presence. When she saw protesters who could have been her grandparents outside her workplace, she thought about what larger powers had gotten them into that position. "It makes me think we were forced to fight each other for somebody's gain," she said, and implied that somebody was the U.S. and Japanese governments.

10

CHIE

ON A BAY AS FLAT AND GRAY AS THE SKY, CHIE MIYAGI PADDLED OUT to confront the United States and Japan. It was a cold February morning in 2017, eight years after Chie had taken me to a cave where schoolgirls like her mother, Sachiko, had toiled as nurses during the war. Now fifty-eight years old, Chie was still a local high school English teacher and peace activist known for her extroversion, individuality, and collection of rainbow outfits and fake flowers she tucked into her hair. Her English nickname was Sunshine. On Oura Bay, her highlighter-pink jacket and neon-orange kayak were bursts of color, while the other eight kayakers with her were dressed in black. All nine had concealed their faces with hats, sunglasses, and bandanas. Together, they represented a range of ages and backgrounds: those who were young and those who were retired, those who were Okinawan and those who were from mainland Japan. "We were born in different places, and we have different jobs," Chie said. "But our goal is one: we will protect Oura Bay."

The group was called Henoko Blue, and they did this regularly, paddling to where the new mammoth U.S. military base was being built, in a district of Nago called Henoko on the eastern coast. The construction site was the bay, which was—for the moment at least—gorgeous and biologically diverse, home to coral-reef ecosystems and the endangered Okinawa dugong, a revered, manatee-like creature that grazed on rare seagrass. The U.S. military wanted to fill in the bay with 21 million cubic meters of rocks, sand, and gravel and build a double-runway, state-of-the-art behemoth. The landfill work had resumed recently after a hiatus, with the crew drilling for survey work and dropping concrete blocks into the water. Henoko Blue's mission for the day was to stop or slow any scheduled construction. Chie's larger mission was to end the U.S. military presence in Okinawa. She, like the other kayakers, was willing to risk her life to achieve it.

I had seen the bay from a lookout point on a bluff nearby. Oura Bay was glittering teal and sapphire, with little rugged islands at its mouth. The construction zone jutted out from the small cape on its south side. After the war, the U.S. military turned the cape into an internment camp for thousands of Okinawan civilians. In 1957 they began building a marine corps base there, Camp Schwab, which still occupies the small peninsula with its drab buildings. Off the coast, ominous-looking ships loaded with equipment for drilling, dredging, and building were anchored, guarded by concentric rings of defense. While Chie and the other kayakers wanted to protect the bay's flora and fauna, another, much larger and better-financed group had been hired to protect the construction site. Every day was a showdown between these guardians on the water.

The innermost ring defending the construction area was the Japanese Coast Guard and the Okinawa Defense Bureau (ODB), the local arm of the Japanese Ministry of Defense. The ODB were the ones charged with building the base, while the coast guard served as the muscle to patrol the site. I was surprised to learn the U.S. military had no presence at the scene, able to stay out of the fray. The ODB and coast guard deployed speedboats that stayed mostly within the next ring, a system of rigged-together orange buoys. Little white monitor boats, about seven of them, were anchored farther out, forming the first line of defense and delineating the exclusion zone.

An activist had explained to me the monitors were local fishermen, paid $500 a day by the Japanese government to stand watch over the bay instead of catching fish. The local fishing cooperative had caved to Tokyo a few years earlier, giving up their fishing rights in exchange for compensation.

Chie had told me the ODB were local people, just like many of the protesters, and sometimes they connected and joked around on the water. But with time the interactions had grown tenser. "The Japanese and U.S. governments want us Okinawan people to be divided and criticize each other," she said. As for the coast guard, she said it used to be neutral, but under the administration of Shinzo Abe—who was committed to fulfilling the wishes of the United States and willing to use more strong-armed tactics against the demonstrators—the organization had been deployed to side with Tokyo. Officials had realized Okinawan coast guard members were more congenial toward the protesters and had begun replacing them with ones from the mainland. Chie said the mainlanders were the ones she couldn't joke with, who weren't sympathetic, who sometimes got violent.

Lately, protesting had grown more dangerous for Henoko Blue. Members of the coast guard had held protesters' faces in the water, choked necks, flipped kayaks. Men and women said they'd almost drowned, they'd thought they were going to die when someone from the coast guard held their faces beneath the surface. When I asked one of the female kayakers if she had experienced violence, she laughed. "Of course!" she said. Sometimes, Chie said, the coast guard would haul the activists onto their boat and keep them there for long stretches of time. Once, too many coast guard members boarded the activists' Peace Boat and caused it to capsize. The captain got trapped underneath the boat and struggled to swim out. Another time, as retribution for Chie's filming them, men had taken her and her kayak far out toward the mouth of the bay. She'd pleaded with them to stop, saying she wasn't sure if she could paddle back, she might get lost, she might die. They ignored her and left her there. Terrified, she somehow made it back to shore.

Because of this, Chie was always armed with her camera or cell phone, ready to document what happened. Once, she filmed a particularly brutal incident of a Japanese coast guard member choking a young male activist. In the video, a man in a black wetsuit and white helmet with a camera strapped to it grabs the other man by the throat, forcing his head back. The coast guard member kneels over the slumped man and screams in his face, their noses an inch apart. Chie and another female kayaker entreat him to back off, Chie's friend wailing and Chie repeating, "Please stop." The camera goes askew, and we see another man grab Chie, in her pink windbreaker, by her arm. She sent the video to a newspaper, which published it, saying the injured man had needed two weeks to heal. "We worried he was going to kill him," Chie said.

No one knew what this February morning would bring: more violence or relative peace. As Chie paddled out, I boarded the Peace Boat, an old fishing boat that always accompanied the kayakers. We'd meet them on the water. The Peace Boat's captain was an elderly Nago native and legal consultant who helmed the boat to protest three times a week. A fourth day of the week, he demonstrated outside Camp Schwab. Another older man on board was a sociology professor from Tokyo who had been studying the Henoko protest for thirteen years. He was about to retire and live full-time in Nago. The other two passengers were young photographers from the two local newspapers. They settled in at the bow of the boat with their telephoto lenses, ready to capture any clashes that happened.

The temperature was in the fifties, and the two older men stuck heating packs to their stomachs under their jackets. In the bay, the Peace Boat gunned for the orange buoys, passing the hired fishermen and moving straight into the first ring of the off-limits zone. Immediately, someone on a monitor boat started yelling into his microphone for us to leave. I tensed, knowing we had become vulnerable, but the captain and professor ignored them.

The boat rammed into the orange buoy system. Up close, I saw how treacherous it was. Every third or fourth buoy was outfitted with two metal rods that slanted out like TV antennas. Chie later described the danger of those rods, how when the sea moved, they could maim a boat, a kayak, a person. Strung between the rods were ropes, another barrier. These rods and ropes had been installed after kayakers had kept slipping past the buoys. The rods knocked against the side of the Peace Boat. The professor went to the edge and unknotted a red and yellow banner from the ropes. A week before, activists had held a large land and sea demonstration here, with three hundred people on the beach cheering on eighty who took to the water. To the buoy system they had tied banners proclaiming "Stop submerging blocks" and "Protect the beautiful sea." They had yelled in concert when a crane dropped concrete into the bay.

The banner had gotten waterlogged and twisted, and the professor hauled the dripping mass into the boat. The captain got on his microphone and broadcast a message to the ODB, who was now watching from the deck of a gray trawler on the other side of the buoys and yelling into their own PA system. Dressed in dark uniforms, the ODB guards were faceless behind white masks and sunglasses. The Peace Boat captain explained they were removing something that wasn't supposed to be there, and the guards backed off for the moment. There's one more, the captain said, and when we pulled up alongside it and one of the photographers moved to help, the captain said better let Sensei do it—they're filming us, and you're shimpo-san, a newspaper man.

The guards had been filming us from the start. All along the borders around Camp Schwab, where the demonstrators and guards face off, cameras are a constant weapon. Each side keeps lenses trained on the other—the activists waiting for the guards to become violent or spit slurs, the guards waiting for the activists to break the law or reveal their faces. The ODB had all the demonstrators' photos, Chie told me, and had figured out the identity of each. Through the U.S. Freedom of Information Act, journalist Jon Mitchell had found the U.S. military was also compiling and distributing intelligence reports on organizations and individuals engaged in anti-base protest and on reporters covering it, including Mitchell. Critics questioned whether this type of surveillance outside the jurisdiction of the bases was legal.

The coast guard approached the Peace Boat in a black speedboat, looking menacing. The men and women wore all black, outfitted for a tumble overboard: wetsuits and snorkel gear, gloves, bandanas that covered everything but their eyes. One had her camera trained on us, but the Peace Boat captain said something to a male guard, and he motioned for her to stop filming. There was a convivial exchange between the captain and other man, the only one I'd see all morning.

Next, we were speeding along the buoys to the north end of the bay, where green cliffs rose above a narrow beach. When an ODB guard shouted at us to leave, his voice echoed off the rock, making it sound like we were surrounded. In fact, a guard in black materialized on the shore as well. He yelled into a megaphone, the angry voices bouncing around, amplified.

We turned and followed the orange buoys in the other direction. Wherever the Peace Boat went, the ODB mirrored its movements from inside the buoys. At the end of the cape, we motored past craggy islets and joined the kayakers in the shallow waters on the other side. Chie and the others were floating there, holding on to the buoy system and staring down a fleet of guards who were droning on about leaving the area and not touching the "floats" for their own safety. The professor dropped anchor. The boat's rainbow peace flag snapped in the wind. The captain played music from his phone into the microphone, broadcasting to everyone. Light, twangy Okinawan tunes drowned out the monotone of the uniforms reading their script. The cheery, traditional music did the trick of drawing out the poignancy of the scene—of the construction equipment already beginning to foul this breathtaking bay, of these Okinawans battling each other in someone else's war.

A cover of "Blowin' in the Wind" began, the singer mixing Japanese lyrics with the English. The captain sang along into the microphone. Over the edge of the boat I could see straight to the sea floor, which looked aquamarine, marbled with shadows. "The ocean is beautiful," offered the captain in English. As activists point out, Oura Bay is a thriving marine ecosystem that supports a vast array of creatures—coral, fish, crabs, sea turtles, and of course the dugong. The slow, gentle mammal was revered in the era of the Ryukyu Kingdom, its meat seen as the "elixir of life" (not helping its population numbers). This bay was the only place left in the region where dugong could feed on seagrass; already, there were maybe only a handful left. With the construction, they'd surely be wiped out.

Chie paddled over and hung off the side of the Peace Boat. "We feel like the Japanese constitution doesn't apply to us," she told me, alluding to their right to peaceful assembly. "Security is more important to them."

The faceoff continued, everyone floating to the music. The guards never let up on their demands to leave, but didn't make any moves toward the kayakers or Peace Boat. Henoko Blue was waiting to see if any action would happen—if the construction crews were going to drop any blocks that day. If so, the kayakers might enter the innermost ring and try to stop them, which would be when the guards would intervene. Eventually, the group realized it didn't look like any construction work was scheduled and took off for one more lap around the buoys. Again, the ODB tracked the protesters, yelling. At the beach, more than a dozen black figures had collected on the rocks. Seeing us, they scrambled toward the water, screaming into megaphones that we were in an off-limits area, it was dangerous, get out immediately. The captain and kayakers yelled back. "Let's protect Oura Bay together!" Chie shouted.

The modern-day plan to build a base at Henoko started in the aftermath of the 1995 rape, when the United States and Japan agreed to close Air Station Futenma on the condition of "moving" it to a less populated area of the island. The roots of the Henoko plan, however, stretch back further. The U.S. military began eyeing the bay, with its remote location and deep waters ideal for aircraft carriers, as early as 1966, when the U.S. Navy drew up plans for an "all-weather, jet-capable" airfield and port there. But with the United States occupying the island, Washington would have had to fund the project—hard to make happen during the ballooning costs of the Vietnam War. The Henoko plan was tabled for thirty years, until the political and financial opportunity came to revive it. In the post-1995 bilateral negotiations, Japan agreed to foot the bill for the new land, sea, and air base, which would be a giant upgrade from aging, landlocked Futenma. Construction was estimated at $10 billion.

As long as the United States and Japan have made clear their intention to build the base, local politicians and activists have opposed it, along with something like 80 percent of Okinawans, according to various polls. Municipal, prefectural, and even federal government opposition has risen and fallen with elections and political dealings, but since 1997 Okinawan citizens have established their presence near the construction site, organizing, demonstrating, staking tents that turned into more lasting structures, waging a sit-in, and trying to physically block the movement of transport trucks with their bodies. When construction workers tried to circumvent the sit-in by embarking on boats from Camp Schwab, activists met them there, on the water. At times, the men and women manned a round-the-clock presence around scaffolding erected in the bay for drilling; some chained themselves to the structures in protest. Tens of thousands of people took part in these early efforts in Henoko, which succeeded in catching Tokyo's attention. In 2005, Prime Minister Junichiro Koizumi announced the central government "was unable to implement the relocation because of a lot of opposition."

Before long, however, the Japanese and U.S. governments were back at it, armed with a new base design that centered the construction in the water off Camp Schwab, making it harder for protesters to access and requiring tons of trucked-in material to create "reclaimed land," to the delight of the gravel industry. The activists continued their sit-in. In the coming years, Japanese and U.S. lawmakers parried back and forth on the details of their plan, while Okinawans maintained their vigil outside Camp Schwab.

In mainland Japan, protests over the new base also took place, though not in the same focused, sustained way. The issue was often a presence—in signs, in speeches—at other rallies, such as ones against the central government or nuclear power. "Any protest rally I've been to in Japan in the last eight, nine years I've seen people speaking about Okinawa and Henoko," Dustin Wright told me in 2018. Wright was a historian who had researched anti-base movements on the mainland. He said there the Henoko issue was largely forgotten after the 1996 post-rape agreement seemed to settle the issue—until 2009, when Prime Minister Yukio Hatoyama brought the issue back into the national spotlight. Like Obama the year before, Hatoyama had run on a platform of change. Since 1955, the Liberal Democratic Party (LDP) had ruled the country almost without interruption, and Hatoyama and the Democratic Party of Japan offered a revolutionary vision for U.S.–Japan policy. To the alarm of Washington, Hatoyama advocated for a more "equal" relationship between the two countries and called for the new base in Henoko to be relocated "at least outside of Okinawa, if not outside the country." When the Democratic Party won the 2009 election in a historic upset, activists in Okinawa celebrated, hopeful that change was on its way. Once Hatoyama became prime minister, however, Washington succeeded in pressuring him and his administration to maintain the status quo and accept U.S. demands. After only eight months in office, Hatoyama signed an agreement accepting the Henoko plan and resigned in shame, saying he had failed.

In local Okinawa politics, what ignited a new round of protest was when then–Okinawa governor Hirokazu Nakaima reneged on his 2010 campaign pledge to build the new base outside the prefecture. In 2012, the LDP regained power and Shinzo Abe became prime minister, vowing to restore the U.S.–Japan relationship that Hatoyama had tried to shake up. This included getting the Henoko base plan back on track. In late 2013, Tokyo agreed to increase its economic subsidies to Okinawa by 15 percent, and Nakaima agreed to reverse course. The governor granted the federal government approval to begin landfill work in Oura Bay. Chie Miyagi, along with many others, was outraged. That December, she joined a crowd outside Nakaima's house, demonstrating against his betrayal of the voters' wishes. After that, Chie didn't stop. She started protesting outside the Schwab gate in Henoko and signed up for a kayaking class, then began protesting on the water. At times, when the land demonstration heated up, she left home at 5 a.m. for the hour's drive north and joined the group outside the gates. The more bodies there, the more likely they were to stop the construction trucks from entering the base. After protesting, she'd drive south to school for a twelve- to fourteen-hour work day.

In 2014, voters ousted Governor Nakaima for his flip-flop and elected Takeshi Onaga on his anti-base platform, along with a Nago mayor and other local politicians who were also against the Henoko base. This became the most concrete proof that the majority of Okinawans stood behind reducing or eliminating the U.S. military presence— even if they didn't march outside bases with protest signs. The next year, Governor Onaga ordered the ODB to stop its work in Oura Bay. The ODB disregarded him, kicking off a protracted legal showdown between Okinawa and Tokyo. "We will use every means available to us to prevent a new base from being built in Henoko," Onaga declared. At the end of 2016, he suffered a blow when the Japanese Supreme Court sided with the central government and ruled Onaga couldn't revoke the permission Nakaima had granted. Onaga pushed on, taking his campaign to the United States and seeking other legal means to stop the construction. But by the time I visited Oura Bay in 2017, nothing the governor had done had worked, and the fate of the bay seemed to be in the hands of these scrappy kayakers and the mostly elderly men and women who camped outside Schwab's gates.

After their morning on the bay, the Henoko Blue members retreated to their nearby headquarters. They hadn't intervened in any construction, but maybe their presence had been a deterrent. And no one had gotten injured: a successful day.

That afternoon, Chie took me to a tent near the beach that was one of the movement's public protest structures. Inside, the walls were covered with yellowed newspaper articles, photos, and charts, along with colorful strands of origami peace cranes and origami dugong. A sign announced the sit-in had been going on for 4,696 days.

Outside the tent, walking along a terraced sea wall, we came upon a group of about ten marines. Chie instantly engaged them. "You look so young," she said. They regarded her with amusement. At that point, she was dressed in a T-shirt and tutu that were both bright pink, along with maroon pants and a white flower pinned in her black bob.

"You look so young," shot back one of the marines, and she laughed.

"That was good," she said, and they high-fived. Everyone was smiling. She asked if they were eighteen, and they said twenty-one. She repeated that they looked so young.

The men were on a training tour, they said, rotating through different international locations. They never knew where they'd be next. They'd been at Camp Schwab about a week, and this was their first day off when they could venture off base. They had no cell-phone data and seemed culture shocked and desperate for something to happen. They were looking for a restaurant called Oceans, but were clearly off track.

Chie went into the tent to ask about Oceans. A Latino marine asked me in a low voice, "Are these protesters?" I told him yes, but not to worry. They didn't hate Americans. He still seemed nervous, but also eager to talk. After Chie returned and described where the restaurant was, the marines thanked her but didn't leave. It was about 1:30 p.m., and Oceans didn't open until five. The men said they'd heard of three restaurants they could go to in town and had already eaten at one that day. The townsperson there had been nice, welcoming them and presenting them with lots of food. I'd driven through Henoko and seen how empty and economically depressed it seemed. I imagined how grateful a restaurant owner might be to have ten hungry young men stroll in.

Chie addressed the marines like her students, as they stood before her in a semi-circle. "Your lives are precious," she told them. "Make sure you stay safe. Don't go to the battlefield." The muscled marines with baby faces nodded politely and said they wouldn't, they wanted to stay safe.

She asked one if he liked nature, then told him she was trying to protect the bay. She asked others why they had joined the military and listened as one talked about the economy.

"I'm sorry to hear about that Osprey that went down," she said. "Was everyone okay?"

The men looked confused. They had just arrived, and most hadn't heard about the accident. The activists had been using it as proof of the danger of Ospreys, of the loss of life that could happen if one crashed not into the sea but into a town.

The marines assured Chie they were okay. As a group, they seemed searching, looking for some kind of guidance or approval from Chie. They answered more of her questions.

"Do you like to kayak?" Chie asked. "Have you kayaked in the bay and seen the beautiful fish?"

Oblivious of what was going on outside their base, the aquatic confrontations that happened daily, the men said yes, they liked to kayak. Maybe they'd go out kayaking tomorrow.

At the school where Chie taught, her colleagues joked about needing sunglasses to look at her. They quipped that next week she would come dressed as Cleopatra. Or the Sphinx. Or a pyramid. Chie didn't mind. She wore whatever she wanted. The photographer Mao Ishikawa, who had documented Okinawan bargirls and Filipina hostesses, had singled out Chie because of this quality, asking to take her picture. Mao saw Chie as a symbol of Okinawa, free-spirited and vibrant, in contrast to conformist mainland Japan. While many other Okinawans who shared Chie's individualistic and outgoing nature had gravitated toward the bases for their window into American culture, Chie had forged her own path within Okinawan society. Two photos of her appear in Mao's work. In one, Chie is teaching her students, who are wearing their navy-colored uniforms, while she's dressed in an orange cardigan over a green sequined top, combined with a red tutu and orange leggings. In another, she is with her niece Yoshi, a graduate student focusing on the preservation of Okinawan languages. The two of them are wearing colorful garb in a field of sunflowers, strumming the sanshin and belting out Okinawan songs.

Chie was constantly trying to get her students to feel proud of their Okinawan identities instead of looking to the mainland for standards of beauty and culture. She denounced what she saw as an attack on Okinawa through Japanese cultural assimilation. She hated how young Okinawans idolized mainland celebrities, like the giant pop group of dolled-up, light-skinned waifs, AKB48. "You are much cuter than those girls," she told her students. She dreamed of an Okinawan broadcasting company that would promote local language and culture instead of mainland media imports.

As a result of her outfits and outspokenness, Chie was a well-known figure around the island. She was often light and silly, even when engaged in serious things. At a talk, she was the one to shoot up her hand to ask a question. She never seemed to run out of energy—zipping from engagement to engagement in her yellow car—until suddenly she did. Sometimes, driving, she would start to fall asleep and ask me to swap seats and take the wheel. After a ten-minute nap, she'd be revived, ready to hit the next event or stop by the next friend's house.

"I'm always trying to become friends with people," she told me. This was her own tactic to stop construction of the new base. She sought to engage on a personal level with the guards who patrolled Oura Bay and the Schwab gate. She wanted to make them see her and other activists as human, to connect with them and nudge them toward glimpsing her point of view. She wanted to win the battle individual by individual, not through intimidation or shame but through empathy.

This was easier to achieve when the guards were Okinawan. The first time she went to protest in a kayak, she and four other Henoko Blue members decided to swim inside the exclusion zone. They tied their kayaks to the buoys and jumped in, the water a relief from the summer heat. At first, they swam unbothered. Then three to four coast guard vessels arrived, and the men physically hauled the swimmers out of the water and onto one of their ships. On board, they split up the activists and interrogated each separately. Chie could tell the other Henoko Blue members were frightened. "But I was having fun," she said. Because of her curious nature, she wanted to explore the ship and talk with the two guards assigned to her. They were both Okinawan, so making the connection was easy. They seemed sympathetic to her cause and spoke to her in native Okinawan. They were kind. When she asked for a jacket, they gave her one. Still, she didn't comply with their orders. She gave a false name and said she was a dancer who performed at parties and weddings. They asked her to promise to never enter the restricted area again, and she refused. When the construction stopped, she would stop, she told them. They asked her to write a state-ment, and she wrote, "We shall overcome. We will never give up."

At other times, she'd chat with Okinawan coast guard members on the water. She told one she was an opera singer, and he asked her to sing a tune. "You're not very good," he joked after hearing her. Another day, she belted out a song and a local guard on a nearby boat danced along.

When Chie managed to talk to mainland guards, the conversations were more serious. "You are here to protect nature and our lives," she told them. "You are not here to destroy nature and our lives. Stop doing this." On land, outside the gate, activists and riot police got physically closer, creating more chances for communication. Chie ini-tiated philosophical discussions, asking them to think about what was right. *We don't have guns or weapons, but so many people come from the Japanese mainland to serve as police,* she'd say. *See what the Japanese government does to us. Next election, please think about this when you vote for the prime minister.* She asked them to learn Okinawan history. *If you know, you will understand.* Many times, the men remained silent, but sometimes she could tell she'd gotten through. She said once she had a conversation with a guard just with their eyes. He told her he was sympathetic with his eyes. Others cried. They tipped their heads toward the sky to hold back tears.

The men sent from the mainland to stand at the Henoko gates were young, and Chie felt sorry for them. Some protesters yelled "Shame on you!" but Chie never engaged in that kind of talk. "They are pure," she said. Like the marines, they were there to do a job.

Some police, however, she could never reach. No matter what she said, they stood there, stone-faced. She remembered one contingent from Osaka who were like robots. They struck in her a rare seed of fear. They didn't seem human, and they didn't seem to respect Okinawans as human, either. They saw Okinawans as primitive, as Others. Activ-ists got proof of this when mainland riot police were recorded calling protesters "dojin," a slur meaning something like "dirty native," and "shinajin," a derogatory name for a Chinese person, like "Chink." Many activists felt like these comments exemplified the whole thing, how mainlanders had been seeing Okinawans as less-than all along. The Japanese had taken over their kingdom, erased their culture, sacrificed them in war, stolen their land, and now were grabbing more of the island using these uniformed young men.

Men and women demonstrated at Henoko for different reasons: to protect the environment, to prevent sexual violence, to stop the noise and accidents and toxic waste that bled from the bases, to promote demilitarization, to fight for democracy. Some protesters were motivated by one cause, others by a combination or all of them. Suzuyo Takazato, who fought against military sexual violence, led one of the regular demonstrations outside the Schwab gates. She thought it was important for people to see a woman in that leadership position. "There are many women sitting in protest, but organizations are always represented by men," she told me. Hideki Yoshikawa, an anthropologist, focused on the environment and the plight of the dugong, because those were causes backed by international NGOs and legal cases he thought they could win. Fumiko Shimabukuro, who was in her eighties and a frequent media voice, often brought up her experience during the Battle of Okinawa, which drove her to try to prevent anything like that from happening again. "In Okinawa, we believe in 'Nuchi du takara'—life is precious," she said. "If this new base is built, it will be used to kill people. So I owe it to all those who died in [the] Battle of Okinawa to stop construction." Those who had lived through that nightmare said they knew what militaries were for—killing, destruction—and didn't want younger generations to be lulled into thinking otherwise. They didn't want the hellish experience to fade from public consciousness, any lessons it could impart lost, all those deaths for nothing.

Chie, too, was deeply motivated by the legacy of the war that her mother, Sachiko, had survived. Over the years, Chie had participated in various activities to help keep the memory of that time alive. She had been part of a group that bought video footage of the battle from the U.S. National Archives and created educational films. She had rallied against the Japanese Ministry of Education's whitewashing of high school textbooks, which in Japan are standardized across the country and undergo a screening process before government approval. In writing the national narrative of the Pacific War—and pushing for the remilitarization of Japan—right-wing leaders, including Shinzo Abe, have long sought to downplay or delete atrocities committed by Japanese soldiers. Along with edits like erasing the story of comfort women and changing the word "invasion" to "advance" in reference to Japan's actions in China, the ministry has repeatedly called for the removal of information about the Imperial Army's killing Okinawans or coercing them into suicide during the Battle of Okinawa. In response to Okinawan and Japanese students using these false textbooks, Chie and other teachers marched through the streets, demanding the government tell the truth.

Chie also co-founded a forum called Nuchi du Takara with the mission of listening to war survivors before they were gone. Despite annual prefecture-wide events and ceremonies to remember the war, Chie thought younger generations stayed emotionally removed from the history. "It's like they're watching a movie," she said. She endeavored to bring it closer. To that end, she had written a bilingual children's book called *A Letter from Okinawa*, which told her mother's story as a student nurse during the war. In it, she invites readers to draw pictures and write text. Kids are asked to pen letters to their parents, imagining being separated during wartime. This way, Chie thought, readers take ownership of the story. They move from observers to participants. It was the only way to begin to understand war without enduring it. In essence, Chie was trying to bridge the generation gap around the war—the great divide between those who had experienced it and those who hadn't. Those who remembered the genesis of the bases, and those who didn't connect the current situation to the islands' past.

Henoko is a small fishing village, technically a part of Nago City, but separated from the populated urban area, on the other side of the island, by seven miles of jungle and mountains. Before the war, Henoko residents lived off the bounty of the forest and sea. After villagers suffered through the Battle of Okinawa, the area became the site of an internment camp for 29,000 Okinawan survivors. Many perished there due to a lack of food and clean water, and their family members were forced to bury their bodies in shallow graves still thought to inhabit the area. By the 1950s, Henoko was a quiet village again—and became notorious for the being the first community to accept a U.S. military base during the mass protest known as the All-Island Struggle. With towns everywhere fighting to prevent the takeover of their land by the U.S. military government, Henoko leaders calculated they were on the losing side and chose to negotiate with USCAR rather than risk losing their land anyway, without significant gains. Once Henoko caved, other towns followed, and the "all-island" alliance was broken and sputtered out. During the Vietnam War, Henoko saw the full expression of this hoped-for prosperity when Camp Schwab swelled with troops. In perhaps an expression of gratitude or recognition, the entertainment area outside the base became known as Apple Town after Major Apple, the USCAR official who had bargained for the town's land. Soon, the number of military-approved "A-sign" bars, restaurants, and brothels reached as many as two hundred. Apple Town became a place where dollar bills were plentiful, bathrooms boasted flush toilets, neon signs lit the night sky, and creative energies sizzled with bands that performed rock and roll. With all that came violence. U.S. soldiers murdered two women during that time and committed an unknown number of sexual assaults.

After the Vietnam War, Henoko grew quiet again. Base workers were laid off. Bars were shuttered and fell into disrepair. Musicians and hostesses migrated to Kin or Okinawa City. Young people left for work on the mainland or in the island's cities. Many remaining residents continued to benefit from Camp Schwab rental payments, but as I saw in Henoko, not many businesses still entertained U.S. military customers. In this context, some locals embraced the possibility of a new, bigger base. They chose the prospect of returned economic prosperity, of more base and construction jobs and cash flowing off base, over the degradation of the bay, military aircraft in the sky, and U.S. soldiers in the streets. Anthropologist Masamichi S. Inoue points out that base supporters in Henoko have been largely working class, while residents who oppose the base tend to enjoy more financial security.

This has caused inter-class friction within the town. "Our life is more important than the dugong's," base supporters told Inoue, upset that activists were rallying around this animal but didn't consider their unemployed neighbors. "Without jobs, we can't live." Another local commented, "Camp Schwab gives hiring preferences to local people. Groups opposing the base come here from outside the prefecture and raise a ruckus about protecting the bay, where they've never gone swimming or fishing." At times, the tension between the two groups grew so thick one resident remarked the air had "gotten so suffocating" it was hard to breathe.

By the time I visited Henoko, it was widely known that most protesters outside the gates and on the water were not town residents, but people who had driven or flown in. Local community leaders had officially accepted the new base, while residents who opposed it had incentive to keep quiet to avoid ratcheting up the tension that had been choking the area for years. "It's been such a long time, people are sort of accustomed to the tension," anthropologist and activist Hideki Yoshikawa told me. "They know what his or her opinions are, so they avoid talking about this particular topic."

Hideki said many local communities around U.S. military bases grapple with dueling ideas of their neighbors. Both the bases and Okinawan towns host regular cross-cultural get-togethers—festivals and "Friendship Days"—where people are invited to cross the fence line. On base, locals eat corn dogs and hamburgers, go bowling, watch movies. Off base, marines eat goya champuru and try Okinawan traditions like tug-of-war, sumo wrestling, and dragon-boat racing. Members of the military and local communities tout these events as proof of good relations. But, as Hideki pointed out, relations are changeable. "I think the Okinawan townships . . . have a very difficult task of living with the base," he said. "They have to get along to a certain extent, but sometimes a bad traffic accident occurs, or a local is injured or killed, and then they have to . . . take a position of anti-base in that particular situation. . . . The communities will switch their positions depending upon the situation." A Kin government worker told me something similar. Noboru Afuso, director of Kin's planning section, which handles public relations between Camp Hansen and the townspeople, mentioned the Friendship Days that happen on base every couple of months. "We're trying to make the relationship friendly," he said. "But sometimes the helicopters are noisy. At that time we have to protest the base." When aircraft taking off from Hansen get too loud, he explained, Kin residents call the town office to complain. The town then complains to the Japanese government, and the government tells the base. The air gets quieter—for a time. Then the loud training exercises resume, the residents complain, and the cycle repeats. Afuso said this cycle happens not only in Kin, but also in communities around Futenma and Kadena. Once in a while, this low-level, regular protest erupts into a large-scale one. He thought the most recent in Kin had been about fifteen years earlier in 2003, over a new training area.

Hideki said this mix of protest and friendship is the only way to live alongside the bases. "You cannot always be anti-base," he said. "Given that we already have the military bases and we have to live with them, they are part of our communities, whether we like it or not."

I visited the protest site outside Camp Schwab on a chilly March morning in 2017. With me was Reiko, a local university student. We'd heard the action took place early, so we arrived around seven, when daylight was breaking over Henoko. As usual, the region's landscapes arrested me: the blue water, the wild-looking coastline, the foliage that feels prehistoric, with oversized ferns and twisting trees. To see it is to understand viscerally what a loss it would be to fill it in, cut it down, bulldoze it away.

Outside Schwab, a handful of protesters stood around the gate that was open. They were older Okinawans or Japanese and held signs with slogans like "NO MARINES" and "Close all bases." Nearby was a crate of laminated signs that people could pick through. One woman, rooting through them, asked us what various English words meant. Another woman had selected one that read, in English, "good neighbors don't rape," and on the other side, "don't rape Okinawa." The most vocal protester in that bunch was an older man I'd seen at

many anti-base demonstrations. He sported a gray beard and traditional topknot and yelled "Marines OUT!" aggressively in English at
vehicles leaving the base.

The main action of the sit-in was at another, closed gate down the
road. This was a wider entrance where transport trucks carrying construction supplies passed through. The bulk of the protesters settled here,
with the mission of blocking the trucks' entrance. A couple of activists
had told me it took two hundred to three hundred people to make the
trucks turn away, so the goal was to have high numbers at the sit-in.
The day before, ten trucks carting gravel had gotten through the gate at
three different times. This morning, there were only about fifty people,
with one group that had been bused in from the island's south. It seemed
doubtful they'd be able to stop the trucks. Most protesters were elderly,
people who had the time and freedom to demonstrate, along with wartime memories as motivation. They sat on folding chairs and makeshift
benches put together with cinderblocks and two-by-fours. Behind them,
a line of police vehicles was parked in front of the gate, and the protesters had decorated the vans with signs opposing the oppression of citizens and Prime Minister Abe. For many, Abe stood against everything
they were fighting for, with his aim to rewrite the peace constitution and
expand the role of the Japanese military, his actions to whitewash history
and pay respect to war criminals at Yasukuni Shrine, his disregard for
the democratic demands of Okinawan people, and his subservience to
the United States. One common joke was that the prime minister was the
lapdog of Donald Trump, slobbering at his feet and obeying whatever
his master said.

More protesters arrived as the morning went on, strengthening
their numbers. One carried a giant inflatable dugong on her head.
They all listened as an older man wearing a conical straw hat made
announcements on a microphone. Today and tomorrow were high
school entrance exams, he said, so they needed to make sure the road
stayed clear for students. He commented that a few of the base security
guards were Okinawan, and he believed these men shared the protesters' passion. He and some others were going to try to talk to them. He

greeted cars driving by: "Good morning, let's stand together!" Some drivers waved, but many passed with their eyes straight ahead.

Reiko and I talked with a seventy-five-year-old man from west of Henoko, on the opposite coast. He held a "NO BASE" sign, wore a khaki bucket hat, and sat on a little plastic stool. His eyes were sad but determined. He told us he came a few times a week to protest, because whoever kills someone should be responsible for their actions. Japan started the war, he said, but put the burden of the bases on Okinawa. He had been born in Micronesia during World War II to Okinawan parents. His leg got injured during the fighting and still gave him trouble, but his two brothers paid a much higher price, losing their lives. He cited this loss as the reason his anger was bigger than others'. He said he had absorbed into his body everything his parents had told him about the war.

"We might lose, we might win," he said of the movement against the new base. He didn't care so much about the outcome. Taking action was what mattered. "America shouldn't bully Okinawa," he said. If American people had a heart, they wouldn't build their bases in Okinawa.

A police car rolled by. Activists explained they were counting the number of people outside the gates. If it was high enough they'd call off the trucks for the day. A low number meant they'd order the white-gloved security guards to haul away the men and women.

The leader on the mic announced details about the trial for three detained people, including Hiroji Yamashiro, one of the movement's leaders who had been arrested for a series of supposed offenses. These included cutting a wire fence outside a military construction zone, injuring an ODB worker, and obstructing the road in front of Camp Schwab. Sixty-four years old, Yamashiro had been held without bail and without visitation rights since October, suffering from lymphoma and apparently declining in health. People had rallied around his detention as a human-rights violation, an unconstitutional ploy to scare others from exercising their free speech and peaceful assembly rights. Amnesty International put out a statement advocating for his release.

"We don't know who will be the next," Suzuyo Takazato had told me. The activists had a sense the police could arrest any one of them.

The man announced that two other people had gotten arrested recently when blocking a vehicle, but both had been released. It was becoming clear, he said, that the Japanese government, the police, and the courts were working together to suppress their protest activities.

Reiko and I met one of the few young people at the sit-in, a twenty-seven-year-old indigo farmer from Nakajin Village, a half hour's drive west. Unlike the rest of Japan, Okinawa still has a positive growth rate, with more births per year than deaths, although that rate is slowing. An abundance of young people, however, won't matter for the future of the anti-base movement if they aren't involved. This young woman said she came once a week to protest with her father. When we asked why she came, she said she didn't know where to start. "I'm allergic to politics," she said. In this, she wasn't alone. The most recent national election had seen the lowest-ever voter turnout—under 53 percent—with an even lower figure—32.6 percent—for people in their twenties. But things had changed for the farmer two years earlier, when she returned to northern Okinawa after living on the mainland and in Naha and started learning about the base issues. Her farm work wasn't directly related to the bases, but she saw everything on the island as connected. Filling in the bay would disrupt the delicate cycle of life. Lately, she had been trying to attract more young people to the cause by holding events in Naha with themes like hip hop. She wasn't having much success. Young people had weak imaginations, she said, and no place for politics in their minds. They had to make a living. Plus, people in Naha were physically removed from the bases. Ospreys didn't fly over their homes. And it was more complicated for young people than for older generations. She herself had friends in the U.S. military. Older Okinawans without personal connections could be more resolutely against the marines.

The indigo farmer was resigned to the building of the new base. She said the point of the sit-in was to postpone the construction and raise awareness so people from all over the world saw what the Japanese government was doing, and maybe in the next election mainlanders would vote in support of Okinawa.

A black van driven by right-wing counter-protesters drove by. Vans like these are a common sight throughout the country, and this one flew the Japanese imperial flag and broadcast patriotic songs and a man's voice. The only part of his message we could hear was "Go home." The indigo farmer told us that in the past the van had played the sound of the wartime sirens that had wailed during attacks. That had triggered bone-chilling memories for the elderly protesters. I had heard some mainland right-wing groups were against the U.S. bases in Japan, because as Japanese nationalists they didn't want a foreign military on their soil. Some older conservatives in Okinawa also opposed the bases because of their wartime experiences. But many Japanese and Okinawans on the right, including Abe, supported the U.S. military presence, even while they advocated for the buildup of Japan's military. The indigo farmer said this right-wing van was affiliated with Happy Science, purportedly a cult that supported the bases and specialized in fake news. They were some of the ones who put out rumors that the protesters were the paid workers of the Chinese Communist Party, which they said was trying to dislodge the bases from Okinawa to make it easier to invade.

Between pro- and anti-base Okinawans, China is a sticking point. Many supporters of the U.S. military presence cite the threat of China as a reason to maintain the bases as a deterrent. South of Okinawa, in the East China Sea, a territorial battle has been waging between China and Japan over some rocky outcroppings known as Diaoyu in China, Diaoyutai in Taiwan, and Senkaku in Japan. A maritime showdown has been taking place between Tokyo and Beijing around the uninhabited islets, and some in Okinawa reason that base closures would trigger this land struggle to move north. In recent years, China has questioned Japan's sovereignty over Okinawa, saying the islands' historic tribute relationship with China predated their subordination to Japan. The exit of the U.S. military, some people fear, would create a vacuum China would rush to fill.

Anti-base Okinawans generally regard China as friendly. Governor Onaga was working to create new economic ties with China, and tourists from China and Taiwan now flood Okinawa on cheap, direct flights with cash to spend. China never invaded us, sacrificed us, bombed us, took our land, these people argue. Why should we be afraid of China? (If anything, Chie said, she fears the United States, not China or North Korea.) Many of these thinkers reason the U.S. military presence acts not as a deterrent, but as a bullseye, making Okinawa more likely to be targeted in the event of war.

Some also doubt whether the U.S. military would step up for Japan in a conflict, though that protection is pledged in the U.S.–Japan Security Treaty. "Do you think American people will support the U.S. military going to war against China for the Senkaku [Islands]?" asked Tomohiro Yara, a journalist and board member of the think tank New Diplomacy Initiative. He thought most Japanese people believe the U.S. military would get involved in the territory dispute between China and Japan—but Yara thought the idea that the American public would let their sons and daughters die for this cause was "ridiculous." Talking about it when we'd met for coffee, he had laughed. "Totally strange."

For more than twenty years, Yara had been investigating why the marines were in Okinawa. He had concluded that on the side of Tokyo it was because of NIMBYism—mainlanders with more political clout didn't want the bases in their backyards. On the side of Washington, it was because the bases were convenient and cheap to maintain in Okinawa, thanks to Japanese "sympathy" payments. And the bases project soft power. The marines participate in humanitarian missions in the region after natural disasters. This relief is important, Yara said—both for the communities in need and for regional peacekeeping. But there is no genuine security reason for all these marines to be in Okinawa. Political science professor Manabu Sato agreed. He told me that building the new base in Henoko had nothing to do with a rising China or nuclear North Korea. In the event of a war with Japan's neighbors, the air force would be the one to launch an attack, not the marines. Another marine base wasn't going to help. "Those people who think that if they don't build Henoko, then China will [attack], they don't know," Sato said. "I feel sorry for them."

Okinawa's self-confidence is another common topic among activists, who believe too many islanders have internalized the view of themselves as Japan's "country cousins," subordinate to and dependent on the mainland. Many locals also think Okinawa needs the U.S. military presence for economic reasons—the Americans' spending power, on-base jobs for locals, and hefty subsidies from the Japanese government. There are also the sizeable rent payments some Okinawans receive; the land under each base still belongs to hundreds or thousands of people forced to rent to the U.S. military after their land or family's land was taken during the Cold War. One local described a popular image of these landowners. "They get free money, every year," the man told me. "So they don't work.... The image is that they spend their lives playing pachinko and drinking it away.... When they finally die, all their kids try to get as much land as they can in their name." The oldest son, the chōnan, usually wins out, inheriting the land. "And so the chōnan becomes the next drunk in the family." Some Okinawans feel conflicted about their forced rental agreements. More than one person with anti-base views admitted to me that part of their personal success—their college tuition, say—was tied to money their families earned from the bases.

Despite these sources of income, in recent years economists have shown the bases account for only about 5 percent of the local economy and a more prosperous future lies with other kinds of development. Landowners can earn more money, for instance, renting to commercial ventures. Yara predicted within the next five years Okinawa's economy would transform due to trade with China and those tourists flying over on direct flights from Taiwan, China, and Hong Kong. Then, he said, an economically and psychically stronger Okinawa could better stand up to the central government, demanding an end to the U.S. bases—or even seeking independence.

For years, intellectuals, activists, and politicians have explored the possibility of restoring an independent Ryukyus—not reinstating a monarchy, but separating the prefecture from Japan to become a sovereign state once again. Masaki Tomochi, an economics professor at Okinawa International University, is a founding member of the Association of Comprehensive Studies for Independence of the Lew Chewan peoples (ACSILs), a group with a few hundred members that advocates for independence, using the traditional spelling of the islands. When I met with Tomochi, they were in the process of trying to meet with the UN to garner support and learn about their options. Tomochi likened the situation to one of domestic violence. "You cannot solve the problem inside the house," he told me. "You have to open the door and go next door to ask for help." That was why ACSILs wasn't going to Tokyo or DC. The UN recognized Okinawans as indigenous people, while the Japanese government officially denied them this status, all while unofficially treating them as different.

Tomochi told me public polls and ones he'd conducted with his students showed only 8 percent of Okinawans favored the idea of independence. But when he asked a few hundred of his students a conditional question—do you agree with Okinawan independence if economic, political, and security issues are solved?—around 40 percent said yes. He thought the Okinawan public would similarly support independence if their two main worries—making a living and being safe from attack—were taken care of.

Tomochi rejected the idea of a paternal Japan. "When we talk about independence, a lot of people have the image of young kids becoming independent from their parents," he said. But he liked to turn it around. Japan, in fact, was depending on Okinawa to host U.S. military bases. Tokyo was the one that needed to learn to stand on its own.

Outside the open Schwab gate, the number of protesters had grown close to twenty. Most of them were middle-aged to elderly women wearing sunhats and face masks. Whenever a car carrying Americans drove up to leave base, they stood in front of it. "Please go home!" one woman yelled at a carful of marines. I watched another driver almost hit a woman. The guards made him reverse behind the yellow line and wait. This was the general protocol. The cars waited on the safety of the base while security guards commanded the protesters to leave. The marines, sitting in their cars, smiled or laughed or stared, expressionless. The guards filmed the protesters, who ignored their commands. Finally, reinforcements arrived. A contingent of guards in blue uniforms and white gloves marched out of the base, young men who physically removed the demonstrators from the road. Sometimes the protesters would get in their faces, but I didn't see the guards use force. One demonstrator pushed back at a guard, but it didn't escalate. The guards herded the activists away by holding up their white gloves and walking forward, while another guard waved the marines out of the gate. "Get out!" one woman screamed at the cars as they escaped. As soon as the cars were gone, the men strode back to base, the whole thing over in less than a minute.

I watched one protester step to the side and talk to an Okinawan guard through the base fence. They looked like friends. The reality was that the demonstrators outside the gates and the hired security inside the gates were often friends, neighbors, or family members. Because of this, I'd heard, the government had been importing more guards from the mainland, as they'd done on Oura Bay.

And like at sea, the guards on land got violent, people told me. The riot police had grabbed and sprained wrists, broken fingers, caused bruises. Ambulances had driven away people with a broken rib or busted hand. Fumiko Shimabukuro, the octogenarian activist, said guards had used one of their common tactics on her as she tried to stop a transport truck. They had crowded close around her, pulled her off balance, and then stepped back, causing her to fall. When she hit the ground, she was knocked unconscious and later suffered lingering pain. Activists attributed this brutality to Prime Minister Abe, whom they unanimously detested. Whereas in 2005 Koizumi had called off construction because of the protesters, Abe seemed bent on powering through, using whatever force necessary. Some activists, too, believed an extreme path was the way to end the decades-long stalemate. The only way things will change is when a demonstrator is killed, Yara told me. At first, I was shocked at this thought, but the more I learned and thought about it, I wondered if a death would really change anything—or if each side would continue to explain away their version of events.

All morning, every five minutes or so, the scene outside the open Schwab gate replayed. The demonstrators blocked the cars, the guards yelled at them to move, and the white-gloved men appeared and retreated. Reiko and I talked to other protesters, who told us why they participated: for their kids and grandkids, for the animals in the bay, because the United States was vast and American bases should be in America, because Okinawa hadn't yet healed from its sacrifice during World War II. A middle-aged man from Osaka told us he had become disillusioned with the federal government after the 2011 Fukushima nuclear accident and had traveled to Okinawa after watching a few films on Henoko and developing a vague desire to live in the countryside. He'd been shocked by the protests that were happening then in Takae, the northern village where the U.S. military was cutting helipads out of the dense, biodiverse forest, and he'd gotten involved in the movement, spending months outside Schwab sleeping in a tent.

Mainland interlopers like this sometimes came across as patronizing or superficial to locals. One Okinawan grad student, doing research at the sit-in, wrote about "the awkwardness" of Japanese people who lectured Okinawans about their own history. "Time to time I would feel the Japanese people's colonial attitude at the sit-in; generous, self-righteous, and friendly Japanese helping quiet, poor, weak Okinawans," Rinda Yamashiro writes. Yamashiro also found Japanese visitors would participate in the movement in Okinawa, but not try to engage mainlanders in the cause after they returned home. They saw the whole thing as "Okinawa's problem," not a national security issue. Many didn't feel a particular passion for Okinawans' fight for justice; it could have been any movement, really. Okinawa was convenient—a short plane ride away within Japan, but still exotic and remote-feeling. It was like they were volunteering in a less developed land; they could leave when they wanted, feeling good about their service, and return home and forget about Okinawans' struggles, save for a boost to their egos and their dinner party stories. The most egregious sight Yamashiro witnessed was chartered buses of Japanese "protest tourists" who would roll up to the sit-in, stay half an hour, then climb back into the AC for their next stop, maybe a pineapple garden. As a result, one faction of the protest movement cut ties with anyone deemed to be Japanese and not Okinawan.

The Osaka man I met clearly had been looking for escape, coming to Okinawa, but he seemed genuinely committed to the cause, ferrying protesters to and from a nearby parking lot and grimly stating he'd keep protesting another five years, if the construction took another five years.

Reiko and I left the sit-in around noon, when many of the demonstrators were breaking for lunch. Before we went, we saw three security buses leave the base. Activists said the buses would drive around and then surprise them, suddenly showing up to remove them from their sit-in when their numbers had dwindled. It seemed clear to me and Reiko that the construction trucks were going to make their move during the lunch break, and we wondered why everyone didn't eat their lunches in front of the gate to prevent this. I realized it wasn't necessarily an all-out, sacrifice-everything struggle for the demonstrators. They were willing to risk their limbs and even lives facing down the security guards—but they still wanted a lunch break. As many people had told us, they didn't believe they could stop the construction. They could slow it, though, and were doing their part, day by day. Ten trucks entering again today was better than the unknown number that might have if they weren't there.

Many demonstrators protested not just in Henoko but also outside other U.S. military bases on the island, in a kind of circuit. The Henoko organizers had conceived of these offshoot protests to project what was happening outside Schwab to more-populated areas of the island. At one I witnessed outside Camp Courtney in Uruma City, about twenty elderly people lined up outside the gate in a rainstorm, at 4 p.m. sharp, for their weekly demonstration. They carried banners expressing their opposition to the new base, and repeated chants after the leader, pumping their fists into the air. A few security guards kept watch, but didn't seem concerned. The demonstrators sang a few songs demanding the return of base land, then did a "fifty-meter" protest, which was basically crossing the street in front of the base gate and returning. "No Camp Courtney!" they yelled in English. I spoke with one participant, an Uruma City councilman in his late sixties. He had short gray hair and a silver tooth that flashed in his mouth as he spoke. He came to the protest every week, along with going once a week to Kadena and twice a week to Henoko. When I asked him about getting paid from China to do this, he chuckled. If he got 20,000 yen a day, he would quit his job as councilman, he said.

Speaking with men and women at the protests, I couldn't imagine them as the paid lackeys of China. The activists did receive donations of money and food, and perhaps some of those donors had political interests in sticking a wrench in the U.S.–Japan security alliance or fighting against the Abe administration. The Japanese Communist Party, which has about three hundred thousand members and promotes anti-militarism and "breaking away from the Japan-U.S. military alliance," supports the protesters in Okinawa, whether financially or just politically. I attended one Henoko meeting where activists met with a national Communist Party leader who promised to take their concerns back to Tokyo.

I didn't meet anyone who seemed to be doing it for money. When people talked about why they were protesting, why they were spending their time and risking their well-being on this cause, their eyes glinted with conviction. For many, this was nothing short of a fight for democracy. Okinawa's voters had made clear their opposition to the new base by electing Onaga and other anti-base leaders, but the central government was ignoring their mandate. One woman at the Henoko protest explained she had come from the mainland, after living for fifteen years in New York City, because she felt like the fight for democracy, justice, and peace was taking place in Okinawa more than anywhere else in Japan. Retired now, she was renting a room in Naha and regularly riding the bus to Henoko, "doing as much as I can as a citizen." Anthropologist and activist Hideki Yoshikawa told me that while in mainland Japan democracy might be taken for granted,

Okinawans knew it was something citizens had to be vigilant about, to fight for. "Democracy is never free," he said.

Every year, people travel to Ie-jima, a small island off the northwest coast of Okinawa, to celebrate "the Gandhi of Okinawa." Also known as the father of Okinawa's civil rights movement, Shoko Ahagon is the late activist commemorated for his commitment to nonviolent protest. After he died in 2002, activists and supporters began organizing the annual gathering to keep his memory and message alive. Chie Miyagi had been twice, and in March 2017 she went a third time. She told me she attended because the weekend was "nuchi gusui," Okinawan for what she interpreted as "medicine for the soul." "Ie-jima is facing a very severe situation," she said, alluding to the U.S. military presence on the island. "But Shoko Ahagon's spirit gives us power."

Ie Island, just two by five miles, is flat save for one mountain that, from afar, seems to float on the ocean like a straw hat. It's accessed by a thirty-minute ferry ride from the main island, and tourists come over to visit the beach resort or attend the spring Lily Festival. What visitors might not realize, at least not at first, is that over a third of the island is controlled by the U.S. military. In the 1950s, Ahagon helped lead an organized front against the building of these bases, with some success but much defeat.

The wartime and postwar history of the island is perhaps more acutely troubled than that of the main island. In the buildup to the Battle of Okinawa, the Imperial Japanese Army commandeered much of Ie-jima for its operations, building a runway and kicking off three thousand of the eight thousand residents. Other civilians were drafted into military service and made to fight in the brutal battle that ensued when American soldiers invaded in April 1945. Some Okinawans were forced into close combat armed only with wooden clubs. Others received hand grenades from Japanese soldiers, who said there was only one honorable way out: to take the lives of yourself and your family. Imperial Army soldiers enforced this order for "suicide" by shooting islanders who tried to surrender. In one cave, 150 villagers detonated an explosive gifted to them by Japanese soldiers. Only about twenty survived.

After six days of fighting, U.S. forces prevailed. About fifteen hundred Ie-jima civilians had lost their lives, along with two thousand Japanese soldiers and three hundred Americans. The battle for Ie Island gained some attention in the United States because Ernie Pyle, the well-known war correspondent, was among the dead.

The U.S. military took control of Ie-jima as a strategic launching point to invade the main island, and American leaders decided all civilians needed to go. They ordered the remaining islanders from their homes and sent them by ship to the islands of Zamami, Toka-shiki, and Kerama, which the U.S. military had already taken over (setting off the mass "suicides" that had killed Chie's grandparents). Ie Island became one big military base.

After the war, residents eventually returned to the island, but the U.S. military didn't leave—or clean up its mess. Veteran M.D. Morris describes visiting Ie-jima in 1946 "to survey, examine, and evaluate all U.S. Army property there." In his report, he "noted that the munitions dumps . . . were in extremely bad shape." He writes that "things like napalm or jelly gas . . . were lying out in mountainous stacks. The outer skins of these metal drums were eroding from the effects of general weathering . . . [and] jelly gas began to creep out and run down the sides." He says he recommended the military dispose of the substances before an accident occurred. Two years later, however, he read that two U.S. soldiers, eleven Filipino workers, and fifty or more "natives" had been killed in an ammunition explosion on the island. He concluded no one had taken his advice.

Still, residents of Ie-jima managed to rebuild their homes and resume some semblance of their former lives—until 1953, when American military officials decided they wanted to build an air force missile practice range on the northwestern portion of the island. This was where the farmers of Maja Village had their houses and fields—as Ahagon writes, "fields green with sugar cane, wheat and potatoes . . . [and] forested hills and uncultivated fields to provide material for compost and feed for animals and firewood." USCAR tricked the villagers into signing an agreement to evacuate, and then, when the farmers realized what had happened and resisted, USCAR took the land by force. They arrested resisters and forced pleading families out of their homes at bayonet-point. They burned and razed the villager's homes, fields, water tanks, and livestock pens. They shot goats. They thrust consolation money into the hands of shocked and terrified people. By the end of their violent campaign, USCAR had taken 63 percent of the island.

"It was as if another battle had occurred," remembered C. Harold Rickard, an American missionary who visited the island in the aftermath. "Houses and livestock sheds were demolished. People were living in tents under the searing sun. We visited a little six-year-old girl who had been injured by rifle fire from U.S. soldiers." Displaced islanders lived in tent villages, where the land was unsuitable for cultivating and hardships included poisonous snakes, a lack of clean drinking water, and little protection from rain and sun. Many people grew sick. In response to their protest over what had happened, a U.S. Air Force official issued a statement saying, "The Air Force can sympathize with and understand the farmers' attachment to their houses and agricultural fields." But, the major general wrote, those individual losses were not as important as the bigger issue of security—for the residents of Ie Island and, in fact, the entire free world: "The purpose of stationing our troops is to protect those farm fields and homes. We have a great trust and responsibility for the Far East and Okinawa, and that is more important than the relatively petty dispute in which the . . . households are engaged. Strong air defense is an important issue, both for the Free World and for all Ryukyuan people."

Of course, Maja wasn't the only community to experience takeover by "bulldozer and bayonet." Rickard describes a place called Isahama, "a beautiful rural village in southern Okinawa which had miraculously escaped destruction during the Battle of Okinawa." He appealed to the USCAR high commissioner and other officials to spare the village, but his petitioning was in vain. He writes, "On July 19, 1955 I personally witnessed the village of Isahama taken at gunpoint and destroyed. The people's productive rice fields were filled by heavy equipment and turned into a U.S. military area. I felt ashamed to be an American."

From this situation, Shoko Ahagon emerged as the Maja farmers' leader. With others from Ie-jima, he staged a sit-in outside the Government of Ryukyu Islands building in Naha. Then they went on the road in what was known as the Beggars' March, twenty to thirty people at a time, for seven months, traversing the main island of Okinawa, trying to raise awareness of their plight. They brandished placards with their message, "An apology and a request." "The road of our livelihoods is completely closed off," the message began. It explained the villagers of Ie Island had considered all their options and, "having overcome all sense of shame," made a decision to call on the "sympathy and support" of other Okinawans and "fight to the end." "There is no way for [us] to live except to beg," they proclaimed. "Begging is shameful, to be sure; but taking land by military force and causing us to beg is especially shameful." Some Japanese mainlanders who heard about the situation on Ie-jima sent relief items to the grateful islanders.

Life was treacherous on Ie Island for those who remained. With the missile practice range, falling bombs were frequent, even outside the military area. With no other way to make a living, men and women foraged for scrap metal from these explosives, collecting bullets and shells from around the practice range. They had to dismantle unexploded shells, risking injury or death. More than a dozen villagers were severely wounded or killed from exploding ordnance and machine-gun strafing. Still, throughout their struggle, citizens resisted in what ways they could. They tried to farm land taken by the U.S. military. They erected crosses to try to appeal to U.S. soldiers who were Christian. They answered U.S. military base signs declaring "Entrance by Other Than U.S. Personnel Is Prohibited" with their own signs: "Entrance by Other Than Land-owners Is Prohibited!" They alerted the media of abuses. "When [U.S. soldiers] came to the island and spoke wildly about how they would kill us with poison gas or shoot us down with guns, we went directly to the newspaper office and had their words published, making the devil's behavior public and bringing shame down on the U.S. military," Ahagon writes.

As in later times, the U.S. military tried to dismiss the Okinawans' movement as being orchestrated by an outside force. In one recorded exchange, an American officer questions an islander taken into custody for resisting. "Aren't you being agitated by the Communist Party?" he asks. "We aren't such fools!" the prisoner replies. "We aren't people who can be manipulated like robots. Because we can't live if we don't have land, we are protecting the land handed down from our ancestors."

Ahagon and other activists eventually succeeded in getting back half the land taken by the U.S. military, leaving about a third of the island still under its control. The coalition of farmers and villagers hadn't given up, driven by a fiery sense of injustice, even though their odds were long. Rickard, who became a friend of Ahagon, writes that the leader "exhibited the spirit of Mahatma Gandhi, of Martin Luther King, Jr., of Chief Seattle, and of Jesus—love, patience, forgiveness, active peacemaking, common sense and simple wisdom, and committed and courageous leadership." Ahagon emphasized the islanders' status as ningen, human beings, saying, "We are attempting to live the quality of life on Iejima which enables us to call ourselves true 'human beings,' and we call on those who have taken our land to think about what it means to act as human beings." He helped popularize that Okinawan saying, nuchi du takara, setting the notion that life is treasure in stark opposition to soldiers trained to kill.

During the whole weekend on Ie-jima Chie wore her neon pink Nuchi du Takara T-shirt. That first afternoon, in a community center situated amid fields of tobacco and sugar cane, she gathered with other conference participants, mostly elderly activists fighting for various causes. There was the famous Okinawan sculptor Minoru Kinjo. There was the woman who had taken over leadership of Ahagon's peace museum, white-haired Etsuko Jahana, who used a wheelchair. There was a Korean-Japanese man from Osaka who was involved in Okinawa's anti-base movement. There was an elegant woman from the mainland who had relocated to Nago after retiring and joined Henoko Blue.

While aircraft droned overhead, an Ie-jima assembly member from the Japanese Communist Party told the group the U.S. military still regarded the whole island as a training site. He showed clips of U.S. military training maneuvers he had filmed around the island. A fighter jet roared, almost unbearably loud, even through the speakers. Figures jumped from an airplane, falling then floating on parachutes. An Osprey carted a three-ton cannon through the sky, causing gasps around the room. The assemblyman passed around photos showing dust or sediment kicked up by aircraft and deposited on plants, and Ospreys flying together like a flock of predatory birds.

Despite all this, many islanders had come to support the U.S. military presence. The assemblyman was the only one in the assembly who was anti-base. Only a few locals worked on the island's base, but, like in Henoko, residents had come to feel they needed the subsidies Tokyo doled out. This made reviving organized protest difficult.

Activists explained Ie-jima was connected to the struggle in Henoko because the idea was that once the new base was completed, it would complete a triangle that included Ie-jima and Takae. Military aircraft would fly among all three points, rendering the whole area, including the city of Nago, a training zone. One irony of this, activists pointed out, was that the Japanese government supported a bid to designate the region's Yanbaru forest as a UNESCO World Heritage site. For its great biodiversity and endemic species of frogs, birds, insects, and other animals, it was being considered. But swaths of it were still controlled by the U.S. military for its jungle training exercises, and soon aircraft would be flying overhead.

After the assemblyman, another local leader talked about how Ospreys scorched and killed the grass as they took off and landed. He talked about noise pollution and cows miscarrying or having still-births. He described the dangers of low-wave sound emitted from aircraft near residential areas. The U.S. military conducted fierce training around their homes. "The U.S. doesn't regard us as human beings," he said.

A University of the Ryukyus professor shared his research on noise pollution. Ie-jima might look peaceful, he said, but it wasn't. Extreme low and high sound waves couldn't be heard, but they harmed people.

He demonstrated by playing the noise of an Osprey through a speaker, on which a glass jar filled with Styrofoam peanuts sat. The Osprey recording made the peanuts jump and bubble. This is what happens to the body and mind as well, the professor said. Chronic noise pollution hurt children's memories, caused headaches, disrupted sleep and concentration, and irritated people. As he spoke, planes thundered outside.

Many speakers talked about military bases in the United States, how they were situated away from residential areas and schools, but no such considerations were extended to Okinawa.

After the presentations, everyone marched down the deserted country road, waving banners, yelling call-and-response chants, and thrusting fists into the air. The march ended at Solidarity Hall, a modest concrete structure where Ahagon and other resisters had kept an eye on the nearby base and waged their activism. Parts of the facade were dark with mildew, but its front had been freshly painted with lines of Japanese text: the guidelines farmers had established for non-violent protest. The guidelines included advice like don't raise your hands above your ears, reasoning that the U.S. military could take a photo and use it as proof of your violence. Others included, "Do not become anti-American," "Never be afraid of the military," "Do not lie," "Never lose your temper," and "With love in your heart and doing your best to be reasonable, talk together with the attitude of teaching and leading young children." Chie squinted in the sun, reading the rules, and sighed with admiration. She wished she had met Ahagon while he was alive.

That June, I traveled to the south of the main island with Chie for Irei no Hi, the prefectural Memorial Day to commemorate those who died in the Battle of Okinawa. Many ceremonies take place in the south because the heaviest, final fighting occurred there during the war, and a circuit of war monuments and museums have sprouted up in remembrance. The main one is Peace Memorial Park—vast, manicured grounds above seaside cliffs with an echoing museum and various monuments. On the expanse where many were slaughtered, an eternal peace flame burns and black granite slabs carved with names of the dead zigzag in row after row. The latter, called the Cornerstone of Peace and unveiled in 1995, was the project of Governor Ota and includes not just Japanese and Okinawan deceased, but also Americans, Koreans, and anyone of any nationality who perished in the battle—civilian and soldier. New names are still being added.

Irei no Hi was the only time I saw Chie wear a subdued outfit. Like most who visited Peace Memorial Park that day, she dressed in funeral black. A gray flower hair ornament was the only nod to her usual style. She arrived early to the park, finding it crawling with police. Law enforcement buses and vans with Tokyo license plates filled parking lots, and men in blue uniforms lined the streets. Chie grew angry. "It's our right to visit," she said. It was like mainlanders thought Okinawans were terrorists, she fumed. How much money had the federal government spent on security, protecting one man? Like every year, the keynote speaker that morning would be the prime minister. "His life is just as precious as ours," she said, alluding to her motto, Nuchi du Takara.

The park was also packed with elderly Okinawans and families. Women with canes and in wheelchairs were dressed up in dark blouses and slacks. "People come even if they're in a wheelchair," Chie said. "I want to hear their stories." Chie was the kind of person who engaged any stranger in conversation—marines outside Camp Schwab, students from Hong Kong on Ie Island, Japanese police sent to subdue her and other activists. War survivors were her biggest passion, though, so on Irei no Hi she wanted to talk to everyone. Right away, she spotted an older man she knew from Henoko. She waved him down and asked for his story. The man had two pens clipped into his breast pocket, and his eyes were cloudy. He said during the war his father was sent to Ie-jima, where he leapt from a cliff with two other soldiers, trying to escape the Americans. One man survived to tell the tale, but no one saw his father again. Later, bones were found at the base of that cliff. After the war, the man told us, he lived in poverty with his mother and two younger sisters. He looked forward to Sports Day twice a year, because then the school supplied lunch: the only time he could eat a bento. Because of this poverty, he said, he grew up lacking in height and self-confidence. There was a girl he loved at school, but he never had the nerve to approach her.

In the shade outside the museum, Chie and I guzzled water. The day was already hot. The temperature was in the eighties, and with a cloudless sky and high humidity, it felt stifling. We watched an NHK reporter film a dispatch in English; along with the heavy police presence, there were legions of reporters and camera crews at the park. This reporter talked about why this year's Irei no Hi was different: the construction was moving ahead in Henoko. "That must be in the minds of many people attending the ceremony," she said.

At the Cornerstone of Peace, grandparents, parents, and children found and gathered around their ancestors' names. They laid out offerings of bentos, flowers, cups of tea, bananas, and oranges. They poured water over their loved ones' names and wiped at the stone, cleaning it. They squatted in front of the wall and prayed, hands together and eyes closed. Chie found her mother's family names and went through these gestures, crying when she thought about her uncle, Sachiko's brother, who had perished. She found the names from her father's family and recalled what she knew about them, her relatives she had never met. Her Aunt Fumi, a studious girl, had been drafted into what would become the most famous student nursing corps, the Himeyuri. The most elite girls' schools formed the Himeyuri, and among the twenty-one schools of student soldiers, the "Princess Lily Corps" became the most widely mourned, revered, and romanticized for the horrors they endured and the selflessness with which they served, getting a sleek museum that chronicled their nightmare. Like other high school students, they became mobilized during the battle, indoctrinated to take their own lives before surrendering. Chie's family never learned the details of Fumi's death.

Chie's late father also had been conscripted into a student corps, the same one as Governor Masahide Ota. Both teenagers had been messenger boys, delivering communications between the Imperial Army headquarters and soldiers in the battlefield. Both men survived to lead long lives. Chie remarked on the miracle of that, how lucky she was to have been born. She grew quiet and then whispered something to the names, tracing the engravings with her fingertip.

We walked to the park's entrance, where a small demonstration against Shinzo Abe was taking place. Chie and other activists didn't want Abe at the ceremony, with his false words of support toward Okinawa, the place he was squashing with his determination to build a new base. The dozen or so protesters, some of whom I recognized from outside Camp Schwab, were hoping Abe would drive by behind his tinted windows and, for a moment, hear their cries.

Next, Chie visited the Peace Hall, a soaring white tower inside of which a giant Buddha presided over artwork. Vents pumped out what felt like life-saving air conditioning. Security approached to say we had to clear the building—Abe was coming. Chie stalled. She continued taking pictures and video and slipped into the bathroom. By the time she came out, we were on the inside of a police blockade along with an Okinawan Girl Scout troop and their families. The girls were practicing lining up to greet Abe, and Chie grew tense, working out what she would shout at the prime minister if he walked by. The year before, she had voiced her concerns to his wife when she paid an unexpected visit to a protest site. Chie had talked about Ospreys flying late at night and Rina Shimabukuro's murder. The first lady had nodded and thanked Chie, gifting her with a business card. For a while Chie had been hopeful Akie Abe would be moved by their cause, but nothing came about from their interaction.

Abe never came. We heard he had entered the hall another way, killing Chie's chance to confront him. She shrugged it off and ran to her car to make her next engagement, a ceremony at the Zuisen monument nearby. In the oven of Chie's car, I started to feel a bit delirious. I was draining bottle after bottle of water and sports drinks, and still, I couldn't drink enough. One war survivor had pointed out this had been the weather seventy-two years before, at the end of the battle, and I couldn't imagine it—surviving combat while suffering through this heat, without shelter or water, let alone AC.

The Zuisen monument honored the student nursing corps in which Chie's mother had served. Sachiko was there, wearing a black and white print blouse and black pants. As on the other occasions I'd met her, she was good-humored and warm, chuckling when I spoke to her and mangled my Japanese. Eighty-nine years old now, she remained in good health and lived independently, the matriarch of a big family. She and her late husband had five kids, four of whom lived in Okinawa and often visited her home, one of the former U.S. military bungalows built mid-century. Sachiko's family reflected the diversity of the island. Her son had married a woman from Tokyo, and one of her daughters had married a South Asian man; their biracial daughters had wed U.S. servicemen. Some family members, including Chie and her niece Yoshi, protested the U.S. military presence and were fierce advocates of protecting Okinawa's history, language, and culture. Despite these differences, everyone in the family seemed to get along well, the U.S. servicemen celebrating and laughing alongside the activists at gatherings. In fact, the Miyagi family was one of the friendliest and most welcoming I met in Okinawa.

The Zuisen monument, a modest stone structure in a grove of greenery, was bedecked that day with flowers. An awning and folding chairs had been set up in front, and about fifty people had gathered for the ceremony. The surviving members of Zuisen sat at the front—about ten women in their eighties and nineties. Every year, the number grew smaller. The program included speakers and songs, a moment of silence. Then everyone lined up to take a turn at the altar to pray. For a long time, I learned, Sachiko hadn't talked about the war, as was common for survivors. In her later years, though, she began to remember and became something of a spokesperson, relating her wartime tale and speaking out against the U.S. military presence. After the ceremony that day, Sachiko conducted media interviews and ended up on the national news that night.

No one knew it yet, but that would be Sachiko's last time at the Zuisen memorial service. In June 2018, just four days before the next Irei no Hi, she passed away suddenly at age ninety. The night before, she had been dancing with Chie and Yoshi in her living room, laughing and posing for photos. They had been practicing for an event the next day at the high school where Chie taught. Yoshi was going to interview Sachiko about her student days before the war, that carefree time of study and friends that was cut short by the battle. Chie hoped the interview would inspire her students to ask their own grandparents, great-grandparents, and elderly neighbors about the past, while they still had the chance. Sachiko had her own mission. She worried over the new base in Henoko and the remilitarizing of Japan, feeling as though the country was approaching another war. She wanted to impress upon the students that if another war broke out, they would be among the first ones drafted to fight. If war could happen to her, it could happen to them, and so they had to advocate for peace.

But before Sachiko had a chance to speak, she suffered a heart attack in the school parking lot, just as Yoshi was bringing her to the event. A couple of hours later, she died at the hospital. It would be up to the younger generations to pass on her message of peace.

11

AI

LIKE RINA SHIMABUKURO, AI TAMAKI HAD JUST ENTERED HER TWEN-
ties and lived in Uruma City. These similarities meant news of the
murder hit Ai especially hard. As she read on her cell phone that the
missing woman had been killed, the suspect an ex-marine, her hand
started trembling. It was the first time her body had acted like that,
moving without her direction, taken over by a feeling so strong and
unfamiliar she couldn't name it. She could only feel it coursing through
her, shaking the small screen at which she stared.

Ai had heard about the missing woman on social media—the spec-
ulation that she had been kidnapped by a cult, or that her boyfriend
had harmed her. Ai had never imagined an American could have killed
her. That kind of danger hadn't been on Ai's mind. Like others of her
and Rina's generation, Ai had grown up seeing the U.S. bases not as
a hazard, a reminder of war, or a great injustice, but as a fixture of the
landscape. Driving by their barbed-wire-topped fences was as normal as passing a Starbucks. Ai had heard about the negative effects
of the U.S. military presence—the crimes, the accidents. In 1959, a
U.S. military fighter jet had crashed into the elementary school Ai

later attended. The F-100 killed seventeen people, including eleven students, and injured a couple hundred more. Family members of the deceased, community members, and students held annual memorials at the school. But still, the base issues seemed distant, unconnected to Ai's life. And, like most people in Uruma, Ai's parents were more conservative. They didn't question the bases, and neither did Ai.

This started to change when Ai was in college. She was a student at Meio University, in the island's north, when then-governor Hirokazu Nakaima backed out of his campaign promise and granted permission to the U.S. military to fill in Oura Bay to build the new base. Ai heard about the mass protests that erupted and, driven mostly by curiosity, went to see them at Camp Schwab and Takae. She had the impression the protestors were "activists," a label with negative connotations born from the videos that circulated on social media. In the videos, irate demonstrators hit the cars of U.S. soldiers leaving base. They yelled things like *Yankee, go home*. Many Okinawans of Ai's generation found these videos distasteful. They felt for the Americans, whom they had grown up alongside, who could have been their friends. Some categorized the rants of these activists as hate speech.

But when Ai met the protesters, she learned the people in the videos were outliers. More often, those outside the base gates were elderly survivors of World War II, motivated not by hate but by a desire for peace and a commitment to not repeat the horrors of the past. Talking to them was eye-opening. Like most Okinawans, Ai hadn't learned much about the prefecture's wartime and postwar history in school. Under the national curriculum, students learn about ancient Japanese history, but not about the Ryukyu Kingdom or the recent history of where they live. They don't study the occupation years or the reversion movement—the previous seven decades that have led to Okinawa's current situation. "They have no idea," said political science professor Manabu Sato. He had verified this by quizzing his students, asking them what the term *fukki undo* meant, or the significance of the date May 15. Zero out of one hundred students had heard of the term that means reversion movement—the mass movement that swept Okinawa in the 1960s and helped lead to the return of the islands to Japan. "I was shocked," Sato said. As for May 15—the date Okinawa reverted to Japan in 1972—only about 30 percent knew that was Fukki no Hi, Reversion Day, even though the local newspapers always ran a history series leading up to it. His students didn't read the newspapers. And they never studied that period of history in school. Sato thought part of the reason young people aren't involved in the Henoko movement is because they don't know Okinawan history.

Ai got her education at the sit-in, talking with protestors. Her thinking about the bases began to evolve. She got more and more involved in the anti-base movement, recognizing her role as one of the few young people. She joined the local contingent of SEALDS, a national student organization fighting to protect Japan's peace constitution. From there she was asked to serve alongside well-known older activists as a co-representative of the All-Okinawa Coalition, which worked to stop construction of the new base. She started making media appearances. For the local television station, she interviewed her grandfather about his experiences fighting in the Battle of Okinawa, the type of intergenerational conversation that's rare on the island. On screen, she asked him, point blank, whether he had killed anyone. Maybe, he said. Later, in private, he said yes.

The news about Rina Shimabukuro's murder was a new turning point—a story that hit close to home. It could have been Ai.

The first person she called after seeing the news was Suzuyo Takazato, the co-chair of Okinawa Women Act Against Military Violence. Suzuyo hadn't yet heard, so Ai was the one to tell her: another murder. Another rape. They met that night to strategize. The women wanted to act, but also to remain respectful of the victim's family during a time of mourning. They decided to hold a press conference the next day and, a couple of days later, a silent protest. At the press conference, Ai said, "I'm speechless with fear, anger and sadness after someone of my generation was killed. As residents of Okinawa, which hosts many bases, we must continue to try and convey our feelings to the Japanese and U.S. governments." At the silent protest outside the U.S. Marine Corps base Camp Foster, she gathered with a couple thousand demonstrators dressed in black and white. They held up signs that read, "Don't rape Okinawa," "Unforgivable," and "You killer go home right now!" They held up pictures of butterflies, which in Okinawan lore carry the dead to the next world. As they marched, women wept. Elderly protesters held up fists of resistance. A gray-haired man banged his umbrella against the base fence, keeping time like a tinny marching drum. Holding a banner that demanded the withdrawal of the U.S. military from the island, Ai bowed her head, her face scrunched in sorrow.

When I first met Ai the next year in a Naha café, she was dressed in a crisp white blouse and tailored jeans and carried a ladylike beige handbag. Her long, reddish-brown hair and makeup were carefully done. She was friendly, polite, and rather soft-spoken. Her laugh was light and sparkling. She periodically checked her appearance in a hand mirror, and had the kind of inward focus that people in their early twenties often do. Like Ai, I had a certain image of an activist, and this wasn't it. I had expected someone more fiery, less demure. But to underestimate Ai based on these stereotypes would be a mistake.

On a blazing Sunday afternoon in June a couple of months after Rina's death, Ai took the stage in front of 65,000 people at a rally in Naha. The temperature climbed toward 95 degrees, but the crowds filled the athletic park in support of the rally's goals: to mourn Rina and demand the withdrawal of all marines from Okinawa. Brandishing signs in yellow, black, and red that said, on one side, "Our anger has passed its limit," and "Pull out the marines" on the other, they sat on the ground under umbrellas and sunhats, listening to the speakers. In Tokyo, a sister rally outside the Japanese parliament building attracted more than seven thousand people.

In Naha, after a moment of silence, Suzuyo Takazato read a letter from Rina's father: "Why was it our daughter? Why did she have to die?" When it was Ai's turn to speak, she bowed to the governor and other leaders seated on stage, then took her place behind the lectern. For a second, a look of terror passed over her face. Although people never believed her, Ai hated public speaking, whether in front of 65,000 people or six. But as a co-representative of the All-Okinawa

Coalition, she had the opportunity to speak, and she wanted to take advantage of it. She wanted to tell the country how she felt. At the lectern, she squinted in the sun. Like others, she was dressed in black, a funeral outfit. The ends of her hair were curled. Tens of thousands of people spread out before her, fanning themselves, waiting.

From the beginning of her eight-minute speech, she seemed emotional, a bit breathless, her brow furrowed. First, she addressed all women who had been sexually assaulted by U.S. military personnel. She wanted to give them a voice. Then she spoke directly to Rina: "Thinking about you, many people in this prefecture wept, got angry, felt sadness and held feelings of depression that cannot be described with words. I have had conflicted feelings in my mind every day, thinking that if I speak, I could hurt you or your loved ones because I did not know you. But I don't want to remain silent."

Not even two minutes in, she delivered an explosive line. Addressing the Japanese prime minister, Shinzo Abe, and all Japanese people on the mainland, she asked, "Who is the second perpetrator of this crime?" She paused. Her face grew more contorted, her voice shaky. She continued, loud: "It's you." There were audible gasps and scattered applause from the otherwise subdued crowd. She seemed to have woken them from their grief- and heat-induced torpor. After that, they were with her, letting out more sounds of approval as her voice grew stronger. She asked how much longer Tokyo would make Okinawans look like fools. She called the actions by the U.S. military to prevent incidents like this "worn-out, childish, simplistic," and "meaningless." She addressed then–U.S. president Barack Obama, asking him to liberate Japan from America.

Halfway through, she started to cry, emitting a sob and pausing to wipe her eyes with a handkerchief. She sniffed. The crowd encouraged her with whistles and applause. She was weeping, but not stopping. "The woman who was killed was around my age," she said. "This could happen to me or one of my friends. . . . How long do we have to put up with them treating us like this?"

Later, she shouted the message on the protest signs, "Our anger has passed its limit," then held a sign over her head, along with everyone else on stage. The tens of thousands of people in the park did the same, like Ai was looking into an infinity mirror.

In the aftermath of Rina's death, Obama and Abe discussed the incident in a mainland Japan meeting, with both condemning the crime. Okinawa's prefectural assembly adopted a resolution demanding the United States and Japan remove all marines from Okinawa, the first such resolution ever. Federal officials increased the number of police patrolling the streets of Okinawa, and the U.S. military banned all servicemembers on the island from drinking off base for thirty days and required them to be back on base by midnight ("Cinderella Liberty"). *Stars and Stripes* reported a "strange new silence" on Gate 2 Street. The Fourth of July that summer was quiet, too, after the military cancelled fireworks and concerts in order to "demonstrate unwavering respect for the loss our friends on Okinawa experienced."

Meanwhile, many women reported feeling less safe. "It's now become difficult for me to go out at night because I'm too scared," one female college student said. In Uruma, walkers avoided the area around the river. An annual women's self-defense class in the city had five times as many participants as the year before. Women recalled past experiences with U.S. soldiers through a new, eerie lens, imagining *what if.* "I could have been the one who was assaulted," a twenty-one-year-old office worker said. She remembered a time when American servicemen approached her near Kadena Air Base; she "became stiff and couldn't move." Another woman recalled a U.S. soldier coming up to her car while she was stopped at a traffic light. "I felt a chill," said the thirty-six-year-old mother of two. After that, she didn't drive with her windows down.

In the neighborhood where the accused killer, Kenneth Franklin Gadson, lived with his wife, baby, and in-laws, some residents were shocked that the dark side of the bases could almost touch them like that. "It is beyond our imagination that someone who committed such a horrible crime lived in our neighborhood," a local community leader said. "Yonabaru is not a place where many foreigners live like in the central section of the island. Whenever an incident involving [a] military member occurs in the central area, we used to feel sorry for the people in the area, but we have always thought it was something like fire on the other side of the river."

People's shock and fear increased when, ten months after the murder, details of that night finally emerged. Kenneth Gadson gave his account of what happened to the U.S. military–affiliated newspaper, *Stars and Stripes*. He had been jailed since the Naha District Court indicted him for abandonment of a body, then homicide and rape resulting in murder. Awaiting trial, he communicated through his Japanese lawyer, who passed on the story to the paper. It ran under the headline, "Former Kadena Worker Reveals Gruesome Details of Okinawan Woman's Death." In an accompanying photo, Rina looks like she's in high school, dressed in a standard navy-colored uniform. Her face, up close and unguarded, is full of youth and hope.

Gadson and his lawyer, Toshimitsu Takaesu, had already been telling the newspaper the story of Gadson's childhood in New York City. The account spoke of mental illness, abuse, and a disturbing relationship toward women that stemmed from Gadson's experience with his mother. His father had never been in his life. According to Gadson's statements, as a child he heard voices and was treated for ADHD and "socialized, non-aggressive, conduct disorder," which, according to the American Psychiatric Association, "is characterized by behavior that violates either the rights of others or major societal norms." It can include aggression, property destruction, and deceitfulness. By high school, Gadson was fantasizing about "kidnapping, restraining and raping women." Women were "sneaky." "For him, women are either good or they are his enemy," Takaesu told *Stars and Stripes*. "There is no gray zone. Asked how he can tell if the woman is a good person or not, he said, 'It's in the eye. You can tell.'" Takaesu implied these issues circled back to Gadson's relationship with his mother and foster mother. As a teenager, he "often inflicted violence on his mother." He thought about killing himself and a foster mother he said was abusive. Later, Gadson traded his mother's surname for his wife's Japanese one in order to distance himself from his mother.

His impulses to kill didn't stop. He said when he applied to join the marine corps in 2007, he announced in a group interview he wanted to become a marine "to kill people." If true, the remark didn't alarm the recruiter; Gadson became a marine. Later, training at Camp Lejuene, he fought the urge to commit suicide by attacking his comrades. "Out on the [shooting] range, I had the urge to go into the bushes and shoot at others and I could get shot," he said. His suicidal impulses continued, and he claimed to be impaired by recent suicide attempts—overdoses of sleeping pills—when he confessed to Rina's murder.

When it came to his account of the death, *Stars and Stripes* told readers they were "withholding some alleged details of the crime because of their graphic nature." Forensic evidence couldn't corroborate or disprove his version of events, because by the time he directed police to her body, the Okinawan elements had left little to examine. Dental records were needed to identify her.

According to Gadson, the incident began when he spotted Rina on the street in Uruma. "When she passed my car and I saw her more clearly, I heard the voice in my head tell me, 'It's her' and that she's the one that will fulfill my fantasy," read his statement, transcribed by Takaesu. "I wasn't 100 percent sure that she was the right one, but when I looked up, I saw a red, full moon and I just knew that that was a sign." He left his car and assaulted her. "I intended to hit her with the stick and make her lose consciousness, then put her in the suitcase, take her to a hotel and then rape her." He believed he could get away with rape because he knew women in Japan rarely reported the crime to police.

He said he didn't mean to kill her. He said he never got the chance to rape her. He said she hit her head in the struggle, as he dragged her out of sight from passing cars. When she tried to speak, he choked her. She lost consciousness. He searched her, taking her keys and cellphone. Before he tossed them, along with the stick, into the river, he snapped a photo of her phone. Then he stuffed her into the suitcase and drove north. In the woods, he dumped her onto the ground. "When I disposed of her, I thought she may have said something," he said.

"I thought that she may be alive, so I stabbed her with a knife to find out." He stabbed her again and again. "She did not let out a sound." He figured she was already dead.

"During the drive home, I was thinking that the effort required to play out my fantasy was more than I expected and the fatigue and stress was not worth it," he said. "I was expecting the police to come for me in a few days, but since they didn't I stopped worrying about it. I continued with my daily routine and went to work as usual. I didn't really think about the girl."

Later, after questioning him, police said they found the stick and keychain in the riverbed, and a photo of Rina's phone on his. They said they found blood matching Rina's DNA in his car.

Of course, Okinawans reacted with horror and outrage at Gadson's account. "It's disgusting," a local journalist told me. "By saying that, he tried to escape being jailed or being sentenced to death." Many believed Gadson released the statements as a preemptive for his defense, to start establishing his case for mental illness. He had already been denied a change of venue and believed the six-person jury, if chosen in Okinawa, would be biased. "All women on Okinawa . . . have the victim's mindset with a feeling that the victim could have been me," Takaesu wrote in the change-of-venue petition. "Men and women alike share the mourning feeling with the victim's parents and feel a close kinship with the victim's family." In his statement, Gadson acknowledged the demonstrations that had taken place after Rina's murder—"so when the trial starts, the Okinawan people will surround the court, attend the hearings, and place pressure on the jurors. . . . They believe that the case is cold-blooded and heinous, and will decide to give me the death sentence."

In Japan, the death sentence is usually reserved for those found guilty of more than one slaying. But Rina's father made public that he wanted the ultimate punishment for his daughter's killer. A few days before what would have been her birthday, he released his own statement: "July 18 is our daughter's 21st birthday, but her smiling face is gone forever. We hope that the assailant receives a death sentence and experiences the pains, agonies and fear that our daughter [went] through."

The *Stars and Stripes* story seemed like a strange way for Gadson to garner sympathy. People focused on one quotation from Takaesu, who may have been trying to show Gadson couldn't tell right from wrong: "[Gadson] is competent enough to feel that he has not been treated fairly in the way the incident has been reported, but he is incompetent to recognize the seriousness of his conduct. He has no sense of guilt for the victim. To him, it was her fault for having been there at the time."

Gadson says it was her fault, the local papers reported. A *Stars and Stripes* reporter expressed frustration to me over this reading of the article. She thought the point wasn't that Gadson was blaming his victim; it was that he was insane. "When I read the reaction in the Japanese-language paper, I was so disappointed," she told me. "What he's saying is that he's insane. He's not normal. . . . We clearly explained in [the article] how insane he is. . . . He shouldn't have been in society from the beginning." She insisted that *Stars and Stripes* wasn't Gadson's "mouthpiece"—they were just conveying the fact of his insanity.

The question of fault—his, hers, the U.S. military's, the Japanese government's, the Japanese people's—was what people debated following the murder. There were those who spread rumors Gadson and Rina were dating, implying that would make Rina somehow culpable. There was Ai, who accused the Japanese prime minister and mainland citizens. After that speech, she received death threats. Some Japanese conservatives pointed the finger back at her: "People in Okinawa have also caused incidents." Some threatened, illogically, to take over Okinawa again. She had expected responses like that. What she hadn't been ready for, what was new, were the angry messages from mainland liberals. They wrote her saying they were on the side of Okinawans, they were the ones who cared about Okinawa. They felt betrayed by her accusation. They couldn't see what Ai could see, which was that they were complicit. They didn't work to change politics at the national level, so the burden of U.S. military bases in Okinawa could be reduced. They wanted to help Okinawans, but not enough to fight to have bases moved to the mainland.

"I wanted the people of mainland Japan to think about the pain Okinawa suffers," Ai said the following year. But the responses from mainlanders made her feel like the gap between there and Okinawa was larger than the hundreds of miles of ocean between them.

Others in Okinawa debated whether the U.S. military should be implicated in the crime. Gadson had left the marines two years earlier. He was a civilian now, and a resident of Japan. This was a Japanese matter, some argued. Online, a *Stars and Stripes* reader, "Bill," wrote, "The Japanese accepted him into their society after he got out of the Military. He left American society because he didn't like it. He blended into Japanese society and became one of them, even marrying one and having a Japanese child. . . . The bases and military have nothing to do with what happened. It is the fault of the Okinawan government if they accepted him to live there." Another reader responded, "Bill, you're completely wrong." Claiming (contrary to accounts I heard) Gadson's wife had left him, the commenter said Gadson "was never embraced by the Japanese/Okinawans, and was never a part of, or integrated into Japanese/Okinawan society. . . . Gadson was simply a con-artist . . . and a vagrant who [stole] a base job away from a local national while committing a heinous rape and murder in the process that tarnished the image and stained the honor of all who serve honorably." Without Japanese-language skills or an advanced degree, Gadson had only been qualified to work on base. Gadson lived in Okinawa because of the bases.

As part of their coverage of the June rally for Rina, NHK World, Japan's international public broadcaster, aired a segment called "Uncovering the Emotions of Okinawan People." A Japanese reporter in a white pantsuit and high ponytail traveled from Tokyo to interview rally participants, asking them how they felt about Americans. "I don't have anti-U.S. feelings," said a middle-aged man wearing a straw hat and a white hand towel around his neck. A woman, frowning with concentration, said, "I think we don't need the U.S. bases here, but I don't dislike Americans." These comments surprised the reporter. She mentioned a survey of Okinawa residents that found over half had "negative feelings about the U.S. military bases. . . . But when they were asked if they feel close to the U.S., almost 60 percent of the respondents said yes."

This didn't surprise me. Of course Okinawans feel close to the United States. They've been living with Americans for decades. Not wanting a foreign military base in the middle of your city is different than disliking a whole nation of people. In recent years, Okinawans have made clear through democratic elections that they oppose such a heavy U.S. military presence on their island. They have elected anti-base leaders, from the governor to mayors to national representatives, and polls show most residents don't want the new base in Henoko built. In Japanese and international news, this dissent is well known. There are news stories about the mass protests, the angry speeches from politicians. What isn't as well known, what many reporters seemed surprised to discover after Rina's death, is this doesn't mean Okinawans hate Americans. On the contrary.

"Personally, I'd be sad if [the bases] all left," longtime Naha City assemblyman Eisaku Yara told the Los Angeles Times. "After 70 years, we are all family here." He thought there should be more opportunities for meaningful interactions between locals and the American military community, like the cross-cultural exchange he experienced in junior high. "I remember doing a weekend home stay on one of the U.S. bases," Yara said. "I stayed with a black serviceman, his wife and two kids. It was a chance to experience American culture, which I only knew from TV and movies."

A fifty-one-year-old man from Okinawa City told a Japanese newspaper he skipped the rally because it signified "too much opposition to the U.S. bases." The newspaper pointed out the man's cousin was married to a U.S. serviceperson. With "an expression of complexity on his face," the man said, "The recent murder was atrocious—but it doesn't mean that all soldiers are bad people."

In Tokyo, an Okinawan college student said he felt betrayed by the murder. "We are working to get along with U.S. soldiers. Why was there a crime like this now?" He acknowledged, "Some people have been victimized due to the presence of U.S. bases. But I cannot imagine Okinawa without U.S. bases." Because he saw both positive and negative sides to the U.S. military presence, he couldn't decide his stance on the issue.

Ai Tamaki recognized the ambivalence many young people in Okinawa feel. They might oppose the bases because of incidents like Rina's murder, but still have friends in the U.S. military. This perspective causes younger protesters to clash with older ones, she said. Once, Ai brought her American serviceman friend to the Henoko sit-in, and activist Hiroji Yamashiro yelled at her: *I didn't think you were that kind of girl.* For Yamashiro, seeing her with the man evoked popular prejudices about amejo. A woman who associated with American servicemen must be dirty, immoral, traitorous. *That kind of girl.* Narrow-minded thinking like that could be another reason more young people don't get involved in the protest movement.

Despite any ambivalence, Ai's stance toward the bases became clearer after she spoke publicly about Rina's death. Along with receiving hate messages, she was approached by rape survivors who confided they had been sexually assaulted by American soldiers, too. Six women total—one friend and five strangers—approached Ai to share their stories of rape by U.S. servicemen. This made Ai feel the base issue wasn't a matter of international security. It was a matter of local women's security. For their safety, the bases needed to close.

In "Uncovering the Emotions of Okinawan People," the NHK reporter acknowledged the large number of sexual assaults by American soldiers in Okinawa over the years. But she noted that many local women chose to marry Americans, too. "Without a doubt, the women of Okinawa have suffered most at the hands of the U.S. military," she concluded. "But women also know the positive side of American culture more than anyone else in Japan." This was a remarkable comment, coming from the polished Tokyo newscaster. Japan itself has a long, twisting relationship with the United States, stemming from the war and occupation years. After the war, the country became, as historian John Dower puts it, "locked in an almost sensual embrace with its American conquerors," an embrace from which "the Americans could not or would not let go." With her comment, the NHK reporter was elevating Okinawan women over everyone else in the country, even the cosmopolitan men and women in Tokyo, for their intimate knowledge of Americanness, of a country that looms large in the national psyche.

Kenneth Gadson's trial took place in the Naha District Court in November 2017. He pled guilty to rape resulting in death and illegal disposal of a body, but not to murder. He insisted he hadn't planned to kill Rina Shimabukuro—just rape her—while the prosecution argued murder had been his intent all along. In court, Gadson sat wearing his prison-issued white T-shirt, blue pants, and plastic sandals and kept mostly quiet, stating, "I choose to remain silent" when given the chance to testify or respond to Rina's tearful parents, who issued a statement reiterating their wish for the death penalty. "A murderer, who took my daughter's life, should not be allowed to live," Rina's mother said in the statement, read by the prosecution. Gadson's lawyers implored the court not to mix up his case with political issues surrounding the bases. "The defendant on trial is one human being," they said. Later, Gadson's lawyer, Takaesu, said, "I'm not asking for the court to lighten the defendant's sentence. I won't complain if the sentence is the same as what is given to a Japanese person."

At the end of the three-day trial, Gadson finally spoke. "I'm not a bad person," he said, "and I didn't mean for any of this to happen."

A week later, the court announced its decision. The judges and jury convicted Gadson of murder and sentenced him to life in prison with hard labor. Explaining the verdict, the chief judge said, "The life of the victim—who had just celebrated her adulthood—was suddenly taken and her body was abandoned in the bushes. Her body was not found until it was reduced to bone; her sorrow is immeasurable. . . . There is no reason to find a lighter sentence than life imprisonment." During the sentencing, Gadson remained expressionless, while Rina's parents wept. Okinawans in attendance yelled that Gadson "had no remorse" and pointed their fingers at the U.S. military presence. In the local media, newspapers applauded the conviction, but reminded readers of the larger culprit. A *Ryukyu Shimpo* editorial stated, "The U.S. and Japanese governments have a heavy responsibility for not being able to prevent these recurring incidents," and agreed with Rina's father that the U.S. military bases should be closed "as soon as possible." An editorial in the *Okinawa Times* also called for a base reduction and said the sentencing gave locals little comfort: "Why is it that we still feel depressed even though the verdict was given as demanded? One cannot be calm when thinking about the fear, pain and devastation that the victim faced." The "reality," the editorial board said, was that "one cannot safely go for a walk in a private community even 72 years since the Battle of Okinawa."

By the Irei no Hi more than two years after Rina's death, her wooded memorial took up two large tables filled with flowers, bottled drinks, and stuffed animals. The Snoopy clutching a heart was still there, grayed and melted after a life outdoors. He was joined by a teddy bear and giant Hello Kitty heads. Off to one side, where I had seen police tape, strings of paper peace cranes cascaded from the trunk of a tree.

People hadn't forgotten Rina, but in the end her death didn't have the political impact many wanted. The marines didn't go anywhere, and Obama didn't usher in change to the U.S.–Japan security alliance, instead maintaining the status quo. Ironically, the election of Donald Trump in November 2016 got some anti-base liberals in Okinawa hopeful again, because he was a wildcard who had complained that Tokyo wasn't paying enough for U.S. bases and had threatened to close them. Soon, though, Abe and Trump were playing golf together, and Tokyo resumed construction of the new base, dropping concrete blocks into the bay while protesters on kayaks tried to stop them. Governor Takeshi Onaga renewed his fight against the project, in July 2018 announcing he planned to revoke the central government's permission to fill in the bay. Less than two weeks later, however, he died from pancreatic cancer at age sixty-seven. In the months leading up to his death, he had grown skeletal, and I remembered something an activist in Henoko had told me. Etsuko Urashima talked about Nago City mayors who had fought the new base, facing incredible pressure from Tokyo. One ended up dying from cancer at a young age, and people speculated the stress of his position was what really did him in. "I feel like he got killed by the Japanese government," Urashima said.

Many people think it's only a matter of time before anti-base sentiment in Okinawa disappears, a result of the passing of older generations. Younger people are less educated about their history, more accepting of the bases they've known their whole lives, and more focused on the daily work of living, rather than politics. The Japanese government knows about this waiting game, political science professor Manabu Sato told me. "In ten more years, Okinawan society will be totally different," he said, and paused. "If that leads to a happier life for Okinawan young people, it's okay." But he doubted decisions based on ignorance could lead to happiness.

The thing was, I did meet many Okinawans who were happy with the island as it was. Not all were ignorant of the history. Some carried the contradictions of the bases like a quiet, personal struggle, something to be mulled over but not discussed. And I did meet young people—like Ai Tamaki, Maki Sunagawa, and Chie's niece Yoshi—who, on their own, were studying the history of their island. In learning the history, they were rethinking the present day, questioning and challenging the U.S. military presence. They were in the minority, to be sure, and vulnerable to getting pulled away from activism by various pressures. That was what happened to Maki Sunagawa, the young Okinawa Christian University instructor. She got involved in the national student organization SEALDS and made media appearances opposing the Henoko base. She said she and Ai Tamaki were two of only about ten young people in Okinawa involved in activism like that. "I know all of them," she told me with a rueful laugh when we met in the university café. Though she felt a responsibility to continue her activism because of this scarcity, she had stepped aside due to family pressure. Her relatives didn't support the base presence, but objected to Maki speaking about the issue in public. "They don't want to see me in the newspapers. . . . because it's really complicated," she said. Her family thought that by speaking out she was risking her reputation and relationships, as well as theirs. They saw the issue as taboo. In private, you could be against the bases. But in public, among neighbors and co-workers, you didn't talk about it, out of fear of criticism or offending someone. Maki said she could accept that her activism had severed friendships and attracted angry messages from strangers. But she couldn't risk alienating her family. Elderly people, she said, had more freedom. Retired and at the ends of their lives, they didn't have to answer to anyone.

As for Ai Tamaki, her family did support her activism. But Ai, too, started stepping away from the anti-base movement. She told me she had shifted her focus to her studies, enrolling in a political science master's program. She aspired to become a journalist and report on the base issues. One activist told me that other activists had pushed Ai too hard, getting her to do too much before she was ready, excited to have a beautiful young face in their midst and before the cameras. Many people wanted Ai to go into politics, but she was resisting. The national exposure and backlash she had experienced must have taken their toll, although when I asked her if the death threats scared her, she said she got used to them, with a little laugh. She joked about a time someone left a vibrator on her car around Christmas, wrapped like a present.

"She is strong," a male Okinawan journalist said to me. "I couldn't take it."

After Onaga's death, the governor's race to replace him was closely watched by the nation, as it would determine whether the prefecture would continue to oppose the new base or accept it. The outcome would also answer a larger question: Was the anti-base movement fading out, a show of a small minority? Or did the majority of Okinawans oppose another base, even if they did so quietly? Candidates on both sides of the race supported closing Air Station Futenma because of its hazardous location. Everyone agreed on that. The debate was whether its "replacement" would be in Okinawa or elsewhere in Japan. On one side was the Abe-backed LDP candidate, Atsushi Sakima, a former

Ginowan City mayor. He supported building the new base in Henoko, but devised a campaign strategy of not mentioning the issue. Instead, he focused on the economy, promising improvements for Japan's poorest prefecture. On the other side of the race was a former House of Representatives member from the opposition Liberal Party, who was vocally against the Henoko base. In his campaigning, fifty-eight-year-old Denny Tamaki said he had a special ability to negotiate with the United States over the issue because of his mixed-race background. Tamaki is the son of an Okinawan woman and U.S. marine, and has never met his father. "It's not possible that the democracy of the country of my father will reject me," he joked at a rally, seeming to know that wasn't the case. The audience laughed.

Tamaki faced common criticism toward "shima hafu," mixed American-Okinawans who live in Okinawan society and not in the base world. On Twitter, he was called "an incomplete hafu" and jeered at: "You can't even speak English!" Others, however, agreed that his mixed-race background came with advantages. Said one supporter, "I think there are some things only he can do." Still others didn't focus on his heritage, used to seeing him in the public sphere since his days as a radio personality and musician. "He is super popular. It doesn't matter [if] he is half-American," said one Uruma City resident. Tamaki himself said he was a "symbol of postwar Okinawa," and emphasized the importance of revitalizing the islands' traditional culture, proposing an annual "Ryukyu History and Culture Day." Unlike others in his position, who are linked to the U.S. bases by blood, he didn't seem conflicted about expressing his Okinawan identity and opposition to the U.S. military presence. Being half American didn't mean he couldn't be Okinawan and advocate for the bases' closure. He proudly carried all these truths within him at once.

Tokyo worked hard to defeat Tamaki, sending high-profile mainland politicians to Okinawa to campaign for Sakima. Their efforts didn't work. In September 2018 Tamaki won the election, becoming the next governor of Okinawa. Again, the people of the prefecture had made clear through their votes that they opposed another base on the island. "Filling [the sea] with earth in Henoko is an action of destroy-

ing democracy," Tamaki said outside Camp Schwab a few days after
the election. "I want to put forth all of my energy to show the entire
world that our democracy starts here."

Recently, I attended an event in Seattle with leaders from Japan and
the United States. At a lunch overlooking Puget Sound, I met a Japanese government official from Tokyo and brought up the topic of Okinawa. His eyes lit up. He had a special interest in the issue.

"Of course we feel for the people of Okinawa," he said, and I smiled,
thinking he might express support for their struggle in Henoko. He
didn't. "But the best place for the new base is on the island."

"You don't think they have enough bases already?" I asked.

He talked about geopolitics and national security, the importance
of that location. The second part of his answer surprised me. "Plus,
Okinawans are already used to living with American bases," he said
lightly.

This irked me. Refusing to relieve someone of a burden because
you think they must be used to it seemed callous and condescending.
Later, though, I saw the truth in his answer. It was what I had realized,
too: keeping the bases in Okinawa is easier because they have become
embedded there. Over the decades they have become entwined with
the local population, making them harder to uproot and plant in a new
community, starting the process over. In fact, the way Okinawans
were "used to" the bases was what drew me to Okinawa in the first
place. I fell in love with the melding of cultures, the contradictions,
complexities, and unexpected worlds. I understood why some people
on the island like it the way it is. The U.S. military presence creates
social spaces and opportunities otherwise hard to find in Japan. This is
part of its staying power.

But the more I learned about the situation and history, the more I
felt bases in Okinawa need to close. Knowing how Okinawans suffered through World War II; how the United States snatched their
land; how mainlanders relegate bases to Okinawa to keep them out of
their own backyards; how there's no strategic reason for such a heavy
military concentration on one small island; how pervasive sexual

assault is; and how Okinawans have demonstrated their opposition, time and again, through democratic means, I know it's an injustice to have so many U.S. bases continue to exist in Okinawa. Okinawans are as deserving of a political voice and personal security as any other citizen.

Although after Denny Tamaki's election the Japanese government promptly resumed ignoring Okinawa's demands to stop construction of the new base, his governorship left me hopeful. Tamaki, Japan's first mixed-race governor, embodies Okinawa's contradictions, how someone can be intimately tied to the U.S. military presence but fight for its reduction. This is the kind of ambiguity that's needed in Okinawa. Too often, the conversation is oversimplified, and people are silenced. More recognition of the contradictions, the gray spaces—the thorny realities instead of simplistic illusions—will allow more people to speak. Maybe his governorship will open up the dialogue. Maybe young people who live more fully in these gray spaces will feel comfortable joining the conversation. Tamaki's personal story also conjures up the prefecture's postwar history, which far too few people in Okinawa, Japan, and the United States know. More awareness of this history will mean more awareness of what the anti-base movement is really about.

At that Seattle lunch, I didn't have a response for the government official from Tokyo. There was so much I wanted to say about Okinawa, about its history and injustices and beauty, but we were gazing at sailboats and making polite talk over shrimp. To have him understand, I needed to tell him the whole story. I needed to bring to life the people I had met there, the women in dialogue with two of the world's superpowers, the ones telling truths others don't want to hear.

ACKNOWLEDGMENTS

THE BEGINNINGS OF THIS BOOK STRETCH BACK MORE THAN FIFTEEN years, and so there are countless people who supported, encouraged, helped, and influenced me along the way. Though I can't name everyone here, I'm grateful to you all.

First and foremost, thank you to everyone in Okinawa who was in some way part of this book. Your openness and generosity in inviting me into your lives and helping me understand the island made this work possible. Special thanks to the women profiled in these pages, as well as to the entire Miyagi family, the McGowan family, Ayano Kayo, Chota Takamine, Chieri Matsuda, Yuki Kokubo, Charlotte Murakami, Vera Fry, and Naomi Noiri.

Thank you to the institutions that have supported me: the Fulbright program for the grant that allowed me to spend a year in Okinawa, and the Brown University East Asian Studies Department, which funded my first summer on the island. My time at the Kyoto Consortium for Japanese Studies (KCJS) and, later, at the Iowa Writer's Workshop was foundational and transformative; my time at Playa was like a dream.

At The New Press, I'm grateful to Ben Woodward for contributing his keen insight into book-writing and Japan, and to Emily Albarillo, Jessica Yu, and the rest of the team that helped bring this book into the world. Thank you for believing in books like this.

To Ayesha Pande, for championing this project from the start and shepherding it through its many iterations with grace, fortitude, and wisdom: my deepest thanks.

Thank you to my early readers and writing comrades: Katie Chase, Elizabeth Cowan, Jennifer duBois, Soma Mei Sheng Frazier, Matt Griffin, James Han Mattson, Keija Parssinen, Rinku Patel, Shawna Yang Ryan, and Karina Salem. Thanks also to Lisa Ayabe and Nancy Lee for venturing with me into the field.

Lily Welty Tamai has been a generous friend, mentor, and research partner since we were fellow Fulbrighters—I appreciate you so much. I'm also grateful to Stephen Murphy-Shigematsu, who has been an inspiration for years. At Brown, Kerry Smith and Steve Rabson guided my first Okinawa research project; much more recently, Steve kindly shared his time, feedback, and expertise. Thank you.

I'm grateful to those who published my previous work on Okinawa, pieces of which appear in this book. These publications include *The Nation*, *Travel + Leisure*, *Roads & Kingdoms*, *Explore Parts Unknown*, *Kyoto Journal*, *Hotel Okinawa*, *Hapa Japan*, *Off Assignment*, *Asian American Literary Review*, and *Brown Alumni Magazine*.

Much love and gratitude goes to my friends and family, especially my parents, Nadine Narita and Nick Johnson, who gave me my first books and blank notebooks and supported me down this uncertain path; and to Mari Johnson, Kenji Johnson, Kim Ries, Joe Fitzgerald, and Katrina Kelley. In loving memory of George and Mary Narita and Bob Johnson.

Finally, thank you to Rei, for your love, support, and braininess, and for building a home with me in which this book could be born, and to Nina, also just born—we love you.

NOTES

This book is based on interviews, my own observations, and sources that are noted below. Throughout the book, Japanese names are written in the Western style, with the given name preceding the family name. Some individuals' names have been changed to protect their privacy. I often use "Okinawan" to refer to the people of Okinawa, though I recognize that many may identify as Japanese or something else or prefer multiple labels.

1: Rina

3. **"land, sea, and air forces, as well as other war potential"** Quoted in Masamichi S. Inoue, *Okinawa and the U.S. Military: Identity Making in the Age of Globalization* (New York: Columbia University Press, 2017), 63.

3. **Tokyo pays billions of dollars** Calculations about how much Japan pays differ, as official numbers don't exist. See, for example, Ayako Mie, "How Much Does Japan Pay to Host U.S. Forces? Depends on Who You Ask," *Japan Times*, January 31, 2017; Taoka Shunji, "Trump's Threat to Charge Japan More for U.S. Forces: Taoka Shunji Says 'Let Them Leave,'" *Asia-Pacific Journal: Japan Focus*, Vol. 15, Iss. 1, No. 5 (January 1, 2017).

3. **While most countries receive money** Kent E. Calder, *Embattled Garrisons: Comparative Base Politics and American Globalism* (Princeton, N.J.: Princeton University Press, 2007), 190, 195, 200.

4. **The highest concentration of marine corps units** Newcomers' Orientation Welcome Aboard, Camp Foster, Okinawa, June 7, 2017.

5. **the air force, not the marines, would be the ones to respond** Former U.S. Army Colonel Lawrence Wilkerson, who served as chief of staff to U.S. Secretary of State Colin Powell during the George W. Bush administration, recently explained why the marines in Okinawa wouldn't be useful during a conflict on the Korean peninsula: "We used to say we'd probably get there after [the conflict] was over. Or if they did get there at all, they would simply be a minor addition to 600,000 Koreans." He said the United States maintains marine corps bases in Okinawa because they cost less there, thanks to Japanese sympathy payments: "There was no genuine strategic need for those Marines on Okinawa. It was all about money and keeping them." See Yukiyo Zaha, "Former Army Colonel Wilkerson Says Marine Corps in Okinawa Is 'Strategically Unnecessary,'" *Ryukyu Shimpo*, December 23, 2018.

6. **overseas bases cost American taxpayers as much as 100 billion dollars a year** David Vine, *Base Nation: How U.S. Military Bases Abroad Harm America and the World* (New York: Metropolitan Books, 2015), 211. See this source for more on the argument against U.S. bases abroad.

9. **"The relationships between Okinawa, America, Japan and me. . . ."** Naobumi Okamoto, *A Night in America* (Tokyo: Life Goes On, 2016).

9. **On the evening of April 28, 2016** My account of this incident draws on interviews, first-hand reporting, the police's missing-person flyer, and the following sources: Matthew M. Burke and Chiyomi Sumida, "Okinawans Shaken by News Marine Veteran May Have Killed Woman," *Stars and Stripes*, May 21, 2016; Matthew M. Burke and Chiyomi Sumida, "Attorney: Former Marine Charged with Rape, Murder Suffered Mental Illness," *Stars and Stripes*, September 4, 2016; Matthew M. Burke and Chiyomi Sumida, "Defense Attorney Says Okinawa Confession Made in a Daze," *Stars and Stripes*, May 20, 2016; "Kadena Worker Admits Strangling, Stabbing Woman Found Dead in Okinawa," *Kyodo News*, May 20, 2016.

11. **under police questioning, Gadson confessed** "Confession is king" in the Japanese judicial system, as Richard Lloyd Parry explains when writing about the 2000 murder of Lucie Blackman, a British woman who was working as a hostess in Tokyo. Police hold suspects for days without access to lawyers, sometimes depriving them of food, sleep, and water, sometimes using violence—all to get a confession, which usually comes, one way or

another. Especially valuable is any information about the crime that the police don't know but can verify. See Richard Lloyd Parry, *People Who Eat Darkness: The True Story of a Young Woman Who Vanished from the Streets of Tokyo—and the Evil that Swallowed Her Up* (New York: Farrar, Straus and Giroux, 2011), 254–255.

11. **"If you get the community relations right"** Julie Makinen, "Finding US-Japanese Harmony amid the Discord of a Death in Okinawa," *Los Angeles Times*, June 6, 2016.

12. **Eldridge reportedly had been fired** Jon Mitchell, "U.S. Marines Official Dismissed over Okinawa Protest Video Leak," *Japan Times*, March 23, 2015.

12. **"the most dangerous base in the world"** Allegedly attributed to Donald Rumsfeld.

2: Eve

20. **a 1969 *New York Times* article** Takashi Oka, "Okinawa Mon Amour," *New York Times*, April 6, 1969.

22. **The Ryukyu Kingdom was a thriving civilization** This description of the Ryukyu Kingdom comes from George Kerr, *Okinawa: The History of an Island People* (Boston: Tuttle Publishing, 2000), 90, 94–95, 96, 99, 109.

23. **Leaders in Tokyo showed little concern** Sources for this section include Masamichi S. Inoue, *Okinawa and the U.S. Military: Identity Making in the Age of Globalization* (New York: Columbia University Press, 2017), 57–58; Mark Brazil, "Cycads: 'Living Fossils' with a Deadly Twist," *Japan Times*, June 16, 2013; Laura Hein and Mark Seldon, "Culture, Power, and Identity in Contemporary Okinawa," in *Islands of Discontent: Okinawan Responses to Japanese and American Power*, ed. Laura Hein and Mark Seldon (Lanham: Rowman & Littlefield, 2003), 5; Steve Rabson, "Assimilation Policy in Okinawa: Promotion, Resistance, and 'Reconstruction,'" in *Okinawa: Cold War Island*, ed. Chalmers Johnson (Cardiff, CA: Japan Policy Research Institute, 1999), 140.

24. **"devil beasts"** Etsuko Takushi Crissey, *Okinawa's GI Brides: Their Lives in America*, translated by Steve Rabson (Honolulu: University of Hawaii Press, 2017), 34.

24. **When the Americans invaded in late March 1945** U.S. forces invaded the Kerama Islands, off the southwestern coast of the main island, at the end of March 1945, before landing on the beaches of Okinawa Island on April 1.

24. **Okinawa transformed into a battlefield** Sources for this summary of the battle include Danielle Glassmeyer, "'The Wisdom of Gracious

Acceptance:' Okinawa, Mass Suicide, and the Cultural Work of *Teahouse of the August Moon*," *Soundings*, Vol. 96, No. 4 (2013), 406; Inoue, *Okinawa and the U.S. Military*, 62; Masahide Ota, "Introduction," in *Ryukyu Shimpo, Descent into Hell: Civilian Memories of the Battle of Okinawa*, trans. by Mark Ealey & Alastair McLauchlan (Portland, ME: MerwinAsia, 2014), xvii.

25. **"What's the difference between Okinawans and people from outside the prefecture?"** Haruko Taya Cook and Theodore F. Cook, *Japan at War: An Oral History* (New York: The New Press, 1992), 372.

25. **In their hasty pre-invasion research** David John Obermiller, "The U.S. Military Occupation of Okinawa: Politicizing and Contesting Okinawan Identity 1945–1955," University of Iowa dissertation (2006), 31.

25. **dropping on the island millions of leaflets** Arnold G. Fisch, Jr., *Military Government in the Ryukyu Islands: 1945–1950* (Washington, D.C.: Center of Military History, 1988), 42.

25. **Describing the postwar scene, an American navy doctor wrote** Obermiller, "U.S. Military Occupation," 159, 160.

25. **The only remnant of the former Ryukyu Kingdom's great Shuri Castle** Frank Gibney, "Okinawa: Forgotten Island," *Time*, November 28, 1949.

25. **Rapes, killings, and atrocities did occur** See, for example, John W. Dower, *War Without Mercy: Race and Power in the Pacific War* (New York: Pantheon Books, 1986).

26. **120,000 Okinawans were in refugee camps** Etsuko Takushi Crissey, *Okinawa's GI Brides*, 21.

26. **"Had it not been for this American policy"** Masahide Ota, "Re-Examining the History of the Battle of Okinawa," in *Okinawa: Cold War Island*, ed. Chalmers Johnson (Cardiff, CA: Japan Policy Research Institute, 1999), 18.

26. **"American forces treated Okinawans"** Quoted in Etsuko Takushi Crissey, *Okinawa's GI Brides*, 19.

26. **One American veteran remembered** Glassmeyer, "'The Wisdom of Gracious Acceptance,'" 414.

26. **the American victors confined almost all Okinawan survivors in these refugee or internment camps** Refugee camp sources include Chris Ames, "*Amkerikamun*: Consuming America and Ambivalence Toward the U.S. Presence in Postwar Okinawa," *Journal of Asian Studies* Vol. 75, No. 1 (February 2016), 41; Michael S. Molasky, *The American Occupation of Japan and Okinawa: Literature and Memory* (London: Routledge, 1999), 19; Fisch,

Military Government in the Ryukyu Islands, 48–49; Nicholas Evan Sarantakes, *Keystone: The American Occupation of Okinawa and U.S.–Japanese Relations* (College Station: Texas A&M University Press, 2000), 30; *Ryukyu Shimpo, Descent into Hell*, 401, 404; Okinawa-shi Gallery of Postwar Culture and History, *Watching History from the Street: Histreet* (Okinawa City Hall, 2011), 9, 12; Peace Park Museum and Histreet Museum exhibits; Ruth Ann Keyso, *Women of Okinawa: Nine Voices from a Garrison Island* (Ithaca, NY: Cornell University Press, 2000), 22; Warner Berthoff, "Memories of Okinawa," *Sewanee Review*, Vol. 12, No. 1 (Winter 2013), 145.

27. **"As far as we could see"** Quoted in Asato, "Okinawan Identity and Resistance to Militarization and Maldevelopment," in *Islands of Discontent: Okinawan Responses to Japanese and American Power*, ed. Laura Hein and Mark Seldon (Lanham: Rowman & Littlefield, 2003), 228.

27. **"everything looked white like snow"** Asato, 229.

27. **Americans had taken tens of thousands of acres from tens of thousands of landowners** Kozue Akibayashi and Suzuyo Takazato, "Okinawa: Women's Struggle for Demilitarization," in *Bases of Empire: The Global Struggle Against U.S. Military Posts*, ed. Catherine Lutz (New York: NYU Press, 2009), 251; Gavan McCormack and Satoko Oka Norimatsu, *Resistant Islands: Okinawa Confronts Japan and the United States* (Lanham: Rowman & Littlefield, 2012), 78.

27. **the local population tripled** Obermiller, "U.S. Military Occupation," 333.

27. **"The students here are too puzzled"** Gibney, "Okinawa: Forgotten Island."

28. **The occupying government, the United States Civil Administration of the Ryukyu Islands** Sources on USCAR activities include Rabson, "Assimilation Policy in Okinawa," 145; Obermiller, "U.S. Military Occupation;" Mire Koikari, "Cultivating Feminine Affinity: Women, Domesticity, and Cold War Transnationality in the U.S. Military Occupation of Okinawa," *Journal of Women's History*, Vol. 27, No. 4 (Winter 2015), 122.

29. **The prefecture's per capita GDP came to surpass that of countries like Italy and Canada** Sarah Kovner, "The Soundproofed Superpower: American Bases and Japanese Communities, 1945–1972," *Journal of Asian Studies*, Vol. 75, No. 1 (February 2016), 91.

30. **national homogeneity is more myth than reality** See, for example, Stephen Murphy-Shigematsu, "Multiethnic Japan and the Monoethnic Myth," *MELUS* Vol. 18, No. 4 (Winter 1993), 63–80.

30. **The larger area is known as Koza** Koza history sources include Okinawa-shi Gallery, *Watching History from the Street*, 3; Linda Angst, "In a

Dark Time: Community, Memory, and the Making of Ethnic Selves in Oki-
nawan Women's Narratives," Yale University dissertation (2001), 276, 289;
Molasky, *American Occupation of Japan and Okinawa*, 53, 55; Kina, "Subal-
tern Knowledge," 450; Emerson Chapin, "Negro G.I. Area on Okinawa
Typifies Unofficial Segregation," *New York Times*, March 29, 1964; Rafael
Steinberg, "Okinawa's Americans Enjoy Luxury Living," *Washington Post*,
May 4, 1964.

31. **White gangs battled black gangs, resulting in deaths** In February
1964, the arrest of a black marine by a white MP seemed to set off a series
of retaliatory attacks. In protest of the arrest, according to the *Washington
Post*, a group of black marines "stormed" the police box of the MP, "hurling
rocks" at him. Weeks later, a black marine's body was discovered in an on-
base reservoir. Police ruled the death an accident, though evidence showed
he had died before entering the water. Then, a white marine was beaten to
death one night outside his barracks. Police charged four black marines. By
May, a serviceman said the next hit was brewing. "Something's going to
happen," a white marine from the American South told a reporter. "We're
just playing it cool, now. Not saying anything, just passing 'em by. But I can
tell you, there's going to be trouble." See Steinberg, "Okinawa's Americans
Enjoy Luxury Living."

31. **"where the Third World grates against the First and bleeds"** Gloria Anzaldúa, *Borderlands/La Frontera* (San Francisco: Aunt Lute Books,
1999), 25.

34. **"normally refers to one's food preference"** Makoto Arakaki,
"Romancing the Occupation: Concepts of 'Internationalisation' Among
Female University Students in Okinawa," in *Under Occupation: Resistance
and Struggle in a Militarized Asia-Pacific*, ed. Daniel Broudy, Peter Simpson,
and Makoto Arakaki (Newcastle upon Tyne: Cambridge Scholars Publishing, 2013), 43.

34. **"sex-hungry military-man-eating machine"** Arakaki, "Romancing
the Occupation," 39.

36. **114th in gender equality** World Economic Forum, *Global Gender Gap
Report 2017*, http://reports.weforum.org/global-gender-gap-report-2017.

36. **In Japan, there's a history** Sources for this history include Dower,
War Without Mercy, 209–10; John G. Russell, "Historically, Japan Is No
Stranger to Blacks, Nor to Blackface," *Japan Times*, April 19, 2015; Susan
Chira, "2 Papers Quote Japanese Leader on Abilities of Minorities in U.S.,"
New York Times, September 24, 1986; Bruce Wallace, "Once Shunned as
Racist, Storybook Bestseller in Japan," *Los Angeles Times*, June 12, 2005;
John G. Russell, "Playing with Race/Authenticating Alterity: Authentic-

ity, Mimesis, and Racial Performance in the Transcultural Diaspora," *CR: The New Centennial Review*, Vol. 12, No. 1 (Spring 2012), 44, 48, 49; Nina Cornyetz, "Fetishized Blackness: Hip Hop and Racial Desire in Contemporary Japan," *Social Text*, No. 41 (Winter, 1994), 122.

37. **"sambo, saru (ape), kaibutsu (monster), and kuronbo (nigger)"** John G. Russell, "Narratives of Denial: Racial Chauvinism and the Black Other in Japan," *Japan Quarterly* (October 1991), 419. Some have questioned whether "kuronbo" should be translated as Russell does, because Japan lacks the same racial/racist history toward black people that the United States has. See Mitzi Carter and Aina Hunter, "A Critical Review of Academic Perspectives of Blackness in Japan," in *Multiculturalism in the New Japan: Crossing the Boundaries Within*, ed. Nelson H. Graburn, John Ertl, and R. Kenji Tierney (New York: Berghahn Books, 2008), 196–7.

37. **Many African American people have said they prefer living in Japan** See, for example, *Struggle and Success: The African-American Experience in Japan*, dir. Regge Life, 1993; "Reel Life & Real Life," interview by Stewart Wachs, *Kyoto Journal*, October 26, 2011. Also see later in this book.

37. **"During my entire year in Tokyo"** Carter and Hunter, "A Critical Review," 194.

37. **"I came to understand that some students . . . "** Carter and Hunter, "A Critical Review," 190.

37. **"I was totally in awe of his dick"** Amy Yamada, *Bedtime Eyes*, trans. Yumi Gunji and Marc Jardine (New York: St. Martin's Press, 2006), 6.

38. **"cooler than cool"** Yamada, *Bedtime Eyes*, 4.

38. **"It was the saddest color in the world"** Yamada, *Bedtime Eyes*, 23.

38. **"As if by being assaulted by a dirty thing"** Quoted in Russell, "Narratives of Denial," 423. (Russell's translation, which differs from Gunji & Jardine's.)

38. **"loads and loads"** Yamada, *Bedtime Eyes*, 63.

38. **"Had *Bedtime Eyes* depicted a relationship"** Russell, "Narratives of Denial," 424.

39. **The same type of Sambo doll** Russell, "Playing with Race/Authenticating Alterity," 50–51.

40. **"We support the riot"** Inoue, *Okinawa and the U.S. Military*, 54–55.

40. **Okinawans were seeking solace** See, for example, Shigeaki Kinjo's story in Cook and Cook, *Japan at War: An Oral History*, 366.

40. **the percentage of Christians climbed higher** Angst, "In a Dark Time," 74–75, 76.

44. "American guys are like nicotine" Arakaki, "Romancing the Occupation," 39.

44. "treated me as though I were a 'bitch'" Arakaki, "Romancing the Occupation," 35.

44. "the 'enemy' [as] he who would ravage women as booty" Mary Louise Roberts, *What Soldiers Do: Sex and the American GI in World War II France* (Chicago: University of Chicago Press, 2013), 87.

44. French men were grappling with their defeat Roberts, *What Soldiers Do*, 9.

45. "From an Okinawan man's perspective" Arakaki, "Romancing the Occupation," 44.

45. "Young women who had engaged in sexual relationships" Roberts, *What Soldiers Do*, 79.

45. "The tonte was massively photographed" Roberts, *What Soldiers Do*, 79.

45. These photographs, "widely distributed" Roberts, *What Soldiers Do*, 80.

45. "Usually, the militarization process" Ayano Ginoza, "Articulations of Okinawan Indigeneities, Activism, and Militourism: A Study of Interdependencies of U.S. and Japanese Empires," Washington State University dissertation (May 2010), 92–93.

45. "males in society who, like Ame-jo, remain hungry" Arakaki, "Romancing the Occupation," 48.

3: Ashley

49. The U.S. military began reshaping Okinawa Sources for this history include "Roads on Okinawa Built as You Wait," *New York Times*, April 3, 1945; Annmaria Shimabuku, "Petitioning Subjects: Miscegenation in Okinawa from 1945 to 1952 and the Crisis of Sovereignty," *Inter-Asia Cultural Studies*, Vol. 11, No. 3 (2010), 360, 362; John Dower, *Embracing Defeat: Japan in the Wake of World War II* (New York: W.W. Norton & Co., 1999), 224, 624n60; Frank Gibney, "Okinawa: Forgotten Island," *Time*, November 28, 1949; Robert Trumbull, "Okinawa's Charm and Comforts Make Troops Vie for Duty There," *New York Times*, April 24, 1956; M.D. Morris, *Okinawa: A Tiger by the Tail* (New York: Hawthorn Books, Inc., 1968), 81, 91–92; David John Obermiller, "The U.S. Military Occupation of Okinawa: Politicizing and Contesting Okinawan Identity 1945–1955," University of Iowa dissertation (2006), 165; Annmaria Shimabuku, "Transpacific Colonialism: An Intimate View of Transnational Activism in Okinawa," *CR: The New Centen-*

nial Review, Vol. 12, No. 1 (Spring 2012), 132–3; Kensei Yoshida, *Democracy Betrayed: Okinawa Under U.S. Occupation* (Bellingham, WA: East Asian Studies Press, 2001), xi–xii, 117; William L. Worden, "Rugged Bachelors of Okinawa," *Saturday Evening Post*, March 30, 1957, 86; Rafael Steinberg, "Okinawa's Americans Enjoy Luxury Living," *Washington Post*, May 4, 1964; Michael S. Molasky, *The American Occupation of Japan and Okinawa: Literature and Memory* (London: Routledge, 1999), 25.

49. **"Okinawa glitters as [a] military prize"** "Okinawa Glitters as Military Prize," *New York Times*, April 6, 1945.

49. **"the southern half of the island still presented a scene of almost total destruction"** David John Obermiller, "The U.S. Military Occupation of Okinawa: Politicizing and Contesting Okinawan Identity 1945–1955," University of Iowa dissertation (2006), 161.

49. **"hovels" and "run-down Quonset communities"** Frank Gibney, "Okinawa: Forgotten Island," *Time*, November 28, 1949.

49. **"a dumping ground for Army misfits"** Gibney, "Okinawa: Forgotten Island."

49. **"Only the worst were sent to 'The Rock'"** Morris, *Okinawa: A Tiger by the Tail*, 81.

50. **Those on Okinawa were "of lower caliber"** Arnold G. Fisch, Jr., *Military Government in the Ryukyu Islands: 1945–1950* (Washington, D.C.: Center of Military History, 1988), 81.

50. **"more than 15,000 U.S. troops"** Gibney, "Okinawa: Forgotten Island."

50. **"putting up white organdy curtains"** Doris Fleeson, "2000 American Women and Children Live on Okinawa," *Daily Boston Globe (1928–1960)*, November 4, 1949 (ProQuest Historical Newspapers: *Boston Globe*), 26.

50. **"Boredom set in"** Morris, *Okinawa: A Tiger by the Tail*, 81.

50. **"living is so cheap"** Faubion Bowers, "Letter from Okinawa," *New Yorker*, October 23, 1954, 139.

51. **"The Commissaries . . . can supply"** Quoted in Morris, *Okinawa: A Tiger by the Tail*, 103.

51. **"space for a maid's cot"** Morris, *Okinawa: A Tiger by the Tail*, 104.

51. **"prepared by Japanese maids"** "Rosemead Girl Finds Okinawa No Paradise," *Los Angeles Times*, November 18, 1956.

51. **"This is a long way from home"** Nicholas Evan Sarantakes, *Keystone: The American Occupation of Okinawa and U.S.–Japanese Relations* (College Station: Texas A&M University Press, 2000), 71.

52. **Kadena Air Base is eight times less dense** Mark L. Gillem, *America*

Town: Building the Outposts of Empire (Minneapolis: University of Minnesota Press, 2007), 241.

52. **younger generations have grown fatter and sicker** Interview with Chota Takamine, May 29, 2017. See also Colin Joyce, "Japanese Get a Taste for Western Food and Fall Victim to Obesity and Early Death," *The Telegraph*, September 4, 2006.

53. **Jon Mitchell obtained slides from a presentation** Jon Mitchell, "U.S. Marines Briefing Links Crimes to 'Gaijin Power'; for Okinawans, 'It Pays to Complain,'" *Japan Times*, May 25, 2016.

53. **"a prime example of [the U.S. military's] arrogant attitude"** Jon Mitchell, "U.S. to Review Okinawa Training Procedures After Report Reveals Sessions Downplayed Military Crimes, Disparaged Locals," *Japan Times*, May 28, 2016.

56. **earlier trainings that had characterized** See Jon Mitchell, "Okinawa: U.S. Marines Corps Training Lectures Denigrate Local Residents, Hide Military Crimes," *Asia-Pacific Journal: Japan Focus*, Vol. 14, Iss. 13, No. 4 (July 1, 2016).

57. **he allegedly made a number of disparaging remarks** David Vine, *Base Nation: How U.S. Military Bases Abroad Harm America and the World* (New York: Metropolitan Books, 2015), 257.

57. **"The perception that Okinawans were permanent wards of the U.S."** Obermiller, "U.S. Military Occupation," 171.

58. **a story the local papers reported** David Allen and Chiyomi Sumida, "Dependents Suspected in Vandalism of Home," *Stars and Stripes*, February 13, 2009; "Chatan Woman Accuses Americans of Hurling Rocks at Her Residence," *Japan Update*, February 12, 2009; "Marines' Kids Step Forward, Admit to Throwing Rocks," *Japan Update*, February 18, 2009.

58. **"When someone under the [Status of Forces] agreement commits a crime"** Erik Slavin and Chiyomi Sumida, "Politics Play Role in Tokyo's Reaction to U.S. Crime on Okinawa," *Stars and Stripes*, June 16, 2016.

59. **"SOFA status personnel make up less than 4%"** Mitchell, "Okinawa: U.S. Marines Corps Training Lectures."

59. **"Between 2006 and 2015, members of the U.S. military"** Mitchell, "Okinawa: U.S. Marines Corps Training Lectures."

59. **Releases of crime statistics on other marine corps bases** See, for example, Mark Walker, "Military: Crime Inside Gates of Camp Pendleton," *San Diego Union-Tribune*, May 1, 2010.

60. **"Hi, Sexy!"** Nika Nashiro, "What's Going On Behind Those Blue Eyes? The Perception of Okinawa Women by U.S. Military Personnel,"

University of Hawaii master's thesis (May 2013), 1.

60. "cheap electronics, HONDA & TOYOTA" Nashiro, "What's Going On Behind Those Blue Eyes?," 34.

60. "beautiful" and "heavily cultured" Nashiro, "What's Going On Behind Those Blue Eyes?," 17.

61. "'good care-takers,' willing to 'serve the [GIs],'" Nashiro, "What's Going On Behind Those Blue Eyes?," 54.

61. "I love Okinawa, it's easy to flirt with people" Nashiro, "What's Going On Behind Those Blue Eyes?," 55.

61. "The more English they speak" Nashiro, "What's Going On Behind Those Blue Eyes?," 57.

62. He didn't think America was a "caring society" Matthew M. Burke and Chiyomi Sumida, "Attorney: Former Marine Charged with Rape, Murder Suffered Mental Illness," Stars and Stripes, September 4, 2016.

66. As scholars have argued See Rebecca Forgash, "Negotiating Marriage: Cultural Citizenship and the Reproduction of American Empire in Okinawa," Ethnology, Vol. 48, No. 3 (Summer 2009), 218.

67. Americans marrying Japanese citizens Scholar Rebecca Forgash notes that during a two-year period starting in 2000, over half of the 387 active-duty servicemen who attended the premarital seminar on Okinawa were marrying Japanese citizens. See Forgash, "Negotiating Marriage," 227.

68. "The company commander told them" Etsuko Takushi Crissey, Okinawa's GI Brides: Their Lives in America, translated by Steve Rabson (Honolulu: University of Hawaii Press, 2017), 36.

69. the one to deploy families See Vine, Base Nation, 49–51.

69. "Out here I have to live with my wife" Worden, "Rugged Bachelors of Okinawa," 88.

4: Sachiko

76. education was also in service to the emperor Sources on education during this time include Saburō Ienaga, The Pacific War, 1931–1945 (New York: Pantheon Books, 1978), 21, 107, 124, 153; Himeyuri Peace Museum: The Guidebook, trans. Ikue Kina and Timothy Kelly (Himeyuri Peace Museum, 2016), 10, 11; John W. Dower, War Without Mercy: Race and Power in the Pacific War (New York: Pantheon Books, 1986).

76. The government pushed this wartime propaganda Sources on wartime propaganda include Ryukyu Shimpo, Descent into Hell: Civilian

Memories of the Battle of Okinawa, trans. by Mark Ealey & Alastair McLauchlan (Portland, ME: MerwinAsia, 2014), 230; Dower, *War Without Mercy*, 61, 231–2; Ienaga, *The Pacific War*, 100, 101, 102, 103, 114; Ruth Ann Keyso, *Women of Okinawa: Nine Voices from a Garrison Island* (Ithaca, NY: Cornell University Press, 2000), 6, 36.

77. **Okinawans became increasingly militarized** Sources on the militarization of Okinawans include Keyso, *Women of Okinawa*, 37–38; Yoshiko Sakumoto Crandell, "Surviving the Battle of Okinawa: Memories of a Schoolgirl," *Asia-Pacific Journal*, Vol. 12, Iss. 14, No. 2, April 7, 2014; *Himeyuri Peace Museum: The Guidebook*, 11, 13, 20; Ienaga, *The Pacific War*, 195; *Ryukyu Shimpo, Descent into Hell*, 217, 221;

77. **They were seen as the homes of deities** Christopher Nelson, *Dancing with the Dead: Memory, Performance, and Everyday Life in Postwar Okinawa* (Durham: Duke University Press, 2008), 123.

78. **a U.S. submarine torpedoed and sunk the *Tsushima Maru*** *Ryukyu Shimpo, Descent into Hell*, 16–18. A total of 4,500 Okinawans died on ships during this time, and 80,000 people successfully evacuated to Kyushu or Taiwan. Thirty-two evacuation ships were hit or sunk by U.S. forces, including the *Tsushima Maru*.

78. **Girls aged fifteen to nineteen joined nursing corps** My account of the student nurses draws on sources that include *Himeyuri Peace Museum: The Guidebook*; Haruko Taya Cook and Theodore F. Cook, *Japan at War: An Oral History* (New York: The New Press, 1992); *Ryukyu Shimpo, Descent into Hell*; *17 Short Lived*, dir. Saiki Takao, 2014; Keyso, *Women of Okinawa*; Ienaga, *The Pacific War*.

79. **their own military's atrocities** For descriptions and accounts of atrocities, see, for example, Ienaga, *The Pacific War*; Dower, *War Without Mercy*; Cook and Cook, *Japan at War*.

79. **Some recounted to Okinawans the brutal rapes** *Ryukyu Shimpo, Descent into Hell*, 31.

79. **The Imperial Japanese Army forbade its soldiers** Ienaga, *The Pacific War*, 49.

79. **"one hundred million Special Attack Force"** Dower, *War Without Mercy*, 232–3. Dower (323n17) notes that at that time, Japan's population was actually just over seventy million. "The phrase 'hundred million' (ichioku) was poetic license, and carried a classical and heroic aura fully in keeping with the wartime ideology."

79. **"We were consumed by a burning desire"** *Ryukyu Shimpo, Descent into Hell*, 26.

79. "The militarist education had affected" *Ryukyu Shimpo, Descent into Hell*, 40.

79. "Give your life for the sake of the Emperor" Cook and Cook, *Japan at War*, 355.

80. "We sang the school song" *Ryukyu Shimpo, Descent into Hell*, 254.

80. "You girls will all die" *Ryukyu Shimpo, Descent into Hell*, 256.

80. Another graduate remembered the ceremony differently *17 Short Lived*, dir. Saiki Takao, 2014, 28:30–29:35.

80. "They petrified us all" Cook and Cook, *Japan at War*, 355.

81. "I hear that Okinawan girls are hooking up" *Ryukyu Shimpo, Descent into Hell*, 303.

81. "I felt more dead than alive" *Himeyuri Peace Museum: The Guidebook*, 47.

82. "the kind of sound you hear" *Himeyuri Peace Museum: The Guidebook*, 44.

83. a World War II bomb that had detonated recently *Ryukyu Shimpo, Descent into Hell*, 185.

83. "All of southern Okinawa has the same problem" "Excavation Triggers WWII Bomb Blast," *Japan Update*, January 23, 2009.

83. one outside a Naha kindergarten in 1974 *Ryukyu Shimpo, Descent into Hell*, 175.

83. Over 2,500 tons of unexploded ordnance See David Allen and Chiyomi Sumida, "More Unexploded WWII Ordnance Disposed of on Okinawa," *Stars and Stripes*, December 13, 2008.

83. The strategy of the Imperial Japanese Army My account of the battle draws on sources that include *Ryukyu Shimpo, Descent into Hell*, 219, 221, 240, 266, 394; *Himeyuri Peace Museum: The Guidebook*, 18–19, 30; Keyso, *Women of Okinawa*, 5.

85. "The thing that frightened me most was myself" *Ryukyu Shimpo, Descent into Hell*, 315.

85. "I felt nothing at all" *17 Short Lived*, dir. Saiki Takao, 2014, 43:54.

85. "The battlefield is now in such chaos" *Ryukyu Shimpo, Descent into Hell*, 222.

86. "Americans will protect you" See *Himeyuri Peace Museum: The Guidebook*, 47; Cook and Cook, *Japan at War*, 360.

86. "Never live to suffer the disgrace" *Himeyuri Peace Museum: The Guidebook*, 49.

86. One Japanese soldier taught Sachiko Mie Sakamoto, "Twist in Okinawa Mass Suicides Tale," *Japan Times*, June 26, 2008.

86. "We thought we were hearing the voices of demons" Cook and Cook, *Japan at War*, 360.

86. some 300,000 to 400,000 civilians lost their lives Ienaga, *The Pacific War*, 202; Dower, *War Without Mercy*, 298.

86. nearly one in three Okinawans Dower, *War Without Mercy*, 298; Masahide Ota, "Introduction," in *Ryukyu Shimpo, Descent into Hell*, xvii.

87. Sixty percent of the 22,000 untrained Home Guard *Ryukyu Shimpo, Descent into Hell*, 217; Masahide Ota, "Introduction," in *Ryukyu Shimpo, Descent into Hell*, xvii. The Imperial Japanese Army forced perhaps half a million Koreans to fight and work during the Pacific War. Koreans suffered high casualty rates because they were made to perform the most dangerous work and treated as less-than ("peninsula peasants") or suspicious by Japanese soldiers. Some Koreans were murdered outright by Japanese soldiers. See *Ryukyu Shimpo, Descent into Hell*, 37, 168, 169, 432–3.

87. Of the sixty-one girls The estimated number of deaths among all mobilized students varies. Some sources say about half of the approximately two thousand students died. Another says more than two thousand students total were killed. See Cook and Cook, *Japan at War*, 354; *Ryukyu Shimpo, Descent into Hell*, 25–26; *Himeyuri Peace Museum: The Guidebook*, 20.

87. they had died in a scene My account of the Tokashiki compulsory mass suicide draws on sources that include *Ryukyu Shimpo, Descent into Hell*, 33–37; Cook and Cook, *Japan at War*, 363–6; Ienaga, *The Pacific War*, 33, 34, 185.

88. "As if by chain reaction" Cook and Cook, *Japan at War*, 365.

89. "I just couldn't believe it" *Ryukyu Shimpo, Descent into Hell*, 36.

89. "the Japanese more than the Americans" Cook and Cook, *Japan at War*, 366.

89. known as Goat Eyes Norma Field, *In the Realm of a Dying Emperor: Japan at Century's End* (New York: Vintage Books, 1993), 57.

89. "I'm not afraid of dying" *Himeyuri Peace Museum: The Guidebook*, 51.

5: Arisa

90. When anti-base demonstrators joined hands Saundra Sturdevant, "Okinawa Then and Now," in *Let the Good Times Roll: Prostitution and the U.S. Military in Asia*, ed. Saundra Pollack Sturdevant and Brenda Stoltzfus

(New York: The New Press, 1992), 248.

93. **The first marriage between an Okinawan woman and an American serviceman** Etsuko Takushi Crissey, *Okinawa's GI Brides: Their Lives in America*, translated by Steve Rabson (Honolulu: University of Hawaii Press, 2017), 33–34. The marriage between Hatsuko Higa and Frank Anderson of Ohio was short-lived, lasting not even a month before the U.S. military annulled it.

93. **"I hated and feared those Americans"** Haruko Taya Cook and Theodore F. Cook, *Japan at War: An Oral History* (New York: The New Press, 1992), 359.

93. **"Half a century later"** Yoshiko Sakumoto Crandell, "Surviving the Battle of Okinawa: Memories of a Schoolgirl," *Asia-Pacific Journal*, Vol. 12, Iss. 14, No. 2 (April 7, 2014).

93. **"What a strange race"** Crandell, "Surviving the Battle of Okinawa."

93. **Another woman recalled that she was attracted** Crissey, *Okinawa's GI Brides*, 53.

94. **"When I was carrying boxes"** Crissey, *Okinawa's GI Brides*, 75.

94. **"The new story is of passion blooming"** Quoted in Crissey, *Okinawa's GI Brides*, 34.

94. **Locals celebrated the first international marriage in one village** Crissey, *Okinawa's GI Brides*, 51.

94. **marriages between Okinawans and Americans numbered more than two hundred a year** Takashi Oka, "Okinawa Mon Amour," *New York Times*, April 6, 1969.

103. *Stars and Stripes*, **the military newspaper, had reported the whole story** See David Allen and Chiyomi Sumida, "Seeking a Father's Presence," *Stars and Stripes*, September 7, 2008; Chiyomi Sumida, "To the Okinawan Widow of a Fallen Marine, a Son Is Born," *Stars and Stripes*, January 14, 2009.

6: Suzuyo

109. **the incident that changed everything** My account of the 1995 rape draws on interviews with Suzuyo Takazato, as well as sources that include Gwyn Kirk, "Women Oppose U.S. Militarism: Toward a New Definition of Security," in *Gender Camouflage: Women and the U.S. Military*, ed. Francine D'Amico and Laurie Weinstein (New York: New York University Press, 1999), 230; Elizabeth Naoko MacLachlan, "Protesting the 1994 Okinawa Rape Incident: Women, Democracy and Television News in Japan,"

in *Journalism and Democracy in Asia*, ed. Angela Romano and Michael Bromley (London: Routledge, 2005), 150; Teresa Watanabe, "Okinawa Rape Suspect's Lawyer Gives Dark Account: Japan: Attorney of Accused Marine Says Co-defendant Admitted Assaulting 12-Year-Old Girl 'Just for Fun,'" *Los Angeles Times*, October 28, 1995; Kevin Sullivan, "3 Servicemen Admit Roles in Rape of Okinawan Girl," *Washington Post*, November 8, 1995; Linda Isako Angst, "The Rape of a Schoolgirl: Discourses of Power and Gendered National Identity in Okinawa," in *Islands of Discontent: Okinawan Responses to Japanese and American Power*, ed. Laura Hein and Mark Selden (Lanham: Rowman & Littlefield, 2003), 136; Masamichi S. Inoue, *Okinawa and the U.S. Military: Identity Making in the Age of Globalization* (New York: Columbia University Press, 2017), 32; *Okinawa: The Afterburn*, dir. John Junkerman (Siglo, 2016), 1:38:23–27, 1:39:27–36; AP, "In Okinawa Rape Trial, a Plea from 2 Mothers," *New York Times*, December 28, 1995; Ronald Smothers, "Accused Marines' Kin Incredulous," *New York Times*, November 6, 1995; Chalmers Johnson, *Blowback: The Costs and Consequences of American Empire* (New York: Holt, 2000), 34; Andrew Pollack, "One Pleads Guilty to Okinawa Rape; 2 Others Admit Role," *New York Times*, November 8, 1995.

110. **Ledet "was a Boy Scout"** Watanabe, "Okinawa Rape Suspect's Lawyer."

110. **"He always wanted to go into the Marine Corps"** Smothers, "Accused Marines' Kin Incredulous."

111. **"lock the bad soldiers in the jail"** Rinda Yamashiro, "Anti-Futenma Relocation Movement in Okinawa: Women's Involvement and the Impact of Sit-In Protest," University of Hawaii master's thesis (2008), 26.

111. **"It almost makes it more arrogant"** Richard Lloyd Parry, "The Unwanted Yankees of Okinawa," *Independent*, October 19, 1995.

112. ***April 6, 1946*** Okinawa Women Act Against Military Violence, "Postwar U.S. Military Crimes Against Women in Okinawa" (July 2016), 3.

112. **One of the first known sexual assaults by an American in Okinawa** Sources for this section include George Kerr, *Okinawa: The History of an Island People* (Boston: Tuttle Publishing, 2000), 331; Chris Ames, "Crossfire Couples: Marginality and Agency Among Okinawan Women in Relationships with U.S. Military Men," in *Over There: Living with the U.S. Military Empire from World War Two to the Present*, ed. Maria Höhn and Seungsook Moon (Durham: Duke University Press, 2010), 199–200n5; Steve Rabson, "Okinawa in American Literature," *Oxford Research Encyclopedia of Literature* (May 2017) [online].

113. **"soon became convinced that the man's death"** Quoted in Kerr, *Okinawa: The History of an Island People*, 331.

113. **"The average Okinawan is a docile, rustic citizen"** Quoted in David John Obermiller, "The U.S. Military Occupation of Okinawa: Politicizing and Contesting Okinawan Identity 1945–1955," University of Iowa dissertation (2006), iii.

113. **"picture of contentment and simplicity"** "Yonabaru Naval Air Station: 1945–1946," Remembering Okinawa History, http://www.rememberingokinawa.com/page/1945_yonabaru_nas.

113. **"simple and good-natured people"** Quoted in Steve Rabson, "Introduction," in Oshiro Tatsuhiro and Higashi Mineo, *Okinawa: Two Postwar Novellas* (Berkeley: Institute of East Asian Studies, 1989), 7.

113. **"Fortunately, life is more peaceful"** M.D. Morris, *Okinawa: A Tiger by the Tail* (New York: Hawthorn Books, Inc., 1968), 87.

114. **The first major anti-base movement took place in the 1950s** At least one scholar argues that mass protest began earlier, in the late 1940s. See Obermiller, "U.S. Military Occupation."

114. **The United States Civil Administration of the Ryukyu Islands (USCAR)** My sources on USCAR include Ikue Kina, "Subaltern Knowledge and Transnational American Studies: Postwar Japan and Okinawa under U.S. Rule," *American Quarterly*, Vol. 68, No. 2 (June 2016), 452, 454n1; Mire Koikari, "Cultivating Feminine Affinity: Women, Domesticity, and Cold War Transnationality in the U.S. Military Occupation of Okinawa," *Journal of Women's History*, Vol. 27, No. 4 (Winter 2015), 123, 134n26; Obermiller, "U.S. Military Occupation," 2n5; Inoue, *Okinawa and the U.S. Military*, 47, 49; Faubion Bowers, "Letter from Okinawa," *New Yorker*, October 23, 1954, 142; interview with Dustin Wright, June 5, 2018.

114. **"It may be denied by some who are skilled political scientists"** Quoted in Nicholas Evan Sarantakes, *Keystone: The American Occupation of Okinawa and U.S.–Japanese Relations* (College Station: Texas A&M University Press, 2000), 61.

114. **"island is actually controlled by the military"** William L. Worden, "Rugged Bachelors of Okinawa," *Saturday Evening Post*, March 30, 1957, 87.

114. **"so that the will to war will not continue"** Quoted in John Dower, *Embracing Defeat: Japan in the Wake of World War II* (New York: W.W. Norton & Co., 1999), 77.

114. **"prenatal form" with the "color"** Worden, "Rugged Bachelors of Okinawa," 87.

115. **as many as one in three employed Okinawans worked in base-related jobs** Hideaki Tobe, "Military Bases and Modernity: An Aspect of Americanization in Okinawa," *Transforming Anthropology*, April 2006, 91.

115. **In its hierarchical pay structure, the U.S. military paid** Tobe, "Military Bases and Modernity," 91.

115. **When Bolivia offered four hundred Okinawans the chance** Bowers, "Letter from Okinawa," 147.

115. **mainland anti–U.S. military base demonstrations** Sources for this section include Dustin Wright, "The Sunagawa Struggle: A Century of Anti-base Protest in a Tokyo Suburb," UC Santa Cruz dissertation (2015), https://escholarship.org/uc/item/08g3h0wc, 255; J. Victor Koschmann, "Anti-U.S. Bases Movements," in *Encyclopedia of Contemporary Japanese Culture*, ed. Sandra Buckley (London: Routledge, 2002), 21–22; Dustin Wright, "'Sunagawa Struggle' Ignited Anti-U.S. Base Resistance Across Japan," *Japan Times*, May 3, 2015; Dower, *Embracing Defeat*, 553–4.

116. **"scotch the idea so prevalent in Japan"** Quoted in Sarah Kovner, "The Soundproofed Superpower: American Bases and Japanese Communities, 1945–1972," *Journal of Asian Studies*, Vol. 75, No. 1 (February 2016), 96.

116. **One Okinawa Prefecture account** Quoted in Michael S Molasky, *The American Occupation of Japan and Okinawa: Literature and Memory* (London: Routledge, 1999), 93.

117. **"It is not a commodity"** Quoted in Mark L. Gillem, *America Town: Building the Outposts of Empire* (Minneapolis: University of Minnesota Press, 2007), 36.

117. **By 1955 the number of displaced Okinawans reached a quarter million** Gillem, *America Town: Building the Outposts of Empire*, 37.

117. **"All-Island Struggle"** Sources on the All-Island Struggle include Inoue, *Okinawa and the U.S. Military*, xii, 44–45; Etsuko Takushi Crissey, *Okinawa's GI Brides: Their Lives in America*, translated by Steve Rabson (Honolulu: University of Hawaii Press, 2017), 23; Okinawa Historical Film Society; Kerr, *Okinawa: The History of an Island People*, 553; Obermiller, "U.S. Military Occupation," 405.

117. **A local newspaper described the crowd** Quoted in Inoue, *Okinawa and the U.S. Military*, 45.

118. *September 6, 1955* Okinawa Women Act Against Military Violence, "Postwar U.S. Military Crimes," 21.

118. **the occupation years were a time of widespread sexual assault** Sources for this section include Calvin Sims, "3 Dead Marines and a Secret of

Wartime Okinawa," *New York Times*, June 1, 2000; Arnold G. Fisch, Jr., *Military Government in the Ryukyu Islands: 1945–1950* (Washington, D.C.: Center of Military History, 1988), 82; *Ryukyu Shimpo, Descent into Hell: Civilian Memories of the Battle of Okinawa*, trans. by Mark Ealey & Alastair McLauchlan (Portland, ME: MerwinAsia, 2014), 453; Crissey, *Okinawa's GI Brides*, 30; Ruth Ann Keyso, *Women of Okinawa: Nine Voices from a Garrison Island* (Ithaca, NY: Cornell University Press, 2000), 86; Obermiller, "U.S. Military Occupation," 181, 182–3, 182n404.

118. **"There were so many cases of rape"** Ruth Ann Keyso, *Women of Okinawa: Nine Voices from a Garrison Island*, 86.

119. **"Because they were female . . . they had to live inside a stockade"** Morris, *Okinawa: A Tiger by the Tail*, 63.

119. **"protect our women from the poor docile natives"** Quoted in Obermiller, "U.S. Military Occupation," 166, 182.

119. **"the natural attention of the vast majority of enlisted men"** Morris, *Okinawa: A Tiger by the Tail*, 60.

119. **In response to the rash of rapes, the U.S. military found a scapegoat** Sources for this section include Arnold G. Fisch, Jr., *Military Government in the Ryukyu Islands: 1945–1950* (Washington, D.C.: Center of Military History, 1988), 83, 84–85, 86.

120. **"extreme ill will"** Quoted in Fisch, *Military Government in the Ryukyu Islands: 1945–1950*, 83.

120. **"Black troops, some at least"** Warner Berthoff, "Memories of Okinawa," *Sewanee Review*, Vol. 121, No. 1 (Winter 2013), 150.

120. **"It is impossible to determine"** Mary Louise Roberts, *What Soldiers Do: Sex and the American GI in World War II France* (Chicago: University of Chicago Press, 2013), 196.

120. **"in many cases . . . charges against black soldiers"** Roberts, *What Soldiers Do*, 196–7.

121. **"cooperation between French civilians and U.S. military authorities"** Roberts, *What Soldiers Do*, 197.

121. **"When a suspect is black and from the military"** Lisa Takeuchi Cullen, "Sex and Race in Okinawa," *Time*, August 27, 2001.

121. **One legendary story** See Sims, "3 Dead Marines"; Eric Talmadge, "Okinawa Legend Leaves Unsettling Questions About Marines' Deaths," Associated Press, May 07, 2000. http://onlineathens.com/stories/050700/new_0507000024.shtml.

122. **"You know, that is why so many Okinawans are afraid of black men"** Rebecca Forgash, "Military Transnational Marriage in Okinawa: Intimacy Across Boundaries of Nation, Race, and Class," University of Arizona dissertation (2004), 149.

123. *February 22, 1969* Okinawa Women Act Against Military Violence, "Postwar U.S. Military Crimes," 24.

123. **"Okinawa is to be one huge depot"** Arthur J. Dommen, "Viet War Supplies Stored on Okinawa," *Los Angeles Times*, April 25, 1966.

124. **"In effect, all Okinawa is one tremendous American base"** Morris, *Okinawa: A Tiger by the Tail*, 88.

124. **"Literally, there is no place in the islands"** Morris, *Okinawa: A Tiger by the Tail*, 2.

124. **Living amid a giant weapons depot** Sources for this section include Wesley Iwao Ueunten, "Rising Up from a Sea of Discontent: The 1970 Koza Uprising in U.S.-Occupied Okinawa," in *Militarized Currents: Toward a Decolonized Future in Asia and the Pacific*, ed. Setsu Shigematsu and Keith L. Camacho (Minneapolis: University of Minnesota Press, 2010), 106; Gavan McCormack and Satoko Oka Norimatsu, *Resistant Islands: Okinawa Confronts Japan and the United States* (Lanham: Rowman & Littlefield, 2012), 83; Takashi Oka, "Okinawa Issue Called a 'Tumor' Afflicting Japanese-U.S. Ties," *New York Times*, February 1, 1969; Okinawa-shi Gallery of Postwar Culture and History, *Watching History from the Street: Histreet* (Okinawa City Hall, 2011), 25.

124. **the presence of U.S. servicemen on the island reached its highest postwar number** Linda Angst, "In a Dark Time: Community, Memory, and the Making of Ethnic Selves in Okinawan Women's Narratives," Yale University dissertation (2001), 48.

124. **second major movement** Sources on the reversion movement include Inoue, *Okinawa and the U.S. Military*, 51, 52; Obermiller, "U.S. Military Occupation," 405–6.

124. **one Saturday night in December 1970 on the streets of Koza** My description of this incident draws on sources that include Jon Mitchell, "Koza Remembered," *Japan Times*, December 27, 2009; Inoue, *Okinawa and the U.S. Military*, 53–54; Okinawa Historical Film Society; McCormack and Norimatsu, *Resistant Islands*, 83; Ueunten, "Rising Up from a Sea of Discontent"; Okinawa-shi Gallery, *Watching History from the Street*, 27. Some details in these accounts are contradictory.

125. **"It felt just like a festival"** Mitchell, "Koza Remembered."

125. **for the sake of "deterrence"** McCormack and Norimatsu, *Resistant Islands*, 59.

125. Japan paid about $685 million to the United States McCormack and Norimatsu, *Resistant Islands*, 7, 59.

125. only some of Okinawans' demands were met Sources for this section include Teresa Watanabe, "Okinawa Marks 20 Years of Freedom from U.S.," *Los Angeles Times*, May 15, 1992; Inoue, *Okinawa and the U.S. Military*, xv, 35–36.

126. "As a social worker and counselor" Suzuyo Takazato, "Trials of Okinawa: A Feminist Perspective," *Race, Poverty & the Environment*, Vol. 4/5, No. 4/1 (Special Military Conversion Issue; Spring–Summer 1994), 10.

126. the story of one woman she counseled "Interview: Why Is There No End to Sexual Violence by U.S. Military Personnel in Okinawa?" *The Mainichi*, September 15, 2016.

127. "Looking back, I realize that the reversion movement" Takazato, "Trials of Okinawa," 10.

127. *September 4, 1995* Okinawa Women Act Against Military Violence, "Postwar U.S. Military Crimes," 27.

127. the prefectural government didn't want the rape publicized Additional sources for this section on the aftermath of the rape include Elizabeth Naoko MacLachlan, "Protesting the 1994 Okinawa Rape Incident: Women, Democracy and Television News in Japan," in *Journalism and Democracy in Asia*, ed. Angela Romano and Michael Bromley (London: Routledge, 2005), 150–1; Linda Isako Angst, "Loudmouth Feminists and Unchaste Prostitutes: 'Bad Girls' Misbehaving in Postwar Okinawa," *U.S.–Japan Women's Journal*, No. 36 (2009), 129; Kozue Akibayashi and Suzuyo Takazato, "Okinawa: Women's Struggle for Demilitarization," in *Bases of Empire: The Global Struggle Against U.S. Military Posts*, ed. Catherine Lutz (New York: New York University Press, 2009), 264; Suzuyo Takazato, "Report from Okinawa: Long-Term U.S. Military Presence," *Canadian Woman Studies/Les Cahiers De La Femme*, Vol. 19, No. 4 (2000), 46–47; Angst, "The Rape of a Schoolgirl," 135, 138; Inoue, *Okinawa and the U.S. Military*, xviii, 1, 68; Angst, "In a Dark Time," 356–7; Obermiller, "U.S. Military Occupation," 14; Akibayashi and Takazato, "Okinawa: Women's Struggle for Demilitarization," 255.

128. "When demanding the withdrawal of the U.S. military" MacLachlan, "Protesting the 1994 Okinawa Rape Incident," 154.

128. "Rape is only reported when it leads to murder" MacLachlan, "Protesting the 1994 Okinawa Rape Incident," 155.

129. "because the victim was young, innocent, and female" Michael S. Molasky, *The American Occupation of Japan and Okinawa: Literature and Memory* (London: Routledge, 1999), 51.

129. **The incident has been cited as a turning point** See, for example, Inoue, *Okinawa and the U.S. Military*, 38.

130. **the first Okinawa Women Act Against Military Violence meeting** Information about the early days of Okinawa Women Act Against Military Violence from Carolyn Bowen Francis, "Women and Military Violence," in *Okinawa: Cold War Island*, ed. Chalmers Johnson (Cardiff, CA: Japan Policy Research Institute, 1999), 192–4.

131. **there were 6,172 reported cases of sexual assault** "U.S. Military Sexual Assaults Down as Reports Reach Record High," Reuters, May 1, 2017.

132. *March 13, 2016* Okinawa Women Act Against Military Violence, "Postwar U.S. Military Crimes," 30.

133. **A 2014 Japanese government survey** Motoko Rich, "She Broke Japan's Silence on Rape," *New York Times*, December 29, 2017.

133. **the men had admitted that knowing these odds** Takazato, "Report from Okinawa," 45. According to Suzuyo, during their trial the men testified with further detail about why they had decided to commit rape. "Brothels are drab and reminded them of their poverty-stricken childhoods," she writes. Additionally, they knew local women weren't likely to carry weapons or report a rape—fellow servicemen had raped and gotten away with it. The men also thought their non-Asian features all looked the same to local people, so the victim wouldn't be able to identify them.

135. **"something wrong with the girl"** Lisa Takeuchi Cullen, "Sex and Race in Okinawa," *Time*, August 27, 2001.

135. **"The worst comments seemed to come from older women"** Matthew Hernon, "Shiori Ito, the Face of the #MeToo Movement in Japan, Speaks Out," *Tokyo Weekender*, February 2, 2018.

135. **the ways sexual abuse is legislated, investigated, and tried in Japan** Sources for this section include United States Department of State, Bureau of Democracy, Human Rights and Labor, *Japan 2017 Human Rights Report*, Country Reports on Human Rights Practices for 2017, https://www.state.gov/documents/organization/277329.pdf, 13; Tomohiro Osaki, "Diet Makes Historic Revision to Century-Old Sex-Crime Laws," *Japan Times*, June 16, 2017; Megha Wadhwa and Ben Stubbings, "Surviving Sexual Assault in Japan, Then Victimized Again," *Japan Times*, September 27, 2017.

136. **"If we had a society in which anyone could complain"** "Interview: Why Is There No End to Sexual Violence by U.S. Military Personnel in Okinawa?" *The Mainichi*, September 15, 2016.

136. **In 1996, three Naha District Court judges** Sources for this section on Gill, Harp, and Ledet include Andrew Pollack, "March 3–9; U.S. Service-

men Sentenced in Rape on Okinawa," *New York Times*, March 10, 1996; Michael A. Lev, "3 GIs Convicted in Okinawa Rape," *Chicago Tribune*, March 7, 1996; David Allen, "Ex-marine Decries Nature of Japan Prison Work," *Stars and Stripes*, July 18, 2004; David Allen, "Former Marine Who Sparked Okinawa Furor Is Dead in Suspected Murder-Suicide," *Stars and Stripes*, August 25, 2006.

136. **"I think it is inhumane"** Pollack, "3 U.S. Servicemen Convicted of Rape of Okinawa Girl," *New York Times*, March 7, 1996.

137. **"That's because if you don't have the perception of discriminating against others"** "Interview: Why Is There No End to Sexual Violence by U.S. Military Personnel in Okinawa?" *The Mainichi*, September 15, 2016.

137. **"Education does not help"** MacLachlan, "Protesting the 1994 Okinawa Rape Incident," 153–4.

137. **"The problem is mostly with the marines"** Forgash, *Military Transnational Marriage*, 126.

138. **One instance where this recipe led to violence** Nika Nashiro, "What's Going On Behind Those Blue Eyes? The Perception of Okinawa Women by U.S. Military Personnel," University of Hawaii Master's thesis (May 2013), 25; Travis J. Tritten and Chiyomi Sumida, "Sailors Sentenced for Gang-Rape in Case That Sparked Curfew," *Stars and Stripes*, March 1, 2013.

138. **"raises the suspicion that they timed the attack"** Quoted in Nashiro, "What's Going On Behind Those Blue Eyes?," 25.

138. **"He said this was his last tour overseas"** *Okinawa: The Afterburn*, dir. John Junkerman (Siglo, 2016), 1:36:42–1:40:57.

139. **"You!" a man shouted at her once** Cynthia Enloe, *Maneuvers: The International Politics of Militarizing Women's Lives* (Berkeley: University of California Press, 2000), 120.

139. **Chris Ames argues that her "oft-quoted remark"** Ames, "Crossfire Couples," 186.

139. **"sting[s] Okinawans with a U.S. military husband"** Ames, "Crossfire Couples," 187.

139. **"Okinawan activism has come to the point"** Annmaria Shimabuku, "Petitioning Subjects: Miscegenation in Okinawa from 1945 to 1952 and the Crisis of Sovereignty," *Inter-Asia Cultural Studies*, Vol. 11, No. 3 (2010), 371.

139. **Linda Angst has criticized Suzuyo** Angst, "The Rape of a Schoolgirl," 143.

139. **Angst also calls out "protest leaders"** Angst, "The Rape of a Schoolgirl," 152.

7: Daisy

143. **the Japanese military notoriously set up a "comfort women" system** For more on comfort women, see Yoshiaki Yoshimi, *Comfort Women: Sexual Slavery in the Japanese Military during World War II*, trans. Suzanne O'Brien (New York: Columbia University Press, 2002). For information on comfort women in Okinawa, see *Ryukyu Shimpo, Descent into Hell: Civilian Memories of the Battle of Okinawa*, trans. by Mark Ealey & Alastair McLauchlan (Portland, ME: MerwinAsia, 2014), 433.

144. **"A hundred million yen is cheap"** John Dower, *Embracing Defeat: Japan in the Wake of World War II* (New York: W.W. Norton & Co., 1999), 126.

144. **"To New Japanese Women"** Dower, *Embracing Defeat: Japan in the Wake of World War II*, 126–7.

144. **"recreation and amusement" centers** On this topic see Dower, *Embracing Defeat: Japan in the Wake of World War II*, 130–2, 133.

144. **firsthand account of occupied Okinawa** M.D. Morris, *Okinawa: A Tiger by the Tail* (New York: Hawthorn Books, Inc., 1968), 60–1.

145. **"They're just healthy, red-blooded young GIs"** Etsuko Takushi Crissey, *Okinawa's GI Brides: Their Lives in America*, translated by Steve Rabson (Honolulu: University of Hawaii Press, 2017), 32–33.

145. **Okinawan officials began collaborating with the U.S. military in building prostitution districts** Crissey, *Okinawa's GI Brides: Their Lives in America*, 31, 32.

146. **one marine corps division reported that a quarter of its troops** Nicholas Evan Sarantakes, *Keystone: The American Occupation of Okinawa and U.S.-Japanese Relations* (College Station: Texas A&M University Press, 2000), 104.

146. **the VD rate among all marines on-island was "so high"** Rafael Steinberg, "Okinawa's Americans Enjoy Luxury Living," *Washington Post*, May 4, 1964.

146. **"a neon-lit nirvana for Neanderthals"** Morris, *Okinawa: A Tiger by the Tail*, 102.

146. **"joy palaces"** William L. Worden, "Rugged Bachelors of Okinawa," *Saturday Evening Post*, March 30, 1957, 88.

146. **debt-bondage system** In addition to interviews with Suzuyo Takazato, my sources on the debt-bondage system include Saundra Pollack Sturdevant and Brenda Stoltzfus, *Let the Good Times Roll: Prostitution and the U.S. Military in Asia* (New York: The New Press, 1992), 307; Linda Angst, "In a Dark Time: Community, Memory, and the Making of Ethnic Selves in Okinawan Women's Narratives," Yale University dissertation (2001), 258.

147. **"gifts of chocolate, soaps, and face creams"** David John Obermiller, "The U.S. Military Occupation of Okinawa: Politicizing and Contesting Okinawan Identity 1945–1955," University of Iowa dissertation (2006), 192.

147. **"On Okinawa the number of prostitutes"** *Okinawa: The Afterburn*, dir. John Junkerman (Siglo, 2016), 1:32:39–1:33:32.

147. **A 1967 police survey** Crissey, *Okinawa's GI Brides*, 33.

147. **Another source estimated the number was double that** Yuki Fujime, "Japanese Feminism and Commercialized Sex: The Union of Militarism and Prohibitionism," *Social Science Japan Journal*, Vol. 9, No. 1 (Apr., 2006), 45.

147. **one in every twenty to twenty-five women** Angst, "In a Dark Time," 309.

147. **more than pineapple and sugarcane farming** Okinawa Women Act Against Military Violence, "Okinawa: Effects of Long-term U.S. Military Presence" (2007), 2.

148. **"We stuffed [the bills] into buckets"** Crissey, *Okinawa's GI Brides*, 25.

148. **These women were the ones who pulled their families** Linda Isako Angst, "Loudmouth Feminists and Unchaste Prostitutes: 'Bad Girls' Misbehaving in Postwar Okinawa," *U.S.-Japan Women's Journal*, No. 36 (2009), 119.

149. **"Every time he said he wanted something"** Ruth Ann Keyso, *Women of Okinawa: Nine Voices from a Garrison Island* (Ithaca, NY: Cornell University Press, 2000), 107.

150. **militarized masculinity** See, for example, David Vine, *Base Nation: How U.S. Military Bases Abroad Harm America and the World* (New York: Metropolitan Books, 2015), 182.

150. **Meanwhile, in the Philippines** My account of the migration and work of Filipina entertainers draws on sources that include Saundra Pollack Sturdevant and Brenda Stoltzfus, *Let the Good Times Roll: Prostitution and the U.S. Military in Asia* (New York: The New Press, 1992), 252, 254, 255, 268, 270, 292, 294, 327; Sealing Cheng, *On the Move for Love: Migrant Entertainers and the U.S. Military in South Korea* (Philadelphia: University of Pennsylvania Press, 2010), 76, 77–78, 81.

150. **in 1981 there were 11,656; in 1987 there were 33,791** Cheng, *On the Move for Love*, 80.

151. **"My salary is $400 a month"** Sturdevant and Stoltzfus, *Let the Good Times Roll: Prostitution and the U.S. Military in Asia*, 269.

151. **Her mama-san also turned out to be kind** One scholar points out that kind mama-sans like Daisy's may have cultivated their familial, protective

treatment of Filipina workers as a means of control. Workers who felt loyal toward their "mama" or "papa"-san were more likely to do as they wanted. See Cheng, *On the Move for Love*, 107.

153. **"the bargain-basement version"** Okinawa Soba (Rob), "Girls Day Off in Okinawa—Kicked Out of Japan by Misogynist Bureaucrats," Flickr, https://www.flickr.com/photos/okinawa-soba/6676515999.

153. **"Back in the States, when I go to a bar"** Cheng, *On the Move for Love*, 146.

154. **U.S. servicemen could be spotted wearing T-shirts** Katherine H.S. Moon, *Sex Among Allies: Military Prostitution in U.S.–Korea Relations* (New York: Columbia University Press, 1997), 34, 177n80.

154. **"Two slanted eyes look into mine"** Sturdevant and Stoltzfus, *Let the Good Times Roll*, 287.

156. **"a people they could feel superior to"** Warner Berthoff, "Memories of Okinawa," *Sewanee Review*, Vol. 121, No. 1 (Winter 2013), 150.

156. **"White customers who came to the bar"** Ayako Mizumura, "Reflecting [on] the Orientalist Gaze: A Feminist Analysis of Japanese–U.S. GIs Intimacy in Postwar Japan and Contemporary Okinawa," University of Kansas dissertation (2009), 167.

156. **a Filipina entertainer said when she lied that she was a virgin** Cheng, *On the Move for Love*, 143.

157. **"You can see the real Okinawa"** taka0302hg, "Mao Ishikawa Fences, OKINAWA November 2007–July 2008," July 4, 2012, YouTube, https://www.youtube.com/watch?v=aZyLJ1oA1hw, 4:36.

157. **"There are those who look down on women who work at military bars"** Mao Ishikawa, *Red Flower: The Women of Okinawa* (New York: Session Press, 2017), 1.

158. **In the black and white photographs Mao took** Mao Ishikawa, *Fences, Okinawa* (Tokyo: Miraisha, 2010), 112–3.

159. **Twenty-one-year-old "Hazel" had been in Japan** My sources on Hazel's story include interviews with Suzuyo Takazato and the following articles: David Allen and Chiyomi Sumida, "Okinawa Police Call for Kadena Soldier to Be Charged with Rape of Filipina," *Stars and Stripes*, April 27, 2008; David Allen and Chiyomi Sumida, "The Toll of Trafficking?," *Stars and Stripes*, June 20, 2007; David Allen, "Testimony for Defense Disputes Rape Account," *Stars and Stripes*, October 5, 2008; David Allen, "Kadena Servicemembers Article 32 Begins with Revelations," *Stars and Stripes*, October 4, 2008; Natasha Lee, "Church Members to Rally for Rape Accuser," *Stars and Stripes*, May 23, 2008; David Allen, "Rape Case Against GI Dismissed," *Stars and Stripes*, February 26, 2009.

159. **"Three points at issue"** Natasha Lee and Chiyomi Sumida, "Rape Charges Against Soldier Dropped," *Stars and Stripes*, May 18, 2008.

160. **"I believe there will be some legal action"** David Allen, "Backers of Rape Accuser Wanted Japan to Prosecute," *Stars and Stripes*, July 21, 2008.

160. **"to facilitate the movement and exploitation of trafficking victims"** *Trafficking in Persons Report* (U.S. Department of State, June 2004), 14.

161. **Embarrassed, Japanese lawmakers responded** This section draws on Rhacel Salazar Parreñas, *Illicit Flirtations: Labor, Migration, and Sex Trafficking in Tokyo* (Stanford, CA: Stanford University Press, 2011), 4, 54–55, 219, 234.

161. **2006 TIP Report noted Japan's "remarkable progress"** *Trafficking in Persons Report* (U.S. Department Of State, June 2006), 149.

161. **Others, however, maintained the women were not victims** See Parreñas, *Illicit Flirtations*.

164. **"As you walk along Gate [Two] Street"** Quoted in Angst, "In a Dark Time," 278–9.

164. **"For the price they paid to rent the car"** Irvin Molotsky, "Admiral Has to Quit Over His Comments on Okinawa Rape," *New York Times*, November 18, 1995.

164. **"When soldiers are risking their lives"** Hiroko Tabuchi, "Women Forced into WWII Brothels Served Necessary Role, Osaka Mayor Says," *New York Times*, May 13, 2013.

167. **more than 16 percent in 2017** "Table of Active Duty Females by Rank/Grade and Service," Defense Manpower Data Center (November 2017), https://www.dmdc.osd.mil/appj/dwp/dwp_reports.jsp.

8: Miyo

171. **stories of unwanted babies** See Annmaria Shimabuku, "Petitioning Subjects: Miscegenation in Okinawa from 1945 to 1952 and the Crisis of Sovereignty," *Inter-Asia Cultural Studies*, Vol. 11, No. 3 (2010), 369.

171. **illegal abortions** Whereas on the mainland the Japanese government enacted family-planning policies that legalized abortion and promoted contraceptives in order to control the rising postwar population, the U.S. occupation government in Okinawa kept abortion illegal—though it looked the other way when doctors began performing them, to the point that Okinawa became known as "a heaven for illegal abortions." See Kayo Sawada, "Cold War Geopolitics of Population and Reproduction in Okinawa Under U.S. Military Occupation, 1945–1972," *East Asian Science, Technology and Society: An International Journal* (2016), 402–3, 404, 411.

171. **"When she realized it was an illegitimate child"** Quoted in Shimabuku, "Petitioning Subjects: Miscegenation in Okinawa," 369.

171. **"The women were outraged at the investigator's assertion"** Quoted in Shimabuku, "Petitioning Subjects: Miscegenation in Okinawa," 369.

171. **"strengthen the Ryukyuan people"** Sawada, "Cold War Geopolitics," 407.

171. **Of ninety-four biracial children** Shimabuku, "Petitioning Subjects: Miscegenation in Okinawa," 370.

172. **the first government survey of mixed-race children** Crissey, *Okinawa's GI Brides*, 37–38.

172. **"the welcome fruits of love"** Quoted in Crissey, *Okinawa's GI Brides*, 37.

172. **"Commonly, you would see grandmothers"** Rebecca Forgash, "Negotiating Marriage: Cultural Citizenship and the Reproduction of American Empire in Okinawa," *Ethnology*, Vol. 48, No. 3 (Summer 2009), 221.

172. *January 1946* Okinawa Women Act Against Military Violence, "Postwar U.S. Military Crimes Against Women in Okinawa" (July 2016), 3.

172. *September 23, 1949* Okinawa Women Act Against Military Violence, "Postwar U.S. Military Crimes Against Women in Okinawa" (July 2016), 15.

173. **Some Okinawan women left the men** See Crissey, *Okinawa's GI Brides*, 39.

173. **Her classmates soaked this in and asked** Quoted in Akemi Johnson, "From Shima Hafu to Daburu: Learning English at the AmerAsian School in Okinawa," in *Hapa Japan, Volume Two: Identities and Representations*, ed. Duncan Ryūken Williams (Los Angeles: USC Shinso Ito Center for Japanese Religions and Culture/Kaya Press, 2017), 111.

173. **"the plight of the Amerasian children"** Calvin Sims, "A Hard Life for Amerasian Children," *New York Times*, July 23, 2000.

173. **"A Hard Life for Amerasian Children"** Sims, "A Hard Life for Amerasian Children."

174. **A *Time* magazine article** Tim Larimer, "Identity Crisis," *Time*, July 24, 2000.

175. **"She didn't understand that we were telling her that we were fine"** Mitzi Uehara Carter, "Routing, Repeating, and Hacking Mixed Race in Okinawa," in *Hapa Japan, Volume Two: Identities and Representations*, ed. Duncan Ryūken Williams (Los Angeles: USC Shinso Ito Center for Japanese Religions and Culture/Kaya Press, 2017), 144.

176. **Until 1985, under Japanese law** My sources for this law include Crissey, *Okinawa's GI Brides*, 40, 41; Johanna O. Zulueta, "Living as Migrants in a Place That Was Once Home the Nisei, the U.S. Bases, and Okinawan Society," *Philippine Studies: Historical & Ethnographic Viewpoints*, Vol. 60, No. 3, Transnational Migration: Part 2: Imperial and Personal Histories (September 2012), 374.

177. **The writer Pearl Buck** My sources on Pearl Buck and the Pearl S. Buck Foundation include Lily Anne Yumi Welty, "Advantage Through Crisis: Multiracial American Japanese in Post-World War II Japan, Okinawa and America 1945–1972," University of California, Santa Barbara dissertation (December 2012), 20, 135; Peter Conn, *Pearl S. Buck: A Cultural Biography* (Cambridge: Cambridge University Press, 1996), 354, 359; Angst, "In a Dark Time," 351.

180. **"I feel myself to be a Japanese"** Takashi Oka, "Okinawa Mon Amour," *New York Times*, April 6, 1969.

181. **What do I see?** Quoted in Naomi Noiri, "Two Worlds: The Amerasian and the Okinawan," in *Uchinaanchu Diaspora: Memories, Continuities, and Constructions*, ed. Joyce N. Chinen, *Social Process in Hawai'i*, Vol. 42 (2007), 225.

182. **Christ the King International School** Shoji Kudaka, "'This Is a Family': Christ the King International School Hosts Reunion Party," *Stripes Okinawa*, November 21, 2016. Zulueta writes that many Okinawan-Filipino families moved back to the Philippines once the father's work contract expired. Some Okinawan-Filipinos who were Japanese citizens later returned to Okinawa as adults to work, often on the U.S. military bases. See Zulueta, "Living as Migrants."

182. **The majority of students at Okinawa Christian School International are mixed American-Okinawan** This is based on my own observation at the school and interviews with graduates. See also Masae Yonamine, "As Parent of an Amerasian," University of the Ryukyus, http://ir.lib.u-ryukyu .ac.jp/bitstream/20.500.12000/9007/4/12871024-4.pdf, 36.

182. **In 1998, five Okinawan mothers** Some of this section is adapted from Akemi Johnson, "From Shima Hafu to Daburu: Learning English at the AmerAsian School in Okinawa," in *Hapa Japan, Volume Two: Identities and Representations*, ed. Duncan Ryūken Williams (Los Angeles: USC Shinso Ito Center for Japanese Religions and Culture/Kaya Press, 2017). See also Yonamine, "As Parent of an Amerasian," 39.

183. **"The 48 students have found a haven"** Tim Larimer, "Identity Crisis," *Time*, July 24, 2000.

183. **"provided a nurturing atmosphere"** Sims, "A Hard Life for Amerasian Children."

183. **"Dream School"** Interview with Naomi Noiri, January 22, 2009.

184. **"If an Amerasian child goes to a Japanese school"** Midori Thayer, "The Goal of the AmerAsian School," in *The Educational Rights of Amerasians in Okinawa*, ed. Naomi Noiri (Okinawa: Ryukyu Daigaku, March 2002), 49.

184. **"Amerasians get lumped into two categories"** Naomi Noiri, "The Educational Rights of Amerasians," in *The Educational Rights of Amerasians in Okinawa*, ed. Naomi Noiri (Okinawa: Ryukyu Daigaku, March 2002), 72.

185. **"When you hear my name, Denny Tamaki"** Quoted in Naomi Noiri, "Two Worlds: The Amerasian and the Okinawan," in *Uchinaanchu Diaspora: Memories, Continuities, and Constructions*, ed. Joyce N. Chinen, *Social Process in Hawai'i*, Volume 42 (2007), 218.

187. **the school was using them as examples of what *not* to be** See Stephen Murphy-Shigematsu, *When Half Is Whole: Multiethnic Asian American Identities* (Stanford, CA: Stanford University Press, 2012), 66, 72.

189. **"people who can assist Okinawans"** Noiri, "Two Worlds: The Amerasian and the Okinawan," 222, 224.

190. **I saw it wasn't quite the mixed-person's utopia I had imagined** My account of the AASO in this chapter is based on first-person research and interviews I conducted in 2003 and 2008 to 2009. Ways in which the school may have changed since then are outside the scope of this work.

9: Kiki

199. **Jon Mitchell and others have exposed the high levels of contamination** Jon Mitchell, "Environmental Contamination at USMC Bases on Okinawa," *Asia-Pacific Journal | Japan Focus*, Vol. 15, Iss. 4, No. 2 (February 15, 2017); Jon Mitchell, "Contamination at Largest U.S. Air Force Base in Asia: Kadena, Okinawa," *Asia-Pacific Journal | Japan Focus*, Vol. 14, Iss. 9, No. 1 (May 1, 2016).

200. **People who work as MLCs and IHAs represent a small fraction of Okinawa's workforce** In 2011, there were more than nine thousand MLCs in Okinawa (see Nika Nashiro, "What's Going On Behind Those Blue Eyes? The Perception of Okinawa Women by U.S. Military Personnel," University of Hawaii Master's thesis [May 2013], 43), while in 2010 the workforce of Okinawa was approximately 622,000 (see Nobuhiro Fujisawa, "The Okinawan Economy and Its Employment Issues," https://ci.nii.ac.jp/els/contentscinii_20180904232436.pdf?id=ART0009860876). In 2004, there were about 8,900 MLC and IHA employees on Okinawa (see Chiyomi Sumida, "Online manual Assists U.S. Managers of Japanese

Employees on Okinawa," *Stars and Stripes*, October 28, 2004).

200. **Christianity, with its history of persecution** The religion was banned until 1873, with practitioners subject to exile, torture, and death. Before World War II, the Japanese state viewed Christians as practitioners of a foreign faith that could subvert national propaganda efforts. Christian leaders were arrested and Christian schools harassed. See Anthony Kuhn, "Driven Underground Years Ago, Japan's 'Hidden Christians' Maintain Faith," NPR's Weekend Edition Sunday, October 11, 2015; Norma Field, *In the Realm of a Dying Emperor: Japan at Century's End* (New York: Vintage Books, 1993), 115; Saburō Ienaga, *The Pacific War, 1931–1945* (New York: Pantheon Books, 1978), 109.

206. **550 full-time jobs on base had attracted more than 20,000 applications** Mizumura, "Reflecting [on] the Orientalist Gaze," 137.

207. **they were little more than dirt encampments** For photos of this time period, see Remembering Okinawa History, www.rememberingokinawa .com.

207. **"dream world"** Ruth Ann Keyso, *Women of Okinawa: Nine Voices from a Garrison Island* (Ithaca, NY: Cornell University Press, 2000), 25.

207. **"I'll never forget stepping inside that house for the first time"** Keyso, *Women of Okinawa*, 25.

207. **"flush toilet, shower, and running water"** Mizumura, "Reflecting [on] the Orientalist Gaze," 95.

207. **"I wanted to work at the PX"** Keyso, *Women of Okinawa*, 12.

207. **Some Okinawans, especially men, imagined that these local women** See David John Obermiller, "The U.S. Military Occupation of Okinawa: Politicizing and Contesting Okinawan Identity 1945–1955," University of Iowa dissertation (2006), 192.

208. **Okinawans weren't even paid in money** Okinawa Prefectural Peace Memorial Museum exhibit.

208. **"In the military, Okinawans are always at the short end"** Kensei Yoshida, "Grievances of Okinawa Workers Are a Major Issue at American Bases," *New York Times*, June 7, 1969.

208. **"the humiliations of separate toilets"** Teresa Watanabe, "Okinawa Marks 20 Years of Freedom from U.S.," *Los Angeles Times*, May 15, 1992.

208. **the situations that caused Okinawan base employees to organize** See Yoshida, "Grievances of Okinawa Workers"; Masamichi S. Inoue, *Okinawa and the U.S. Military: Identity Making in the Age of Globalization* (New York: Columbia University Press, 2017), 47; Obermiller, "U.S. Military Occupation of Okinawa," 215.

209. **"I just didn't like being bossed around"** Kozy K. Amemiya, "The Bolivian Connection: U.S. Bases and Okinawan Emigration," in *Okinawa: Cold War Island*, ed. Chalmers Johnson (Cardiff, CA: Japan Policy Research Institute, 1999), 58.

209. **"(a) nearly all of them were employed at one time or another"** Amemiya, "The Bolivian Connection: U.S. Bases and Okinawan Emigration," 58.

215. **"I have to admit that my remarks might be biased"** Keyso, *Women of Okinawa*, 110–111.

10: Chie

221. **The local fishing cooperative had caved to Tokyo** Communication with Steve Rabson; "Nago's Fishing Cooperative Gives Thumbs Up to Henoko Landfill," *Japan Update*, March 8, 2013.

222. **"We worried he was going to kill him"** Jon Mitchell, "Injuries to Okinawa Anti-base Protesters 'Laughable,' Says U.S. Military Spokesman," *Japan Times*, February 9, 2015.

223. **three hundred people on the beach cheering on eighty** "Don't Destroy the Beautiful Henoko Sea: 450 People Protest Against Construction of New US Base Both on Sea and Land," *Ryukyu Shimpo*, February 19, 2017.

223. **Jon Mitchell had found the U.S. military was also compiling and distributing intelligence reports** Jon Mitchell, "How the U.S. Military Spies on Okinawans and Me," *Japan Times*, October 19, 2016.

224. **"elixir of life"** Masamichi S. Inoue, *Okinawa and the U.S. Military: Identity Making in the Age of Globalization* (New York: Columbia University Press, 2017), 176–7.

225. **The U.S. military began eyeing the bay** Gavan McCormack & Satoko Oka Norimatsu, *Resistant Islands: Okinawa Confronts Japan and the United States* (Lanham: Rowman & Littlefield Publishers, 2012), 92-93.

226. **Construction was estimated at $10 billion** Masamichi S. Inoue, *Okinawa and the US Military: Identity Making in the Age of Globalization* (New York: Columbia University Press, 2017), xxx n1. Later, this estimate more than doubled.

226. **80 percent of Okinawans** See, for example, Inoue, *Okinawa and the US Military: Identity Making in the Age of Globalization*, xx; Martin Fackler, "Amid Image of Ire Toward U.S. Bases, Okinawans' True Views Vary," *New York Times*, February 14, 2012.

226. **since 1997 Okinawan citizens have established their presence near the construction site** Masamichi S. Inoue, *Okinawa and the US Military:*

Identity Making in the Age of Globalization (New York: Columbia University Press, 2017), 137; Gavan McCormack and Satoko Oka Norimatsu, *Resistant Islands: Okinawa Confronts Japan and the United States* (Lanham: Rowman & Littlefield Publishers, 2012), 98, 101–102.

226. **"was unable to implement the relocation"** Quoted in McCormack and Norimatsu, *Resistant Islands*, 98.

227. **Hatoyama advocated for a more "equal" relationship** McCormack and Norimatsu, *Resistant Islands*, 114.

228. **"We will use every means available to us"** "Governor Raps Renewed Deal on Okinawa Base," *Japan Times*, April 29, 2015.

232. **calling protesters "dojin"** "Osaka Police Warn 2 Officers Who Insulted Anti-base Protesters in Okinawa," *The Mainichi*, October 22, 2016.

233. **"In Okinawa, we believe in 'Nuchi du takara'"** Mitchell, "Injuries to Okinawa Anti-base Protesters 'Laughable.'"

234. **Along with edits like erasing the story of comfort women** McCormack and Norimatsu, *Resistant Islands*, 32–35; Norma Field, *In the Realm of a Dying Emperor: Japan at Century's End* (New York: Vintage Books, 1993), 62.

234. **Before the war, Henoko residents** This history of Henoko draws on sources that include Inoue, *Okinawa and the U.S. Military*, 14–19, 100, 102, 131; Steve Rabson, "Henoko and the U.S. Military: A History of Dependence and Resistance," *Asia-Pacific Journal | Japan Focus*, Vol. 10, Iss. 4, No. 2 (January 16, 2012), 6, 7; Go Katono, "Henoko Project Prolongs Pain of Woman, 89, Over Human Remains," *Asahi Shimbun*, August 23, 2018.

236. **"Our life is more important than the dugong's"** Inoue, *Okinawa and the U.S. Military*, 188.

236. **"Camp Schwab gives hiring preferences"** Quoted in Rabson, "Henoko and the U.S. Military," 13.

236. **"gotten so suffocating"** Inoue, *Okinawa and the U.S. Military*, 188.

240. **The most recent national election had seen the lowest-ever voter turnout** "Election Turnout Likely Second-Lowest in Postwar Period, Estimate Says," *Japan Times*, October 23, 2017; Reiji Yoshida and Tomohiro Osaki, "Young Voters Hope to Reform Japan's 'Silver Democracy,'" *Japan Times*, July 8, 2016.

242. **there is no genuine security reason for all these marines to be in Okinawa** See also Yukiyo Zaha, "Former Army Colonel Wilkerson Says Marine Corps in Okinawa Is 'Strategically Unnecessary,'" *Ryukyu Shimpo*, December 23, 2018.

245. **Fumiko Shimabukuro, the octogenarian activist** Mitchell, "Injuries to Okinawa Anti-base Protesters 'Laughable.'"

246. **One Okinawan grad student, doing research at the sit-in** Rinda Yamashiro, "Anti-Futenma Relocation Movement in Okinawa: Women's Involvement and the Impact of Sit-In Protest," University of Hawaii master's thesis (May 2008), 75, 88, 89, 90, 95–96.

248. **The Japanese Communist Party** "What Is the JCP?," Japanese Communist Party, http://www.jcp.or.jp/english.

249. **wartime and postwar history of the island** My sources for this history of Ie Island include Shoko Ahagon, *The Island Where People Live*, trans. C. Harold Rickard (Hong Kong: Christian Conference of Asia, 1989), 5, 69, 100–101, 121, 167, 171n4; *Ryukyu Shimpo, Descent into Hell: Civilian Memories of the Battle of Okinawa*, trans. by Mark Ealey & Alastair McLauchlan (Portland, ME: MerwinAsia, 2014), 247; Jon Mitchell, "Beggars' Belief: The Farmers' Resistance Movement on Iejima Island, Okinawa," *Asia-Pacific Journal: Japan Focus*, Vol. 8, Iss. 23, No. 2, June 7, 2010; M.D. Morris, *Okinawa: A Tiger by the Tail* (New York: Hawthorn Books, Inc, 1968), 31, 71.

250. **M.D. Morris describes visiting Ie-jima** Morris, *Okinawa: A Tiger by the Tail*, 71.

250. **two U.S. soldiers, eleven Filipino workers, and fifty or more "natives" had been killed** Morris, *Okinawa: A Tiger by the Tail*, 72. Shoko Ahagon writes of another U.S. military accident that killed 102 people in 1947. See Ahagon, *The Island Where People Live*, 5.

250. **"fields green with sugar cane"** Shoko Ahagon, "I Lost My Only Son in the War: Prelude to the Okinawan Anti-base Movement," trans. by C. Douglas Lummis, *Asia-Pacific Journal: Japan Focus*, Vol. 8, Iss. 23, No. 1 (June 7, 2010), 9.

251. **They thrust consolation money** Ahagon, *The Island Where People Live*, 9–10. Villagers received 10,000 to 50,000 yen, according to Ahagon, 169n16.

251. **USCAR had taken 63 percent of the island** C. Harold Rickard, "Translator's Introduction," in Shoko Ahagon, *The Island Where People Live*, trans. C. Harold Rickard (Hong Kong: Christian Conference of Asia, 1989), xi.

251. **"It was as if another battle had occurred"** Rickard, "Translator's Introduction," in Ahagon, *The Island Where People Live*, ix.

251. **"The Air Force can sympathize with and understand the farmers' attachment"** Ahagon, *The Island Where People Live*, 22.

251. **"a beautiful rural village"** Rickard, "Translator's Introduction," in Ahagon, *The Island Where People Live*, ix.

252. **"The road of our livelihoods is completely closed off"** Ahagon, *The Island Where People Live*, 71.

252. **"When [U.S. soldiers] came to the island"** Ahagon, "I Lost My Only Son in the War," 14.

253. **"Aren't you being agitated by the Communist Party?"** Ahagon, *The Island Where People Live*, 58.

253. **"exhibited the spirit of Mahatma Gandhi"** Rickard, "Translator's Introduction," in Ahagon, *The Island Where People Live*, xi.

253. **"We are attempting to live the quality of life"** Rickard, "Translator's Introduction," in Ahagon, *The Island Where People Live*, xii.

253. **He helped popularize that Okinawan saying** Inoue, *Okinawa and the U.S. Military: Identity Making in the Age of Globalization* (New York: Columbia University Press, 2017), 243n9.

255. **"Do not become anti-American"** Ahagon, *The Island Where People Live*, 23; Ahagon, "I Lost My Only Son in the War," 18.

11: Ai

262. **The F-100 killed seventeen people** "Okinawa School Marks 50th Year Since Deadly U.S. Fighter Crash," *Japan Times*, July 1, 2009; interview with Ai Tamaki.

262. **but not about the Ryukyu Kingdom** For one exception see Kenta Masuda, "Schools to Teach History of the Ryukyu Islands," *Ryukyu Shimpo*, March 4, 2013.

263. **SEALDS** See *sealdseng.strikingly.com*.

263. **"I'm speechless with fear, anger and sadness"** "Angry Okinawans Rally at Kadena Air Base Following Ex-marine's Arrest," *Japan Times*, May 20, 2016.

263. **At the silent protest** My sources on the silent protest include "2,000 Rally in Silent Protest in Front of U.S. Base, Mourning the Death of a Woman," *Ryukyu Shimpo*, May 23, 2016; Matthew M. Burke and Chiyomi Sumida, "Okinawans Protest Slaying Outside Base Gate," *Stars and Stripes*, May 22, 2016; *Ryukyu Shimpo* video, https://www.youtube.com/watch?v=whQR8XKfxZo.

264. **On a blazing Sunday afternoon in June** My sources on this protest rally include "Editorial: Okinawans at Mass Rally Protesting Base Employee Incident Say No to Marines and Bases as Their Anger Has Surpassed Tipping

Point," *Ryukyu Shimpo*, June 20, 2016; "65,000 People in Rally Mourn and Demand Withdrawal of Marines from Okinawa," *Ryukyu Shimpo* Digital Edition, June 19, 2016; Dave Ornauer and Chiyomi Sumida, "Anti-US Military Protests Attract Thousands in Naha, Tokyo," *Stars and Stripes*, June 19, 2016; "Okinawans Lament Murder of Woman, Ask Japan Mainlanders for Consideration," *Mainichi Japan*, June 20, 2016; "Anger Directed at Japan Mainland at Anti-U.S. Base Rally in Okinawa," *Asahi Shimbun*, June 20, 2016; "Straining Under the Burden," NHK World, June 20, 2016.

266. **Okinawa's prefectural assembly adopted a resolution** Interview with Tomo Yara; Chiyomi Sumida, "Okinawa Lawmakers Pass Protest Resolution Against Marines," *Stars and Stripes*, May 27, 2016.

266. **Federal officials increased the number of police** Ayako Mie, "Police to Step Up Patrols in Okinawa After Woman's Murder," *Japan Times*, June 3, 2016.

266. **the U.S. military banned all servicemembers** James Kimber, "Restaurants, Bars Hurting Outside U.S. Bases on Okinawa," *Stars and Stripes*, June 21, 2016.

266. **"strange new silence"** Kimber, "Restaurants, Bars Hurting Outside U.S. Bases on Okinawa."

266. **"demonstrate unwavering respect"** Seth Robson, "July 4 Fireworks, Live Concerts Canceled at U.S. Bases in Japan," *Stars and Stripes*, June 22, 2016.

266. **"It's now become difficult for me to go out at night"** "Okinawans Lament Murder of Woman, Ask Japan Mainlanders for Consideration," *Mainichi Japan*, June 20, 2016.

266. **In Uruma, walkers avoided the area** Interview with Chiyomi Sumida, February 22, 2107.

266. **An annual women's self-defense class** "Okinawa Women Pack Self-defense Seminar Following Murder of 20-Year-Old Local Woman," Kyodo News, June 2, 2017.

266. **Women recalled past experiences** "Okinawa Women Pack Self-defense Seminar Following Murder of 20-Year-Old Local Woman."

266. **"It is beyond our imagination"** Matthew M. Burke and Chiyomi Sumida, "Defense Attorney Says Okinawa Confession Made in a Daze," *Stars and Stripes*, May 20, 2016.

267. **gave his account of what happened to the U.S. military–affiliated newspaper, *Stars and Stripes*** Matthew M. Burke and Chiyomi Sumida, "Former Kadena Worker Reveals Gruesome Details of Okinawan Woman's Death," *Stars and Stripes*, February 13, 2017.

267. **telling the newspaper the story of Gadson's childhood** Matthew M. Burke and Chiyomi Sumida, "Attorney: Former Marine Charged with Rape, Murder Suffered Mental Illness," *Stars and Stripes*, September 4, 2016.

267. **"is characterized by behavior that violates either the rights of others or major societal norms"** American Psychiatric Association, "Conduct Disorder," *DSM-5* Fact Sheet, 2013.

267. **aggression, property destruction, and deceitfulness** American Academy of Child & Adolescent Psychiatry, "Conduct Disorder," August 2013. http://www.aacap.org/aacap/families_and_youth/facts_for_families /fff-guide/conduct-disorder-033.aspx.

267. **"For him, women are either good or they are his enemy"** Matthew M. Burke and Chiyomi Sumida, "Attorney: Former Marine Charged with Rape, Murder Suffered Mental Illness," *Stars and Stripes*, September 4, 2016.

268. **"Out on the [shooting] range, I had the urge"** Matthew M. Burke and Chiyomi Sumida, "Former Kadena Worker Reveals Gruesome Details of Okinawan Woman's Death," *Stars and Stripes*, February 13, 2017.

268. **he claimed to be impaired by recent suicide attempts** Burke and Sumida, "Defense Attorney Says Okinawa Confession Made in a Daze."

268. **"withholding some alleged details of the crime"** Burke and Sumida, "Former Kadena Worker Reveals Gruesome Details." The following account draws on this article as well as Burke and Sumida, "Defense Attorney Says Okinawa Confession Made in a Daze;" "Kadena Worker Admits Strangling, Stabbing Woman Found Dead in Okinawa," Kyodo News, May 20, 2016.

269. **"All women on Okinawa . . . have the victim's mindset"** Matthew M. Burke and Chiyomi Sumida, "Defendant in Okinawa Slaying Seeks Change of Venue," *Stars and Stripes*, July 5, 2016.

269. **"July 18 is our daughter's 21st birthday"** Matthew M. Burke and Chiyomi Sumida, "Father of Okinawa Homicide Victim Wants Execution for Suspect," *Stars and Stripes*, July 15, 2016.

270. **"[Gadson] is competent enough to feel that he has not been treated fairly** Burke and Sumida, "Former Kadena Worker Reveals Gruesome Details."

270. **"People in Okinawa have also caused incidents"** Keiko Yasuda, "April 28: A Day of Pain, Separation for Many Okinawans," *Asahi Shimbun*, April 28, 2017.

271. **"I wanted the people of mainland Japan to think about the pain Okinawa suffers"** Yasuda, "April 28: A Day of Pain, Separation for Many Okinawans."

271. **Online, a *Stars and Stripes* reader, "Bill," wrote** This exchange was posted in response to Burke and Sumida, "Attorney: Former Marine Charged with Rape, Murder Suffered Mental Illness."

271. **"Uncovering the Emotions of Okinawan People"** "Straining Under the Burden," NHK World, June 20, 2016.

272. **"Personally, I'd be sad if [the bases] all left"** Julie Makinen, "Finding U.S.–Japanese Harmony amid the Discord of a Death in Okinawa," *Los Angeles Times*, June 6, 2016.

272. **A fifty-one-year-old man from Okinawa City told a Japanese newspaper** "Okinawans Lament Murder of Woman, Ask Japan Mainlanders for Consideration," *Mainichi Japan*, June 20, 2016.

273. **"We are working to get along with U.S. soldiers"** "Straining Under the Burden," NHK World.

273. **"Without a doubt, the women of Okinawa have suffered most"** "Straining Under the Burden," NHK World.

274. **"locked in an almost sensual embrace with its American conquerors"** John Dower, *Embracing Defeat: Japan in the Wake of World War II*, 23.

274. **Kenneth Gadson's trial** My sources on Gadson's trial include Hana Kusumoto, "Gadson Pleads Not Guilty to Okinawan Woman's Murder, but Admits Other Charges," *Stars and Stripes*, November 16, 2017; Hana Kusumoto, "Gadson 'Should Not Be Allowed to Live,' Victim's Parents Say as Trial Continues," *Stars and Stripes*, November 17, 2017; Matthew M. Burke, "Gadson Attempts to Show Remorse as Murder Trial Wraps Up on Okinawa," *Stars and Stripes*, November 24, 2017; Matthew M. Burke and Hana Kusumoto, "Base Worker Sentenced to Life with Hard Labor for Slaying of Okinawan Woman," *Stars and Stripes*, December 1, 2017; "Ex-marine Kenneth Shinzato Sentenced to Life in Okinawa Rape and Murder Trial," *Ryukyu Shimpo*, December 2, 2017.

275. **"The U.S. and Japanese governments have a heavy responsibility"** Quoted in Burke and Kusumoto, "Base Worker Sentenced to Life."

275. **"Why is it that we still feel depressed"** Quoted in Burke and Kusumoto, "Base Worker Sentenced to Life."

278. **"It's not possible that the democracy of the country of my father will reject me"** Motoko Rich, "A Marine's Son Takes on U.S. Military Bases in Okinawa," *New York Times*, September 25, 2018.

278. **"I think there are some things only he can do"** Rich, "A Marine's Son Takes on U.S. Military Bases in Okinawa."

278. **"He is super popular"** Yuri Kageyama, Associated Press, "New Okinawa Chief Embodies Complexity of Japan's U.S. Bases," *Stars and Stripes*, October 2, 2018.

278. **"symbol of postwar Okinawa"** Rich, "A Marine's Son Takes on U.S. Military Bases in Okinawa."

278. **proposing an annual "Ryukyu History and Culture Day"** Eric Johnston, "Meet the Top Contenders Seeking to Lead Okinawa: Atsushi Sakima and Denny Tamaki," *Japan Times*, September 13, 2018.

278. **"Filling [the sea] with earth in Henoko"** Takao Nogami, "Tamaki in Nago: U.S. Base Plan 'Destroying Democracy,'" *Asahi Shimbun*, October 4, 2018.

ABOUT THE AUTHOR

Akemi Johnson is a former Fulbright scholar in Okinawa and has written about the island for *The Nation*, *Travel + Leisure*, *Explore Parts Unknown*, and other publications. She has also contributed to NPR's *All Things Considered* and *Code Switch*. A graduate of the Iowa Writers' Workshop and Brown University, she lives in Northern California.

PUBLISHING IN THE PUBLIC INTEREST

Thank you for reading this book published by The New Press. The New Press is a nonprofit, public interest publisher. New Press books and authors play a crucial role in sparking conversations about the key political and social issues of our day.

We hope you enjoyed this book and that you will stay in touch with The New Press. Here are a few ways to stay up to date with our books, events, and the issues we cover:

- Sign up at www.thenewpress.com/subscribe to receive updates on New Press authors and issues and to be notified about local events
- Like us on Facebook: www.facebook.com/newpressbooks
- Follow us on Twitter: www.twitter.com/thenewpress

Please consider buying New Press books for yourself; for friends and family; or to donate to schools, libraries, community centers, prison libraries, and other organizations involved with the issues our authors write about.

The New Press is a 501(c)(3) nonprofit organization. You can also support our work with a tax-deductible gift by visiting www.thenewpress.com/donate.